D0948884

CATALOGUE OF THE SLAVONIC MANUSCRIPTS OF THE NATIONAL SZÉCHÉNYI LIBRARY

CEU MEDIEVALIA 9

Series Editor: József Laszlovszky
Series Technical Editor: Annabella Pál

Catalogue of the Slavonic Cyrillic Manuscripts of the National Széchényi Library

Edited by
Ralph Cleminson
Elissaveta Moussakova
Nina Voutova

with a historical essay by Orsolya Karsay

Central European University
Department of Medieval Studies
&
Central European University Press
Budapest · New York
&
National Széchényi Library

Budapest, 2006

© Editors and Contributors 2007

1st edition

Technical Editor: Péter Banyó

Cover design for the series by Péter Tóth

The cover illustration shows OSZK MS Oct. Serb. 1, f.2
(no.41 in the catalogue).

Joint publication by:

**Central European University
Department of Medieval Studies**
Nádor u. 9, H-1051 Budapest, Hungary
Telephone: (+36-1) 327-3051, Fax: (+36-1) 327-3055
E-mail: medstud@ceu.hu, Website: http://medstud.ceu.hu

Central European University Press
An imprint of the Central European University Share Company
Nádor u. 11, H-1051 Budapest, Hungary
Telephone: (+36-1) 327-3138, Fax: (+36-1) 327-3183
E-mail: ceupress@ceu.hu, Website: http://www.ceupress.com

400 West 59th Street, New York NY 10019, USA
Telephone (+1-212) 547-6932, Fax: (+1-646) 557-2416
E-mail: mgreenwald@sorosny.org

National Széchényi Library
Budavári Palota F épület, 1827 Budapest, Hungary
Telephone: (+36-1) 224-3700, Fax: (+36-1) 202-0804
E-mail: inform@oszk.hu, Website: http://www.oszk.hu

Research on the project was supported under the 'Changing Places' scheme of the Arts and Humanities Research Board of the United Kingdom.

ISSN 1587-6470 CEU MEDIEVALIA
ISBN ISBN 978 963 7326 97 4 (cloth)

Library of Congress Cataloging-in-Publication Data

Cleminson, R. M.
Catalogue of the Slavonic cyrillic manuscripts of the National Széchényi Library / compiled by Ralph Cleminson, Elissaveta Moussakova, Nina Voutova; with a historical essay by Orsolya Karsay.
p. cm.
Includes bibliographical references (p. 263) and indexes.
ISBN 978-9637326974 (cloth) -- ISBN 978-9637326837 (pbk.)
1. Manuscripts, Cyrillic--Hungary--Budapest--History. 2. Manuscripts, Church Slavic--Hungary--Budapest--History. 3. Manuscripts--Hungary--Budapest--History. I. Moussakova, Elissaveta. II. Voutova, Nina. III. Karsay, Orsolya. IV. Országos Széchényi Könyvtár. V. Title.

Z6621.S943S53 2006
015.439031--dc22
2006015440

Printed in Hungary
by Akaprint, Budapest

TABLE OF CONTENTS

List of Plates	vi
Introduction	ix
Orsolya Karsay: On the History of our Slavonic Cyrillic Manuscripts	xxv
Conspectus of Shelfmarks	xl
Descriptions	I
Plates	133
Colour Plates	209
Watermark Album	219
Index to the Watermark Album	259
List of Publications and Other Sources for Watermark Identification	261
Bibliography	263
Index of Persons	267
Index of Placenames	276
Index of Titles	278
Index of Incipits	284
Chronological Index	287
Index of Manuscripts by Origin	288

LIST OF PLATES

Black-and-white plates

1.   Oct. Eccl. Slav. 2, f.2 (cat. 1)
2.   Quart. Eccl. Slav. 7, f.87v (cat. 2)
3.   Fol. Eccl. Slav. 3, f.170 (cat. 4)
4.   Fol. Eccl. Slav. 20, f.68 (cat. 5)
5.   Fol. Eccl. Slav. 20, f.200 (cat. 5)
6.   Fol. Eccl. Slav. 1, f.8 (cat. 6)
7.   Fol. Eccl. Slav. 11, f.3v (cat. 7)
8.   Fol. Eccl. Slav. 11, f.78 (cat. 7)
9.   Fol. Eccl. Slav. 7, f.14 (cat. 8)
10. Fol. Eccl. Slav. 13, f.5 (cat. 9)
11. Fol. Eccl. Slav. 6, f.16 (cat. 10)
12. Fol. Eccl. Slav. 6, lower cover (cat. 10)
13. Fol. Eccl. Slav. 2, f.71 (cat. 11)
14. Quart. Eccl. Slav. 10, f.14 (cat. 12)
15. Quart. Eccl. Slav. 10, lower cover (cat. 12)
16. Fol. Eccl. Slav. 12, f.106 (cat. 14)
17. Fol. Eccl. Slav. 18, f.18v (cat. 15)
18. Fol. Eccl. Slav. 18, f.58 (cat. 15)
19. Fol. Eccl. Slav. 9, f.4v (cat. 16)
20. Fol. Eccl. Slav. 19, f.140 (cat. 17)
21. Fol. Eccl. Slav. 19, f.330v (cat. 17)
22. Fol. Eccl. Slav. 22, f.3 (cat. 18)
23. Fol. Eccl. Slav. 22, f.105v (cat. 18)
24. Fol. Eccl. Slav. 8, f.10v (cat. 19)
25. Fol. Eccl. Slav. 8, f.82v (cat. 19)
26. Fol. Eccl. Slav. 5, f.4v (cat. 20)
27. Fol. Eccl. Slav. 5, f.57v (cat. 20)
28. Fol. Eccl. Slav. 5, f.109 (cat. 20)
29. Fol. Eccl. Slav. 10, f.9 (cat. 21)
30. Fol. Eccl. Slav. 15, ff.65v-66 (cat. 22)
31. Fol. Eccl. Slav. 15, ff.92v-93 (cat. 22)
32. Fol. Eccl. Slav. 15, ff.167v-168 (cat. 22)

33.   Fol. Eccl. Slav. 15, ff.216v-217 (cat. 22)
34.   Fol. Eccl. Slav. 25, f.46v (cat. 23)
35.   Fol. Eccl. Slav. 26, f.69 (cat. 24)
36.   Fol. Eccl. Slav. 26, f.411v (cat. 24)
37.   Fol. Eccl. Slav. 4, f.51v (cat. 25)
38.   Fol. Eccl. Slav. 4, f.56 (cat. 25)
39.   Fol. Eccl. Slav. 14, f.71 (cat. 26)
40.   Fol. Eccl. Slav. 14, f.158v (cat. 26)
41.   Fol. Eccl. Slav. 23, f.47 (cat. 27)
42.   Fol. Eccl. Slav. 27, f.21 (cat. 28)
43.   Fol. Eccl. Slav. 16, f.28v (cat. 29)
44.   Fol. Eccl. Slav. 28, f.83 (cat. 30)
45.   Quart. Eccl. Slav. 13, f.55v (cat. 31)
46.   Quart. Eccl. Slav. 13, f.134v (cat. 31)
47.   Quart. Eccl. Slav. 13, f.161 (cat. 31)
48.   Quart. Eccl. Slav. 12, f.25 (cat. 32)
49.   Quart. Eccl. Slav. 12, f.62v (cat. 32)
50.   Quart. Eccl. Slav. 12, f.177v (cat. 32)
51.   Quart. Eccl. Slav. 15, f.5 (cat. 33)
52.   Quart. Eccl. Slav. 11, f.24v (cat. 34)
53.   Quart. Eccl. Slav. 11, f.58v (cat. 34)
54.   Quart. Eccl. Slav. 11, f.274 (cat. 34)
55.   Quart. Eccl. Slav. 9, f.4 (cat. 35)
56.   Fol. Eccl. Slav. 21, f.5 (cat. 36)
57.   Quart. Eccl. Slav. 17, f.2 (cat. 37)
58.   Quart. Eccl. Slav. 6, f.1 (cat. 39)
59.   Quart. Eccl. Slav. 19, f.89v (cat. 40)
60.   Oct. Serb. 1, f.1 (cat. 41)
61.   Oct. Serb. 1, upper cover (cat. 41)
62.   Duod. Eccl. Slav. 1, ff.47v-48 (cat. 42)
63.   Quart. Eccl. Slav. 16, f.7 (cat. 43)
64.   Quart. Eccl. Slav. 1, f.48 (cat. 44)
65.   Quart. Eccl. Slav. 2, f.35 (cat. 45)
66.   Quart. Eccl. Slav. 4, f.4 (cat. 46)
67.   Quart. Eccl. Slav. 3, f.38 (cat. 47)
68.   Quart. Serb. 2, f.59 (cat. 48)
69.   Oct. Eccl. Slav. 1, f.4 (cat. 49)
70.   Quart. Eccl. Slav. 5, f.5 (cat. 50)

71.   Quart. Serb. 6, f.15v (cat. 51)
72.   Quart. Eccl. Slav. 18, f.8v (cat. 52)
73.   Frag. Eccl. Slav. 3, №II, recto (cat. 53)
74.   Frag. Eccl. Slav. 3, №II, verso (cat. 53)
75.   Frag. Eccl. Slav. 1, verso (cat. 54)
76.   Frag. Eccl. Slav. 2, verso (cat. 55)

Colour plates

I.   Quart. Eccl. Slav. 7, f.120v (cat. 2)
II.   Fol. Eccl. Slav. 17, f.175 (cat. 3)
III.   Fol. Eccl. Slav. 3, upper cover (cat. 4)
IV.   Fol. Eccl. Slav. 6, f.225v (cat. 10)
V.   Fol. Eccl. Slav. 24, f.115 (cat. 13)
VI.   Fol. Eccl. Slav. 9, f.5 (cat. 16)
VII.   Quart. Eccl. Slav. 19, upper cover (cat. 40)
VIII.   Oct. Serb. 1, f.2 (cat. 41)
IX.   Oct. Serb. 1, f.68v (cat. 41)
X.   Oct. Serb. 1, f.72v (cat. 41)

This catalogue contains descriptions of the cyrillic Slavonic manuscripts of the National Széchényi Library in Budapest. Though it describes basically mediæval manuscripts, it does include more recent material insofar as this can be regarded as a continuation of earlier traditions. It restricts itself moreover to codices and fragments of codices, thus excluding charters and other archival documents, and to manuscripts written principally in Slavonic languages: the Library's collection of Rumanian cyrillic manuscripts is not described.

The collection thus defined includes fifty-six manuscripts, the vast majority of which have never been described before and, it is fair to say, have been hitherto unknown to scholarship. They represent nevertheless one of the most important collections of such material in present-day Hungary. The only other collection of comparable size and importance is that of the Serbian Orthodox Diocese of Buda at Szentendre; there are nine such manuscripts in the University Library in Budapest, and a number of other collections which have only one or two examples of them.[1] It is by no means unlikely that there are other individual manuscripts in other collections which are yet to be discovered; indeed, some of the items here described came to light only in the course of work on this catalogue.

Considering that this group of manuscripts represents only a small fraction of the Library's holdings, and that they are held outside the main centres of Slavonic studies, it is perhaps not surprising that they have received little scholarly attention. One manuscript, indeed, had been the object of close study even before it entered the Library. This is Fol. Eccl. Slav. 19, which was acquired in 1787 by Juraj (György) Ribay, who immediately set about studying its text. He communicated the results of his labours to Josef Dobrovský, who cites the manuscript ("[eine] Handschrift, die Herr Ribay, evangelischer Prediger zu Czinkota in Ungarn, betsitzt") as one of his sources for one of the very first attempts at the textual criticism of the Slavonic New Testament (Dobrovský 1790). Dobrovský's article is dated 15.

---

[1] The manuscripts in Szentendre have been thoroughly described in Sindik, Grozdanović-Pajić, Mano-Zisi 1991, the introduction to which also surveys the previous literature relating to this collection, supplemented by Sindik 2002. The general survey by Tóth 1980 relies largely on previously published material. For the University Library see Cleminson 1995, Stefanović 1998, Velčeva and Musakova 2003. A manuscript in the library of the Academy of Sciences is described by Anguševa and Dimitrova 1995, 1997. Isolated manuscripts outside Budapest are described in Baleczki 1958, Hauptová 1961, Somogyi 1970, Ojtozi 1982, Pandur 1990, Kocsis 1994, 1999, Földvári 1995 and Stefanović 2001. Very brief notices of some of the above are also found in Nyomárkay 1990- .

Sept. 1788, which shows how quick Ribay had been to realise the importance of his acquisition and to make it known to scholarship, and he continued to investigate its text as part of his wider Biblical studies.[2] In June 1794 Dobrovský had the opportunity to examine the manuscript *de visu* and make a closer study of it ("diligentius codicem hunc examinavi atque integrum contuli"). The results were communicated to J. J. Griesbach (a member of the same circle: Ribay had been his student at Jena in 1780-2), and variants from this manuscript are included in the critical apparatus to his edition of the Greek New Testament.[3]

The first study to mention any of the Library's Slavonic holdings as such was Ivan Boynychich's description of the only two mediæval MSS then in the collection, Fol. Eccl. Slav. 17 and 19, which is far superior to the descriptions of the same two manuscripts published in the recent catalogue of the Jankovich exhibition (Boynychich 1878, Jankovich catalogue 2002, № 234, 235). After this promising start, however, there were only a brief survey article (Kočubinskij 1882) and an even more perfunctory note of the collection's existence (Conev 1927) until László Dezső returned to Fol. Eccl. Slav. 19, which is also the subject of an article by Mária Szarvas, making it the most-studied MS in the collection (Dezső 1955, Szarvas 1986). Péter Király published articles on two manuscripts, Fragm. Eccl. Slav. 3 and Fol. Eccl. Slav. 3 (Király 1968, 1974), and Imre Tóth published an article with the same title as Király's second on Quart. Eccl. Slav. 7 (Tóth 1983). This last manuscript has lately been edited, with descriptions of its language and script, by a group of scholars led by Tóth (Zaimov, Tóth, Balázs 2003). The Gospel Homiliary of 1588 has been edited by Mihály Kocsis, who has also devoted a number of small articles to it (Kocsis 1997, 2004). Attention has thus been mainly focused on the older manuscripts in the collection, and on Biblical texts; however, Quart. Serb. 6, a late eighteenth-century Serbian songbook, was the subject of an article by I. Póth (Póth 1961), and another Serbian manuscript, the beautifully produced miscellany compiled c. 1680 by Hristofor Račanin, has recently merited a monograph by Á. Kacziba (Kacziba 1999). One manuscript, Quart. Eccl. Slav. 14, has been the subject of study not so much for its own sake, as for the sake of its extensive inscriptions (Chivu 1978, 1997), which contain some interesting Rumanian literary texts. Finally, the authors of the present volume have contributed a survey article

[2] OSZK MS Quart. Slav 1 is a collection of "Biblicae Collationes" by Ribay, the fifth of which (ff.56-70v) is a "Collatio Codicis Cyrillici [...] apostol [i.e. Fol. Eccl. Slav. 19] cum Bibliis Ostrorogiensibus" covering the book of Acts and dated August 1789.
[3] Griesbach 1806; the manuscript is no.5 in the list on p.xix of Slavonic MSS of the Acts and Epistles "quorum catalogum et lectiones multas mecum communicavit celeb. I. Dobrowskius."

(Cleminson, Moussakova, Voutova 2003) which goes into some detail about the nature and origins of the collection.

The manuscripts date from the end of the thirteenth to the beginning of the nineteenth centuries, though almost half are from the sixteenth; this is not an unusual distribution for a collection of this kind. Nearly half of them came to the library from the collections of Miklós Jankovich in 1836 and Antal Hodinka in 1890-1909 (nine and eighteen manuscripts respectively); the remainder were acquired through sporadic gifts and purchases in the late nineteenth and twentieth centuries. For a detailed study of the collection's history, see the essay by Orsolya Karsay elsewhere in this volume.

Hardly any of the manuscripts contain explicit evidence about their origins. Only four manuscripts earlier than the eighteenth century are dated, and of these only one, the earliest, Fol. Eccl. Slav. 11, has a regular colophon. This provides little information beyond the date (1553) and the name of the scribe (the priest Lazar). The other three manuscripts, Fol. Eccl. Slav. 9, 12 and 4, have nothing more than the bare date (1588, 1648-9 and 1678 respectively).

In the eighteenth century scribes became more informative, and indeed half the manuscripts from this century are provided with a date, and often other information about their creation as well. The first of these, Fol. Eccl. Slav. 25, written in 1707, has an inscription by the scribe following the pattern of a traditional colophon, and indeed continues older traditions of book production, having been written in the Uniate monastery of Mielec for a church in Kowel 160 miles distant in Volhynia. A similar inscription, with the date 1726, is found in Fol. Eccl. Slav. 26. Regrettably, the name of the community who commissioned the manuscript has been obliterated, presumably when it passed from their possession.

The remaining dated eighteenth-century manuscripts were produced by the Hungarian Serb community. The first of these is Duod. Eccl. Slav. 1, written in 1713 in Buda apparently by a team of scribes. Next are Quart. Eccl. Slav. 3 and 5, both written in 1769, the first in Esztergom by Grigorije Tirović and the second in Buda by Ilija Radišić, and Quart. Serb. 6, which was written in 1793/4, possibly by Georgije Antonić, who certainly owned it. The date 1743 found in Quart. Eccl. Slav. 4 is not original, but it is plausible.

Of the two nineteenth-century manuscripts in the catalogue, Quart. Eccl. Slav. 18 is dated 1835 and Fol. Eccl. Slav. 21 is datable to the reign of Ferdinand I (1835-48).

There remains one manuscript to which a date and named scribe can be assigned, even though neither is explicitly mentioned in the book. This is Oct. Serb. 1, written by the renowned Hristofor Račanin and with a calendar beginning in 1679.

It is apparent from the above that hardly any direct information about the places where the manuscripts were written is to be found in the manuscripts themselves. Circumstantial evidence strongly suggests that by far the greater part of them was produced by the minority communities of the Kingdom of Hungary, Ruthenians (русини), Rumanians and Serbs. Of these the Ruthenian manuscripts comprise a considerable majority, to the extent that they could even be said to be typical of the collection as a whole. Besides their contents, their common tradition is chiefly visible in their appearance (hands, layout and decoration). They are an expression of the cultural and religious traditions of the south-western edge of the East Slavonic population, whose communities often intermingled with communities of other populations or existed as discontinuous enclaves within them, so that although it is possible to identify the geographical area which they inhabited, it is hardly possible to assign precise borders to it. Still less do the shifting political frontiers of the region bear any relevance to the shared culture of the speakers of East Slavonic dialects and followers of Eastern Christianity who lived there. They nevertheless maintained a functioning ecclesiastical structure until the end of the seventeenth century, and continued to produce manuscripts with varying degrees of professionalism even later.

It is likely that the older Serbian manuscripts were brought with them by Serbian immigrants to Hungary in the seventeenth century. This is suggested in the case of Quart. Eccl. Slav. 15 and 19 by inscriptions connecting them respectively with Hunyad megye by 1640 and with the village of Töttös in the eighteenth century. It is quite possible that Oct. Serb. 1 was brought to Hungary by the scribe Hristofor Račanin himself, or by other monks from Rača, after the destruction of their monastery c. 1690 (Kacziba 1999: 4). Fragm. Eccl. Slav. 3 is a case apart, as it was extracted from a binding made probably at Vác in 1615, and binders commonly used scrap materials that had originated at a considerable distance from where they were working (Zinčenko 2004: 13-14). The eighteenth-century Serbian MSS were produced in Hungary by the Serbian communities by then established there.

There remain three other "imported" manuscripts: the origins of two of these, the Bulgarian Fol. Eccl. Slav. 19 and the Muscovite Russian Quart. Eccl. Slav. 17, can be traced back as far as their acquisition by the collector Juraj Ribay, while the provenance of the other Bulgarian manuscript, Quart. Eccl. Slav. 7, remains a mystery.

While they provide no direct evidence for where the manuscripts were written, later inscriptions do show where they were used, and give provenances throughout the Ruthenian area, from Kwiatoń in the North-West to the three south-eastern counties of Máramaros, Szolnok-Doboka and Beszterce-Naszód, where the Ruthenian population intermingled with Rumanian speakers.[4] There are indeed close affinities between the Ruthenian and Rumanian Slavonic (which we have conventionally designated "Moldavian", though strictly speaking Máramaros and the adjoining counties are in Transylvania) traditions, and not only in their styles of writing and decoration. It is clear that the two communities were each prepared to accept and use the other's manuscripts: two of the five Moldavian manuscripts have Slavonic inscriptions, and there are Rumanian inscriptions in six Ruthenian manuscripts. There are even inscriptions which mix Rumanian and Slavonic. Quart. Eccl. Slav. 14 is even more cosmopolitan: it is a Ruthenian manuscript with extensive Rumanian inscriptions which show contact with the Serbian linguistic area, specifically in the Bács region (Chivu 1978, 1997). Somewhat geographically isolated from the rest of the manuscripts are the numerous inscriptions in Fol. Eccl. Slav. 4, which begin within thirty years of the date of the manuscript and relate to places within the *powiat* of Biała Podlaska in eastern Poland. It is quite possible that the manuscript was also written here, and in such a case it would serve as a reminder that the Ruthenian manuscript tradition within the Kingdom of Hungary did not exist in isolation from the wider world.

There are only three manuscripts written on parchment (Quart. Eccl. Slav. 7, Fol. Eccl. Slav. 17, Frag. Eccl. Slav. 3), though parchment is also used for the illuminated leaves of Fol. Eccl. Slav. 3. The majority are, as one would expect, on paper, mostly of Western or Central European manufacture, from the fifteenth to nineteenth centuries. The profile of the collection is reflected in the predominance of two classes of watermarks, namely the various coats of arms and the boar. There is a remarkable diversity of other classes of marks, but none is represented by more than half a dozen specimens. We also find a number of twentieth-century marks in the endpapers which shed some light on the manuscripts' restoration history. By and large, the paper on which the manuscripts are written is not of a particularly high quality, being ordinary paper for ordinary manuscripts intended for ordinary use. For this reason (as well as the physical damage which the books have inevitably suffered over the years), the watermarks are often fragmentary, hard to see and hard to identify. Nevertheless, total excerption of the material has allowed us to assign most of the undated manuscripts to within relatively narrow chronological

---

[4] Kwiatoń is a little way north of the mediæval Hungarian frontier, in that part of Poland which became a Habsburg possession after the First Partition of Poland in 1772. From here the territory passes in a broad arc through what is now north-eastern Slovakia and the Transcarpathian *oblast'* of the Ukraine into the border provinces of modern Rumania.

limits, and to give an approximate date even in those cases where certain data is lacking.

The catalogue includes a watermark album containing full-scale copies of all the watermarks contained in the codices (except those from a few manuscripts which came to light late in the compilation of this catalogue and were consequently not seen by Dr Voutova.) To ensure a minimum of omissions, excerption was carried out leaf by leaf, including endpapers and additional leaves, and all visible marks noted, whatever their state of preservation. The marks were copied by hand in the traditional manner, the only method possible in our case, not to mention that this is the only way to proceed when the marks are partly hidden by the sewing of the quires. In spite of all our efforts, some marks remain unidentified for lack of any comparable specimens in the published repertories, but their inclusion in the album allows us to hope that further investigation may lead to their recognition.

In content, the manuscripts are almost entirely religious: there are occasional items on secular subjects in some of the eighteenth-century miscellanies and song-books, but they are very much the exception. The text found most frequently is the four Gospels – fourteen manuscripts. These are all continuous texts: the Evangelistary or *Aprakos* is not represented, except in a modified form as the Gospel Homiliary (Fol. Eccl. Slav. 9), which is arranged according to the calendar, and as the much abbreviated Gospel and Epistle lectionary appended to one of the Euchologia (Quart. Eccl. Slav. 15). Although these texts can be and certainly were used for reading in a non-liturgical context (an inscription in Fol. Eccl. Slav. 12 enjoins the reader to read it through four times a year), they are equally adapted for liturgical use, with indications of pericopes, their numbers, opening words and the occasions for which they are prescribed. It is interesting to note that in the oldest Gospel codex, Quart. Eccl. Slav. 7, the pericope numbers are a later addition, replacing the Ammonian sections which the manuscript originally indicated. This change reflects liturgical revisions following the adoption of the Jerusalem Typicon. The early date of this manuscript is likewise reflected in the absence of the tables of kephalaia and the prefaces of Theophylact, Archbishop of Ohrid, which normally accompany the Gospel texts in later manuscripts.[5] (The usual lectionaries are also absent, but this may be due to damage to the manuscript.) Curiously, the prefaces and kephalaia are also missing from the most recent Gospel manuscript, Fol. Eccl. Slav. 18.

There are three manuscripts and three fragments of the Acts and Epistles, including the oldest manuscript in the collection (Fragm. Eccl. Slav. 3), and two

---

[5] Cf. Dogramadžieva 1993, 11, 19.

manuscripts of the Psalter. The rest of the Bible is not represented by individual books, although some of the Menaia and the Lenten Triodion include a limited number of Old Testament parœmiæ.

Almost as well represented in the collection are liturgical books. With the exception of two short and comparatively late *ad hoc* collections of services (Quart. Eccl. Slav. 8 and 17), they are standard service books of the Eastern Rite – the Festal Menaion, Lenten Triodion, Octoechos and Euchologion. Although these are standard collections ("сборници с устойчив състав"), the structure of each of them permits considerable variation, the Menaion and Euchologion in particular being especially susceptible to local requirements. Fol. Eccl. Slav. 15, a peculiarly rustic manuscript in many respects, stretches the structure of the Menaion to its limits, combining it with material which properly belongs in other books: one can only assume that it was written very far from the main centres of culture where the traditions were maintained. Another Menaion, Fol. Eccl. Slav. 25, by contrast, is a much more professionally produced manuscript, but its remarkably eclectic content leaves the strong impression that it was written specifically in order to fill in the gaps in the books of the church for which it was commissioned. The remaining Menaia are much more traditional in content; however, the presence of a number of synaxarion readings in Fol. Eccl. Slav. 10 (which as a Moldavian manuscript represents a slightly different tradition) is worthy of note. Regional differences may also be observed amongst the Euchologia, where Quart. Eccl. Slav. 15, a Serbian manuscript, has a much more restricted selection of occasional offices than its Ruthenian congeners, to the extent that it might be better termed an Hieraticon or Liturgicon. Similarly isolated is Fol. Eccl. Slav. 21, though in this case it is time rather than distance that separates it: it is the most recent manuscript in the collection.

Canon law is represented by Quart. Eccl. Slav. 6, and also by a short penitential nomocanon inserted into the order for confession in Quart. Eccl. Slav. 12.

Two extensive Serbian compendia provide the most important sources in the collection for mediæval Slavonic literature other than hymnography. The first of these, Quart. Eccl. Slav. 19, is a Panegyricon, a genre particularly popular in the Serbian tradition, and contains no less than fifty homiletic and hagiographical texts. The other is Hristofor Račanin's miscellany, a less extensive but more varied selection of works, the first half of which is taken up by the Slavonic translation of the *Fiore di virtù*, a moral treatise believed to have been compiled by the Bolognese friar Tommaso Gozzadini. The rest contains a number of short texts, mostly of

Russian origin, on historical and other subjects, and is particularly noteworthy for the finely executed calendar and the tables accompanying it.

The remaining manuscripts may be grouped together by virtue of their age (all written after 1700), origin (all but two written by the Serbs of Hungary) and content, which is radically different from that of the earlier manuscripts. Two, admittedly, contain texts which had been current earlier, namely the *Dioptra* of Philip Monotropus (Duod. Eccl. Slav. 1, copied from a seventeenth-century printed book) and the Страсти Христовы which had been very popular in the later seventeenth century, but these are still not the scriptural and liturgical texts which had dominated the manuscript tradition hitherto. Above all these manuscripts document the religious culture of the Orthodox minority in eighteenth-century Hungary, and particularly its educational activity. Among them the four "Popović manuscripts", Quart. Eccl. Slav. 1, 2, and 4 and Quart. Serb. 2, form a distinct group. All came from the collection of Miklós Jankovich; the bindings of three of them are practically the same, while that of the fourth, Quart. Serb. 2, while not identical, is very similar. The name of Arsenije Popović is found in all but Quart. Eccl. Slav. 1. Quart. Eccl. Slav. 2 and 4 have a text in common. However, there is *internal* evidence to identify Arsenije only as the author of parts of Quart. Serb. 2; he may well be the third scribe, who has dated the items he has written. The latest date (which may be of composition, not necessarily of writing in this MS) is 1754. Quart. Eccl. Slav. 4 is dated (in a later inscription) 1743, and the paper agrees with this. However, Quart. Eccl. Slav. 1 and 2 are written on paper with à la mode watermarks which appear to date from the second decade of the eighteenth century; the MSS themselves are undated, but there is nothing in them that makes this date unlikely.

According to Jankovich's biographical note on Arsenije in Quart. Serb. 2, he took part in Franz von der Trenck's Moravian campaigns in the 1740s, first as soldier, then as army chaplain. If he was ordained at the canonical age of thirty, this means he was born about the same time as Quart. Eccl. Slav. 1 and 2 were written. On the other hand, if he was studying theology in the second decade of the eighteenth century, he would have been rather old for the wars by the time Trenck was recruiting his Illyrian legion. Clearly if Jankovich's note in Quart. Serb. 2 is to be trusted, his note in Quart. Eccl. Slav. 2 ("*Popovich Arsenii opera varia theologica*") is not, unless it is taken to mean merely ownership of the MS. The balance of probability, therefore, indicates that it is reasonable to believe that Arsenije owned all four MSS, and was very likely responsible for having them bound, but that he wrote only parts of Quart. Serb. 2.

Within the catalogue, the manuscripts are arranged in the usual manner according to type, manuscripts of the same type being ordered chronologically. This not only gives for the first time an organised view of the whole collection, but has entailed the re-identification of a number of manuscripts, and a revision (sometimes a very radical revision) of the dating of many more.

In the structure of the descriptions we have endeavoured to follow current best practice throughout, though this has required the exercise of a certain amount of judgment, particularly where there is no universally accepted norm. This was particularly acutely felt in the summary heading that introduces each description, which in Western European catalogues usually includes some indication of its geographical origin, while in Eastern European practice it is more usual to give some indication of its linguistic character ("извод"). Neither is really appropriate for the present collection. While the place of origin of Western European manuscripts can often be determined quite closely, even to the scriptorium, this is rarely the case in the East; and even when it can be done, to describe such manuscripts as Quart. Eccl. Slav. 3 or 5 as "Hungarian", though geographically accurate, might create something of a false impression. The vast majority of our manuscripts would have to be ascribed to a vague "Ruthenia" without any properly defined borders. One could indeed make a case for ascribing these manuscripts to a common Ruthenian tradition, but since the implications of this are both geographically and linguistically imprecise, to do so in the header might mislead as much as it informed. Classification by linguistic tradition would give even worse results. The tradition, as far as sixteenth- and seventeenth-century Ruthenia was concerned, was too fluid and inconsistent for summary description, and any attempt at it is likely to be inadequate as far as individual manuscripts are concerned, and to create a very false impression of the manuscripts as a whole. Our solution has been to limit the information in the header to title and date, indicating both origin and language in the body of the description.

After the summary heading, the description proper begins with the physical characteristics of the manuscript, starting with the material on which it is written. In the case of paper, the watermarks are identified by reference to the corresponding figure in the watermark album included in this volume. They are also related to similar marks in published watermark repertories. The index to the album allows the figures to be referred to the manuscripts in which the marks occur.

The next part of the description gives the number of leaves in the manuscript and their numeration (which is rarely original). In accordance with the usual library practice, flyleaves are indicated by Roman numerals in the leaf count, and their numeration is indicated by Roman numerals at the front, but as a continuation of the main sequence at the end. Thus if we have, say, a manuscript of 196 leaves with two flyleaves at each end, this is expressed as "ii+196+ii leaves, foliated i-ii, 1-198". In practice, flyleaves are more often than not unfoliated. In such cases square brackets are used to indicate the suppositious numeration of the unfoliated leaves (as indeed they are for unnumbered leaves in the body of the book), for example "i+146+i leaves; modern stamped foliation, [i], 1-146, [147]".

After this comes the collation formula, in which gatherings are numbered consecutively in Roman numerals, the original number of leaves in each gathering being indicated by a superscript arabic numeral and any changes to this in brackets immediately following, thus $XIV^8(-1 \pm 5)$ means that the fourteenth gathering was of eight leaves, of which the first is now lost and the fifth is a cancel. Signatures, whether original or later additions, are also indicated here. In a number of cases manuscripts have been reconstructed so that their present composition differs from their original structure, which may or may not be recoverable; this is likewise mentioned at this point.

While description of the layout and ink used in the manuscripts is relatively straightforward, description of their hands is extremely problematic, not least because of the highly unsatisfactory state of the terminology. There is no consensus as to the meaning of the terms in current use, to the extent that the *same* hand can be described as полуустав by one authority and скоропись by another (for example in the descriptions of GIM Čud. 71 in Protas'eva 1980: 50, and Šul'gina 2000: 53-55 and pl.72). The introduction, or reintroduction, of the term книжное письмо by Kostjuchina (1974) to designate the type of hand regularly used for writing codices, is much to be welcomed. We have used the roughly equivalent English term "bookhand" in precisely this sense, reserving "semiuncial" for the more formal and conservative hands. This can certainly not be regarded as a final resolution of the terminological problem, which probably requires a complete revision of cyrillic palæography going back to its Greek models, but it is perhaps a small step in the right direction. In any case, since all the manuscripts in this catalogue are illustrated, the reader may refer to the plates to see what we mean by our description of the hand in any particular instance. We have frequently had equally great problems in distinguishing between hands within a single manuscript, either because different scribes may adhere strictly to a common style of writing, or because a single scribe may have been inconsistent. We have nevertheless listed and briefly characterised the various hands to the best of our ability.

While there is no established hierarchical format for the description of bindings, we have adhered to a fixed order within each description: materials and measurements, technical characteristics, and details of the tooling or other ornamentation. Most of the bindings have been restored, generally following the practice of the

Library's restoration laboratories. According to this the original leather, if preserved, is reapplied on the original wooden boards (or on new ones if they must be replaced), and new leather is used for repairs. The descriptions therefore make it clear whether the binding has been restored. The probable date of the original work is given on the basis of comparative analysis, as far as our available sources have allowed. Since many of the manuscripts had undergone previous repairs before the modern restoration, the problem with the dating persists: there are cases in which the data from the bindings allow their dating roughly to the same time as the manuscripts themselves, but the date of the paper mendings cannot be determined. For this reason we have preferred in certain cases to avoid firm statements concerning the originality of a binding.

In regard to the ornamentation, there are interesting examples of bindings on which different ornamental systems occur together. The implements used for tooling combine Western and Eastern patterns in such a way as to result in an eclectic design reflecting an Eastern Orthodox milieu existing in close proximity to its Catholic neighbours. One such example is the binding of Fol. Eccl. Slav. 3 with a border consisting of small human heads in oval medallions – this is a common motif in Western European bindings of the second half of the sixteenth century, and spread to the Polish-Lithuanian Commonwealth (including much of the present-day Ukraine and West and South-West Russia). The medallions with the Virgin within the central panel also belong rather to Western iconography, but adapted to satisfy Eastern perceptions, while the traditional images of the Evangelists in the corners have Greek captions. The upper cover of Quart. Eccl. Slav. 10 is a similar case, but its lower cover is decorated entirely with popular Western stamps with four images of Apostles and Evangelists, each related to a Biblical quotation in form of a caption. These were widespread amongst German binders and also in Poland (Kraków) in the late sixteenth century. Maybe the most curious example is the binding of the Serbian miscellany (see below) which, being a masterpiece of Oriental craftsmanship, is a witness (not unique for its time and area of production) to cooperation between Christians and Muslims in the sphere of book production.

The decoration of the manuscripts, i.e. their artistic content, is treated as an element at the same level as their literary content or physical structure. Its description normally begins with a brief unstructured overview of its general characteristics (in the case of manuscripts with extremely modest decoration this may be sufficient for the entire description) followed by a structured list of decorative elements fully described. The advantage of this scheme is that it enables the encoding of the description at a level appropriate to the actual complexity of the decoration.

The usual order of description has been followed, beginning with the miniatures, and proceeding with the headpieces, initials, tailpieces and marginal ornaments/drawings. As several manuscripts include ornamental borders, they are described as a separate decorative element. Titles are described here only if they constitute a particular decorative element; otherwise, if they are written in simple majuscules, they are included in the discussion of the script under "Hand". We have retained Ščepkin's term "vjaz'" for the form of script where characters share ascenders and descenders, no better term having so far been introduced.

In contrast to the long established practice of Slavonic palæography, we have avoided the term "style" by reason of the great inconsistency that prevails in its use; instead, we have preferred the more neutral term "type" to classify the stylistic features of any particular ornamental device. The great majority of the manuscripts reveal the diffusion of what is commonly known as the "Balkan interlaced style", to which we refer in the descriptions as "ornament of Balkan interlaced type" or "Balkan interlaced ornament". One of the most refined artistic expressions of the late Balkan ornament, executed by the masterly hand of Hristofor Račanin, is the Serbian miscellany of 1679 (Oct. Serb. 1), a manuscript unrivalled in the collection for its calligraphic quality, the use of gold and the miniature representations of the signs of the zodiac in the Calendar. The Gospel manuscript Fol. Eccl. Slav. 17, though it has lost most of its ornamentation, reveals the richness and elaboration of the Moldavian version of Balkan ornament. When appropriate, the term "Neobyzantine" is also used to describe the red initials with vegetal ornamentation. Several manuscripts, Gospels mainly, are illuminated following the pattern developed in the sixteenth-century Ukrainian and Belarusian manuscripts, that is filling the margins of the opening page with a rich vegetal border. In various cases the illumination demonstrates the intermingling of the South Slavonic traditions with East Slavonic ones, the latter adapting some so-called "Western" elements as well. One such example is Fol. Eccl. Slav 4, whose illumination combines heterogeneous patterns, among which are Gothic-style-like floral motifs and one teratological headpiece with obvious predecessors in the thirteenth century. On the whole, the Széchényi Slavonic collection does not show the best of the late mediæval artistic achievements. Nevertheless, the only illustrated Gospel (Fol. Eccl. Slav. 6) must be mentioned because of its full-page miniatures of the Evangelists. Their bright colouring, simple tempera technique and stylistic features point to a provincial workshop the location of which cannot be established at the moment, but it is possible that comparison with other manuscripts preserved in the region may enable other scholars to identify even the hand of the painter.

The contents of each manuscript are listed in full, with an indication of the leaves which each item occupies. Incipits and explicits are not given for standard texts (church services, books of the Bible, etc.), but only in those cases where they may be of use in assisting the reader in identifying the text. Any attempt at textual criticism or literary history would be quite beyond the scope of a catalogue such as this, which aims for no more than to make the texts identifiable to those who may be interested in them.

Our characterisation of the language of the texts is similarly limited, and indeed the collection contains relatively few manuscripts which are likely to be of particular interest to the linguist. The vast majority of the manuscripts, being scriptural or liturgical texts of Ruthenian provenance, are written in Church Slavonic of the type current amongst the Eastern Slavs. The Ruthenian scribes participated in the linguistic processes of the whole East Slavonic area, which included the wholesale adoption in the early fifteenth century of Tărnovo orthographic norms, which then gradually declined as East Slavonic features reasserted themselves, though they persisted longer in the West than in Muscovy. The sixteenth- and seventeenth-century manuscripts that predominate in our collection thus present a mixture of Bulgarian and East Slavonic features in various proportions. Perfect adherence to Tărnovo orthography is virtually unknown, as it was an artificial system for this region; most noticeably, there was clearly no distinction between оу and ѫ in pronunciation, and it is a very rare scribe who manages to maintain this distinction completely in orthography. Our material displays no particular correlation between the age of the manuscript and the extent of Bulgarian influence: on the contrary, the evidence of these manuscripts suggests rather that orthography depended primarily on the tastes and competence of the individual scribe, and the extent to which he chose to reproduce the usage of his original or accommodate it to his own habits. It is particularly noteworthy that even within a single manuscript one can find significant divergence between scribes' practice, which must mean that at this period there was no accepted standard even within particular scriptoria, let alone the region as a whole.

Exceptional amongst the Ruthenian material is the vernacular Gospel Homiliary of 1588 (Fol. Eccl. Slav. 9), which reflects the practice of preaching in the проста мова at this time. Its language has been the subject of a series of short articles by M. Kocsis.[6] In the eighteenth and nineteenth centuries the vernacular continued to be used in less formal religious contexts (Quart. Eccl. Slav. 16, 18),

---

[6] The most recent of these (Kocsis 2004) includes a full list of previous work on the manuscript.

while all the Eastern Slavs adopted the standardised Muscovite norm that has come to be known as Synodal Church Slavonic[7] for their official religious texts.

The Middle Bulgarian language of the two Bulgarian manuscripts in the collection has been described in some detail in the articles devoted to them (Tóth 1983, Szarvas 1986, Zaimov, Tóth, Balázs 2003); as one would expect, the Moldavian manuscripts belong to the same linguistic tradition. The mediæval Serbian manuscripts follow the Serbian recension of Church Slavonic, though one of them, Quart. Serb. 1, has a number of features indicative of the Russian antecedents of the texts it includes. The manuscripts produced by the Serbian community in eighteenth-century Hungary exhibit a considerable linguistic diversity. The *slavenosrpski* language of Serbian literary activity of that period predominates, though that of some texts reflects their Russian and Belarusian origins. These books also incorporate items in Rumanian, and a lesser amount of Latin and German.

The treatment of inscriptions in the manuscripts is much more complete. All legible inscriptions (with the exception of utterly trivial scrawls and jottings, and the presence even of these is noted) are reproduced in full. Where possible, persons and places mentioned in the inscriptions are identified, though there has been much more success with the places than the persons, who do not, as a rule, appear to have been involved in public life beyond their own villages. The most prominent person mentioned in the inscription is apparently Ferenc Rákóczy (ракoвцѣ Ферєнцъ) in Quart. Eccl. Slav. 11, f.5v, though why his name should appear in a list of unknown persons we can only guess: perhaps it reflects the political sympathies of the writer. The eminent bishop Andrej Bačins'kyj is mentioned in Quart. Eccl. Slav. 12, f.35v, but apart from such individuals even the episcopate is shrouded in obscurity: Miklós Jankovich's biographical note in Quart. Serb. 2 (if indeed it can be trusted) is our main source at present for the career of Arsenije Popović, and the bare statement that "From 1653-1663, the bishop of Máramaros was Mychajil Molodec'" (Pekar 1992: 64), which seems to be the extent of the information about him in published sources, should perhaps be reconsidered in the light of the inscription on f.347v of Fol. Eccl. Slav. 24, Михаи҆ молодє҆ арх҃їеп҃кпь | Маромор8шѣнского ѡⷠⷣА҆рⷤъ | рѡ҇ сп҃н҃їа ҂ах҃н҃в. а҃ца а҃. г҃. дн҃ь, i.e. 1652.

In most cases the inscriptions record the ownership, purchase or donation of a manuscript, or list persons who are to be commemorated in prayer – sometimes all of these things in one inscription. Having a book rebound could be considered a pious act similar to its donation (Fol. Eccl. Slav. 13, 15, 28). Sometimes the price paid for the manuscript is recorded, and frequently anathemas are invoked against anyone who removes the manuscript from the church to which it has been given.

---

[7] For the use of this term see Mathiesen 1972, especially pp.70-72.

Other inscriptions have nothing to do with the manuscript in which they are found, and record remarkable climatic phenomena, political or local events: Fol. Eccl. Slav. 4 and 11 have a particularly fine selection. Even fragments of popular songs may be written in the margins of books to which they bear no relation, and there are of course the inevitable trivial jottings and *probationes calami.*

The inscriptions are also the only source for the history of the manuscripts before their acquisition by the library. The date of their acquisition and the person from whom they were acquired is known (and stated) in almost every case, but other evidence for their recent history is rather sketchy. Documentation of restoration and other events within the OSZK has in recent years been exemplary, and is referred to in the descriptions, but for earlier times there are very few records. They can, however, sometimes be supplemented by information from the manuscripts themselves. In particular, there are two watermarks that can be found in the endpapers of a number of manuscripts: an oak twig (fig.34 in the watermark album in this volume) and a coat of arms (fig.20). The former is found in three manuscripts, Fol. Eccl. Slav. 6, 10 and 16, of which the first is known to have been restored in the Library in 1956; the latter is found in no less than twelve (Fol. Eccl. Slav. 1, 2, 4, 5, 9, 11, 12, 13, 23, 26, Quart. Eccl. Slav. 10 and 15). Fol. Eccl. Slav. 23 and 26 were acquired in 1956 and 1962 respectively, and consequently restored after these dates. This points to an extensive programme of conservation in the Library during the 1950s and 1960s. Such other information as can be retrieved about the manuscripts' fate is also adduced, and in those few cases where there are publications on the manuscripts, these are cited.

Following the precedent of the catalogue of early-printed cyrillic books in the British Isles,[8] we originally produced the descriptions in electronic form; the printed version which this book represents is generated from the electronic descriptions. The electronic descriptions will remain in existence and may be used for future research, whether integrated into larger electronic catalogues of one kind or another, used for the extrapolation of data for more narrowly focused studies, "quantitive codicology"[9] or other purposes. The format used for the descriptions is XML. In terms of the structure of the descriptions, we have endeavoured to adhere to the best practice in current manuscript studies, in which there have been considerable advances in recent years. Since the discipline of computer-assisted manuscript studies is still in its infancy, there is no standard for the construction

[8] R.M. Cleminson, D.Radoslavova, C.G.Thomas, A.V.Voznesenskij, *Cyrillic Books Printed Before 1701 in British and Irish Collections: A Union Catalogue*, London: The British Library, 2000.
[9] This term was introduced by D.J. Birnbaum at the Thirteenth International Congress of Slavists in Ljubljana, August 2003.

of electronic descriptions,[10] but a model has been devised for the project which allows the data recorded to be presented in conformity with traditional manuscript descriptions and the *de facto* standards which have been developed over many years of scholarship. Experience gained in the *Repertorium of Old Bulgarian Literature* and the description of early-printed cyrillic books in the British Isles has been valuable in this respect.

While the compilation of the catalogue was essentially a collaborative endeavour, there was a certain division of labour amongst the compilers. In particular, the identification and study of the watermarks was carried out by Nina Voutova, who also drew the album. All aspects of the visual appearance of the manuscripts, particularly the decoration and bindings, were the prime responsibility of Elissaveta Moussakova, while the more strictly codicological parts of the descriptions were mostly in the hands of Ralph Cleminson, who was also responsible for the technical aspects of the XML encoding.

The authors have been assisted in their work by numerous colleagues, whose expertise and generosity are gratefully acknowledged here. Special thanks are due to Dr István Monok, Director of the National Széchényi Library, Dr Orsolya Karsay, Head of the Manuscript Department, Dr Beatrix Kastaly of the Conservation and Restoration Laboratory, and to all the people in the Manuscript Department for their patience and readiness to make our work easier. We are most indebted to Professor Borjana Velčeva, originally expected to be a member of our team, but whom various circumstances prevented from taking part in the work, for her invaluable comments on the language of the manuscripts, even in cases where our views differed considerably. Outside the Library, we are grateful to Dr Louise Barrick, Cristian Gaşpar, Dr Dorotej Getov, Dr Marija Jovčeva, Dr Ágnes Kacziba, who kindly sent us copies of her monograph on MS Oct. Serb. 1, Professor József Laszlovszky, Dana Prioteasa, Dilyana Radoslavova, Professor Dimitrije Stefanović, Dr Elena Uzunova, and colleagues from the Dept of Manuscripts and Early-Printed Books at the National Library of Bulgaria. The final presentation of the printed volume owes much to the typographical skill of Péter Banyó. Most importantly, financial assistance without which the project could not have been carried out was provided by the Arts and Humanities Research Board and by the Central European University, and our debt to both these bodies is most gratefully acknowledged.

---

[10] Such claims have been advanced for the MASTER DTD, but practical experience shows that it is not at all suitable for this purpose; however, there are hopeful signs that developments being carried out under the auspices of the Text Encoding Initiative may eventually produce a usable interchange format.

On the History of our Slavonic Cyrillic Manuscripts

Orsolya Karsay

Although the collections of the National Széchényi Library have always included books and manuscripts in Slavonic languages, collecting them has never been part of the main focus of the acquisitions policy of the National Library. Therefore the collection is not the outcome of a planned system, but our Slavonic material has rather grown by itself, finding its natural place among Hungarica as a regional Hungaricum within the "Patriotica" materials, i.e. those relating to the historical Kingdom of Hungary. This means it is made up of documents written in languages other than Hungarian resulting from the cultural activities of ethnic groups living within the historical Hungary or in countries adjacent to it. In this sense, the holdings of the Manuscript Collection of the National Széchényi Library, which number over one million items, include manuscripts in various Slavonic languages (i.e. Russian, Serbian, Croatian, Czech, Slovak, Polish, etc.), as well as a group of Rumanian, Greek, Hebrew and other works. As within the Manuscript Collection these are regarded as exotic or minority languages in comparison with the bulky Hungarian, Latin and German units, documents written in them have never received the professional treatment due to them, partly because of a shortage of specialist experts. Their cataloguing has remained superficial, and most of them have been hiding in our storerooms almost unknown. The only reference in the manuscript department providing information on them has been a hand-written inventory called *Variæ linguæ*, also listing manuscripts in the other minority languages. The situation is further complicated by the fact that the Slavonic manuscripts have often been reclassified, with their call numbers changed, which makes the identification of individual items rather difficult even within the inventory. This is one of the reasons why the present undertaking by Professor Cleminson and his colleagues is of such significance. Applying the most up-to-date methods of processing, they are making a detailed content, linguistic, historical, codicological and palæographic examination of our collection of fifty-six manuscripts written in Church Slavonic, which is the most valuable and at the same time least accessible section of our Slavonic holdings.

It would be unfair towards old collectors of Hungarian books to suggest that their collections of Church Slavonic manuscripts grew only through accidental acquisitions. This was certainly not the case. They knew that the value of any collection is determined by pieces of international significance. So did the scholarly curators and officials of the Hungarian National Museum, whose donations also very considerably enriched the numbers of Slavonic codices. Later on, old Slavonic materials were deposited in our Manuscript Collection by several private individuals who were in close contact with Slavonic traditions because of their family or personal connections, political activities, religious denomination or birthplace. There are a few items that have reached us from booksellers or through other channels. In one case, all we know is the year of arrival, and in another even that date is not clear.

We have thus outlined five distinct groups through whom Church Slavonic codices came to be among the manuscript collections housed by the National Széchényi Library. The first group is made up of the great nineteenth-century bibliophiles, with Miklós Jankovich the most outstanding among them. The second group includes curators of the museum, and the third is made up of private persons. A fourth group of manuscripts contains items of mixed provenance, and finally in the fifth we have those whose provenance is uncertain.

The aim of this paper is to show how the history of these groups is related to the main trends in the history of the National Széchényi Library. The history of each item will be dealt with only insofar as it is relevant to the history of collection. In all the cases where present research is unable to solve the problems of provenance, attention will be drawn to further possibilities of clarifying those issues. Even with this approach, certain questions will have to be left unanswered and their solution left to future research.

1. Old Hungarian book collectors

1.1. Ferenc Széchényi

It was in the late eighteenth and early nineteenth centuries that the earliest group of our Church Slavonic manuscripts came into the collections that have for 200 years formed the basis of the Hungarian National Library, called the National Széchényi Library today. This means that their acquisition had begun long before the National Library was actually founded. Although we have no knowledge of any Church Slavonic manuscripts in the core collection of Count Ferenc Széchényi (1754-1820), his interest in Slavonic literacy is apparent from the large number of his Slavonic printed books. Among the old Slavonic printed books in Ferenc Széchényi's core collection, the Breviarium Zagrabiense is an outstanding cimelium (the term used for the most precious items in the Library's collections), an incunabulum printed in 1484 in Erhard Ratdolt's Venetian printing house. This rarity, of which there is only one other copy extant, in the Vatican Library, exhibits many features of the art of the book in Renaissance Italy. Its pages, printed on parchment, are decorated with rich floral ornaments, gilded initials and delicate frames in the margins. The book had been commissioned by the generous patron of Zagreb Cathedral, bishop Osvát Thuz.

Besides this internationally acclaimed incunabulum of Ferenc Széchényi's, mention should be made here of two equally valuable Slavonic items, an early printed book and a codex. Although neither reached us through the "founding fathers", both add to the prestige of the National Library. The former is the most complete copy of the famous Missale Glagoliticum, the first book printed on Croatian land, which was printed in 1494 in Senj with the participation of canon Blaž Baromić. The latter is a Latin codex purchased in 1979 (Cod. Lat. 540), on the last page of which one of the earliest examples of Croatian poetry, a Passion Song, was written down at the beginning of the twelfth century. This Croatian Song of Mary is a "twin" of the first known Hungarian verse, the Old Hungarian Lament of Mary dating back to the last quarter of the thirteenth century. The Hungarian poem is also an added text in one of our Latin codices, known as the Leuven Codex after its previous location.

1.2. Miklós Jankovich

As regards our Church Slavonic manuscripts, Miklós Jankovich (1772-1846), "the greatest Hungarian art collector of all time", had an even more prominent role than Ferenc Széchényi, as it was through his collections that the very first Church Slavonic manuscripts were obtained. After Ferenc Széchényi, Jankovich is rightly called "the second founder" of the Hungarian National Museum and the National Széchényi Library. He devoted all his life and wealth to his passion for collecting. The paradigmatic significance of his life's work was recently illustrated by the comprehensive exhibition "The Collections of Miklós Jankovich (1772-1846)" held in the Hungarian National Gallery. The best pieces from Jankovich's varied collection available in present-day Hungarian museums, libraries and archives were exhibited with the intention of demonstrating some less well-known characteristics of the collector and scholar. The aim was to show how he managed to combine the discovery and study of Hungarian historical relics with considerations of universal art history. It was thanks to his efforts that a number of internationally acknowledged sets of artefacts and individual items of outstanding value ended up in Hungarian museums and libraries, thus entering the cultural bloodstream of this country.

Jankovich's collection may be divided into three parts: firstly paintings and carvings, secondly the treasury, and thirdly the library. The first category comprises paintings, statues, ivory carvings, incrustations and stone carvings. The treasury contains examples of goldsmith's work, jewellery, ceramics and glassware. Finally, the library is made up of manuscripts, early-printed books, old Hungarian printed materials (the so-called "Régi Magyar Könyvtár"), early editions of classical authors, old prints, sources for the Lutheran reform movement, archival sources and the coins, banknotes and medals that were traditionally collected side by side with books. The manuscripts are further divided into mediæval and works written in modern Latin, German, Hungarian, Greek, Church Slavonic and Oriental languages.

Although a mere list does not give a clear idea of either the quantity or the quality of these collections, it does throw a light on the dimensions of the undertaking and the collector's wide national and international interests that extended to Corvinas (three in number), Hungarian linguistic records, German books on alchemy and Turkish defters, just to mention a few of the manuscripts. And on top of all that, there are the nine Slavonic manuscripts.

These nine manuscripts entered public ownership as part of Jankovich's so-called first collection when in 1836, on Palatine József's initiative, parliament purchased for the Hungarian National Museum Jankovich's collections, to the creation of which he had devoted all his wealth from the 1790s onwards, sometimes pushing himself to the brink of bankruptcy. Jankovich immediately started creating another collection, but the second collection was auctioned off after his death and only a few fragments reached the National Museum. The two vast collections are today in the National Museum, the National Széchényi Library, the Library of the Hungarian Academy of Sciences and the three institutions that once formed part of the National Museum: the Museum of Applied Art, the Museum of Fine Art and the Hungarian National Gallery. A large number of artefacts, however, can no longer be identified as having been his.

From this point of view, the manuscripts enjoy the best position, as they usually bear Jankovich's oval or rhomboid stamp or hand-written record of his source of purchase. Jankovich originally intended to hand over the library with annotations, but this plan was only partially realised. Nevertheless, the list of his Slavonic books is available (Fol. Boch. Slav. 1), as is the list of György Ribay's Slavonic books, which had ended up in Jankovich's possession together with Ribay's other books (Fol. Boch. Slav. 7).

Two of the nine Church Slavonic manuscripts in Jankovich's possession had originated from Ribay's large collection of Slavonica (mainly Bohemica). The special significance of these two items for the history of collecting is that through Ribay's contacts they give us an insight into some chapters of Hungarian and European collecting in Jankovich's time and before.

An evangelical pastor, György Ribay (1754-1812) was also a well-known collector and literary figure of his age. He was a student at Western European universities, studying in Jena between 1780 and 1782 with Professor Johann Gottfried Eichhorn. On his return home, he worked as a pastor, taking an active part in organising the Evangelical Church in northern Hungary and in establishing its congregations there. From 1785 he was a pastor in Cinkota. In 1798 he opened a lucrative art shop in Pest, which he ran for a few years, and then returned to his profession in the Church. He maintained strong contacts with contemporary scholars in Hungary and abroad, conducted serious Slavonic research and collected a very considerable number of Slavonic books from Bohemia and Hungary. He sold his stock to Jankovich in 1807.

The older of the two Ribay manuscripts is a paper codex, dating back to the middle of the fifteenth century, which contains the Acts and Epistles, followed by the cycle of antiphons (Fol. Eccl. Slav. 19). Bound into the end of the codex are two modern leaves (foliated 1-2) containing two Latin texts by two different hands. The first was written by György Ribay, who is uncertain as regards the age of the codex (fifteenth or sixteenth century), as is indicated by the crossed-out dates on the inside of the wooden binding. Ribay goes on to describe in the first person how he managed to acquire the codex, namely from Dániel Cornides (1732-1787) in 1787, in exchange for very rare and valuable Hungarian historical works. As well as being an eminent member of the generation of great eighteenth-century historians, Dániel Cornides was a significant book collector. After his death, his collection, which reflected his wide interests, went to the Pest library of Count József Teleki (1738-1796), and later to the Library of the Hungarian Academy of Sciences. It is important to note that Cornides had a very special relationship with Miklós Jankovich. As a schoolboy, the young Jankovich would often call on the famous professor, to whom he was truly grateful and whom he always respected as his master, although Cornides was never officially his tutor. The influence of the middle-class historian is evident in Jankovich's later development, both as regards the universal character of his collection and its religious tolerance.

In connexion with this item it is also noteworthy that on the other leaf bound at the end of the volume are philological comments and critical remarks made by the Czech scholar Josef Dobrovský (1753-1829) about the Old Church Slavonic translation of the original Greek text. Dobrovský was an outstanding linguist, literary man and historian, the founder of comparative Slavonic studies, well-versed in Oriental languages and a strong believer in the Finno-Ugrian language family.

He was born in Hungary and had excellent contacts with Hungarian scholars and language reformers. He knew Ribay personally, and maintained a regular correspondence with him. It was only after Ribay's death that he established contact with Miklós Jankovich. It is even more interesting that he cultivated a true friendship with Ferenc Széchényi, who would always call on him to exchange views when he visited Prague. Fortunately their correspondence has survived. Thus Dobrovský made a considerable intellectual impact on the work of three Hungarian collectors.

The origins of the other manuscript which Jankovich acquired from György Ribay can be traced even further than Prague, namely to Jena. This liturgical book, dating back to the late seventeenth century and written in Russian Church Slavonic, was presented to Ribay by his professor, the theology tutor Johann Gottfried Eichhorn (1752-1827) at the time when Ribay was studying in Jena. Eichhorn was the most influential Bible critic of the turn of the eighteenth and nineteenth centuries, one of the instigators of the trend called "Higher Criticism", according to which sacred books are interpreted as literature, using all the apparatus of professional scholarship. How the manuscript came to be in Jena it is no longer possible to establish – perhaps it was brought by a wandering student.

It is equally impossible to trace the earlier history of one of Jankovich's oldest Slavonic manuscripts (Fol. Eccl. Slav. 17). Disbound and with all its leaves detached, this incomplete Gospel book from Moldavia is most likely to originate from the fifteenth century. There are two nineteenth-century sheets of paper attached to it, with Hungarian and Latin notes written by different hands, but they do not bring us any closer to a solution.

Four of the other six Slavonic manuscripts belonging to Jankovich are related through the person of Arsenije Popović, who must have been their author or owner (Quart. Eccl. Slav. 1, 2. and 4, Quart. Serb. 2). Who was Arsenije Popović? It is briefly noted by Jankovich himself on the first page of Quart.Serb.2. that Popović originally served in the army of Franz von der Trenck (1711-1749), then went into the Church, and finally became bishop in Belgrade, then in Buda. In the Serbian-Hungarian manuscript of mixed contents, you can also read Trenck's German and Latin epitaphs. The romantic hero, Ferenc Trenck, and his nephew Frigyes Trenck, both soldiers in Maria Theresia's army, must have enjoyed great popularity in the nineteenth century, partly thanks to their autobiographies. Jókai wrote about their adventurous lives in two different works (*The Vicissitudes of Ferenc Trenck* and *The Two Trencks*), but later on they were forgotten. If it is permissible at all to talk of a Popović group within Miklós Jankovich's manuscripts, it is to be remembered that only very subtle features might suggest a closer relationship among them. All four of them originate from Hungary. The first three items in quarto format are also connected by the great similarity of their bindings. It is to be hoped that further research will support the joint origin of these four manuscripts.

The last two items in the Jankovich collection are related to the activity of the Hungarian Serbian congregations: one to that in Buda (Duod. Eccl. Slav.1), while the other to the one in Esztergom (Quart. Eccl. Slav. 3). The former, the *Dioptra* of Philip Monotropus, was copied in Buda in 1713 from the edition published in Vilna in 1642. The inscription recording its creation mentions the name of Nestor, clerk and subsequently archpriest of Buda. A further inscription dated 1735 records the name of the priest Nikolaje Milovanović. The *Dioptra* (Speculum, i.e. Looking Glass) was a popular edifying reading for monks, containing the description of human existence. The other work, "The Brief Instruction" was copied by György Tiro(vić) in 1769 in Esztergom.

1.3. Dr. Gyula Todorescu and Aranka Horváth

We are indebted to Dr. Gyula Todorescu and his wife Aranka Horváth for a very precious seventeenth-century manuscript miscellany (Oct. Serb. 1, Accessions register: 1929/40; the later stamp 1953/191 was applied in error and has been cancelled). Gyula Todorescu (1866-1919) was a dedicated and passionate collector, who, like Jankovich, devoted all his life and wealth to the creation of a Hungarian library. He died in the prime of life, impoverished and mentally disturbed.

Todorescu collected all books printed in Hungarian or related to Hungary published up to 1711, and also books published up to 1800 that were of relevance to Hungary. His collection was divided into two main parts: books printed in Hungarian and books in other languages printed in Hungary. These very significant collection of printed Hungarica was presented to the National Széchényi Library in 1919 by his widow, Aranka Horváth. Besides the Todorescu Hungarica, there were seven valuable Cyrillic printed books in his collection. The manuscript in Church Slavonic may have accompanied them, as it was only in 1929 that it reached the Manuscript Collection as a transfer from the Book Collection, together with a few other hand-written volumes. When and how the manuscript entered the Todorescu collection is unfortunately unclear. Ágnes Kacziba is the most recent scholar to have studied this manuscript, a Serbian redaction of texts of Russian origin, which she regards as "one of the oldest Serbian manuscripts in Hungary".

2. Museum officials

To the second category of sources for our Church Slavonic manuscripts belong three officials of the Hungarian National Museum, namely Antal Hodinka, László Réthy and Szilárd Sulica. The three are united in having achieved the highest level of scholarship in their particular fields, and were likewise dedicated guardians of the collections entrusted to them. Although Hodinka worked for the museum only for a short time, his positivist respect for written sources characterised him throughout his career.

2.1. Antal Hodinka

Both chronologically and in order of magnitude, the first of the three is Antal Hodinka (1864-1946). Antal Hodinka was one of the pioneers of Hungarian Slavonic Studies, a historian of positivist outlook, university professor and academician, who at the beginning of his career worked for the Library of the Hungarian National Museum (i.e. the present-day National Széchényi Library, which at that time was still a department of the Museum) for a short while (1888-89), and dealt with the cataloguing of Church Slavonic manuscripts. They must have been the Jankovich items, because at that time we possessed nothing else. The son of the Sub-Carpathian Greek Catholic priest in the village of Ladomírová he was preparing to be a priest himself, studying history and Slavonic philology, in addition to his studies in theology. He had a good command of Ruthenian, Russian, Serbian, Croatian and other languages. His academic career started in Vienna, in the circle of Lajos Thallóczy, and continued in Rome, Pozsony (Bratislava), Pécs and Budapest. On the basis of archival research, he dealt among other things with the history of Sub-Carpathian Ruthenians, the Munkács bishopric, with the sources of Serbian history and with material relating to Hungary in the Russian chronicles.

In 1890 Hodinka sold the National Library a sixteenth-century Ruthenian Gospel book, and another from the seventeenth century (Fol. Eccl. Slav.1 and 18, Accessions register: 1890/4). In 1904, however, he made a considerable donation. Among the material in our archives we have the following note from 1905 regarding the previous year's acquisitions of the Manuscript Collection: "The 14 Slavonic codices that Antal Hodinka has presented to the Manuscript Collection are of great value for linguistics and church history" (Fol. Eccl. Slav. 6, 7, 8, 9, 10, 11, 12, 13, 14, and. Quart. Eccl. Slav. 9, 10, 11, 12, 13, Accessions register: 1904/1). His 1904 donation was followed by another two: in 1907 an Octoechos (Fol. Eccl. Slav.15,

Accessions register: 1907/34) and a Nomocanon in 1909 (Quart. Eccl. Slav. 6, Accessions register: 1909/7).

We do not know why the young scholar first sold and subsequently made donations. It may have been the example set by Jankovich, or the recognition that the right place for the sources in his possession was a public collection where they could be exposed to further scholarly examinations. We do not know either how he got the eighteen Slavonic codices, whether they had been in the family and he inherited them from his father, or whether he collected them in his homeland. Nevertheless, the collection has a uniform image. As far as their genres are concerned, the items in the collection can be divided into two main groups: texts from the New Testament and service books. They are all of Ruthenian origin and are fairly early, dating back to the sixteenth and seventeenth centuries. It is possible that Hodinka's manuscript bequest preserved in the Manuscript Collection of the Hungarian Academy of Sciences has interesting information in store regarding the earlier history of his manuscripts and his motives for donation.

2.2.   László Réthy

Dr. László Réthy (1851-1914) was the curator of the Coin and Medal Collection of the Hungarian National Museum, an academician and the founder of modern Hungarian numismatics. His many-sided, positivist interest extended to questions of ethnography and linguistics, and even to the Daco-Roman theory. Like Hodinka, Réthy had strong ties with Viennese Hungarian historians, primarily with Lajos Thallóczy. The circle of friends made up of serious scholars led a merry social life; at the height of their get-togethers László Réthy would read out some of his coarse-humoured, schoolboyish poetry, written under the pseudonym of Árpád Löwy. Our collection of manuscripts owes two to him, a sixteenth- or seventeenth-century Ruthenian Psalter and a Serbian liturgical manuscript (Quart. Eccl. Slav. 14. and 15, Accessions register: 1912/43), which the scholar donated on his retirement in 1912, together with a printed book. It is not known how they had reached Réthy. His motives for donation may have been similar to Hodinka's: as a scholar he was fully aware of the value of the written sources which came into his hands and, as a museum curator, he also knew that the best place for them was in a collection. Unfortunately, at present the Psalter is hiding, therefore processing it has only been possible from the microfilm that was made of it for conservation reasons.

Professor of Rumanian studies, Szilárd Sulica (1884-c.1945) started his career as an archivist at the Hungarian National Museum and later became Director of the Archives. When his department was merged with the collection of the National Archives, he became involved in a dispute with his superior and left the Museum for good. From 1934 he worked as a professor of Rumanian philology at Szeged and Kolozsvár universities. At the beginning of 1956, his widow placed two Slavonic and one Rumanian manuscript in the Manuscript Collection (Fol. Eccl. Slav. 22, 23, and. Fol. Valach. 8, Accessions register: 1956/15, 1956/22). The modern Hungarian and Rumanian remarks in one of the Slavonic volumes (the Acts and Epistles) may have been made by Sulica. Three nineteenth-century German and Rumanian texts were attached to the other one (an Octoechos), bearing the name of one Jeremiás Papp, possibly a former owner of the manuscript.

We also owe it to Sulica's widow that his substantial manuscript bequest came to our collection. While data was being collected for the present catalogue, three more uncatalogued cyrillic codices were found amongst his manuscripts. Two of them are included here as Fol. Eccl. Slav. 27 and 28; the third is Rumanian. The volumes are badly damaged, and it will be possible to study them properly only after conservation. Sulica's manuscripts may yet conceal more interesting information about the volumes donated by his widow and on others previously catalogued, and perhaps even about Sulica's collecting activities.

3.   Twentieth-century private individuals

The list of twentieth-century donors and vendors begins with those about whom we have succeeded in finding information. Unfortunately they are the minority, only three, while those for whom only names are known number as many as six.

3.1.   Vazul Damján

Teacher, priest, cultural politician and member of parliament, Vazul Damján (1855-1919) sold two sixteenth-century books of Gospels (Fol. Eccl. Slav. 2 and 3, Accessions register: 1910/33, 1910/49) to the Collection of Manuscripts. Damján was a member of the Rumanian Orthodox Synod, as well as of the Rumanian Cultural Association and the Rumanian National Theatre Foundation. In 1905 and 1906 he was elected to Parliament for the Kőrösbánya constituency with his Rumanian national ethnic programme, and re-elected in 1910, this time unanimously. It must have been through his religious and cultural interests that the two codices came into his possession.

3.2.   Gyula Halaváts

Gyula Halaváts (1853-1926) was a mining engineer, geologist, palæontologist and chief mining consultant of the Institute of Geology. He was the first to examine the geology of the Hungarian Plain, on the basis of data from the sources of artesian wells. His feeling for antiquities is shown by his efforts for the preservation of ancient monuments in addition to work in his own field of expertise. We purchased a sixteenth-century Ruthenian Menaion from him in 1918 (Fol. Eccl. Slav. 4, Accessions register: 1918/25).

3.3.   Miklós Pastinszky

Teacher, historian, expert on books and manuscripts, Miklós Pastinszky (1914-1986) sold in 1960 an eighteenth-century Festal Menaion of Ruthenian origin (Fol. Eccl. Slav. 25. Accessions register: 1960/51) to our collection. Up to 1944 Miklós Pastinszky had been an expert for the Budapest Auction Hall; later he worked as an external consultant for various museums. The Collection of Manuscripts and a number of other Hungarian collections owe their acquisition of many valuable items to Miklós Pastinszky's knowledge of book and art collecting. It is possible that he played a part in the acquisition of our manuscript Quart. Serb. 6, which reached us in 1942 from the Auction Hall (see below). Miklós Pastinszky's name is also associated with the discovery of two other important manuscripts, one on music and the other on medicine.

The following six owners are known only by name, since there is not enough data to identify them. We list below the items that have reached our Manuscript Collection through them, and give the year of acquisition. We trust that future research will be able to find out more about the individuals concerned, thus bringing us closer to the origin of the manuscripts they once owned.

3.4.   Mariu Nicora

Mariu Nicora ("Mariu Nicora de Cinkota") of Cinkota was the source of two Slavonic manuscripts that he sold to us in 1925 (Fol. Eccl. Slav. 5, Quart. Eccl. Slav. 7, Accessions register: 1925/47), together with another Rumanian manuscript (Fol. Valach. 6). The Gospel book, Quart. Eccl. Slav. 7, seems to be one of our earliest

Slavonic manuscripts, dating back to the fourteenth century. It is worth noting that Cinkota was György Ribay's home as well.

3.5. Ernő Naményi

In 1952 Ernő Naményi donated to us a nineteenth-century codex of Ruthenian origin (Quart. Eccl. Slav. 18, Accessions register: 1952/109).

3.6. György Egri

An eighteenth-century Ruthenian Psalter (Oct. Eccl. Slav. 2, Accessions register: 1956/51) reached our collection in 1956 as a present from György Egri.

3.7. Gusztáv Seiden

Gusztáv Seiden placed this Ruthenian Gospel book (Fol. Eccl. Slav. 24, Accessions register: 1957/20) in our collection in 1957 as a gift, along with a few Latin manuscripts.

3.8. Mrs. Miklós Oprics

This eighteenth-century Ruthenian Menaion (Fol. Eccl. Slav. 26, Accessions register: 1962/91) was purchased from Mrs. Miklós Oprics in 1962.

3.9. János Krajcsovics

The sixteenth-century Serbian Panegyricon (Quart. Eccl. Slav. 19, Accessions register: 1973/37) was sold to us by János Krajcsovics in 1973.

4. Items of mixed provenance

4.1. Book trade

4.1.1. Antiquarian Dániel Kún

We have acquired two Slavonic volumes from the antiquarian Dániel Kún. We bought one in 1891, along with several other items, but at that time this eighteenth- or nineteenth-century Passion narrative was placed in limbo, and not taken out to be catalogued and classified until 1925 (Quart. Eccl. Slav. 16, Accessions register: 1925/14). The other item, an eighteenth-century Songbook written by Hungarian

Serbs, was purchased from Dániel Kún in 1893 (Quart. Eccl. Slav. 5, Accessions register: 1893/29).

4.1.2. Auction Hall

This eighteenth-century Serbian Miscellany (Quart. Serb. 6, Accessions register: 1942/54) was purchased from the Auction Hall maintained by the Postal Savings Bank, most probably with Miklós Pastinszky's mediation (see above).

4.2. *Nationalisation*
4.2.1. Miscellaneous material

This lot and the next two are closely associated with the events in Hungary in the 1950s, when privately owned libraries (especially church, monastic and school collections) were wound up or nationalised. Members of the National Széchényi Library staff took the initiative in collecting and saving this material from complete destruction, both in the capital and in the country. Later on the Ministry of Culture took over their action and set up the National Library Centre for sorting the mix of loose, mostly old books. This added a large number of titles, including many of outstanding value, to the collection of the National Széchényi Library. Although the books and manuscripts reaching the Centre were saved from decay, if they had no stamp of ownership it was no longer possible to identify the place where they had originally been kept. It was in 1952 that this early Ruthenian Gospel book was picked out of such a miscellaneous lot (Fol. Eccl. Slav. 20, Accessions register: 1952/121). It bears the following stamp: "From the People's Library Centre. Not for sale."

4.2.2. Zirc

The Zirc Cistercian Monastery was in a special position in the 1950s. Its library, as part of a protected monument, together with the libraries of the Keszthely Palace Museum and the Gyöngyös Franciscan Monastery, was taken over by the National Széchényi Library, which meant that its most precious items, mainly manuscripts, were incorporated into the collections of the National Library either as groups of books or individually. It was in 1954 that the nineteenth-century Ukrainian Liturgicon (Fol. Eccl. Slav. 21) reached us as part of the Zirc stock of manuscripts. How it had come to be at Zirc is unknown.

4.3. Inside the Library

4.3.1. Transfer

It was through a 1912 transfer from the "print department" that along with two Rumanian manuscript volumes this sixteenth-century Ruthenian Octoechos (Fol. Eccl. Slav. 16, Accessions register: 1912/56) entered the stocks of the manuscript collection.

4.3.2. Stocktaking

It was during stocktaking in 1948 that the short ecclesiastical history, edited in the form of questions and answers and formerly in the library of the Novi Sad Grammar School (Oct. Eccl. Slav. l, Accessions register: 1948/52), was found. Novi Sad was part of Hungary up to the First World War, and temporarily also during the Second World War.

4.3.3. Discovered in the Library

Seven fragments (Frag. Eccl. Slav. 3) of a thirteenth-century Serbian book of the Acts and Epistles were removed from the binding of a seventeenth-century Hungarian manuscript (Sermons of János Foktövi, Oct. Hung. 380). The manuscript was bought by the library in 1887, and the leaves were removed at some time between 1952 and 1968.

5. Uncertain provenance

5.1. Place of origin

This sixteenth-century Ruthenian fragment (Frag. Eccl. Slav. 1) probably originates from the Esztergom Archiepiscopal Library, and is preserved with a Latin-Hungarian and a Czech fragment. Accompanying the Czech fragment there is a covering letter dated 1955, written by the primate's secretary to Péter Király, later professor of Slavonic Studies, who was then working for the National Széchényi Library. This clue perhaps indicates that the fragment came from Esztergom.

5.2. Year of acquisition

The seventeenth-century Serbian fragment (Frag. Eccl. Slav. 2) can be identified only by its year of arrival: 1936.

5.3.   No data on provenance

Unfortunately, the acquisition stamp of this seventeenth- or eighteenth-century Ruthenian manuscript (Quart. Eccl. Slav. 8) became unrecognisable or disappeared during restoration.

Literature

On the history of the National Széchényi Library: *Aere perennius – Ércnél maradandóbb. Az Országos Széchényi Könyvtár és a Magyar Nemzeti Múzeum 200 éve* [200 years of the National Széchényi Library and the Hungarian National Museum]. Ed. by Endréné Ferenczy. Budapest, 2002.

On the most important Slavonic items: *Cimélia. Az Országos Széchényi Könyvtár kincsei. The Treasures of the National Széchényi Library.* Ed. by Orsolya Karsay. Budapest, 2000.

On Miklós Jankovich: *Jankovich Miklós (1772-1846) gyűjteményei* [The Collections of Miklós Jankovich]. Ed. by Á. Mikó. Budapest, 2002.

On the Todorescu collection: V. Akantisz, *Dr. Todoreszku Gyula és neje Horváth Aranka régi magyar könyvtára* [The Old Hungarian Library of Dr. Gyula Todorescu and his wife Aranka Horváth]. Budapest, 1922.

Current shelfmarks are in roman type, obsolete ones in italics.

Duod. Eccl. Slav. 1	42	*Fol. Slav. 37*	*16*	Quart. Eccl. Slav. 13	31
Fol. Eccl. Slav. 1	6	*Fol. Slav. 38*	*21*	Quart. Eccl. Slav. 14	56
Fol. Eccl. Slav. 2	11	*Fol. Slav. 39*	*7*	Quart. Eccl. Slav. 15	33
Fol. Eccl. Slav. 3	4	*Fol. Slav. 40*	*14*	Quart. Eccl. Slav. 16	43
Fol. Eccl. Slav. 4	25	*Fol. Slav. 41*	*9*	Quart. Eccl. Slav. 17	37
Fol. Eccl. Slav. 5	20	*Fol. Slav. 42*	*26*	Quart. Eccl. Slav. 18	52
Fol. Eccl. Slav. 6	10	*Fol. Slav. 43*	*22*	Quart. Eccl. Slav. 19	40
Fol. Eccl. Slav. 7	8	*Fol. Slav. 46*	*29*	*Quart. Illyr. Serb. 1*	*17*
Fol. Eccl. Slav. 8	19	*Fol. Valach. 3*	*15*	*Quart. Russ. Ruthen. 3*	*37*
Fol. Eccl. Slav. 9	16	*Fol. Vet. Slav. 1*	*6*	Quart. Serb. 2	48
Fol. Eccl. Slav. 10	21	*Fol. Vet. Slav. 2*	*11*	Quart. Serb. 6	51
Fol. Eccl. Slav. 11	7	*Fol. Vet. Slav. 3*	*4*	*Quart. Slav. 67*	*35*
Fol. Eccl. Slav. 12	14	*Fol. Vet. Slav. 4*	*25*	*Quart. Slav. 68*	*12*
Fol. Eccl. Slav. 13	9	*Fol. Vet. Slav. 5*	*20*	*Quart. Slav. 69*	*34*
Fol. Eccl. Slav. 14	26	Fragm. Eccl. Slav. 1	54	*Quart. Slav. 70*	*32*
Fol. Eccl. Slav. 15	22	Fragm. Eccl. Slav. 2	55	*Quart. Slav. 71*	*31*
Fol. Eccl. Slav. 16	29	Fragm. Eccl. Slav. 3	53	*Quart. Slav. 75/1*	*56*
Fol. Eccl. Slav. 17	3	Oct. Eccl. Slav. 1	49	*Quart. Slav. 75/2*	*33*
Fol. Eccl. Slav. 18	15	Oct. Eccl. Slav. 2	1	*Quart. Slav. 77*	*43*
Fol. Eccl. Slav. 19	17	*Oct. Hung. 380*	*53*	*Quart. Vet. Slav. 1*	*44*
Fol. Eccl. Slav. 20	5	Oct. Serb. 1	41	*Quart. Vet. Slav. 2*	*45*
Fol. Eccl. Slav. 21	36	Quart. Eccl. Slav. 1	44	*Quart. Vet. Slav. 3*	*47*
Fol. Eccl. Slav. 22	18	Quart. Eccl. Slav. 2	45	*Quart. Vet. Slav. 4*	*46*
Fol. Eccl. Slav. 23	27	Quart. Eccl. Slav. 3	47	*Quart. Vet. Slav. 5*	*50*
Fol. Eccl. Slav. 24	13	Quart. Eccl. Slav. 4	46	*Quart. Vet. Slav. 6*	*39*
Fol. Eccl. Slav. 25	23	Quart. Eccl. Slav. 5	50	*Quart. Vet. Slav. 7*	*2*
Fol. Eccl. Slav. 26	24	Quart. Eccl. Slav. 6	39	*Quart. Vet. Slav. 8*	*38*
Fol. Eccl. Slav. 27	28	Quart. Eccl. Slav. 7	2		
Fol. Eccl. Slav. 28	30	Quart. Eccl. Slav. 8	38		
Fol. Illyr. Slav. 2	*3*	Quart. Eccl. Slav. 9	35		
Fol. Slav. 34	*10*	Quart. Eccl. Slav. 10	12		
Fol. Slav. 35	*8*	Quart. Eccl. Slav. 11	34		
Fol. Slav. 36	*19*	Quart. Eccl. Slav. 12	32		

Psalter, 18th century (second quarter)

Paper. Watermark: Virgin and Child (fig.1), similar to Laucevičius 2339 (1725-6); postillion (fig.2), similar to Laucevičius 2784 (1728); a fragment of an indistinct watermark.
i+126 leaves; modern stamped foliation 1-127; older foliation а̑-к̑а̑ on ff.2-22. Size of leaves: 187×155 mm.

Collation: I¹², II-VI⁸, VII⁶, VIII⁸, IX¹², X⁸, XI-XIII¹², XIV² (4 leaves). Unsigned.

Layout: 19-21 ll./p. (on ff.124-127, 24-26 ll.), written area 138-150×125 mm. Catchwords. Running titles.

Hand: probably four scribes, 1: ff.1-17v, 2: ff.18-31v.6 and 56.3-67v, 3: ff.31v.7-56.3, 4: ff.68-127. All write a very similar type of late semiuncial; on ff.124v-127 this alternates with cursive. The last scribe writes a somewhat smaller hand than the rest. Majuscule title on f.2 and smaller majuscule titles at the beginning of each kathisma.

Ink: ff.2-17v, 31v-56, 68-127 brown, gradually darkening to blackish after f.111; ff.18-31v, 56-67v black. Red for some (but not all) titles, initials and running titles, more or less faded.

Binding: black leather on cardboard, 195×150 mm. Sewn on four cords, flat spine. One thong (on the back cover, very likely original) and one cord (on the front cover, evidently not original). Blind tooling, identical on both covers: a vase with a tulip and two roses within a simple frame 140×102 mm, with floral motifs at each corner. One old flyleaf at the front.

Condition: very dirty, but seemingly intact.

Decoration: primitive headbands at the beginning of each kathisma, with scribal or simple floral ornament in red or black ink. Three- or four-line initials in red or orange, of geometrical or free shape, with some simple ornamentation including "eyes" and "faces".

Contents:

    (ff.2-111) **Psalms** [followed by "Psalm 151" and a prayer]
    (ff.111v-120v) **Canticles**
    (f.121-121v) молитва сконча́вшї ѱалтирѧ
    (f.122) оүка́зъ како пѣ́ти ѱалтирѧ по вса дни
    (ff.122v-123) У̑ка́зъ како пѣ́ти ѱалты́ в по́ст вели́кїй
    (ff.123v-127) многомл̃́тивое пѣвае́мое во пра́здники | г̑а̑кі̑ѧ и̑ во дни нарочиты́ с̑тыхъ
    (f.127v) [blank]

Language: Synodal Church Slavonic.

Inscriptions:
f.123v: Chceł byc sczensliwjm
There are also a few semi-literate scrawls inside the covers and on the flyleaf.

Provenance: evidently produced within the Ruthenian area. Given on 24th March 1956 by György Egri.
Despite the shelfmark, the manuscript is in fact a quarto.

Plate 1

Gospels, 14th century

Parchment.

i+146+i leaves; modern stamped foliation, [i], 1-146, [147]. Size of leaves: 230×175 mm.

Collation: I^8 (-1), II-III^8, IV^8 (-2 -7 -8), V$^{8?}$ (one fragmentary leaf), VI^8 (-1 -2), VII^8 (-2 -7 -8), VIII^8 (-4 -5 -7 -8), IX^8 (-1), X^8 (-1.8), XI^8, XII^8 (-1), XIII^8 (-1), XIV^8, XV^8 (-1), XVI$^?$ (4 leaves), XVII$^?$ (2 leaves), XVIII^8, XIX^8 (-1), XX^8 (-8), XXI^8 (-1.8 -2.7), XXII^8 (-1), XXIII^8, (3 leaves), (2 leaves). This collation is somewhat conjectural, because there are many missing leaves, and the hinges of those that remain are restored. The rule of Gregory is observed, and on the evidence of the surviving leaves, the first recto and the last verso of each gathering consistently show the hair-side of the parchment. The gatherings are not signed.

Layout: 21-24 ruled ll./p., written area 194-200×130-135 mm. Ammonian sections (subsequently altered to numbers of pericopes) are indicated in the outer margins, and their opening words in the upper and lower margins; both may also occur in the body of the text.

Hand: small upright uncial, 3-4 mm. Very characteristic throughout is the symmetrical v with rectangular cup. Simple majuscules for the titles. There is a certain amount of variation in the hand, but at least some of this is certainly due to changes of pen and inconsistencies in the surface of the parchment. There may have been only one scribe, or possibly more than one writing very similar hands. The most probable distinction is between ff.1-28v, 127-146v on the one hand and ff.29-126v on the other: ꙋ is characteristic for the first, ꙋ for the second.

Ink: black; red for titles, small initials, rubrics, incipits and chapter numbers. There are evidently two types of original red ink, one of which has faded very badly, and the other of which has retained its colour well. There seems to be no system in their distribution: they coexist on ff.68-72, 78v-86v, 98v and 119-133, while only the faded type is present on ff.1-68, 87-98, 99-118v and 133v-146v, and only the unfaded type on ff.72v-78.

Binding: dark brown leather on thin boards, 245×170 mm, restored. Three raised bands on the spine, two clasps now lost. Blind tooling. On the upper cover a border of double fillets and roll-stamped rinceaux with double beaded stems and rich foliage (see also Fol. Eccl. Slav. 22); fillets and a roll-stamped scallop frame the centre panel; within it a Latin cross of linear rinceau stamps. Faintly similar borders on MS Gr 1 from the Library of the Serbian Orthodox Eparchy of Buda, 1730-1896, cf. Sindik, Grozdanović-Pajić, Mano-Zisi 1991:192. Tripartite floral motifs are impressed at the corners. On the lower cover the same framing and corner decoration; the centrepiece is a lozenge enclosing two fleurs-de-lys mirroring each other about the horizontal axis; for identical stamps cf. MSPC Grujić 20 (16th century) and Ljubljana, University Library, Cod. Kop. 15 (18th century), cf. Janc 1974, plate 88; 43,5. One modern flyleaf at each end. The binding was made in the eighteenth century and is contemporary with the restoration of the parchment.

Condition: sporadic losses of leaves throughout, but those that remain are reasonably sound and clean. The manuscript was restored in 1954, and the present sewing and restoration of the leaves date from that time, but there is evidence of earlier repairs to the hinges.

Decoration: simple majuscule title on f.120v with yellow fillings between the letters; 2- or 3-line red marginal initials without ornamentation mark the beginnings of the lessons. There was evidently no other kind of decoration.

Contents: Gospels. The beginnings and ends of the individual gospels are mostly lost, but St John's Gospel follows immediately after the end of St Luke's, indicating that there were no prolegomena. Since both the beginning and the end of the manuscript are lost, it is impossible to tell what lectionaries it may have contained.

(ff.1-43v) **Gospel according to St Matthew** [defective: only vii.14-xviii.9, xviii.23-xx.28, xxi.44-46, xxii.9-12, xxii.17-xxv.21, xxv.38-xxvi.69, xxvii.33-xxviii.20]

(ff.44-72v) **Gospel according to St Mark** [defective: only i.13-32, iii.11-vi.30, vi.50-ix.32, ix.50-xiii.12, xiii.32-xvi.16]

(ff.73-120) **Gospel according to St Luke** [defective: only i.12-vi.49, vii.19-x.9, xi.36-xii.37, xv.20-xx.8, xx.28-end]

(ff.120v-146v) **Gospel according to St John** [defective: only i.1-51, vii.2-viii.29, ix.20-xvii.11, xviii.1-xix.17, xix.34-xx.26]

Language: Middle Bulgarian, two jers (ь predominates), two juses, but not in their etymological positions; ѕ is used, but not consistently.

Inscriptions:

inside front cover: [an inscription in Rumanian, no longer legible]
A later hand has overwritten the faded red in places; at the same time it has systematically obliterated the numbers of the Ammonian Sections, replacing them with pericope numbers.

Provenance: the hand and language indicate a Bulgarian origin for the manuscript. Bought from Mariu Nicora of Cinkota, Pest megye, on 31st August 1925, together with Fol.Eccl. Slav. 5 and Fol. Valach. 6. Restored in July 1954.

Zaimov, Tóth, Balázs 2003; Tóth 1983.

Plates I, 2

3. FOL. ECCL. SLAV. 17
Gospels, 15th century

Parchment. Ff.17-24 are of paper, with boar watermarks, one very similar to Mareş 382 (1594), the other similar to Mareş 383 (1594), and form a gathering of eight, and were evidently added to the book late in the sixteenth century to replace a gathering that had been lost earlier in its history.
232 leaves; modern stamped foliation, 1-232; there is also an earlier modern pencil foliation, reflecting previous disruption of the order of the leaves. Size of leaves: 310×230 mm.

Collation: all the leaves are now detached, so the collation cannot be established with certainty. However, there are signatures (possibly not original) throughout the book, the first barely visible on f.16v (possibly Ӱ), then a complete sequence from Ӡ (f.25) to Ӥ (f.223). These imply that the book was in eights, apart from the 19th, 24th, 26th and 27th gatherings, which had seven, nine, nine and seven leaves respectively.

Layout: 21 ll./p., written area 235×150-180 mm (the width varies, but is mostly about 170 mm); in the menology (ff.230v-232v), 25-26 ll./p., written area 255×170 mm.

Hand: uncial; a large variety of hands, x-height 5-6 mm, some very formal and conservative (symmetrical ѵ, м with loop below the line), others less so, but all of a very high standard.

Ink: black; red for titles, initials and some marginalia.

Binding: disbound.

Condition: lacking the binding and a few leaves at the beginning and end. All the leaves are detached and somewhat distressed at their inner edge, but otherwise they are largely intact, apart from ff.2, 69 and 113, which are severely damaged. These are the first leaves of the first three Gospels, and evidently the headpieces which were on them have been removed.

Decoration: luxury, of headpieces and initials outlined with gold, at the Gospels, representing a typical Moldavian version of the Balkan interlaced ornament. Only one headpiece has survived, the rest have been torn out.

f.175: St John's Gospel: a headpiece composed of four intersecting circles, crossed by stylised double stems with blue median line and rich foliate endings, the area of the whole 70×165mm. The leaves at the corners and the interstices are coloured bright red, blue and green, with small white beads ("pearls").

f.2: St Matthew's Gospel: six-line initial with median lines drawn in blue or red; small tripartite grass ornaments follow the contours.

f.69: St Mark's Gospel: approximately seven-line initial with its upper part missing; the intertwined green stem is filled with linear chain-ornament in yellow; the same grass ornament around the letter.

f.175: St John's Gospel: six-line interlaced initial, composed of intricately intertwined stems, with fillings of red and green with beads between the interlaces and the same grass ornament.

f.66v: a tailpiece consisting of a simple wavy line drawn in black with small red tripartite ornaments following the curve delimits the text of St Matthew's Gospel from the Kephalaia to Mark.

Contents:

(f.1) **End of a lectionary and beginning of the Kephalaia** (up to 43) **to St Matthew's Gospel**

 (ff.2-66v) **Gospel according to St Matthew** [Ch. i 6-10, i 15 - ii 17 is missing because of the damage at the beginning.]

 (ff.66v-67v) **Kephalaia to St Mark's Gospel**

 (ff.67v-69v) Theophylact, Archbishop of Ohrid: **Preface to St Mark's Gospel**

 (ff.69v-111v) **Gospel according to St Mark**

 (ff.111v-113) **Kephalaia to St Luke's Gospel**

 (ff.113v) Theophylact, Archbishop of Ohrid: **Preface to St Luke's Gospel** [Fragment only; the page is damaged, and one leaf is missing immediately after it.]

 (ff.114-174v) **Gospel according to St Luke** [lacking i 1-12]

 (f.174v) **Kephalaia to St John's Gospel** [Beginning only: two leaves are missing.]

 (ff.175-225v) **Gospel according to St John** [Lacks xviii 37-xix 11: one leaf is missing after f.219.]

 (ff.226-230) **Synaxarion**

 (ff.230-232v) **Menology** [the beginning only, up to January 16th]

Language: Middle Bulgarian, Tărnovo orthography: two jers, two juses; ь is used finally, ъ medially, while ѫ and ѧ seem to be more or less interchangeable.

Inscriptions:

f.226: (: Codex Membranae, initio ac fine mutilatus, | in medio charta Gossipina supliens [sic], nunc folia | universim 231 continet :)

Provenance: written in Moldavia or in one of the Rumanian counties of the Kingdom of Hungary. One of nine Slavonic cyrillic manuscripts from the collection of Miklós Jankovich, acquired by the Library in 1836.

Two slips of paper with 19th-century notes accompany the manuscript. The first reads: "Sunt quatuor Evangelia. | cod moldavicus sec.xiv-xv. | folio 8. est finis Evangelii Joannis. | f.10. incipit Matthaeus. | 13. 14 pertinent ad Joannem. | & sic plura folia perperam | sunt posita, quae per otium | quilibet parochus in locum suum | reponere poterit. | praeter Evangelia habet codex, ut solent, | & Synaxarium seu calendarium cum | indicatione lectionum. [in another hand:] Ita cl. Kopitar Biblioth. Caes. Wiennens. Custos. [in a third hand:] Possessor Nicol: Jankovich de Wadass ". There are later pencil additions: "Biblia [illyrica crossed out] novi testa|menti. cod membr. sec. xiv-xv" and "Szláv-Szerb". The second reads: "[crossed out: ꙁⷶⷹⷢⷰ (64) Evang. Ioan. non est integrum. [...] Ioan. | desunt.] | Evangelium Mathei et Lucæ initio parum mutilatum | Marci vero & Ioannis integrum. Omnia vero quatuor sunt | in Ordine. | [in another hand:] írva a leveleken van 231 szám. |Tényleg van: 232 levél = 224 azaz 1-26 és 34-231 | kártya | 8 azaz 27, 28, 29, 30, | 31a, 31b, 32, 33 papi|ros | Összesen 232 levél. | 20/11 72"

Boynychich 1878; Jankovich catalogue, №234 (ff.174v-175 are reproduced (reduced), but the accompanying description of the manuscript is extremely inaccurate).

Plate II

4. Fol. Eccl. Slav. 3
Gospels, 16th century (first quarter)

Paper, and also parchment for the opening leaves of each Gospel (ff.1, 63-64, 103, 170, 177). Watermark: scales (fig.3), very similar to Mareş 1203 (1503) and similar to Briquet 2584 (1501); ladder within a circle surmounted by a star (fig.4), similar to Mareş 1507 (1511). In the endpapers and f.74, coat of arms (fig.5).

i+231 leaves; modern stamped foliation [i], 1-231; earlier, deleted foliation 181-218, 178-180 on the present ff.178-218 indicates a previous disordering of the leaves; cyrillic foliation а̃-р҃ı on ff.1-110, not original. Size of leaves: 265×190 mm.

Collation: I⁷ (4 leaves), II-VIII⁸, IX⁸ (-3 ±4.5), X⁸ (±7), XI-XIII⁸, XIV⁸ (-4.5 +1), XV-XXI⁸, XXII⁸ (-8), XXIII⁸ (±1.8), XXIV-XXIX⁸, XXX⁸ (-7 -8). I₁, IX₄.₅, XIV₄ and XXIII₁.₈ are the parchment leaves. The missing leaves in IX and XXII (but not XXX) involve loss of text, as does the cancel in X, which is a later blank leaf (of the same paper as the flyleaf) replacing one that is missing. I₄ also replaces a lost leaf, but bears the text in a somewhat later hand. I is at present bound as a gathering of 4, but is probably a made-up gathering, as the prolegomena to St Matthew's Gospel are missing, and it is very likely that this gathering too originally had eight leaves. Gatherings signed in the lower outer corner of the first recto and last verso, but only signatures ҃ѕ-ѳ, а҃і-г҃і, к҃д-к҃ѕ survive; the rest are fragmentary or missing altogether.

Layout: 23 ll./p., written area 200×140 mm. Numbers of pericopes and their opening words are indicated in the margins, as are numbers of kephalaia.

Hand: a fine, very clear and elegant semiuncial. The texts of the prolegomena to the Gospels and of the lectionaries are written by the same scribe in a hand slightly smaller than that of the texts of the Gospels themselves, but otherwise identical. Elegant majuscule titles.

Ink: black, faded in places to brownish; red for titles, initials, rubrics and marginalia (apart from numbers of kephalaia). A large red medial point is frequently used for punctuation, in addition to the usual black points and commas. The red ink used for the headpieces, initials and titles at the beginning of the four Gospels (but not of the other sections) is different, and has faded to yellowish brown, and in places even to grey. Elsewhere the red has retained its colour well.

Binding: ornamented brown leather on bevelled boards, 285×195 mm, restored. Four raised bands on the spine with roll-stamped foliage between them; two clasps, one lost. Gold and blind tooling on the centre panel of the upper cover, and traces of gold tooling on the lower cover. On the upper cover a double border, the outer one of Renaissance type, roll-stamped with beaded medallions enclosing men's heads with turbans, helmets and crowns, alternating with linear foliate ornament, cf. Western bindings of the second half of the 16th century. In the inner border roll-stamped rinceau of Renaissance type. A lozenge centre-piece with palmette corners, enclosing an oval medallion with the Crucifixion; five more medallions in the centre panel: another oval one with the Resurrection below the centre-piece, partly overlapping it; two smaller medallions on the left and right with the images respectively of the Virgin with the Child and Christ Pantokrator; the other two bear identical stamps of the Virgin, cf. Laucevičius 1976: 77, №338 (17th century); the Crucifixion is impressed above the central medallion, flanked by two identical stamps of the crowned Virgin; at the corners of the panel are the Evangelists. On the lower cover the composition is similar, with the Resurrection medallion as centrepiece and below it a rectangular stamp with a three-quarter figure of Christ. Rich foliage fills in the space between the medallions. The edges of the leaves are stained greyish-green at the corners and in the middle. The stamps, repairs to the hinges and trimming of the leaves suggest a seventeenth-century date for the binding. One flyleaf at front.

Condition: generally good, apart from discolouring of the first leaf, and damp-staining at the top of the leaves in the second half of the book. Early repairs to the hinges of some of the leaves, mostly towards the beginning and end of the book. Binding becoming slightly detached.

Decoration: rich, of four big, elaborate headpieces at the Gospels, headbands and initials, all of the Balkan interlaced type, outlined in red. In the headpieces the colour of the outlines has faded to yellow.

f.1: St Matthew's Gospel: a ∏-shaped headpiece composed of six intersecting circles formed of vegetal stems and crisscrossed by double stems with endings in form of pointed palmettes; the whole area 100×140 mm; between the endings a small cross-like motif.

f.63: St Mark's Gospel: four intersecting circles, 40×125 mm, crossed and intertwined by stems with small volutes; endings in the form of small branches with buds; on the upper rim the Triumphal Cross inscribed їc χ͞с н̄ к̄.

f.103: St Luke's Gospel: an arch-shaped headpiece of Moldavian pattern, 90×130 mm, with intersecting circles formed of double vegetal stems and crossed by double strips; endings in the form of a branch with an interlaced "bud"; a central interlaced motif above the upper rim.

f.170: St John's Gospel: a ∏-shaped headpiece, 108×130 mm, very similar to that on f.1.

ff.61, 101, 167, 226: four interlaced headbands, unframed and finely outlined, at the kephalaia to Mark, Luke and John, and the Menologion; the intertwined stems form loose loops or heart-shaped figures; a specific motif is a small branch with hanging heart-shaped leaves serving as endings and central motifs. The headband at the Menologion is of intersecting circles crossed by stylised vegetal stems with floral endings.

ff.62, 168: two simple ornamental lines with small floral motifs at the Prefaces.

Four big eight-to eleven-line initials, outlined with red ink, at the Gospels, the biggest one being at St Mark's Gospel; the first three are of the Balkan interlaced type, with some archaic features, while for the last one Byzantine floral and structural elements have been reworked. At the Prefaces three red penwork and pen-flourished initials, the latter with rich floral ornamentation of small wavy leaves and gemmæ.

Contents:

(ff.1-60v) **Gospel according to St Matthew**
(f.61-61v) **Kephalaia to St Mark's Gospel**
(f.62-62v) Theophylact, Archbishop of Ohrid: **Preface to St Mark's Gospel** [lacking the end]
(ff.63-100v) **Gospel according to St Mark**
(ff.101-102) **Kephalaia to St Luke's Gospel**
(f.102v) Theophylact, Archbishop of Ohrid: **Preface to St Luke's Gospel**

(ff.103-166v) **Gospel according to St Luke**

(f.167-167v) **Kephalaia to St John's Gospel**

(ff.168-169v) Theophylact, Archbishop of Ohrid: **Preface to St John's Gospel** [lacking the end]

(ff.170-219) **Gospel according to St John**

(ff.219v-225v) **Synaxarion**

(ff.226-231v) **Menology**, followed by readings for Lent and for sundry occasions [St Sava of Serbia is commemorated on January 14th, and St Simeon of Serbia on February 13th.]

Language: Middle Bulgarian, Tărnovo orthography: two jers, two juses; ь is usual finally, and ъ elsewhere, but ѧ and ѫ are more or less interchangeable.

Inscriptions:

ff.1-9, rectos: + сию книхѹ рекомѹю евд҃хел[..] ⁞ кѹпиⷯ є авраⷣ ѡрмениⷩ. за ѿпѹщение ⁞ грѣхѹⷡ своиⷯ. и родичѹⷡ своиⷯ ⁞ и даⷣ й до храмѹ ѹспениꙗ ⁞ пресвꙗтѣ двѣ вохородици ⁞ до манастирꙗ пѹ҃ноⷡ [?] ⁞ рокѹ вж҃го ҂а҃х҃о҃ѕ [1676] маⷣ є дъ ⁞ хти виⷩ ѡдалиⷩ ѿ храмѹ ⁞ ст҃ага вѹди проклꙗтъ

Provenance: probably written in Moldavia. The inscription may indicate that the manuscript once belonged to the Church of the Dormition at the Monastery of Putna in Moldavia. Purchased in 1910 from Vazul Damján (1855-1919), member of the Hungarian parliament for Kőrösbánya (Baia de Criș), from whom MS Fol. Eccl. Slav. 2 was also purchased in the same year.

Despite the shelfmark, the manuscript is in fact a quarto.

Király 1974.

Plates III, 3

5. FOL. ECCL. SLAV. 20

Gospels, 16th century (first quarter), with additions from the second half of the century

Paper. Watermark: boar (fig.8), very similar to Mareş 336 (1505); oxhead (fig.9) with serpent above, very similar to Mareş 292 (1511); oxhead with crosier above (fig.10), similar to Laucevičius 1491 (1520), Piccard Ochsenkopf 197 (1505-1509); boar (fig.11), similar to Mareş 339 (1527). In the additional leaves, arms of Olkusz (fig.6), identical with Budka 148 (1573); Jastrzębiec (fig.7), similar to Siniarska-Czaplicka 294-299 (1567-1570), type Mareş 1435-1441 (1567-1578).
i+5+137+1+81+9+i=i+233+i leaves; modern stamped foliation [i], 1-219, [1 unfoliated], 220-232, [233]. Size of leaves: 310×195 mm.

Collation: 5 leaves, I-V^{12}, VI^{12} (±1.12 -3-4), VII^{10}, VIII^{12}, IX$^?$ (apparently a regular gathering of 12 leaves, but there is certainly one leaf missing after the ninth (f.106)), X-XI^{12}, XII^{12} (9+1), XIII-XIV^{12}, XV$^?$ (6 leaves), XVI^{12}, XVII^{12} (±1.12), XVIII-XIX^{12}, 9 leaves. VI$_{1.12}$ and XVII$_{1.12}$ evidently replace bifolia lost relatively early in the history of the manuscript, the first, indeed, before it was completed. The first five and last nine leaves are later additions, as is the additional leaf in XII (f.143); they were probably written to supply missing material, though it is not completely impossible that they originally belonged to another manuscript. Unsigned.

Layout: 23 ll./p., written area 235×155 mm. Numbers of pericopes and their opening words are indicated in the margins. Marginal indications of kephalaia are evidently not original. In the additional leaves, 21 or 22 ll./p., written area 225-235×140 mm.

Hand: a rather coarse semiuncial/bookhand; rather crude majuscule titles. The first pair of cancelled leaves (ff.66, 75) seems to have been written by the original scribe later than the rest of this gathering (the ink and paper match those of the later gatherings), but the second (ff.189, 200) is written in a much smaller, more elegant hand. Ff.1-5, 143, 224-232 are written in an elegant light semiuncial; majuscule title on f.143.

Ink: brownish-black, fading to dark brown towards the end of the book. Red for titles, initials, rubrics and marginalia (except for the later kephalaia numbers, which are brown). On ff.1-5, 143, 224-232, black and red, the latter used extensively because of the nature of the text.

Binding: recent, pinkish-brown leather on boards, 305×200 mm; four raised bands on the spine. Blind-stamped border on both covers, consisting of palmette-like motif; a similar motif is stamped between the bands on the spine. Metal cast icon, 48×46 mm in the centre of upper cover, with representation of the Virgin with the Apostles (?) accompanied by the inscription M͞P Θ͞Ȣ, on a foliate background. Pastedown and flyleaf of faded wove paper at each end.

Condition: generally poor. Probably one entire gathering lost at the beginning, and perhaps at the end also, replaced with a smaller number of extraneous leaves. Lacunæ at the beginning of each Gospel, suggesting that some decoration may have been removed. The pages at each end, particularly the additional ones, are somewhat tattered and torn. Extensive staining throughout, worming and other damage.

9

Decoration: crude headpieces and initials, most of them lost with the opening pages of the Gospels, one tailpiece.

f.68: St Mark's Gospel: a rectangular headpiece, 60×140 mm, with thick interlaced stems forming loose loops within the frame and rude vegetal endings; the green coloured interstices are filled with parallel lines drawn in black; a zigzag runs above the interlace; bright yellow, blue, and red stems, parts of them speckled with yellow; brown background. On ff.107 and 176v there are impressions of the now lost headpieces at St Luke's and St John's Gospels.

Two red penwork initials, at St Mark's Gospel and the Preface to St Luke's Gospel, ff.68, 106v; the first one very simple, the second one with foliate finials.

f.176v: a tailpiece at the end of the Preface to St Luke's Gospel, consisting of a pen outlined cross on a postament.

Contents: Gospels, defective, lacking the beginnings of all the Gospels except that of St Mark, and also lacking the lectionaries. The present lectionaries (now also incomplete) were added somewhat later.

> (ff.1-5, 143) **Synaxarion** [Incomplete: lacks the material between the fifth Saturday after Easter and the third Thursday after All Saints, and everything after the twelfth Sunday of the Lucan cycle except for the last four lines, which appear at the beginning of f.143.]
>
> (f.143-143v) **Kephalaia to St Matthew's Gospel** [1-47]
>
> (ff.6-66v) **Gospel according to St Matthew** [Lacks the beginning (up to ch.1 v.17).]
>
> (f.67-67v) **Kephalaia to St Mark's Gospel** [The end is missing, as is the Preface: two leaves are lost after f.67.]
>
> (ff.68-105) **Gospel according to St Mark**
>
> (ff.105-106v) **Kephalaia to St Luke's Gospel**
>
> (f.106v) Theophylact, Archbishop of Ohrid: **Preface to St Luke's Gospel** [The first five lines only: there is apparently one leaf missing.]
>
> (f.107-173v) **Gospel according to St Luke** [Lacks the beginning (up to ch.1, v.5).]
>
> (ff.173v-174) **Kephalaia to St John's Gospel**
>
> (ff.174-176v) Theophylact, Archbishop of Ohrid: **Preface to St John's Gospel**
>
> (ff.177-223) **Gospel according to St John** [Lacks the beginning (up to ch.3, v.24): there is a lacuna of six leaves.]
>
> (f.223v-232) **Menology** [Of the original manuscript, the beginning only (to September 8th) is present, on f.223v: after a short gap (up to September 21st), the remaining leaves continue the menology, followed by lectionaries for Lent and for sundry occasions. F.232v was originally blank.]

Language: Church Slavonic, partly following Tărnovo orthographic norms but with distinct East Slavonic elements.

Inscriptions:

f.2v: ҲXΛ̀

f.60: Kocska | Kocska | Szalasi | Pap | Mih[...]

f.61: Kocska | Szalas Pap | Mihaly Isten

f.61v: Kocska | Szalas | Pap | Mihaly

f.98v: Помощь моꙗ ѿ Г҇да сотворвшего нбо и землю [Similar inscriptions appear on ff.123, 135v, 136v, 137v, 138v, 139v, 140v, 144v, 145 and 146v.]

f.101v: okuli omnyum minden mindenik szeme

ff.103v-104: szolgalok [...] uramnak

f.130: косинꙪо косинки" дꙗкьмо[..] ми[...] мꙋка[?...]

ff.170v: tegnap elveszett

ff.175v: Eunnepnap tegnap tegnap

f.189v: тота кнйга псана есть рокꙋ | Божого перва ҂ахм | Ista librum Skribptum est | anno | 1640 | 1640 [NB this leaf is additional, and the hand of the inscription is not that of the scribe of this leaf, nor of the book as a whole.]

passim: [a number of short and illegible inscriptions throughout the book, apparently of the same trivial nature as those that can still be read; in addition, a few words here and there copied out from the text]

f.232v: Сꙗ Евꙋлꙗ Попо꙯ Поховски꙯ А [...|...] ни нꙗкꙿто нешꙋдали꙯. и ѿ хра[...]внои Мтре параскевй, А[..] | Кто Єго вкраде꙯ то прокꙷлꙗ꙯ анаѳе|ма гарамафà спи꙯ ро꙯ вж | ҂ах꙯ [1640] велйкй по꙯

f.232v: Дне вста꙯ и печати гробꙋ знакꙋ не по꙯с[...|.] со꙯це за хмари вынй꙯ неꙗсно. та꙯ страже|ве помꙗли иже было страꙗно

f.232v: Ѡле смотре бж꙯ꙗ ѿ вꙗка х꙯сꙿ вгꙿь пострада | ради члвека. древле поп꙯шагосꙗ адама и змйны" сов[.]|то꙯ полежаше смꙗти хвы товы ѡвꙗте. О в[...]| че милосꙗдиꙗ Бꙿь не хотꙗ прꙗрꙗти. вꙗно[..]| смꙗтию члвекꙋ оумрꙗти. ради древ[..] | на дрвꙗ сꙗ распинае꙯. и егоже престꙋп[..]|нꙗемꙿ никомꙋ сꙗ не стинае꙯. глаголюꙉꙗ [..|..] мон еси ты снꙋ созданию. хоꙉꙋ тꙗ про|вести ко ѿцꙋ впознанию. à Бꙿь те[..] | ради изволи родитисꙗ смꙗрꙿь в[..] |сити ко кр꙯ꙋ пригвозд[ит]исꙗ

Provenance: both the original manuscript and the additional leaves were written in the Ruthenian area. Acquired in 1952 together with a large quantity of other material.

Plates 4, 5

Gospels, 16th century (second quarter) with 17th-century additions

Paper. Watermark: fleur-de-lys (fig.12), very similar to Briquet 7146 (1524), Budka 17 (1528) and Siniarska-Czaplicka 7 (1529); cross (fig.13), very similar to Budka 5 (1526), Siniarska-Czaplicka 125 (1530), Mareş 1372 (1528); boar (fig.14), very similar to Briquet 13576 (1526), Mareş 340 (1527); boar (fig.15), very similar to Mareş 341 (1528); boar (fig.16), very similar to Mareş 342 (1531); in the newer section, crowned W (fig.17), similar to Laucevičius 3331 (1672); horn within a circle with letter B above (fig.18); coat of arms (fig.19). In the endpapers, coat of arms (fig.20).
i+163+38+84+i=i+285+i leaves; modern stamped foliation, [i], 1-171, 171-284, [285]. Size of leaves: 305×195 mm.

Collation: I$^?$ (7 leaves), II-V^{12}, VI^{12} (-6), VII-VIII^{12}, IX^8 (-8), X-XIII^{12}, XIV$^?$ (7 leaves), XV$^?$ (10 leaves, the 7th a cancel), XVI$^?$ (1 leaf (signed +)), XVII^{12} (-1 -2), XVIII-XIX^{12}, XX$^?$ (4 leaves), XXI$^?$ (5 leaves), XXII-XXIII^{12}, XXIV^{12} (-10), XXV^{12}, XXVI-XXVII^{10}, XXVIII^{12}. Gatherings XVII-XX (ff.164-200v) are additional. Most gatherings signed (apart from XVII-XX) centrally in the upper margin of the first recto, +.

Layout: 20 ll./p., written area 200×130 mm, except for ff.164-200v: 24 ll./p., written area 235×140 mm. Pericopes and their opening words are indicated in the margins, as are kephalaia.

Hand: semiuncial, four hands. 1. (ff.1-97, 201-217) somewhat irregular script, x-height 5 mm; 2. (ff.98-163v) regular script by a practised hand, slightly sloping to the left, x-height 5 mm; 3. (ff.164-200v), smaller, regular script by a later hand, slightly sloping to the right, x-height 3-4 mm; 4. (ff.218-284v) practised, fluent hand using a thick pen, x-height 5 mm. Majuscule titles. While the first, second and fourth scribes write the same general style of large heavy semiuncial, the scribe of the additional leaves belongs to a very different tradition.

Ink: blackish-brown for scribes 1 and 2, grey for scribe 3, and black for scribe 4. Red used for the titles, rubrics, marginalia (except for numbers of kephalaia) and the small initials within the text.

Binding: brown ornamented leather on boards, 320×200 mm, restored. New spine with four raised bands, two new clasps. Blind tooling with traces of gold tooling on the upper cover. Ornamental borders enclosing the centre panel on the upper cover; its centre-piece is a medallion with the Crucifixion within a complicated strap-frame; for a very similar if not identical stamp cf. Simoni 1903, plate XXXI, 43 (17th century). Above and below it, overlapping the border, two round medallions, both bearing an image of the Old Testament Trinity surrounded by the inscription оvѵрєжда патрїарх҃ъ страннъіа ※ оvѵрєди мѣсто ѵелов҃ѣкъ вог҃ъ; on the left and right six smaller medallions with repeating images of the Resurrection, the Virgin and Child enthroned, and one more, very faint (Deesis?); corner stamps with the Evangelists. On the lower cover the same pattern but with another image (a standing figure, now very faint), in the central medallion; the round medallion below bears the image of David seated. All free space is stamped with floral motifs of Renaissance type. Ruthenian bindings of the same general pattern are known from the late

12

16th century, so the binding could be contemporary, or it may date from the restoration when ff.164-200 were replaced. One modern flyleaf at each end.

Condition: severe staining in places on ff.117-144 and especially ff.201-211; ff.212, 278 badly torn; some leaves missing at both front and back. Ff.164-200 are later, and evidently replace leaves damaged early in the manuscript's history.

Decoration: headpieces and initials of the Balkan interlaced type, outlined in red, at the Gospels. The page design with borders belongs to the sixteenth-century Ukrainian tradition of book illumination. The headpiece at St Luke's Gospel is missing, together with the beginning of the text.

f.8: St Matthew's Gospel: three intersecting circles formed by double vegetal stems crisscrossed at their centres, with large half-leaf endings and green, yellow, and brown background, the whole area 80×150 mm.

f.98: St Mark's Gospel: a framed panel, 80×123 mm, with three intersecting circles of double vegetal stems, intertwining in cross-like figures at the centres; red tinted and hatched background; classical rinceaux of half-palmettes in the upper border of the frame and a rude interlaced motif in the lower one.

f.218: St John's Gospel: three intersecting circles similar to those on f.8, with large asymmetrical foliate endings, the whole area 90×120 mm; red tinted and hatched background.

Three big six-line initials, of thick interlaced stems; that on f.8 is coloured in yellow and green.

f.8: a foliate border in the lower and right-hand margins with two big buds and a tuliplike flower from which a long tendril starts; green, yellow, and red-brown colours, the whole pattern similar to Zapasko 1960: fig. 42 (16th century).

A primitive drawing of the Virgin in the margin of f.117v, and by the same hand in the margin of f.118 the Crucifixion represented as a cross with human head and hands.

Contents:

(ff.1-3v) **Synaxarion** [fragment: from the 15th Thursday after All Saints to the 16th Friday of the Lucan cycle only]

(f.4) **Kephalaia to St Matthew's Gospel** [the last five lines only]

(ff.4-7) Theophylact, Archbishop of Ohrid: **Preface to St Matthew's Gospel**

(f.7v) [blank]

(ff.8-94) **Gospel according to St Matthew**

(ff.94v-95v) **Kephalaia to St Mark's Gospel**

(ff.95v-97) Theophylact, Archbishop of Ohrid: **Preface to St Mark's Gospel**

(f.97v) [Originally blank: a later hand has added liturgical instructions for 6th, 7th, 11th, 12th, 14th, 16th January.]

(ff.98-152) **Gospel according to St Mark**

(f.152-152v) **Kephalaia to St Luke's Gospel** [lacking the end]

(ff.153-214) **Gospel according to St Luke** [lacking the beginning (before ch.1, v.10)]

(f.214v) **Kephalaia to St John's Gospel**

(ff.215-217) Theophylact, Archbishop of Ohrid: **Preface to St John's Gospel**

(f.217v) [Originally blank: the same hand as on f.97v has added liturgical instructions

13

[for Sunday before the Nativity, 24th-30th December, 1st January, Saturday and Sunday before Theophany.]

(ff.218-281) **Gospel according to St John**

(ff.281-284v) **Menology** [lacking all after 20th December]

Language: Church Slavonic; the orthography largely follows the Tărnovo norms, but confusion of а and ѧ, оү and ѫ is frequent.

Inscriptions:

ff.1-2: [...]пѣ антонїи премыко . й сабаско дѣднун зр[...]|диловн͠. а при дрьжавѣ в͠е͠к͠о короля пⷱоска жиⷨ[...] | а͠вгоуⷮта й в͠е͠ка͠ кнѧsа литоⷭска по сеⷨмоⷯ тисѧщи | лѣта н͠н. іⷩ͠ н м͠ца і͠ю͠нїа вь г͠ де͠ а то выло в домоу пана ишана поуⷣкы та сѧ ста[...] | тоⷣзапнⷭ. за зоzволѣнаⷨ всⷠ паноⷠ. й громады

7v: Помꙗни господи раба вожого данила г͠а͠рнла | мн͠х͠ила ѳтеѿдора татнанꙋ прокопа марко [?] | йвана михаила микꙋлꙋ аннꙋ настасю амѣнⸯ

f.85v: Коли иереа григориа вꙋрга врганикⸯевⸯ пѣшовⸯ оуроⷭсⸯ та е͠гⸯ | клѣнⸯ оувн[...] рокꙋ вожого ͵ашка [1721] м͠ца ферьвариꙗ дна s

f.97: Коли иере вꙋ|рга поцшово | оуроⷭсⸯ та его | клѣнⸯ оувивⸯ | ѱⷪд͠а| колико еⷮ мⷲестⸯ вогосло|вескихⸯ ѿ а при[...] | принимꙋществⸯ

f.133v: Пⷠкснⸯ ѡ[...] | Гое гое стадемь в коло и весело разⸯмовⸯлꙗгамо випивдимо панове сꙋсѣдⸯкове | не наⷯ доврⷠ буде в гои гои де стꙗ вавишⸯ мои товарицшⸯ хочешⸯ пити | попросити тⷠлⸯко стꙗ вⸯстидаешⸯ во гроши не маешⸯ ве | гои гои [......] но торⸯгꙋи рихло престанⸯ тоⷯговати коли жж в кожⸯꙗии пиво т[...]

passim: [a number of largely illegible scrawls of the type покꙋшаю перо ци довро пише; also a few crude drawings]

Provenance: both the original and additional parts were written in the Ruthenian area. Purchased on 27th February 1890 from Antal Hodinka together with Fol. Eccl. Slav. 18 and an early-printed Slavonic Gospel book. According to a note in the accessions register, they were acquired "magyarországi felvidéki ruthén egyházakból," that is, from Ruthenian churches in Upper Hungary (present-day Slovakia).

Tipped in on f.171a is a receipt for salt issued in Máramaros county and dated 20th July 1784.

Plate 6

7. Fol. Eccl. Slav. 11
Gospels and fragment of Epistles, 1553

Paper. Watermark: boar (fig.21), identical to Mareş 357 (1553); boar (fig.22), very similar to Mareş 355 (1553). Ff.1-6 are of different paper. In the endpapers, coat of arms (fig.20). 4+2+251 leaves; modern stamped foliation, 1-257. Size of leaves: 300×190 mm.

Collation: 4 leaves, 2 leaves, I¹²(-1 -2 -11), II-XIX¹², XX¹²(-11), XXI¹⁰, XXII²(5 leaves). The present ff.1-6 are fragments of other manuscripts. Most gatherings are signed +′ centrally in the upper margin of the first recto. There is a signature ё in the lower left hand corner of f.63v, and traces of signatures in a similar position on ff.159v, 171v, 183v, 219v and 231v, of which the first, second and last were evidently ГІ, ЅІ, ѲІ. Although the gathering represented by the present ff.7-15 would have been numbered as the first in this sequence, it would appear that there was originally material before it, of which the present ff.253 and 256 may have been part, but this is not likely to have been sufficient in extent to form a gathering of twelve leaves.

[FIRST PART, FF.1-4]

Layout: 21 ll./p., written area 200×140 mm. Pericopes and their opening words are indicated in the margins.

Hand: an elegant semiuncial.

Ink: black; red for titles, initials and marginalia.

[SECOND PART, FF.5-6]

Layout: 24 ll./p., written area 250×145 mm.

Hand: a fairly vigorous and freely handled bookhand.

Ink: black; red for title and initials.

[THIRD PART, FF.7-257]

Layout: 22 ruled ll./p., written area 230×140 mm; on ff.117v-118v, 253 (lists of kephalaia), 247-252v (menology), 24 ll./p., written area 250×160 mm; on ff.254-255v, 257, two cols./p., 25 ll./col., written area 250-260×140 mm; on f.256 two cols./p., 24 ll./col., written area 255×140 mm. Pericopes and their openings are indicated in the margins, as are numbers of kephalaia.

Hand: a large, clear, but not too formal semiuncial/bookhand. The size of the letters and thickness of the penstrokes differ at different parts of the manuscript, but since there is never any clear discontinuity, and the colophon appears to indicate only one scribe, it is probably a single rather variable hand.

Ink: black; red for titles, initials and marginalia, except for numbers of kephalaia, which are black.

Binding: modern, brown leather on boards, 310×210 mm, flat spine with five raised bands. Some old paper with fragments of a coloured woodcut is preserved inside the upper and lower covers. The original binding is kept in the Library's binding collection.

Condition: rebound and restored, particularly at the end, where the leaves were quite severely damaged.

15

Decoration: plain, of interlaced headpieces and initials of two kinds.

ff.7, 78, 119v, 194: four rectangular headpieces, at the Gospels; all are of the same simple pattern, composed of tightly intertwined ribbons, outlined with black or red, with black or red beads at the intersecting points, differing stylistically from the initials.

Four big interlaced initials, a version of the Balkan interlaced ornament, at the Gospels.

f.7: a ten-line initial with red outlines, a yellow median line and blue fillings at the intersecting points; at the bottom four small tripartite "grass" motifs, typical of Moldavian illumination, coloured in blue-green.

ff.78, 119v, 194: similar, six- to nine-line initials, of which that at Luke's Gospel is arch-shaped and composed of "joints".

ff.5, 76v, 118v, 191v: red penwork initials at the Prefaces with simple decoration of large wavy vegetal ornaments, buds and tendrils.

Red penwork initials of a smaller size at the readings, occasionally ornamented with vegetal motifs.

Contents: Gospels, slightly defective, lacking the lectionary at the beginning and the prolegomena to St Matthew, and with some damage to the lectionaries at the end; four leaves from the Epistles are bound in at the beginning, followed by two leaves from another MS of the Gospels with part of Theophylact's preface to St Matthew.

(ff.1-4) A fragment of a continuous text of the Acts and Epistles, containing the end of the preface to the Second Epistle of Peter, II Peter i.1-16 and I John ii.2-iii.2—evidently two bifolia from a larger gathering.
(ff.5-6) Theophylact, Archbishop of Ohrid: **Preface to St Matthew's Gospel** [lacking the end]
(ff.7-75) **Gospel according to St Matthew**
(ff.75v-76v) **Kephalaia to St Mark's Gospel**
(ff.76v-77v) Theophylact, Archbishop of Ohrid: **Preface to St Mark's Gospel**
(ff.78-117) **Gospel according to St Mark**
(ff.117v-118v) **Kephalaia to St Luke's Gospel**
(ff.118v-119) Theophylact, Archbishop of Ohrid: **Preface to St Luke's Gospel**
(ff.119v-191) **Gospel according to St Luke**
(ff.191-191v) **Kephalaia to St John's Gospel**
(ff.191v-193) Theophylact, Archbishop of Ohrid: **Preface to St John's Gospel**
(f.193v) [blank]
(ff.194-246) **Gospel according to St John**
(f.246v) [blank]
(ff.247-254) **Menology** [St Sava of Serbia is commemorated on 14th January and St Simeon of Serbia on 13th February. F.253 is misplaced here. It contains the end of the list of kephalaia to St Matthew's Gospel and presumably originally belonged at the beginning of the book.]
(ff.254-257) **Lectionary for Lent and for sundry occasions, followed by Lectionary of Gospels and Epistles** [F.256 is misplaced here. It contains a table of lessons from the Sunday of All Saints to the 14th Thursday thereafter, and presumably originally belonged at the beginning of the book.]
(ff.257v) **Colophon**: [...] в҃. р҃. ѡ҃. т҃. л҃. в҃. д҃. | [...] ѯ҃. л҃. к҃. ц҃. рад҇ ꙁадѧцѣ сѣ|[...]ши. а пс҇арь

ра̇ послѣ̋неи | [...] Исписаса ст҃а книга. е҃ѵг. | [...] Произволенїемь ѿ҃ца. | [...]ѣшенїе̋ сн҃а. И съврѹшенїе̋ | [..]:- й писаса книга много|[...]ы̋. й хѫды̋ й малопотрѣвь|[...] оу҃унижені̋ сщ҃енны̋ лазаре̋. | [...]оньмь. а̇ вы̋ ѿ҃ци ст҃ый аще | [...]жди въ сжѣтѣ ѿписа̇са. или | [...]ъ дрѹго̋ повѣстауй исправлаите | уетѣте. а̇ не килѣнете. да йзвѫдѹ | мѫкы вѣныѧ вашими ст҃ыми мо|литвами. по χαυλѧ ко̋. ами̋ - а | въ лѣ̂, по се̇мо̋ тисѧщ[.] ᵃᵃ и̋дикта | к҃д. ѿврѣте̋ ѵ҃тныя главы. ст҃го | їѡанна пр҃теуѣ: [The extraordinary "и̋дикта | к҃д" is evidently due to an omission on the part of the scribe; the text should presumably have read "и̋дикта а҃і м̇ца фебрѹарїа дн҃га к҃д".]

Language: Church Slavonic, following the Bulgarian orthography but with distinct East Slavonic features, both in the manuscript proper and in the extraneous fragments at the beginning.

Inscriptions:

f.1: Помощь мога ѿ господа сотво|рѹшаго небо и земѣлю | Уесни ѿу[е] | Уесно пре|велевъ|нѣши ѿ|уе [...|...]

f.3: Epistola I. S. Ioannis ap | cap. II,3 III,2

f.7: Hodinka B[...]

f.10: hiányzik egy | sor!

f.63v: Начало премѹдрости | Страхъ гд҃нь [...|...]

f.87v: [illegible]

f.108v: Admodum Reverendissime Dne mihiq⟨ue⟩ Collendissime

f.141v: а҃ѱо [1770] Zaritsó megéget ipen pönköz havának 6 napjan. Ugyanabban az orszagban | 1767 irtóztató hidegek támatok Karátson utan mingyar szeredan. | Birodálmat akor vettik az Uraktúl Kiralynéra És mingyart nagyobb hasadik | az Emberekre | szalt. | а҃ѱз̇таго. [1767]

f.142v: Аве Мариа̇ Грациа̇ Плена Доминѹсъ Текѹмъ Benedicta tu in Mulie[...]

f.158v: [illegible]

f.177: Помощ҃ъ мога ѿ гд҃а Сотворшаго небо и землю | по мощъ ш щъщъщъ | щъ щъ щъ щъ

f.194v: Ѿ пророуества Іа̇ков|лиа̇ утение а҃ѱги | а҃ѱги валаганово[?] пе|нга̇з[?] ѳеодоровиуѹль да̇ | на 12 рокѹв ꙁ̇винацат | Zlatиch

f.195: ѿ проро

f.195v: се вѣ слово

f.205v: Anno Dni 1764 | Adum Reverendo

f.205v: Помощъ мога ѿ гд҃а сотворшаго [...]

f.206: Festa pentecostalia hoc ano sunt pluviosa et ideo pauci | homines fuerant Beresnæ, ibidem ungvariensis græci ritus Archidi|aconus dicebat concionem ibidem ungvarienses homines gladiis | secarunt tres homines Mircsanienses penes judei popina

f.206v: Supremæ Classis! | Adum Reverendo Dno Marheæ [?] Theodorovics, Parocho Græci Ritus unito. Zaricsiensi vigilantissimo | mihique Dno, & patrono Colendissimo | Zaricsó.

17

f.207: Admodum Reverende Dno Marheæ [?] Theodorovics Parocho | Græci Ritus unitorum Zaricsiensis vigilantissimo | mihique Dno & Patrono Colendissimo | Zaricsó.

f.234: TTTT

f.246v: Благословеный тотъ уловєк што прєпиє што ма колвєкъ

f.246v: Господи! не постави сія словеса нещастникови во грѣхъ, не | зналъ ибо онъ когда что творитъ - молитва | В.Медвєцкого Пароха | со года 1867.

f.246v: Agnus Dei qui tollis pecata Mundi parce nobis Domine

Provenance: written in the Ruthenian area, as were the extraneous leaves. Myrča (Mircse, Mércse) and Zaričeve (Zaricsó, Drugetháza), mentioned in the inscriptions, are villages in the Velykyj Bereznyj region of the Transcarpathian oblast' of the Ukraine (formerly Bereznai járás, Ung vármegye); the former is mentioned also in inscriptions in MS Fol. Eccl. Slav. 7. One of fourteen manuscripts donated by Antal Hodinka in 1904.

Plates 7, 8

Gospels, 16th century (middle)

Paper. Watermark: boar (fig.23), similar to Laucevičius 3695 (1545); boar (fig.24), similar to Laucevičius 3658 (1554); boar (fig.25), similar to Lichačev 443 (1555). In the penultimate endpaper (f.293) hart (fig.26), type Piccard Hirsch 853-856 or 879-883 (1587-1651).

292+ii leaves; modern stamped foliation, 1-294. Ff.293-4 are evidently old flyleaves (probably dating from the first half of the seventeenth century), but are of a different paper from the pastedowns. Size of leaves: 280×190 mm.

Collation: I^8, II^2, III-XIV^{12}, XV^{12}(-9), XVI-XXV^{12}, XXVI^{10}(-8-9-10). The missing leaf in XV involves no loss of text. XXII$_{1.2}$ has been misbound inside out as the outermost bifolium of XXIII, so that the present f.261 should in fact come between ff.237 and 238. Later signatures Ⰰ-Ⱌ have been added in the lower margins, but they do not always correspond to reality.

Layout: 20 ruled ll./p., written area 210×140 mm. Kephalaia, and numbers of pericopes and their opening words, are indicated in the margins. Frequent running titles consisting of the abbreviated name of the evangelist in the top outer margin, but often lost through trimming during binding.

Hand: large regular semiuncial/bookhands; there seem to be at least two hands, but there is no clear discontinuity between the two. In the middle of the book there is some variability, possibly the result of the activity of several scribes, possibly of one scribe's attempts to accommodate his hand to the other's.

Ink: blackish-brown; red for titles, initials, rubrics and marginalia, except for the numbers of kephalaia in the margins, which are written in the same ink as the body of the text.

Binding: ornamented brown leather on bevelled boards, 298×198 mm; restored. Sewn on four cords with raised bands on the spine; two new clasps. Gold and blind tooling. On the upper cover a roll-stamped frame of Renaissance vegetal motifs between an outer border of a repeating "bird's-eye" motif and an inner border of linear cresting; the centre-piece is an oval medallion with the Crucifixion; four smaller almond-shaped medallions bearing the same scene are grouped around it; another two almond-shaped ones above and below the centre-piece bear respectively the representations of the Crucifixion and the Virgin with the Child; on the left and right two oval medallions are stamped each with a bust of St Nicholas(?); the corners with complicated strip frames have the images of the Evangelists with their symbols and captions stamped in reverse with cyrillic letters. All the images are very plain. The space between the medallions is filled in by a scroll with small round flowers. On the lower cover a narrow "bird's-eye" border frames the centre panel stamped at the corners with floral motifs. The centre-piece is the same almond-shaped medallion with the Virgin and Child as on the upper cover. The edges of the pages are stained green. The binding is very possibly from the seventeenth century.

Decoration: headpieces and initials of the Balkan interlaced type with archaic patterns at the Gospels, outlined in red-orange ink. Red penwork initials of the Neo-Byzantine type at the Synaxarion and Prefaces.

f.14: St Matthew's Gospel: a headpiece of three big intersecting double circles of thick

19

vegetal stems with large floral endings of rude, irregular shape, the area of the whole 82×124 mm.

f.90: St Mark's Gospel: a headpiece of three thick vertical stems on a common base, each formed of three big knots with a cross on top, the area of the whole 85×135 mm; the middle cross is bigger, with the inscription ĪС Х̄С | НН КА. Around it are more letters: ĪН Ц̄Ī | Ф Н̄| м̄л р̄в; a large floral ending rises from the lower right corner; reddish-orange colour in the interstices.

f.139: St Luke's Gospel: a panel (70×130 mm) composed of tightly intertwined ribbons with a knot above the upper rim; floral endings of irregular shape.

f.220: St John's Gospel: an interlaced composition depicting a cross, 76×126 mm; two large half-leaves at the upper corners; inscriptions around the cross read Ц̄ С̄ | ĪН Ц̄Ī | ĪС Х̄С | НН КА | Б Ц Д Х | Б Ц Д Х | Б Ц Д Х | Б Ц Д Х.

Red majuscule titles with vjaz' and simple ornamentation of small gemmæ and leaves; size varies between 15 and 38 mm.

Four big interlaced initials of varying size – eight, nine, 7½, and 5½ lines respectively; the initial on f.220 is of archaic pattern, constructed of a plain tight interlace; the rest combine interlaces with floral motifs and volutes. The red initials are of varying size, decorated with leaves and tendrils, dots and short lines. The archaising interlaced patterns resemble South Slavonic manuscripts of the 16th century, cf. the earliest part of MS RA 1 at the Library of Serbian Orthodox Eparchy of Buda in Szentendre, Sindik, Grozdanović-Pajić, Mano-Zisi 1991: 129-131, 286.

Contents:

(ff.1-9v) **Synaxarion**
(ff.9v-11) **Kephalaia to St Matthew's Gospel**
(ff.11-13v) Theophylact, Archbishop of Ohrid: **Preface to St Matthew's Gospel**
(ff.14-86v) **Gospel according to St Matthew**
(ff.86v-87v) **Kephalaia to St Mark's Gospel**
(ff.87v-89) Theophylact, Archbishop of Ohrid: **Preface to St Mark's Gospel**
(f.89v) [blank]
(ff.90-135v) **Gospel according to St Mark**
(ff.136-137v) **Kephalaia to St Luke's Gospel**
(ff.137v-138v) Theophylact, Archbishop of Ohrid: **Preface to St Luke's Gospel**
(ff.139-216v) **Gospel according to St Luke**
(ff.216v-217) **Kephalaia to St John's Gospel**
(ff.217-219) Theophylact, Archbishop of Ohrid: **Preface to St John's Gospel**
(f.219v) [blank]
(ff.220-278v) **Gospel according to St John**
(ff.279-287) **Menology**
(ff.287-290v) **Lectionary for Lent and for sundry occasions**
(ff.291-292) **Lectionary of Gospels and Epistles**

Language: Church Slavonic, following Middle Bulgarian Tărnovo orthographic norms but with clear East Slavonic features.

Inscriptions:

f.1: мешканінъ станько

f.1v: [...]їта ѵзы разрѣшаю

ff.12v-14: Сїѧ книга рекомаѧ Еѵангелїе | цр҃кви Миѵанской Аще | Кто бы ю ѿдалилъ ѿ цр҃кви | той да бѫдетъ клѧтва | на немъ юже ѿц҃и ст҃ии | оузаконили

f.14: коитрикто [?]

f.87v: Сотвори[?...] | невинною его Мѫкою

f.89v: Коѵпилъ сїю. бжественую книгу еѵлїе. | Бл҃гоѵсвыи мѫжь дѣко ромаѵнинь василевъ | за в҃ı златы за пана его матти. | гумени аноша. й да ей до цр҃кве. ст҃ы | бесребрьни. козмы. и демана. оу | селѣ миѵу. сщ҃еномоу ерѣови лоукови | иже бы на не. пъ за его дш҃у. й за его | родителии дш҃у. кто бы порѵши сїю | книгоу ѿ цркве той. проклѧ боуде | анаѳема. и списавъсѧ си листъ. ро | бжего а҃·х҃ лд҃ [1634] лѣта | мц҃а априлѧ въ дн҃ь ı҃є | и списа его рабъ бжи. ере лоука | и рука его власьнаѧ

f.89v: и списа рабъ бжи лоука роука его ·в·ла | и з молито ст҃ы ѿц҃ъ наши ги ıс | сне бжи помилоу на

f.89v: Ма|тѳей кленик' которо|му се|ло по|рѵчило | й дала | оу мере|сиц|ку | межи | бѫртками | лѣжок | ѿ пото|ка до верха | межи рѣками лѫка на пѧть | возѵв' загорова и в'хежи | ѿ запуто на два возы сѣна | балажъ + мацко + грицеи [?] | косенко лазаръ аврѣли[?]

f.90: [illegible]

f.138v: Похвали ерѵсалиме гд҃а хвали бг҃а сионе

f.198: [illegible]

f.219v: сїю книгу дав' исправати за ѿ|пущение грѣховъ балажъ юнь и своею | женою и с' федею и з матѳѣумъ и своим' | братомъ и з потом'своим' и федею | мц҃а маиа дн҃а в҃ хз҃г [??] | за ѿц҃а матфѣа

f.264v: восита во серца

f.290v: зѣлѣ церковнѣи на вышни вѣкъ | оу матѣıовци лазъ цѣлый | сего бокъ болота [...] лазок | оу поли три зѣлѣ и прок[...]ѧ | пѫд горпки пѫтъ зѣлѧ й лѫка | на моѵари конец' зѣлѣ на три во|зы лѫка мижи рѣками | на три возы оу мерецъ

f.292: **ПО БЛГОДАТИ БЖ҃И.** зволениı ѿц҃а поспѣшенїı стого дх҃а | кѫпиль сїю. бжественоу книгу еѵлїе. Бл҃гоѵсвыи м(оу)жь дѣко | ромаѵнинь василевъть за в҃ı златы за пана его милости. | гумени аноша[..] и даль ей до цркве. ст҃ы бесребрьни | козмы. и демана оу селѣ мирьѵу сщ҃еномъ ереови | игнатıови. жи бы на немь пı за его дш҃у. и за его ро(ит)ли | дш҃у. кто бы порѵши сїю книгу ѿ цркве той проклѧ боу|де анафема. и списавь си листь. рокѵ бжего | а҃хлд҃ [1634] лѣта мц҃ѣ марьта | во днь в҃ | и списа его рабъ бжи ере игнатий | и рѵка его власьнаѧ

f.292v: Сиѧ книга господниа Ѡица ингнатıѧ | мирѵıньского повине бг҃а просити | за того що еи Коѵпиль

f.292v: великодны хлабъ иванъ | мигашоты. ѡлѣда . миг. | стецъ . игна. адри . павлика . | матѣ . петро . федоръ . анъдри | гриц . маренъка . федоръ | стако . ѡлѣда ива. тимѣко . | [.]рктъ василъ . иддако . иванъ . | [н]гна. михало . анъдри . ива. | костъ . стецъ . васи . грицъ . | иванъ . василъ . станъко . | лазоръ . наста . кани[...] | иванъ . федоръ . иванъ . василецъ . | юрѣко . | вѣкюски.

21

ff.293v-294: Za его милости ар̃хидиѩкона | Иеренцїѩ гꙋменѩнскаго повино|сти Іерейски которїи тꙋтъ ѡписа|саннꙇ za крестины Ꙅ҃ гроши za вѣнꙋанѩ трй марѩшѣ za по|грѣбъ Г҃ марѩшѣ хлѣбъ велико̍нїи Ирⷭ҇тѩньꙇ двѣ мѣрѣꙇ вꙋса. | za города пꙋ̍хиꙁꙋ ꙁѣлѣ оу горвѣхⷭ҇ | шитъ на моуари Е҃ и на̍ва воꙁьꙇ | сѣна при тыхъ ꙁемлꙇи і лꙋка ме|жи рѣками лꙋжокъ оу мерцкⷪ҇ доб|ха на вышне моуари на три воꙁьꙇ | сѣна и пꙋ ꙁѣⷧ҇лѣ............ | оу поли Г҃ ꙁелѣ пробꙋета Е҃ и кꙋтъ | оу матѣꙋвцїй на хотари по воло|то на нижномъ бокꙋ | ꙁамотⷪ҇ лаꙁокъ на кривꙋлꙗ|хъ Г҃ ꙁѣⷧ҇лѣ на вершкꙋ на ‖ І мѣрокъ вꙋса тото | было при старихъ лꙋдий | балажъ старин г[...] | мацко балажъ

f.294v: [illegible]

Provenance: written in the Ruthenian area. The village of Myrča (Mircse, Mércse) is in the Velykyj Bereznyj region of the Transcarpathian oblast' of the Ukraine (formerly Bereznai járás, Ung vármegye); Mátyócz is Maťovské Vojkovce (okr. Michalovce) and Mocsár is Močarany (now part of Michalovce) in present-day Slovakia. Myrča is also mentioned in inscriptions in Fol. Eccl. Slav. 11. One of 14 manuscripts donated by Antal Hodinka in 1904. Restored in 1988 by Zsuzsanna Tóth. At this time 173 small fragments of paper were removed from the binding, and are now kept separately under the shelfmark B72. The fragments bear text, both manuscript and printed, in German, Latin, Slavonic, Hungarian and English. As far as it is possible to tell from such fragmentary texts, they appear to date from the late seventeenth or early eighteenth centuries. Photographs of the manuscript at the time of its restoration are kept separately in the restoration department of the library.

Plate 9

9. FOL. ECCL. SLAV. 13
Gospels, 16th century (middle)

Paper. Watermark: boar (fig.27), identical to Mareş 362 (1558); boar (fig.28), identical to Mareş 363 (1558); coat of arms (fig.29), very similar to Mareş 401 (1557), similar to Laucevičius 3604 (1557). In the endpapers, coat of arms (fig.20).

i+328+i leaves; modern stamped foliation [i], 1-328, [329]. Size of leaves: 320×200 mm.

Collation: I^{12}(-1), II-VI^{12}, VII^{12}(4+2), VIII^{10}, IX-X^{12}, XI^{12}(-7), XII^{12}(6+2), XIII^{12}(-11), XIV-XX^{12}, XXI^{14}, XXII-XXV^{12}, XXVI^{12}(-12), XXVII^{12}(-1.12), 6 leaves. There are signatures in the lower margin, level with the outer edge of the text, on the first recto and last verso of the gatherings, but most have been lost due to damage to the edges of the leaves; the first surviving one is ɓ' on f.325 (originally the first leaf of I), and the last is ќ' on f.227v (XIX_{12}). Of the additional leaves in VII, f.76 is the original XXVII_{12} and belongs after f.322, and f.77 (which is bound back to front) is the first leaf of the lectionary which originally came at the front of the book. The additional leaves in XII (which are bound upside-down) are the original XXVII_1 and XXVI_{12} and should come between ff.312 and 313, of which the latter is bound back to front. Of the six leaves at the end, ff.323, 324 and 326 are the first three leaves of the next gathering, while ff.325, 327 and 328 belong at the front of the book.

Layout: 20 ruled ll./p., written area 215×130 mm. Pericopes and their opening words are indicated in the margins, as are kephalaia.

Hand: a very clear, regular and conservative semiuncial.

Ink: brown to brownish-black, less dark in the earlier pages of the book; red for titles, initials, rubrics and marginalia (except for numbers of kephalaia).

Binding: modern, half-bound over green marbled paper on cardboard, 330×205 mm; one modern flyleaf at each end.

Condition: restored, in particular repairing damage to the edges of the leaves in the outer sections of the book.

Decoration: four red penwork headpieces at the Gospels and initials of two types; the greater part of the decoration uses Balkan interlaced ornament. The incised tracing of the headpieces is visible.

f.5: St Matthew's Gospel: a panel, 70×135 mm, in which stylised vegetal stems form four big intersecting ellipses; red interstices; at the centre of the upper edge there is a composition of the Cross with the Instruments of the Passion, accompanied by the letters IC XC НIКA and to either side of this К͡ and тр͡ (i.e. копїе, тр'ьст'ь).

f.96: St Mark's Gospel: a panel, 69×123 mm, of small intersecting circles in five rows, whose intertwined stems end in the lower part in complicated cut leaves combined with a small trefoil and tendrils; a central tulip-like interlaced motif above the upper rim.

f.155: St Luke's Gospel: four intersecting circles in a frame (46×121 mm) crisscrossed by vegetal stems, with red interstices.

f.254: St John's Gospel: four circles in a frame (51×124 mm) composed of intertwined, stylised vegetal stems with red interstices.

23

Titles of elongated majuscules, 25-33 mm, forming simple vjaz' with small floral or
f-shaped motifs.

Four interlaced initials, at the Gospels; all are composed of thick, tightly intertwined
vegetal stems shaded in parts with short lines; the largest initial, at St Mark's Gospel, is
of the same height (100 mm or nine lines) as the text-column; the rest are five to six lines
high. Smaller red initials of the Neo-Byzantine type, with simple vegetal or f-shaped
motifs, at the Prefaces.

Contents:

(ff.1-4v) Theophylact, Archbishop of Ohrid: **Preface to St Matthew's Gospel**
(ff.5-91v) **Gospel according to St Matthew**
(ff.92-93v) **Kephalaia to St Mark's Gospel**
(ff.93v-95) Theophylact, Archbishop of Ohrid: **Preface to St Mark's Gospel**
(f.95v) [blank]
(ff.96-151v) **Gospel according to St Mark**
(ff.152-154) **Kephalaia to St Luke's Gospel**
(ff.154-154v) Theophylact, Archbishop of Ohrid: **Preface to St Luke's Gospel**
(ff.155-249v) **Gospel according to St Luke**
(f.250-250v) **Kephalaia to St John's Gospel**
(ff.250v-252v) Theophylact, Archbishop of Ohrid: **Preface to St John's Gospel**
(f.253-253v) [blank]
(ff.254-317) **Gospel according to St John**
(ff.317v-322, 76, 323-324) **Menology** [Lacking the end, after August 25th. St Sava of
Serbia is commemorated on January 14th, and St Simeon of Serbia on February 13th.]
(f.325-325v) **Kephalaia to St Matthew's Gospel** [The end only; this leaf originally
immediately preceded the present f.1.]
(ff.77, 327-328v) **Fragments of a synaxarion** [originally at the front of the book]

Language: Church Slavonic, following Middle Bulgarian Tărnovo orthographic norms
but with frequent lapses indicating East Slavonic origin.

Inscriptions:

inside front cover: Evangelium | cyrillicis characteribus scriptum, | ex saeculo [deleted:
XVII] XVI-XVII | (Első bejegyzés: 1697).

ff.5-8, 11-12 rectos, 12v, 13v-14r, 15-19v, 21v-24r: во им҃а ѿц҃а і сн҃а і і ст҃го дх҃а ам҃и: |
Потощ҃аста к҃юпити сїю | книг҃ꙋ | Єѵа҃лїе рабь бж҃їи їереи | петрь плешос҃кїи Со своею | женою
ѳе҃ною до села | стройна Фен'ною ꙁа свое ѿпꙋщенїе | гре҃хо̏ свои и чадь наши҃ преставишис҃ꙗ
пос҃юдꙋ | православн҃ы хр̃тїанъ к҃юпиемъ ꙋ петра ган'к҃юскаго | дае҃мь ем҃ꙋ ꙁа ню коровꙋ и ꙁ᷈ |
выко᷈т̏а была цѣна Єѵа҃лїю, | на што бг҃ь і ст҃ы свод̏о᷈ ꙁа свое правое, | Прош̃ꙋ ꙁа бг҃а ст҃го кто
бꙋде᷈ | на неи ѿпрал҃ꙗти и на᷈ гре҃ш'ныхъ | внеи | неꙁабываи | до цр̃кве кде еи бг҃ь повер̃|не᷈᷈ |
та᷈ нехаи бг҃ꙋ слꙋжи᷈ | рок҃ꙋ бж҃го, аֿхֿ҃ч҃ꙁ [1697], мц҃а | ноев҃рцїа дн҃ꙗ а҃,, | а по се᷈ ꙁдрас҃твꙋйте
ѿ хр̃тѣ | аминъ:-

ff.25r, 26v: Сїе Єѵа҃лїе переви҃ꙁала ан'на | шелесни҃ка дала ꙁа не ві҃, Марїꙗшо̏ ꙁа свое ѿпꙋщенїе
гре҃хꙋ᷈, и ꙁа | свое ꙁдравїе ꙗ, и ꙁапис̃а҃ла рꙋкою свое᷈ | рок҃ꙋ бж҃ого. а҃ѱ҃к҃д [1724]. аминъ:

f.95v: рокъ па᷈: андр҃е креч҃ꙋ | ѿкрещ̃е҃на ѿтроковица марїа декемврїꙗ л҃а | а ꙁродиласта л҃:

f.154: Кто бг҃ъ вели ꙗко бг҃ъ нашъ ты еси бг҃ъ

f.253: рокъ пд҃: | ѡ́крещено стасово василй і́аннѹарі́а 2

Provenance: written in the Ruthenian area. The village mentioned in the inscription on f.8 is evidently Strojne (Malmos) in the former Bereg county, now the Svaljava region of the Transcarpathian oblast' of the Ukraine. One of 14 manuscripts donated by Antal Hodinka in 1904.

Plate 10

Gospels, 16th century (third quarter)

Paper. Watermark: boar (fig.30), very similar to Mareş 636 (1558); boar (fig.31), similar to Laucevičius 3702 (1556); boar (fig.32), similar to Briquet 13580 (1556-60); boar (fig.33), similar to Laucevičius 3684 (1560). In the flyleaves, oak-twig (fig.34), also found in the endpapers of Fol. Eccl. Slav. 10 and 16.
i+292+i leaves; modern stamped foliation, [i], 1-47, [1 unfoliated], 48-291, [292]. Size of leaves: 315×205 mm.

Collation: I^{12}(-1-2), II^{12}(±5), III-VII^{12}, VIII^{12}(±11), IX-X^{12}, XI^{10}, XII^{12}, XIII^{12}(±4), XIV-XIX^{12}, XX^{12}(±2), XXI-XXIV^{12}, XXV^{10}(-9-10). The cancels are the leaves which bear the miniatures. Gatherings signed in the bottom left-hand corner of the last verso: legible are signatures є̄, а̄і, ѕ̄і, ѯ̄і, ѱ̄і, ꙗ̄і, on ff.57v, 127v, 139v, 175v, 187v and 223v respectively. There are also traces of signatures on ff.22v, 46v, 69v, 93v, 117v, 151v, 163v, 199v and 211v.

Layout: 20 ruled ll./p., written area 200×130 mm, except on ff.284-286v, which have 25 ruled ll./p., written area 225×145 mm. Kephalaia, and numbers of pericopes and their opening words, are indicated in the margins. There are frequent but irregular running titles consisting of the abbreviated name of the evangelist.

Hand: a large, regular semiuncial/bookhand. Majuscule titles.

Ink: brownish-black; red for titles, initials, rubrics and marginalia, except for the numbers of kephalaia in the margins, which are written in the same black ink as the body of the text.

Binding: ornamented leather on bevelled boards, 330×215 mm, restored; four raised bands on the flat spine; remains of two clasps. Gold and blind tooling on the upper cover, blind tooling on the lower. The upper cover framed by roll-stamped cresting terminating in floral endings (similar to that on Fol. Eccl. Slav. 9); deeply-impressed centre-piece of the Crucifixion on an architectural background within a complicated strip frame, 125×85 mm; around it six oval medallions with alternating stamps of the Virgin and Child enthroned and Christ enthroned; smaller eight-sided medallions between them bear images of St Nicholas and St Michael, alternating. At the angles are the Evangelists within complicated strip frames, with captions. The free space is stamped with linear floral ornament. On the lower cover a similar composition, with the Second Coming as centre-piece; the small medallions beneath the central one are replaced here by crowned heraldic lions. On the spine a floral motif similar to that on the front cover is impressed between the raised bands. Edges of the leaves stained green. Binding probably contemporary with the bookblock and resewn, or made in the 17th century, cf. Fol. Eccl. Slav. 1 and 3. One modern flyleaf at each end.

Decoration: rich, of four full-page miniatures of the Evangelists, each preceding the appropriate Gospel, four headpieces outlined in red or orange-red ink at the Gospels, representing a variety of Balkan interlaced ornament, and initials in red ink.
f.15v: red-framed full-page miniature, 275×175 mm, with Matthew seated, writing in a book on his left knee, against an architectural background; red halo, red chiton with green himation over it, red socks; the face is outlined in brown and modelled in red, ochre and white; a semi-circular bench painted pink; the buildings in the background are

three-dimensionally rendered and coloured pink and blue; the figure is set on a yellow background and ochre terrain with green grass.

f.92v: red-framed full-page miniature at the beginning of St Mark's Gospel, 281×182 mm, identical in composition and stylistic features to the previous one; the evangelist is clothed in a green chiton with pink himation over it.

f.143v: the same pattern, 288×145 mm; pink chiton and green himation.

f.225v: a similar pattern, 285×175 mm, with John on Patmos, seated, with a book on his knee and his head turned towards the sky; the setting is a mountain landscape, coloured green and blue.

f.16: a lattice, each ribbon with a black median line; three large half-leaves as endings, the whole area 90×135 mm; on the upper rim a central composition with the Cross accompanied by the instruments of the Passion and the inscription ĪC XC ́ Ñ Ќ.

f.93: a framed panel 45×125 mm, with an interlaced motif of thick stems within, drawn on a yellow background; two large half-leaves at the upper corners and two small floral motifs at the lower ones; a central composition above the upper rim with an outlined cross, inscribed ĪC XC ́ Ñ Ќ.

f.144: a frame 50×120 mm, formed by thick interlaced stems with rude floral endings flanking a central cross-like motif; black dots at the intersecting points; the space within the frame is coloured light yellow.

f.226: a panel of intersecting stems forming small rosette-like motifs at the intersecting points, with big floral endings, the whole area 65×130 mm; the central composition on the upper rim is identical with that on f.16; the interstices are coloured light yellow.

Majuscule titles, 25 mm for the Prefaces, 15 mm for the Kephalaia, and 20 mm for the Gospels, simple vjaz' and decoration of parallel lines filling some letters.

Four big, six-line red (orange-red) initials at the Gospels, ornamented with abundant vegetal motifs (shepherd's purse-like motif), leaves, and gemmæ; smaller initials of a similar kind at the Prefaces.

Contents:

(ff.1-9v) **Synaxarion**
(ff.9v-11) **Kephalaia to St Matthew's Gospel**
(ff.11-14) Theophylact, Archbishop of Ohrid: **Preface to St Matthew's Gospel**
(ff.14v-15) [blank]
(f.15v) [miniature]
(ff.16-88) **Gospel according to St Matthew**
(ff.88v-89v) **Kephalaia to St Mark's Gospel**
(ff.89v-91) Theophylact, Archbishop of Ohrid: **Preface to St Mark's Gospel**
(ff.91v-92) [blank]
(f.92v) [miniature]
(ff.93-139v) **Gospel according to St Mark**
(ff.139v-141v) **Kephalaia to St Luke's Gospel**
(ff.141v-142) Theophylact, Archbishop of Ohrid: **Preface to St Luke's Gospel**
(ff.142v-143) [blank]
(f.143v) [miniature]

(ff.144-221v) **Gospel according to St Luke**

(ff.221v-222) **Kephalaia to St John's Gospel**

(ff.222-224v) Theophylact, Archbishop of Ohrid: **Preface to St John's Gospel**

(f.225) [blank]

(f.225v) [miniature]

(ff.226-282v) **Gospel according to St John**

(ff.283-291v) **Menology, followed by readings for Lent and for sundry occasions**

Language: Church Slavonic, following Middle Bulgarian Tărnovo orthographic norms but with clear East Slavonic features.

Inscriptions:

inside front cover: во юности нехо[...]

f.1: и во юности нехо[...]

f.14v: Коренъ ѹченїю корок [sic] пло́же его

f.15: Кто ти Спсе ризу раздра: Арг̄ ти Рече ї̈ | трбцѹ пресѣ́че

f.15: ро̂ бж̄аго ҂а

ff.16-27 rectos, 27v, 28: во има Ѿца и сина и свѧтого | дх̄амінь. | сїю книгѹ рекомѹю евгг̄елиле | кѹпи́ раб божи Ѿлексей | и спору́жие свое̂ ан̈ьною | и прида̂ ей до села уе́ны· | ко храмѹ архистратига | михаила. | и кто ви сѧ важи́ Ѿда|ли ей Ѿ сей церкве | нагай бѹде клат и про | анафтема | сѹд вѹдѹ имати на с̄ра̃̈ном сѹдѣ зни́̄ пома господи дш̄ѹ преста̂̈шихьсѧ Ѿ вѣка ѹмѣ̃ш̈х | помани господи раба божего | иѡ̂ана. настасїю. михаи́̈ фтеѡ̂до̂. ференць . | йѡ̂ань. марїѧ. парасковѣ́ѧ. | ѡ̂ нихже поминают васи | пома господи помѧщихь | помнани господи равожего | василйѧ. марїѧ.

Provenance: written in the Ruthenian area. It is possible that the inscription on ff.16-28 refers to the village of Čorna in the Vynohradiv region of the Transcarpathian oblast' of the present-day Ukraine (formerly Ugocsa megye). One of 14 manuscripts donated by Antal Hodinka in 1904. Restored in 1956 by Magyari Lászlóné.

Plates IV, 11, 12

28

11. Fol. Eccl. Slav. 2

Gospels, 16th century (last quarter)

Paper. Watermark: boar (fig.35), very similar to Briquet 13583 (1562; similar variants 1564/5, 1569-71, 1576); type Mareş 370 (1574-9), 371 (1574, 1579, 1581); coat of arms (fig.36). In the endpapers, coat of arms (fig.20).

i+130+i leaves; modern stamped foliation [i], 1-130, [131]. F.99 was evidently formerly misplaced after f.77, so that the present ff.78-99 bear an older foliation, now deleted, 79-99, 78. Size of leaves: 290×200 mm.

Collation: I^{10} (-1-2-3), $II^?$ (9 leaves: apparently a gathering of 10, lacking the first leaf, but there is no discontinuity of text between it and the previous gathering), III-VI^{10}, VII^8, VIII^{10} (-2-3-4-5), IX^{10} (-1-2), X-XI^{10}, XII^{10} (-4-5-6-7-10), XIII-XIV^{10}, XV^{10} (-8-9-10). One signature survives, $\overline{\text{ЛІ}}$ on f.7v.

Layout: 21 ll./p., written area 225×140 mm. Numbers of pericopes and their opening words appear in the margins, as do numbers of kephalaia.

Hand: a large formal semiuncial, x-height=5mm, with a very slight backward slope. Descenders may be extended into the lower margin. Frequent use of broad о and є, and of м with the loop descending below the line. Majuscule titles on ff.69v, 71, 128v.

Ink: black; red for titles, initials, rubrics and marginalia, apart from kephalaia numbers.

Binding: ornamented dark brown leather on boards, 291×210 mm, restored. Grooves running the whole length of the outer edges of the boards; the bottom edges have three studs each; new spine with five raised bands, two new peg-and-strap fastenings. Blind tooling, faintly visible on the upper cover, consisting of small stamped foliage and rosette motifs forming a cross in the middle of the field; on the lower cover an ornamental border encloses the inner field, which is divided in two by a vertical strip filled in with roll-stamped rinceaux. One modern flyleaf at each end.

Condition: many leaves missing, but those that remain are almost all in very good condition, with the exception of f.118, half of which has been torn away, and some minor damage around the edges of some of the leaves towards the end of the book, all of which have been restored in recent times.

Decoration: headpieces and initials of the Balkan interlaced type outlined in red, at the Gospels. Only one headpiece survives.

f.71: St John's Gospel: a headpiece of three intersecting circles formed by double vegetal stems crisscrossing at their centres, with short quadripartite foliate endings; the area of the whole 55×123 mm.

f.71: a big eight-and-a-half-line initial, composed of a rich vegetal stem, doubled in the lower part, making an unusual form of the letter Б.

Contents:

(ff.1-16v) **Gospel according to St Mark** [fragment: ch.11, v.6 to ch.15, v.39 only]
(ff.17-69v) **Gospel according to St Luke** [fragments: ch.3, v.15 to ch.10, v.42 (ff.17-46v); ch.16, v.13 to ch.22, v.64 (ff.47-65v) and ch.23, v.54 to the end (ff.66-69v)]
(ff.69v-70v) Theophylact, Archbishop of Ohrid: **Preface to St John's Gospel** [lacking the end]

29

(ff.71-128) **Gospel according to St John** [lacking ch.10, v.10 to ch.11, v.34 and ch.12, vv.6-21]

(ff.128v-130v) **Menology** [the beginning only, to November 8th]

Language: Church Slavonic of a strongly Bulgarian tradition; lapses indicating the East Slavonic linguistic milieu are very rare.

Inscriptions:

inside front cover: [illegible]

f.32: Трети | ванде|лъ | сирвес[..]|кȣ[..]| ник[.]| рю[...]

f.70v: сынътате де ла х̄с похтескъ дȣмитале пърй'те попа нѡсн̄ кȣ пауе съ треещи

Provenance: probably written in a Ruthenian community, but possibly in an area of contact with Moldavian traditions. Purchased in 1910 from Vazul Damján (1855-1919), member of the Hungarian parliament for Kőrösbánya (Baia de Criş), from whom MS Fol. Eccl. Slav. 3 was also purchased in the same year.

Plate 13

12. Quart. Eccl. Slav. 10

Gospels, 16th century (middle of second half)

Paper. Watermark: boar (fig.37), identical to Mareş 373 (1574). In the endpapers, coat of arms (fig.20).

i+250+i leaves; modern stamped foliation, [i], 1-250 [251]. Size of leaves: 210×140 mm.

Collation: I^{10} (-1), II^{10} (-5), III^{10}, IV^{12}, V-VIII^{10}, IX^{10} (-1), X-XI^{10}, XII^{10} (-10), XIII-XVIII^{10}, XIX^{10} (-9), XX-XXIV^{10}, XXV^{2} (13 leaves; possibly originally 10+3, but the hinges have been restored and it is no longer possible to tell). Gatherings signed in either the lower right-hand corner of the first recto or the lower left-hand corner of the last verso (but never both), а̄-к̄ѕ̄. XV unsigned. There is an extra signature к̄ѕ̄ on f.249r. The irregular gatherings do not involve any loss of text.

Layout: 22 ll./p., written area 152×100 mm. Pericopes and their opening words areindicated in the margins, as are kephalaia.

Hand: an elegant small semiuncial/bookhand. Majuscule titles.

Ink: in the earlier parts of the book, black, but on f.68 a different ink begins, which has faded generally to grey, and in places to brown. There is some fading to brown in the lectionary at the front also. Red is used throughout for titles, initials, rubrics and marginalia (except for kephalaia numbers) with no visible variations.

Binding: brown leather on thick bevelled boards, 220×150 mm, restored. Three raised bands surrounded by double fillets on the spine, two new clasps. Well preserved, refined blind tooling. On the upper cover a Renaissance roll-stamped border with repeated lion, bird and linear floral motifs; the centrepiece is the Crucifixion within a big oval medallion, 85×65 mm, with a rinceau within its frame. At the corners the images of the Evangelists, with their symbols and Greek captions, are impressed. On the lower cover the border is stamped with four repeating images of Apostles and Evangelists, each under refined foliage and with a caption: APPARV|VITBE, ECCEA|NGNUS [Jn. i 36], TUESPE|TRUSET [Mt xvi 18], or DATAE|STMIH [I Cor. iii 10]. The pattern is known from German, Polish and Lithuanian Renaissance bindings of the second half of the 16th or early 17th century, cf. Laucevičius 1976: №427 (1565). The central panel is divided by triple fillets into three vertical strips ending at two horizontal ones; the vertical strips are impressed with the same roll as on the upper cover, the middle one being overlapped by the figure stamps. The binding is contemporary with the manuscript. It may have been produced in a milieu of mixed Catholic and Orthodox population. One modern flyleaf at each end.

Condition: restored and resewn in the twentieth century, with damage to the edges of the leaves at both the beginning and end repaired. The restoration of the binding is apparently earlier.

Decoration: three headpieces at the Gospels, one teratological and two of the Balkan interlaced type; the headpiece for St Mark's Gospel was never drawn. Initials of different types, with some archaising elements.

f.14: St Matthew's Gospel: a framed ∏-shaped headpiece, 103×50 mm, with a green snake body within it, ending with two symmetrically positioned heads and intertwined with

31

vegetal stems; small floral motifs are set at the upper corners and a central interlaced one on the upper rim. Red outlines, ochre background, dark brown filling in between the stems.

f.119: St Luke's Gospel: a headband consisting of a lattice of tightly intertwined straps, 35×90 mm, with small beads on the outer rim and at the intersecting points; red outlines, green median lines and interstices.

f.187: St John's Gospel: a headpiece of four intersecting circles formed of thick vegetal stems, 55×100 mm; large foliage of Gothic type starts from the left upper corner to bend over the composition. Red outlines, green and ochre fillings between the stems. The headpiece differs in style from the others.

f.238: a pen-drawn interlace dividing bar.

Fine vjaz' titles with letters 9-10 and 15 mm high.

f.14: a five-line interlaced initial, outlined in red and coloured in yellow, green and bluish;

f.78: a red eight-line pen-flourished initial with many buds and tendrils in ochre and green; the whole form differs from the South Slavonic tradition;

f.119: an eight-line initial Π in arch form, composed of joints; red outlines and green and ochre colouring;

f.187: a red pen-flourished eleven-line initial, with rich decoration of tendrils, buds and big foliage; ochre and green colouring;

ff.1, 10v: red nine- and six-line pen-flourished initials at the Synaxarion and the Preface to St Matthew; the first with hatching within the letter, and foliage as finials and small tendrils around it; the second is more elegant, of the Neo-Byzantine type, with stems doubled with fine toothed lines;

ff.76, 184v: red penwork initials with simple ornamentation at the Prefaces to St Mark and St John.

Contents:

(ff.1-8v) **Synaxarion**
(ff.9-10v) **Kephalaia to St Matthew's Gospel**
(ff.10v-13) Theophylact, Archbishop of Ohrid: **Preface to St Matthew's Gospel**
(f.13v) [blank]
(ff.14-75) **Gospel according to St Matthew**
(ff.75-76) **Kephalaia to St Mark's Gospel**
(ff.76-77v) Theophylact, Archbishop of Ohrid: **Preface to St Mark's Gospel**
(ff.78-115v) **Gospel according to St Mark**
(ff.116-117v) **Kephalaia to St Luke's Gospel**
(ff.117v-118) Theophylact, Archbishop of Ohrid: **Preface to St Luke's Gospel**
(f.118v) [blank]
(ff.119-184) **Gospel according to St Luke**
(f.184-184v) **Kephalaia to St John's Gospel**
(ff.184v-186v) Theophylact, Archbishop of Ohrid: **Preface to St John's Gospel**
(ff.187-238) **Gospel according to St John** [F.205v is blank.]
(ff.238-250) **Menology, followed by a lectionary for Lent and for sundry occasions and a table of Gospels and Epistles** [St Sava of Serbia is commemorated on 14th January and St Simeon of Serbia on 13th February. F.250v was originally blank.]

Language: Church Slavonic, following Bulgarian orthographic norms very closely.

Inscriptions:

inside front cover, on a fragment of an old pastedown: Jankovits Ágoston | [...]i lelkésztől | 1893 dec 15

f.2: въдомо [...] Пане шлекъсо же въте [...]

f.2: Сее Єѵлїе кѹпилѧ ѵо҇ его Люби то [...] | занє съпакъ ѵо҇ кошътѕе шлекъсѹ вѹѵкѹ [...]

ff.3v-8v: Во йма̃ ѿца й сина й стаго дѹха | Амйнъ Сию̃ кнйгоѵ к | Єѵангелйе Коѵпилъ рав божйй | Шлексѧ Южйкового йвана Содрѹжїемъ | й со ѹадй своймй И далъ за ню̃ золотй̃ | десѧтъ полнй̃ й прйдалъ ей | до церкве въѵкова до храмоѵ й преⷭтолоѵ стрѣтенїа гⷣа ⁿдⷶшаго їс хса | й далй ей за свое ѿпоѵщенїе грѣхов' | и ꙁⷶⷣ родйтелѧ своѧ кождо по йменй их' | А хто вй [...] ѿдалити [?] | [......]

f.15v: [some illegible scrawls]

ff.14-22: Йꙁволенїеⷨ ѿца. й съпоспѣⷲшенїеⷨ сйⷶ. йсъвⷬшенїеⷨ стго дⷯа | коѵпйⷯ сїю кнйгоѵ ꙁовемаѧ | еѵлїе. Раⷠвжїй [федⷪ erased] съ поⷣдрѹжеⷨ его. и съ ѹады свойⷮ. | [й даⷡꙁа ню̃ ѕ̃ ꙁлатыⷯ erased.] Й прйⷡдали ей до црквй вътоѵ̃цй. [erased] ко храмоѵ й прⷮтлоѵ. аⷬхїераⷴха никольı. й дали ей ꙁа своѐ | ѿпꙗщенїе грѣхо҇ⷠ. й ꙁа роⷣⷩтелѧ своꙗ каж'даⷣ по йменй. н̃.| тѣже кто вы ей смѣⷯ ѿдалйⷮти. ѿ ѡбѣтованного мѣста. | поⷬ йли дїаⷦ йли простыⷩ ѵлⷦ | да вѹдеⷮ анаѳема прокла҇ⷮ. | й ѿ стыⷯ ѡцⷪ. тй⷇. иⷤ въ нїкїй. | въ сеⷨ вѣце й в'вѹдоѵщиⷨ✝

f.138v: Sosendom bo w dom hospes wenit chrystus vetit

f.250v: [?Sp]es mea Chrystus erit donec in orbe fruor | Pastor Talaboriens | Petrus Talabori | Anno 1638 | die 18 Nouembr

f.250v: Martinus Vaynagi

f.250v: доꙁде рѧ ѐвⷶгене ѵели

f.250v: [illegible]

Provenance: written in the Ruthenian area. The erased placename on f.17 may indicate the town of Turka, Lviv oblast'; Vičkovo is a village in the Mižhirja region of the Transcarpathian oblast' of the Ukraine. Talabor is the Hungarian name of one of the tributaries of the Tisza (in Ukrainian Terebja), in the same area. One of fourteen MSS donated in 1904 by Antal Hodinka.

Plates 14, 15

13. Fol. Eccl. Slav. 24

Gospels, 17th century (first quarter)

Paper. Watermark: grapes (fig.38), identical to Piccard Frucht XIV, 1096 (1613). In the flyleaves, sun with letters SA | REGEST (fig.39), type Decker 858-72 (paper produced at Rožňava, 1813-31).

i+374+i leaves; modern stamped foliation, [i], 1-374, [375]. Size of leaves: 292×180 mm.

Collation: I^8 (-1), II-VIII^8, IX-XII^{12}, XIII$^{12?}$ (the first three leaves only), XIV^8 (-1), XV-XVII^{12}, XVIII^{12} (-1.12), XIX^{12} (-1.12), XX^8 (-1.8), XXI-XXVIII^{12}, XXIX^6 (-6), XXX^8 (-1), XXXI^{12} (9+1), XXXII^{12}, XXXIII^{12} (1+1), XXXIV^{12} (-12), XXXV^{12}, XXXVI^{12} (-1.12), XXXVII^8, XXXVIII^4. The extra leaf in XXXIII is the missing XXXVI$_1$. I-XXXV signed in the lower outer corner of the first recto and last verso, а̄-л̄е.

Layout: 20 ll./p., written area 206×125 mm.

Hand: large formal semiuncial, x-height=6 mm, professionally written. Majuscule titles.

Ink: dark brown; red for the titles, rubrics, incipits and explicits.

Binding: recent, brown leather on boards, 306×185 mm. Four raised bands on the spine, two clasps. One nineteenth-century flyleaf at each end.

Condition: thoroughly restored and rebound after restoration. Before the restoration the ink had oxidised, severely corroding many leaves and affecting the legibility of many more. A number of leaves are missing.

Decoration: rich, but of undeveloped ornaments in the headpieces, initials and borders; typologically linked with the Ukrainian manuscript decoration of the sixteenth century.

Six headbands and headpieces transforming the Balkan interlaced ornament into kaleidoscopic geometric patterns.

f.1: Synaxarion: a framed headband within a larger frame, 150×175 mm, of intersecting circles, resembling a garland with rude foliate endings at the upper corners; a motif resembling a coat of arms is set at the middle of the upper rim; coloured in Prussian blue, dark green, dark red (brown-red) and ochre.

f.20: St Matthew's Gospel: a framed headpiece, 124×60 mm, including three intersecting circles with stems crossing them; a mosaic effect is produced by the alternate colouring of each intersection, to which stippled "white" is added; a geometric cross between undeveloped foliage set at the corners adorns the upper rim.

f.115: St Mark's Gospel: a framed headpiece, 131×70 mm, of intersecting small circles enclosing lozenges; the colours alternate in the same way; a large cross-like motif is set at the centre of the upper frame and vegetal endings hang from the upper corners.

f.178: St Luke's Gospel: a framed headpiece, 133×46 mm, with interlaces turned into a mosaic-like pattern of the same colours.

f.285: St John's Gospel: a triple framed headpiece, 143×80 mm, with several rows of intersecting circles combined with coloured spots of irregular shape; the other features are the same as above.

f.363: Menology: a headband, 125×35 mm, composed of six intersecting circles, with alternately coloured intersections as above and a rather big floral ending at the lower right corner.

34

Five big (six- to nine-line) framed initials, at the Synaxarion and the Gospels; some frames are step-like and the letters transform the Balkan interlaced pattern into geometric forms; on f.115 the initial is deconstructed to an abstract form; the colouring is the same as the headpieces. Three 5-6-line red initials, with tendrils, wavy leaves and small buds, at the Prefaces, ff.15, 177, 280; on f.15 a thick half-leaf stems from the letter's base.

Borders, some of which resemble cornucopiæ, are composed of rich but rudimentary floral motifs, stemming from either the headpieces or the initials, on ff.1, 20, 115, 285.

Contents:
(ff.1-12) **Synaxarion**
(ff.12v-14v) **Kephalaia to St Matthew's Gospel**
(ff.14v-18v) Theophylact, Archbishop of Ohrid: **Preface to St Matthew's Gospel**
(f.19) [blank]
(ff.20-114v) **Gospel according to St Matthew** [The end (after ch.28, v.5) is missing.]
(ff.115-174v) **Gospel according to St Mark** [lacking the kephalaia and preface]
(ff.174v-177) **Kephalaia to St Luke's Gospel**
(f.177-177v) Theophylact, Archbishop of Ohrid: **Preface to St Luke's Gospel**
(ff.178-279) **Gospel according to St Luke**
(f. 279v) **Kephalaia to St John's Gospel**
(ff.280-283) Theophylact, Archbishop of Ohrid: **Preface to St John's Gospel**
(ff.283v-284v) [blank]
(ff.285-362) **Gospel according to St John** [The end (after ch.21, v.13) is missing.]
(ff.363-374) **Menology** [Followed by list of Gospel readings for sundry occasions andtable of Gospel and Epistle lessons according to the Octoechos. St Sava of Serbia iscommemorated on 14th January and St Simeon of Serbia on 13th February.]

Language: Church Slavonic, following Middle Bulgarian Tărnovo orthographical norms but with features indicating an East Slavonic origin.

Inscriptions:

f.284-284v: Млтию бжїю. й |влгодѣтїю . ще|дротами . й улко|любїемь . гд̃ . бд̃ . й сп̃са . | нашего . і̃с . х̃д . и млтва|ми . пруѓтыа . влуца . на|шеа . вба . й прно . двы . | мрїа . й млтвами . въсѣхь . сѣтыхь . иже | ѿ вѣка угож'дьши. хви. | стю к'нигѕ . зовемѕа̃ . | еулїе . тетрѓ . | рабь бжїи їѡнь . ревни | й подрѕжїе его парака | й съ сыно свои | ивано | й подрѕжїе его марюца | й ивсѣми уады своими | дали ѕробити . ѕ домѕ | свое́ и заплатйли | съ ѕмиленїемь | и радостїю стю книгѕ

f.374: Аще кто хоще знати кто писа̃ | стю книгѕ. смотри. за стлъпо | їѡановы. Ащели хоще знати | кто кѕпи. смотри. пре стлъпо | їѡановы. Ащели хоще знати | та ѕгіати ѿ цркве смотри пре | стлъпо | маковы. Ащели спо|манѕти кто купи й родителѣ его | смотри пре | стлъпо. стого лукы.

f.374v: Михаи молоде архїепкпь | Маромороушънского ѡбдрѓъ | рѡ спнїа дхн̃в [1652]. мца д. г. днь

Provenance: written in the Ruthenian area. Given in 1957 together with some Latin MSS by Gusztáv Seiden.

Michail Molodec is recorded by Pekar 1992 as Bishop of Máramaros from 1653 to 1662; the inscription on f.374v suggests that these dates may need revision.

Plate V

35

Gospels, 1648-9

Paper. Watermark: coat of arms with "Hagel-Rune", letters SW above (fig.43), similar to Eineder 252, 255 (1620, 1641); a coat of arms (Lubicz?) with letters SR (fig.44); Justice (fig.45); Justice (fig.46); a further, unidentified coat of arms (fig.42). In the pages from the printed book, coat of arms (ryba?), faint, in two variants (figs.40, 41). In the endpapers, coat of arms (fig.20).

i+2+3+329+1+11+i=i+346+i leaves ; modern stamped foliation, [i], 1-346, [347]. Size of leaves: 300×190 mm.

Collation: 2 leaves, 3 leaves, I²(the last 3 leaves), II⁸, III⁸(-1), IV-XXV⁸, XXVI⁸(-8), XXVII-XXXV⁸, XXXVI⁶, XXXVII-XLII⁸, 1 leaf, XLIII⁸, XLIV²(3 leaves). The missing leaf in XXVI involves no loss of text, but does signal a change of hand. XLIV probably originally had ten leaves, of which the present ff.345, 344, 346, 2 and 1 are the 4th, 5th, 6th, 8th and 10th respectively. Ff.3-5 and 335 (the last bound between the 42nd and 43rd gatherings) are extraneous. They are four leaves (ff.397-400) from a printed book, evidently the Gospels printed in Lviv in 1743 (Zapasko, Isajevyč 1984: №1451), bound in reverse order and containing a fragment of a lectionary from the third week after Easter to the tenth after Whitsun. Gatherings II, IV-XLIII signed in the lower margin level with the right-hand edge of the text, Ҕ, Д̄-М̄Г̄. There is a further signature М̄Д̄ on f.1v.

Layout: 18 ruled ll./p., written area 220×125 mm. Numbers of pericopes and their opening words are indicated in the margins, as are kephalaia. Regular running titles consisting of the abbreviated name of the evangelist in the top outer margin of the verso.

Hand: an upright, rather variable semiuncial, written on widely spaced lines, becoming somewhat less elegant towards the end of the book; rather more compressed in the menology. Majuscule titles.

Ink: black; red for titles, initials, rubrics and marginalia, except for numbers of kephalaia, which are black.

Binding: extensively restored, plain brown leather on bevelled boards, 320×200 mm, incorporating some ornamented leather from the previous binding on the upper cover; two new clasps. Blind tooling. Double frame with triple fillets; the outer border is stamped with a lattice pattern, while the inner one is impressed with a repeating stamp of mirroring palmettes within a heart-shaped frame; the centre panel is a narrow rectangle divided into three vertical strips, the outer with the lattice, and two horizontal ones divided into triangles. The pattern on the old leather suggests that the binding from which it was taken could have been the book's original one, though the presence of additional printed leaves of 1743 implies that the book was rebound (or at least resewn) after this date. One modern flyleaf at each end. Other fragments of the previous binding are kept separately in the library.

Decoration: very rude, of coloured headpieces and initials, and black-ink tailpieces.

Four framed rectangular headpieces, and one unframed, 13-50×123-135 mm, with variable geometric or interlaced ornaments, at the Gospels and Kephalaia to Mark, on ff.19, 106v, 109v, 169, 275. Black outlines, colouring in ochre, orange, bluish, yellowish and black.

Four framed initials at the Gospels, 55-83×25-38 mm, with simple ornamentation within the frames or the letters themselves, using geometric or unspecific floral motifs; red outlines, black, orange, and/or greenish ochre backgrounds. Simple penwork initials at the Prefaces.

f.14v: tailpiece at the end of the Synaxarion, consisting of a pen-drawn hand with a "tablet".

f.16: tailpiece at the end of the Kephalaia to Matthew, a floral motif between the figures 1648.

f.106: tailpiece at the end of St. Matthew's Gospel: a frieze consisting of an interlaced foliate saltire, flanked by a small flower and hand with pointing finger on each side; beneath it the date 1648 is written.

ff.107v, 108v, 167: tailpieces at the ends of the Kephalaia to Mark and Luke and of the Preface to Mark, similar to that on f.14v.

f.168: end of the Preface to St Luke's Gospel; interlaced ornament, a flower and the date 1648, written in yellowish ink.

f.346v: end of St. John's Gospel (and of the codex); a hand, holding a twig, accompanied by the inscription: 1649 | Maïa Dzen. 14.

Contents:

(ff.1-2) **Fragments of a menology, from October 26th to November 26th and September 11th to October 3rd** [This would originally have been placed at the end of the book. In its present position it is followed by three of the extraneous leaves.]

(ff.6-14v) **A synaxarion, lacking the beginning** [The extant part begins with the fourth Tuesday after Easter.]

(ff.15-16) Kephalaia to St Matthew's Gospel

(ff.16v-18v) Theophylact, Archbishop of Ohrid: **Preface to St Matthew's Gospel**

(ff.19-106) **Gospel according to St Matthew**

(ff.106v-107v) **Kephalaia to St Mark's Gospel**

(f.108-108v) Theophylact, Archbishop of Ohrid: **Preface to St Mark's Gospel**

(f.109) [blank]

(ff.109v-165) **Gospel according to St Mark**

(ff.165-167) **Kephalaia to St Luke's Gospel**

(ff.167v-168) Theophylact, Archbishop of Ohrid: **Preface to St Luke's Gospel**

(f.168v) [blank]

(ff.169-271v) **Gospel according to St Luke**

(f.272) **Kephalaia to St John's Gospel**

(ff.272v-274) Theophylact, Archbishop of Ohrid: **Preface to St John's Gospel**

(f.274v) [blank]

(ff.275-346v) **Gospel according to St John** [Some leaves are lost after f.343, and the passage from Jn. xix.37 to xx.29 is missing.]

Language: Church Slavonic of an East Slavonic recension.

Inscriptions:

ff.6-19, rectos: и с̃таго дх̃а Ѧминь: | Купиⷮ сию к҆нигу Є̂ѵⷢ҇лїе | раⷠ бж̃їй шимⷪⷩ гано҇ⷭ || и з҆женою своею Ѧн҆ною: | [added on f.9v: ꙇ зсвоиⷯ сⷮѣⷩ҆цⷪⷢ петроⷣ꙼ ꙇ зⷣеⷡнцею | Ѧн҆ною+] || за золотихъ дєвꙗⷮ [added: Ѧнна] || ꙋ старогѡ попа ꙋ ѿц҃а | федора: ꙇ приⷣаⷩ꙼ ен |

37

до цє́квє кара́кой Ст҃гѡ ‖ Ар҅хистратига Михаи́ла ‖ за своє сп҃сєнїє дш҃євноє: и за своих҆: ‖ родитєлє́: А хто бы є́й ‖ има́ ꙋкра́ти такй нєхꙋ́ ‖ бꙋдєт пpоклꙗ́т Ана́фтємою: ‖ I а́рама́фта на вѣки вѣꙋнꙑ́й : А́минъ:

ff.19v, 20, 21, 22: [added to previous inscription] бы́ли при то́мъ лю́дє ꙋ̑є́ный [...] ‖ твєдє́ш гано̑ш стари̅" .в҃. твєдє́ш гано̑ш моло̑ш ‖ .г҃. со̑ноцъ [?] гано̑ш д҃ уг҄тй гано̑ш, ‖ pокъ: вꙁ҃ѡ: ҂а҃х҆п҃в [1682]: ‖ мц҃а : сєп́тє́брїа : дн҃ꙗ л҃: ‖ записова́л ѿц҃ъ василій караскі́й

f.10v-12: За ᵉвоє ѿпꙋ́щєнїє ꙗ за помѣшй҄ ‖ родитєлєй ѿц҃а и матєрє Іꙋа́на й є|лєни ‖ й бра́та̑ своєго лє́дє́ пєтра̑ ‖ й сы́на своєго пєтра̑ ‖ сє́трй своᵉх҄ марѳи́

ff.19-40, rectos: кꙋпи́лъ сїю кни́гꙋ ра́бь бж҃ий ‖ їєрєи фєѡ́доръ ꙋ кара́сѣ ꙋ сѣдє[...]‖ Iз pꙋ́сй любыцкий за своє спасєн[...] ‖ за ѿпощєєннє грѣховъ Т зжоною [...]гафою за золотыхъ Т ‖ кто по мою́й смє́рти бꙋ́дєтъ на сюм єѵⷢлїє ѿправь|ла́ти тоть повинєнь за мєнє многогрѣшнаго б҃а проси҃ти ‖ за єрєꙗ фєѡ́дора + ‖ ктом[...] ‖ ꙋкра́сти а́лбо прода́ти крємⷮъ ‖ мєнє їєрєꙗ фєѡ́дора̑ pꙋского ‖ люцкого во ꙗ за свою вѣр́йнꙋ̑ю ‖ працю кꙋпилъ за҄Т золотыхъ на ст҃ра́шномъ сꙋ́дѣ зо мною бꙋ́дєⷮ ᵉ мати заплатꙋ́ пєрєⷣ стра́ны̑мⷨ анг҄гл҄ай пєрєⷣ стра́шнымь ‖ прє́столомь а́лє ꙗ многогрѣшни ‖ прошꙋ̑ добрый ꙋита́тєлю писма ‖ сг҃о прочитай стоє єѵ҄лїє ‖ ꙋ pокꙋ єди́нъ pазъ ꙋ вєлико̑ ‖ говѣ́на ‖ дрꙋ́гий pазъ ꙋ пєтрово говѣⷩ[.] ‖ трєтий pазъ ꙋ госпожино говѣⷩ[.] ‖ чєтвєртый pазъ ꙋ pозꙋ́дна́ноє ‖ говѣ́на: ‖ сєсє єѵ҄лїє кꙋпи́лъꙗмь собѣ́ ‖ нє добро бы́ти попови бєз єѵ҄лїє ‖ дє схощꙋ̑ своймь єѵ҄лиємь поидꙋ̑ ‖ подписальємь свꙗ́тоє єѵ҄лїє ‖ ꙋ вєликоє говѣ́на ꙋ бю сꙋ́бо|тꙋ

f.71v: [erased]

f.168: 1648 | wasýl wolosiansky. Pop. klia|canowsky

f.182v: Помощъ моꙗ ѿ г҃а вг҃а стѡшаго нб҃о I ꙁємлю ‖ Помощъ моꙗ ѿ г҃а со[...]

f.228v: pд҃ вⷪ҆ Iєрєи Iѡⷩ Ꙁавадо̑скі́й писа̑ ꙋ карасꙋ pⷪ҆ вⷪ҆ ҂а҃х҃ѯ҃є [1665], мц҃а апри̑ є҃ дн҃ꙗ

f.306v: miloserdija dveri

Provenance: written in the Ruthenian area. The dates 1648 and 14th May 1649, given in the tailpieces, appear to be the dates at which these sections of the manuscript were finished. The date in the inscription on f.168, though it imitates these, is not original. The places mentioned in the inscriptions are probably Krásnovce (Karaszna) and Kapušianske Kľačany (Magyarkelecsény), okr. Michalovce in present-day Slovakia, though there are several other places with similar names in the region. One of 14 manuscripts donated by Antal Hodinka in 1904.

Plate 16

38

15. Fol. Eccl. Slav. 18
Gospels, 17th century (first half)

Paper. Watermark: cock (fig.47), similar to Briquet 4483 (1598); cock on a shield (fig.48); coat of arms (fig.49); imperial eagle (fig.50); imperial eagle (fig.51).
ii+236+ii leaves; modern stamped foliation [i-ii], 1-236, [237-238]. Size of leaves: 305×180 mm.

Collation: I^{10} (-1-2), II-XX^{10}, 1 leaf, XXI^{10}, 1 leaf, XXII^{10} (-1.10), XXIII^{10}, XXIV^{10} (-8-9-10), 1 leaf. The stray leaves before and after XXI are the missing outer bifolium of XXII: f.199 should follow f.209, and f.210 (which is bound back to front) should follow f.218. Gatherings signed in the bottom right-hand corner of the first recto, but only signatures ӡ̈, ѳ̈, їѵ̈, х̈ѵ̈ and їѵ̈ (on ff.29, 59, 109, 119 and 159) are intact: the rest are fragmentary or missing altogether.

Layout: 24 ll./p., written area 220×130 mm; numbers of pericopes and their opening words are indicated in the margins.

Hand: two well-formed hands: 1. (ff.1-57, St Matthew's Gospel) a clear practised semiuncial/bookhand, fairly free in its treatment of some of the letters; 2. (ff.58-236) a heavier, more formal hand, but still with distinct affinities to the first in terms of the form of the letters. The second hand becomes somewhat larger and thicker as it progresses. Majuscule titles.

Ink: brownish-black; red for titles, initials, rubrics and marginalia.

Binding: late 19th/early 20th century, 315×190 mm, half-bound over marbled paper on cardboard, marbled endpapers and two modern flyleaves at each end.

Condition: some leaves missing at both front and back. Ff.176 and 236 have been quite seriously damaged, and a few other leaves near the back less seriously so, and mended with pieces of paper bearing fragments of a woodcut picture (a lubok?). Intermittent staining and damage by damp.

Decoration: headpieces, initials and tailpieces of the Balkan interlaced type, at the beginnings and ends of the Gospels. The opening headpiece is missing together with the initial part of St Matthew's Gospel.

f.58: St Mark's Gospel: a headpiece, 56×140 mm, composed of four intersecting circles, crossed by straight vegetal stems and segments; interstices filled with black ink, green and brown.

f.100: St Luke's Gospel: a headpiece, 90×140 mm, composed of eleven intersecting circles in three rows, of the same pattern as above; interstices filled with blue, red, brown and black.

f.177: St John's Gospel: a framed headpiece, 100×140 mm, of a similar pattern, except that the stems hang from the frame; blue, red brown and ochre interstices.

Three initials of varying size, 8½, 10 and 7 lines respectively, composed of interlaces, joints and vegetal elements, with red outlines and coloured stems in blue, red and yellow (or ochre); on f.58 the initial is put entirely within the text-column.

Cross-like interlaced tailpieces on ff.99v and 176, the first one coloured in red, yellow and blue, and the second one outlined in black.

Contents:

(ff.1-57) **Gospel according to St Matthew** [The beginning is missing: the text starts with ch.3 v.5.]

(f.57v) [blank]

(ff.58-99v) **Gospel according to St Mark**

(ff.100-176) **Gospel according to St Luke**

(f.176v) [blank]

(ff.177-231v) **Gospel according to St John**

(ff.232-236v) **Menology** [Lacking the section between 26th March and 4th July; St Simeon of Serbia is commemorated on February 13th.]

(f.236v) **Fragment of a lectionary for Lent**

Language: Church Slavonic, written in an East Slavonic milieu and with Middle Bulgarian Tărnovo orthographical norms not entirely consistently followed.

Inscriptions:

second front flyleaf: Novum Testamentum | MS Saec. XVIII. fol.236 in 2° | Hodinka Antaltól 4/1890

f.1: Hodinka | Antaltól | 10 forintért | megvásarol|tatott. | 1890 febr. 26 | 1890/4

ff.1, 3: йсправʼлъ: сию книгȣ ‖ ркомȣю: ѥванъ [added:] ѥваглиѥ

f.93: ѿцъ васѣлй стȣденскыйн

f.106: помоцръ мога ѿ господа

ff.125, 126, 127: иоан [not a running title, since this is St Luke's Gospel!]

f.127: помоцр моа ѿ гдⷭ҇а

f.129: Сиѥ ѥвглиѥ вышнѥи цѣркве ҂аѱѯз [1767]

f.158: реⷱ҇ гдⷭ҇ъ причʼтȣ сию | чоловѣкъ нѣкыйн | реⷱ҇ гдⷭ҇ъ [...]

f.159: реⷱ҇ гдⷭ҇ъ причʼтȣ сию | чоловѣкъ нѣкыйн

f.167v: Сйноу во юности [...] премȣдростъ

f.176v: [crude drawings of hands, one grasping a branch, and a sort of bird with a human head]

f.180v: абвгдежѕѕи

f.181: панове крайнйц[.] ѕыйчⷩ҇ доброе ѕдова [?]

f.184: да сꙗⷷ йсправйтъ молитвȣ

f.207: возълюбълют|вдйкрѣ [?]

f.208v: водинюин

Provenance: written in the Ruthenian area. Purchased on 27th February 1890 from Antal Hodinka together with an early-printed Slavonic Gospel book and Fol. Eccl. Slav. 1. According to a note in the accessions register, they were acquired "magyarországi felvidéki ruthén egyházakból," that is, from Ruthenian churches in Upper Hungary (present-day Slovakia).

Plates 17, 18

Gospel Homiliary, 1588

Paper. Watermark: coat of arms (fig.52), very similar to Budka 140 (1583), Siniarska-Czaplicka 959 (1599); coat of arms (fig.53), very similar to Siniarska-Czaplicka 961 (1594), Budka 158 (1600). In the endpapers, coat of arms (fig.20).

i+224+i leaves; modern stamped foliation, [i], 1-224, [225]; an inconsistent pencil foliation, wrong on ff.78, 80, 86 and others; most often the even numbers are written. Size of leaves: 298×190 mm.

Collation: I^{12} (-1-2-3), II^{12} (-1-2-12), III-V^{12}, VI^{12} (12+1), VII^{12}, VIII-IX^8, X^{12} (-2), XI-XIX^{12}, XX^{12} (-11-12)

Layout: 27 ruled ll./p., written area 218×125 mm.

Hand: regular professional bookhand, x-height 3 mm. Majuscule titles. The hand on ff.1-6 is fractionally larger and more formal; it may be written by a different scribe of the same school, or by the same scribe using a thicker pen.

Ink: black; red for titles, initials, rubrics. On ff.1-6 red punctuation is also used.

Binding: ornamented dark-brown leather on bevelled boards, 315×193 mm, restored; sewn on four cords with raised bands on the new spine, two fastenings lost and replaced with long leather strips. Blind tooling. On the upper cover a double border of triple fillets, roll-stamped with interlaced cresting with dotted stems ending in leafy tufts; the motif resembles that on Fol. Eccl. Slav. 4; for a very similar example cf. Laucevičius 1976: 54-55, №169 (late 16th century); less similar are Laucevičius 1976: 50, 59, or №117 (1590) and 118 (late 16th century), and №210 (1604). The same stamp is impressed within the centre panel. The centre-piece is an oval medallion with the Crucifixion, 53 mm, within a lozenge of palmette motifs; at its angles four big rosette stamps are imprinted; the panel corners are stamped with small triangles consisting of foliage and flower motifs. On the lower cover there is a triple border, identical to that on the front; the small centre panel is divided by the triple fillets into two vertical strips; all are roll-stamped with the same cresting. One modern flyleaf at each end.

Condition: leaves missing at both front and back; f.1 badly damaged; some leaves have been mended.

Decoration: one headpiece, initials of two kinds and simple tailpieces.

f.5: a headpiece, 60×126 mm, with the frame hatched into triangles; a central medallion within, enclosing tulip- and palmette-like flowers, flanked by foliage with big volutes. Black outlines, red, ochre and "white" fillings.

f.5: the biggest, nine-and-a-half-line outlined initial, with a composite stem; red contours and ochre filling.

Numerous red, pen-flourished, five-to seven-line initials, at the readings and commentaries; variations of the Neo-Byzantine type, ornamented with either small buds and short tendrils centred on the stems or finals in the form of small branches.

Two tailpieces, at the end of the exhortation and of the sermon on the fourth Sunday of Lent.

f.4v: a knot with black outlines and red and ochre fillings, with floral terminations flanked by the inscription: М҃.Г҃.П҃. | С҃.М҃. ҂аф.п҃и [1588].

f.42v: a line of scribal ornaments.

ff.26, 83, 152v: marginal drawings of a hand holding a "tablet" enclosing an additional word of text.

Contents: Gospel Homiliary. One of the original vernacular collections of the sixteenth century, identified as the Przemyśl redaction (Čuba 2002: 87).

(ff.1-2) **Preface** [evidently the second of two prefaces that that book originally had, as indicated by the running title on ff.1v-2: в҃. пре́мова ‖ то́моужь]

> Defective: begins with the words: тє. га́ко й ҁсвъ притүи є҆ѵг҃льскои г҃лє. | ѡ҆ с къ̇щим.

(ff.2-4) До ка́ждого хр̇ттїаньского ү́лка ко́|ро҃кое оу́помина́нѧ, й пре́мо́ва

> Incipit: У҆л҃къ ка́ждый хр̇ттїа́н'скїй. жа́ной ‖ р̇ќүи
>
> Explicit: га҃ намь ѡ҆в къ́цѧти ра́үиль г҃ъ | на́шь і҆ѵ́ ҁс. ко́торомоу е҆҃ у҃тъ· й хва́ла | на в къ̇кы в къ̇ү'ный· а҆мі́нь

(f.4) **Brief exhortation to the reader**

> Incipit: кт̇о хоүе҃ үита́ти й҆ли пє́реписо|ва́ти

(ff.4v) За́клад є҆ѵ҃а́їа

(f.5-224v) По́үүенїа изврана́ ѡ̇ | стого е҆ѵ҃а́їа и ѡ̇ многи҃ бж̇твны҃ пи|санїи. [Sermons on the Gospel lessons for Sundays throughout the year, beginning with the Sunday of the Publican and Pharisee and ending with the 32nd Sunday of the Lucan cycle; these are followed by sermons for the Sundays before and after the Elevation of the Cross, the Sunday of the Forefathers, Sundays before and after Christmas, and the Sunday before Epiphany. The end is missing. Each sermon is preceded by a Ukrainian version of the Gospel for the day.]

Language: Ukrainian проста мова, with limited Church Slavonic influence including remnants of orthographical elements (ж, use of ъ) of Middle Bulgarian origin.

Inscriptions:

f.1: polotno 2 | Kobotö 3 | plat 1 | Katran 1 | Kenderica 3 | pelehö [1] | Mnaso 5

f.9: An 1633 die 10bris pop wi a416 [?]

f.31: [illegible]

f.95v: Jasnie wielmozne miłosciwe Panstwo y Dobrodzie[...] | S pokorną supliką moią upadam do nug Jasniewielmoz[...]g

f.194v: үєснї ѡ҆үє҃аси|лиє талама|ски

f.221: помоцъ

f.222: Үєсни ѡүє [...]

f.224v: около 30 листовъ | вырвано | МГ [?] АН [?]

Provenance: written in the Ruthenian area. The date of the manuscript is given in the tailpiece on f.4v. One of 14 manuscripts donated by Antal Hodinka in 1904.

Kocsis 1997

Plates VI, 19

Acts and Epistles, 15th century (middle)

Paper. Watermark: mountains (fig.54), very similar to Dečani 779 (1430-40), very similar to NBCM 120 (1430-40), very similar to Harlfinger 17 (1431); unicorn (fig.55), similar to Voutova 107 (first quarter 15th c.), similar to Briquet 9962 (1443); star (fig.56), similar to Dečani 62 (1435-45), Zadar 306 (1444), NBCM 541 (middle 15th c.); mountains within a circle (fig.57), similar to Briquet 11877 (1441), Harlfinger 81 (1445); flower (fig.58), similar to Zonghi 1048 (1452); flower (fig.60); unicorn (fig.59); in ff.347-348 only, oxhead (fig.61), very similar to Briquet 14762 (1470/75).

375+II leaves; modern stamped foliation, 3-377, 1-2 (there is an additional stamped foliation 25-48 on ff.26-49); modern pencil foliation, 1-8, 10-376. Size of leaves: 268×205 mm.

Collation: I^8 (-1), II-IV^8, V^8 (±1±2±3), VI-IX^8, X^8 (5+1), XI-XLVI^8, XLVII^6 (6+1). Original signatures in lower left-hand corner of last verso of II-IV Б- Д̄, XIX Ԁ, XXI-XXIII Ԁв-Ԁд̄, XXVII Ԁн, XXIX-XXXII й-йг, XXXVI йз; later signatures centrally in the lower margin of the first recto and last verso of V-XLVII, ї-д̄з; another series of later signatures on XXXIII-XXXV, XLI, XLVII йд-йs, дв, дн. The first series of later signatures corresponds to the present state of the book, but this is the result of extensive repair and reconstruction, when it appears that the hinges of all the leaves were repaired with a later paper. It is certain that the present gatherings V-XVIII do not correspond to the original state of the book. There are original signatures s on f.52v (the present VII$_3$), ї on f.116v (XV$_2$); sї on f.124v (XVI$_2$), зї on f.132v (XVII$_2$), a trace of a signature on f.140v (XVIII$_2$)and s̄ї on f.146v (XVIII$_8$).

Layout: 20 ruled ll./p., written area usually 190×125 mm; on ff.34-36v 24-25 ll./p., written area 195×150 mm; from f.331 onwards 21-22 ruled ll./p., written area 205×130 mm. Rubrics in the upper and lower margins (in most cases no space is left between them and the body of the text); numbers of pericopes in the margins at the sides.

Hand: semiuncial, several hands. 1. Medium-sized, not very regular hand, x-height 5 mm, written with a thick pen and slightly sloping to the right, on ff.3-202v, except for the cancels (ff.34-36), on which there are several hands and ff.37-44v (the original fifth gathering?), which are written by a single, but different scribe. 2. Medium-sized hand of a similar type but slightly smaller, also variable, on ff.203-299.8 (except ff.216.5-225v, 277-282v), and probably also 301-330v. 3. Smaller (x=height 4-3mm) likewise variable hand, on ff.331-377v. The rest of the manuscript was written by a variety of scribes, who have often written only a page or two at a time, with occasional short interpolations in the part written by the second main scribe. Only the third main scribe is really distinctive: all the others belong to a common school or training. All scribes use majuscule titles when appropriate.

Ink: black and dark brown, greyish brown used by the third main scribe; red for titles, initials, rubrics.

Binding: ornamented leather on boards with grooves running the whole length of the edges, 265×200 mm; the spine is even, with the original endbands preserved; two peg-and-strap fastenings of which only the pegs remain. Blind tooling. On the upper cover a triple frame is incised with triple fillets; the borders are decorated with four different motifs: small repeating rosette stamp in the outer border; a rectangular stamp of two alternating heart-shaped palmettes in the middle one; in the inner one the stamps are a bigger eight-petal rosette with pointed leaves and a different, smaller palmette. The centre panel, divided into six triangular sections by the same fillets, is stamped with trefoils ("snowdrops"), the smaller palmette and small round eight-petal rosettes; the small rosettes are also found at the intersecting points and around the centre. On the lower cover the composition is almost identical, only without the outer border; the larger centre panel is stamped with the "snowdrops" and the bigger rosettes. Both the type of binding and the ornament are very similar to Janc 1974: plate 80 (15th century). The binding is original (but resewn).

Condition: well preserved codex, with minor restoration to the binding (small pieces of new leather replacing missing parts). At some point in the book's history the individual leaves became detached and all the hinges were mended; therefore the present conjugate pairs to a great extent do not correspond to the bifolia of the original gatherings. Two or three later restorations of the leaves can be detected, including the modern restoration.

Decoration: simple and somewhat rude, of headpieces, initials and tailpieces, resembling the decoration of the so-called "monastic miscellanies" of the 14th century.

Twenty-five bands, predominantly interlaced (of various kinds), within the text; outlined with red or black and often with a median line in the stems, with simple floral endings; they are put at almost every entry.

Numerous three-to five-line red initials, five of interlaced type, all outlined with red and some with a coloured median line in the stems.

Two tailpieces, on ff.141v and 297; the first one is composed of knots linked by strips with floral endings and outlined with red, while the median line is ochre-green; the second one is a red outlined flower motif with long linear branches.

Contents:

(ff.3-97) The Acts of the Apostles [The beginning is missing (up to Acts i.9).]
(ff.97-353) The Epistles [Each epistle is accompanied (in the case of the Catholic Epistles usually followed, in the case of the Pauline Epistles usually preceded) by its Hypothesis ("сказанїе"), but there is no other apparatus.]
(ff.353-363v) Сказанїе извѣстно їже на | въсѣ дни глава́ дѣани а҃плъ
(ff.363v-366) Начало с҃тꙑи и велицѣи четꙑ|ридесѧтници. сꙙ҃мь. и недѣ́мь.
(ff.366-377v) СЪБоРНІКЬ СЪБоМЬ. Б҃ІМЬ М҃ЦЬ СКАЗАꙖ | главꙑ а҃плоу [Menology, including prokeimena and antiphons for major festivals]

Language: Middle Bulgarian, Tărnovo orthography: two jers, two juses, but not in their etymological positions; ь predominates.

Inscriptions:

f.36: [п]рьвое оубо слwво

f.253v: + С҃ти прадѣю́ кꙋпи́ па́ ю҃а́ названнꙑй ѳѣтиẃ и да|де й въ мо́ себѣ и порти своеи настасїи и ча́ й. и възада́|дꙗшїе родителїе свои. в цр҃квь ѿ него създаннѣи цр҃ви | ꙋспенїе прꙋ́тїа ꙋ своего двора оу ко́нꙗ да е́ непо́|вижно навѣкꙑ. запрѣщенїе с҃тꙑ тꙑ҃ w҃ꙗ в лѣ́ ҂зм҃и [A.M.7047=A.D.1539]

44

inside back cover: Й таи х҃е̅ вим мистикось йкони|зоньдесъ. ке ти҃зопиш҃. | триади. то҃трйсь аг҃ниш҃ | йлино҃ просадон҆десъ пасд҃ | тинь виш҃тики҃ апофо|меѳа меримна | ѿс тонь василеа то҃ | ѡло҃ йподедомѣни тесь | аггли кесь аѡрато҃ | дорифорꙋмено҃ та|ꙁеси алꙗлꙋиа:- три҃

Provenance: of Bulgarian origin. First recorded in the collection of the historian Dániel Cornides (1732-1787). Shortly before his death he gave it to Juraj Ribay (1754-1812) in exchange for some Hungarian historical manuscripts. Ribay's extensive collection was subsequently acquired by Miklós Jankovich, and thus came to the library with Jankovich's other books (including nine Slavonic cyrillic manuscripts) in 1836.

The two additional leaves (ff.1-2, now bound at the end) bear notes on the manuscript in the hands of Juraj Ribay and Josef Dobrovský; these are published in full by Dezső 1955. The same author cites a number of places where the manuscript is mentioned in the correspondence between Ribay and Dobrovský, as published by Patera 1913.

Boynychich 1878; Szarvas 1986; Jankovich catalogue (№235). (The last of these is very inaccurate, but is accompanied by a reproduction of ff.191v-192 (reduced). See also pp.xi-xii of the introduction to the present catalogue.)

Plates 20, 21

Acts and Epistles, 16th century (first half)

Paper. Watermark: crown (fig.62), very similar to Mareş 1331 (1504); boar (fig.63), very similar to Mareş 340 (1527); crown (fig.64), similar to Briquet 4912 (1501), 4913 (1502); boar (fig.65), similar to Mareş 339 (1527); oxhead (fig.66), similar to Piccard Ochsenkopf XVI, 155 (1523); letter G (fig.67), similar to Briquet 8189 (1359—but such marks were still used in the sixteenth century).

i+ii+203+i leaves; modern stamped foliation, 1-2, 107, 3-106, 108-208 (f.208 is the back pastedown); older, but not original foliation on ff.4-71, а̃-ѻ̃і, ѕ̃а-ѻ̃. Size of leaves: 315×205 mm.

Collation: I⁸ (disrupted: the present ff.3, 13-18, 12), II-VI⁸, VII⁸ (disrupted: the present ff.58, 52, 53-57, 51), VIII⁸ (-4-5), IX-X⁸, XI⁸ (-1), XII-XIX⁸, XX⁸ (disrupted: the present ff.160, 154-159, 153), XXI-XXV⁸, XXVI? (6 leaves). II is misplaced inside the outer bifolium of I. I₈ (f.12) is followed by I₂₋₇ (ff.13-18), then IV, then III. The rest of the gatherings are in the correct order. Ff.2 and 107 are modern and extraneous. Gatherings I-X signed by the first scribe in the lower outer corner of the first recto and last verso (not all signatures have survived), according to a most curious system: а̃, б̃, г̃/г̃д̃, д̃е̃, е̃ѕ̃, ѕ̃з̃, ѕ̃з̃/з̃и̃, з̃и̃, з̃ѳ̃ (?!), ѻ̃і. The gatherings in the part written by the second scribe are not signed.

Layout: 24 ruled ll./p., written area 230×135 mm for the first scribe and 230×130 mm for the second.

Hand: semiuncial, by two practised, very distinctive hands. 1. (ff.3-81) with letters of square form, x-height=3mm, lines somewhat widely spaced; 2. (ff.82-206) less formal while no less elegant, more condensed and with a slight curve to its vertical strokes, which lean more definitely to the right. Both scribes use majuscule titles.

Ink: black for the first scribe, brownish-black for the second; red for titles, initials, rubrics and marginalia.

Binding: ornamented brown leather on boards, 300×198 mm; three raised bands on the spine with incised lines above and below them; two fastenings, now lost. Blind tooling. On the upper cover a roll-stamped border between double fillets, consisting of a rinceau with an outlined beaded stem with flowers on it, the same as on Quart. Eccl. Slav. 7; in the centre panel a Latin cross is roll-stamped with cresting enclosing another rinceau motif within the limbs of the cross; small bunches of flowers are stamped at the angles of the panel. On the lower cover a border of the same rinceau as on the front; the central panel is divided by triple fillets into three vertical strips, roll-stamped with the same beaded rinceau, and the area between it and the border is divided into triangles. The binding dates from the eighteenth century, as indicated by its pattern, the mended leaves and traces of old threads, which do not match the new ones. One flyleaf, probably of 18th-century paper, at each end.

Condition: the lower cover is broken into two pieces under the leather. A number of the hinges of the leaves have been mended; where this is not the case, the holes left by the previous sewing are still visible.

Decoration: simple interlaced headbands in red ink in the part of the manuscript written by the first scribe, and red initials of the Neo-Byzantine type at each primary and secondary liturgical division of the text.

f.3: a "rope" headband at the beginning of Acts, with large foliate endings distorted to such an extent as to look like phyto-zoomorphic motifs; between them an interlaced cross with the inscription ī͠с х͠с н͠и к͠а.

f.60: a "rope" at the Preface to James, with very simple vegetal endings. On f.13 an empty space has been left for a headband.

Numerous three-to five-line penwork initials throughout the manuscript, distinctive for each scribe; those of the first one have rude foliate motifs as finials and small buds between short lines on the stems; those of the second scribe are more elegant, with wavy vegetal finials and small buds and tendrils on the stems.

Contents: Acts and Epistles; each book is preceded by the Euthalian hypotheseis ("сказанїа"). The Synaxarion and Menology both give antiphons and prokeimena for major festivals.

(ff.3-60) The Acts of the Apostles
(ff.60-85) The Catholic Epistles
(ff.85-186v) The Epistles of St Paul
(ff.187-197v) Сказанїе и҆звѣстно и҆же по всѧ дн҃и | глава́.. дѣѧнїа ап͡лъ [Synaxarion]
(ff.197v-205) Съборни́к̅ ·вı҃·тимь мц҃омь · сказѹ́ | главы ап͡лѹ [Menology]
(ff.205v-206) ѹ̑ка҃з ѡ̑став́шимь ап͡ломь ї е͡ѵл҃амь | непрꙗн꙼ꙁѣмы̅ с͡ты̅

Language: Church Slavonic of the Bulgarian type, but with features betraying that it was written by East Slavonic scribes; inconsistent diacritics.

Inscriptions:

On the inside of both front and back covers, and also on the front and back flyleaves are written out liturgical texts for Christmas and for the Nativity of the Mother of God. Inside the front cover there is also a Rumanian text beginning "Фрацилорꙋ де ауаста ᲂѵцелепꙋꙗне | съ ꙉ҃е ѧнтрꙋво".

ff.14-16, 17, 18: + въ лѣ͡т :аѱ꙾і: [1719] аѵ҃г ꙗпосто́ | ламъ кꙋпъратъ ѿаре къ͡т | манъ + ѿаре кътъ лаꙋдапо | + дила трꙋка гавを́илъ | + ши милаꙋ да͡т. мне ши фичорилᲂ꙾ + | ши неполорꙋ. сꙑн꙾ꙋ. потꙋ + | + тꙋрна: пе вице. пе съмꙉце ши уине ва ꙁꙋла съ͡т торне. съ ꙉ҃е: афѹрисиꙋтъ. + || де :тиꙉ: ѿтецꙋ. дн꙼некиа + помени ги҃ дш҃е рабе евеселие: || веселие : гавを́илъ : адриика[?] : тодосие : михаю : михꙋилъ

f.206v: по͡т іѡ͡н пома гла҃ та ꙗ꙼ковъ с͡еꙉе

f.206v: [A faint cursive hand has written out the names of the Forty Martyrs, beginning свꙉ҃и꙼ л꙾ м꙼ иже имена съ͡т сїта доме́тета͡н + | але́сандрꙋ + кыри͡н +.]

The disruption to the earlier part of the manuscript is reflected in notes at the foot of ff.18v, 12v, 11v, 34v and 26v indicating where the text continues.

Provenance: written in the Ruthenian area. Bought on 18th January 1956 from the widow of Szilárd Sulica (1884-c.1950) at the same time as MSS Fol. Eccl. Slav. 23 and Fol. Valach 8; Fol. Eccl. Slav. 27 and 28 were also obtained from her.

Two small pieces of modern paper are kept with the manuscript: the first, f.2, is a brief description in Hungarian, and the second, f.107, is a Rumanian transcription of the inscription on ff.14-18.

Plates 22, 23

Acts and Epistles, 16th century (end)

Paper. Watermark: boar (fig.68) similar to Mareş 383 (1594); boar (fig.69) very similar to Mareş 382 (1594); boar (fig.70), very similar to Mareş 382 (1594), but not identical to the previous mark. 248 leaves; modern stamped foliation, 1-249 (f.249 is the back pastedown). Size of leaves: 310×200 mm.

Collation: I^8 (-1), II-VIII^{10}, IX-X^8, XI-XXV^{10}, XXVI$^{6?}$ (-6?). Gatherings signed in the bottom right-hand corner of the first recto: legible are signatures Б-КД.

Layout: 23 ruled ll./p., written area 240×150 mm, except on ff.48 and 65, which have 29ruled ll./p. Pericopes and their opening words are indicated in the margins.

Hand: large semiuncial, x-height up to 5mm, very professionally executed, the letters becoming slightly larger and thicker after f.84. Elegant majuscules of varying size for the titles throughout.

Ink: black; red for titles, initials and rubrics.

Binding: ornamented black leather on thick bevelled boards, 330×200 mm, re-used. The width of the binding is slightly smaller than that of the bookblock. Sewn on four cords, with slightly raised bands on the flat spine and endbands of red and white cotton threads; two peg and strap fastenings, of which only the pegs and part of the straps (which are not original) survive. At the tail of the spine a piece of brown leather, possibly cut from another binding, is pasted onto the present one; the same leather was used for the straps and the corners. Blind tooling. On the upper cover incised borders enclosing stamps of geometric ornaments, now very faint; in the centre panel rude incised letters reading ฀ПฤСТฬ̈. The pastedowns appear to be leaves from an octavo Octoechos. The binding is probably slightly older than the bookblock, but repaired at a later date.

Condition: not very good; the hinges have been mended with strips of different papers, including printed books, woodcuts, and an 18th-century manuscript. The leaves at the front and back of the book are filthy, many are detached from the manuscript body, and from f.294 onwards badly damaged at their lower edges. Severe worming in the upper cover.

Decoration: simple, of red initials at the readings and prefaces.

Numerous pen-flourished initials of varying size (between four and nine lines), skilfully adorned with rinceaux stemming upwards and downwards from a flower bud at the base of many letters; the foliage is often twice as long as the letter itself; the stems of the letters are decorated with small gemmæ set two by two: for the general pattern cf. Zapasko 1960: fig.39 (early 16th century). Red penwork initials at the rest of the text subdivisions, some of them simply decorated with gemmæ.

Contents:

(ff.1-57v) The Acts of the Apostles [lacking any preface]
(ff.57v-86v) The Catholic Epistles [Each is preceded by its hypothesis.]
(ff.87-228v) The Epistles of St Paul [Each is preceded by its hypothesis.]
(ff.229-238v) Сказа́нїе и̇зьвѣ́стно и̇͒ на вса̀ | дн̑и глава́͒ дѣ́анїй апл҃ъ

(ff.238v-240) Нⷶло ст҃ꙑ велиⷰцѣй четверодесⷶн|ци

(ff.240-248) Типикь съворⷩникь сь вⷢо҃ⷢ ѣі мцⷭⷭска|ꙃоѫ глⷶвы апⷪло̆у [Menology]

(ff.248-248v) Readings on sundry occasions [The end is missing.]

Language: Church Slavonic, following Middle Bulgarian Tărnovo orthographic principles but with strong signs of having been written in an East Slavonic area.

Inscriptions:

ff.1-28, rectos: + ⱥтⷬꙋ нꙋмеле татъⷶлꙋи. | ши ⷶ фїюлꙋи ши ⷶ д̆хꙋлꙋи | сѣнть вине ⷶꙋ врꙋть | ровⷩⷩи лꙋи дⷩ҃ꙋ анꙋме | поⷫ геⷳгїе | попь цⷳефⷶнь дⷷⷢ сⷶть | дⷩ҃ хрозⷶгре[?] ⱥ морьмⷶрйⷲ | ⱥ ирⷶшⷷ де сⷳсь лⷶ хⷬⷶм | соворⷩⷩ сⷮ҃и архⷢгⷢⷶⷧ миⷯⷶй | сь фⷧⷶ слꙋжⷷтⷶдⷬⷶⷧⷶ свⷩтⷷи | весⷷречⷩⷩ пⷷⷢрⷳ сⷳⷩⷷⷶⷶ̆тⷶте трⷳⷶ[...] | сⷳⷩⷶⷶ̆тⷶте трꙋпⷩⷶⷶ̆ше ши ⷷⷶ̆тⷶре де | пⷶⷶ̆кⷶте сꙋⷶ̆флетⷷⷶⷶ̆ше ши пⷷⷢрⷳ | сꙋⷶ̆флетⷳⷶ̆ пⷶⷶ̆ⷢрⷩⷩциⷶ̆лⷳⷶ̆ сⷶⷶ̆й | поⷫ миⷯⷶи гⷶфⷮⷶⷶ̆е поⷫ гⷶврⷩⷩиⷶⷧ | ѡдⷩⷩоⷶ̆тⷷⷶ̆ помⷷⷩⷩи гⷢ҃и дⷳⷶ̆ше рⷶⷶ̆вⷶ своⷶ̆ⷯ | цⷷⷶ̆фⷶⷶ̆ⷢ
й жⷷⷩⷩⷶ ѥгⷪ ιⷭⷶⷶ̆ⷩнⷶ мⷶⷶ̆рⷷⷶ̆ꙗ | поⷫ никⷷⷶ̆тⷶ поⷫ лⷳꙋпⷳⷶ̆ⷶ̆ григⷪⷶ̆рⷷⷩ̆е | ⷶⷶ̆мⷶⷶ̆ь плⷶⷶ̆тⷷⷶⷶ̆ть дⷩ҃трⷶ̆ ⷶⷶ̆ мⷷⷶ̆ ⷶⷶ̆гⷩⷩⷩⷩⷶ̆сⷶ̆ⷶ̆тⷶ | поⷫ цⷷⷶⷶ̆фⷶⷶ̆ⷶ̆ поⷫ геⷳⷶ̆рⷢⷢⷶ̆ⷶ̆ⷶⷶ̆е | сⷶ̆ прⷶⷶ̆тⷶⷶ̆мⷶⷶ̆скⷷⷶⷶ̆ дⷶ̆мⷩⷩⷳⷶ̆ⷶ̆ⷶ̆ дⷶ̆мⷩⷩⷳⷶⷶ̆ꙋ | вⷶⷶ̆лⷶⷶ̆ть ꙃⷷⷶⷶ̆лⷶ̆ꙗ де лⷶⷶ̆ х҃с анⷶⷶ̆ⷶⷶ̆ⷶⷶ̆и | ⷶⷶ̆ѱⷶ̆ⷶ̆к҃ѳ [1729]
мⷶⷶ̆ц̆ⷶ̆ь юⷶⷶ̆лⷶⷶ̆и | помⷷⷩⷩⷩⷩⷩⷩⷩⷩⷩⷩⷩⷩⷩⷶⷶ̆и гⷢ҃и дⷶ̆ше рⷶⷶ̆вⷶ своⷶⷶ̆ⷶⷶ̆и рⷶⷶ̆вⷶⷶ̆ь геⷳⷶ̆рⷢⷢⷶⷶ̆ⷶ̆е ⷶ̆ⷶ̆ⷶ̆лⷶⷶ̆ⷶ̆нⷶⷶ̆ꙗ поⷫ тⷪⷶ̆ⷶ̆дⷶⷶ̆ерⷶⷶ̆ⷶⷶ̆ⷶⷶ̆ь | хⷶ̆ⷶ̆нкⷶⷶ̆ ιⷭ̆ⷶ̆ⷶ̆ⷶ̆ⷩⷩⷶ̆лⷶⷶ̆ꙋⷶ̆пⷶⷶ̆ мⷶⷶ̆рⷶⷶ̆ⷶ̆ⷶ̆е | поⷫ григⷪⷶ̆рⷶⷶ̆ⷶⷶ̆ꙗ мⷶⷶ̆рⷶⷶ̆ⷶⷶ̆кⷶ̆ꙗ ιⷭ̆ⷶⷶ̆ гⷶⷶ̆ⷢвⷶⷶ̆рⷶⷶ̆ⷶⷶ̆ⷶⷶ̆н | тⷪⷶⷶ̆дⷶⷶ̆ⷷⷶ̆ крⷶ̆ⷢⷶⷶ̆тⷶⷶ̆ⷶⷶ̆нⷶⷶ̆ⷶⷶ̆ⷶⷶ̆ мⷶⷶ̆рⷶⷶ̆ⷶⷶ̆кⷶ̆ⷩⷩⷶⷶ̆ь дⷶ̆ꙃⷶ̆ⷢⷶⷶ̆нⷶ̆ⷶ̆ⷶ̆ⷶⷶ̆е | й вⷷⷶⷶ̆ⷶ̆ рⷪⷶ̆ⷢⷶ̆ⷶ̆ⷶⷶ̆ⷶ̆ⷶ̆ й дⷶ̆мⷩⷩⷳⷶⷶ̆ⷶ̆ⷶ̆ сⷶ̆ⷶ̆ⷶⷶ̆ь й
помⷷⷩⷩⷶ̆ⷶ̆ⷶⷶ̆ⷶ̆ⷷⷶⷶ̆скⷶ̆ⷶ̆ь ꙃⷶⷶ̆ рⷪⷶⷶ̆ⷢⷶⷶ̆ⷶ̆ⷶⷶ̆ⷶ̆ⷶⷶ̆ⷶ̆ | жⷶⷶ̆ⷶ̆ⷶ̆ⷶⷶ̆ⷶ̆вⷶⷶ̆ⷶⷶ̆ⷶ̆ⷶ̆лⷶⷶ̆ⷶ̆мⷶⷶ̆ь й мⷶ҃ⷶ̆ртⷶⷶ̆ⷶⷶ̆ⷶⷶ̆вⷶⷶ̆й.

ff.29-34: Ezen könyvet Tekénytetes Nemes Maramoros | Vármegyéből Rozávlya névű | Helységnek Templomából Isten | nevében ugyantsak odavaló Paro|chus és Vice Espe-res által adta | Kis Rákotz névű helységnek Tem|plom számára, aravaló nézve | odavaló Tiszt Parochus Ur tartozni | fog isten elöt való imatsagiban | az Istenes jó tselekedetért emlékezet|teni Amen

Provenance: written in the Ruthenian area. The inscriptions link the manuscript with the villages of Rozália (Rozavlea, in Maramureș) and Kis Rákóc in the former Ugocsa vármegye (Malyj Rakovec, in the Vynohradiv region of the Transcarpathian oblast' of the Ukraine). One of 14 MSS donated by Antal Hodinka in 1904.

Plates 24, 25

20. Fol. Eccl. Slav. 5

Festal Menaion, 16th century (3rd quarter)

Paper. Watermark: boar (fig.71), very similar to Mareş 357 (1553); boar (fig.72), similar to Mareş 355 (1553); fleur-de-lys (fig.73), similar to Briquet 6943 (1540-54); oxhead (very faint); two faint circular marks (unidentified). In the endpapers, coat of arms (fig.20). i+151+i leaves; modern stamped foliation, [i], 1-151, [152]. Size of leaves: 300×185 mm.

Collation: the original gatherings have been reconstituted, which makes impossible the reconstruction of the original composition. There are occasional leaves missing. The last two leaves are possibly extraneous. Gatherings signed in the bottom right-hand corner of the first recto: ✦ on f.50 and by small crosses in the upper left-hand corner on ff.33, 50, 121, 147.

Layout: 30 ll./p., written area 235×140 mm, except on f.151 (26 ll./p., written area 225×140 mm).

Hand: a variety of more or less formal bookhands. 1. (ff.1-26v; 60-103v) an upright, squarish, practised bookhand; 2. (ff.27-59; 104.1-9; 104v-105.9; 105v.4-108v.17; 112-149v) a less formal hand of the same type with a tendency to curved stems for the letters; 3. (ff.104.10-30; 105.10-105v.4) a small, square, somewhat irregular semiuncial sloping slightly to the right; 4. (ff.108v.17-111v) a hand similar to the second, but less fluid, slightly sloping to the left in places; 5. (f.150) an upright bookhand of the same type as the first hand; 6. (f.151) a small square semiuncial (x-height=2mm). Majuscule titles for many sections, varying in size.

Ink: yellowish-brown for the first scribe; black or brownish-black for the second scribe; black for scribes 3 and 4, brown for scribes 5 and 6; red for titles, initials and rubrics.

Binding: ornamented brown leather on thick boards, 308×192 mm, restored and largely new, with only two pieces of leather from the original covers. Five raised bands on the new spine; two fastenings, now lost. Blind tooling. On the upper cover a triple border with fillets and roll-stamped scroll; the centre panel is a lozenge formed of fillets with a cross inside it; all are stamped with the same scroll. On the lower cover the same borders with fillets enclose the centre panel, divided into seven vertical strips, all stamped with the scroll; they are terminated above and below by two rectangles divided into triangles. The ornament is very faint. One modern flyleaf at each end.

Condition: the leather of the original binding has been badly damaged, two large parts of it are missing. Many leaves are missing at both the front and the back of the manuscript and sporadically within. The surviving leaves are in good condition.

Decoration: very simple, red or red and black four-to six-line penwork and pen-flourished initials of the Neo-Byzantine type at the Bible readings. Two sub-types are distinguishable, the first with simple ornamentation of small gemmæ and tendrils and the second with "negative" fillings of schematised acanthus (or palmette?) motifs on ff.29v and 57v.

Contents: Selective Festal Menaion for the whole year, according to the Jerusalem Typicon. A number of festivals are provided with parœmiæ and/or multiple canons, the latter being intercalated. There are occasional lacunæ.

(ff.1-7v) 1st September, the New Year and St Symeon Stylites; Isaiah the Monk; the Forty Women

Defective: begins with the words: Иже премꙋдростїю в'са съд'ѣлавый, и | превѣчное слово ...
[three canons, one for each commemoration]

(ff.7v-10v) 6th September, The Miracle of the Archangel Michael at Chonæ [one canon]

(ff.11-19) 8th September, Nativity of the Virgin [two canons; parœmiæ]

(ff.19-21) 9th September, Joachim and Anna [one canon]

(ff.21-27v) 14th September, Elevation of the Cross [two canons; parœmiæ]

(ff.27v-34v) 26th September, Dormition of St John the Theologian [two canons, the first to the Mother of God; parœmiæ]

(ff.35-39v) Veil of the Virgin, Apostle Ananias, Romanus the Melode

Defective: begins with the words: молит҃са въ црькви бца ликꙋнте стыи
[three canons, one for each commemoration]

(ff.39v-42v) празꙋе҇ [sic!] в нелю по памати сто апт҃ла | филипа. въ преидꙋщоую. мца ѡктѐ сътва|рѣемь памат҃ сто сѐго събора [defective; one canon (to St Philip)]

(f.42v-48) 8th November, Synaxis of the Bodiless Powers [one canon; parœmiæ]

(ff.48-53v) 12th November, St John the Almsgiver [one canon]

(ff.53v-56) 20th November, Forefeast of the Presentation of the Virgin [one canon]

(ff.56-65v) 21st November, Presentation of the Virgin [two canons, by George and Basil; parœmiæ]

(ff.65v-76) мца того҇ ѕ [sic] St Nicholas [one canon to the Mother of God and two to St Nicholas; parœmiæ]

(f.76-79) 9th December, Conception of the Mother of God [one canon]

(ff.79-83) Нелѧ стыⷯ праѿȸь [one canon]

(ff.83-87v) Не҇ стыⷯ ѿȸь ѐже ꙇ пре҇ рож҇дество҇| хвⷭ҃ [one canon]

(ff.87v-95v) 20th December, Forefeast of the Nativity; St Ignatius Theophorus [two canons, one for each commemoration]

(f.95v-101) 24th December, Forefeast of the Nativity; St Eugenia [two canons, one for each commemoration]

(f.101-103v) Унⷩ како повае҇ пѣти часы въ навеерїе | рож҇ства хвⷶ [followed by service for Christmas Day, with Gospel readings and parœmiæ; lacking the end]

(ff.104-105) 21st May, SS Constantine and Helena

Defective: begins with the words: сꙗ са, доброю кротостїю ꙗко вѣнцемь оукрасꙗ|са
[one canon]

(ff.105-111v) 12th June, St Onuphrius [two canons, the first to the Mother of God; parœmiæ; lacking the end]

(ff.112-115) 2nd July, Deposition of the Robe

Defective: begins with the words: вьшеє ѿдежоу славы даровавъ
[one canon]

(ff.115-117) 15th July, SS Cyriacus and Julitta ("крика й мтѐре єго҇ | лоулиты"); St Vladimir ("влад҇ мерꙗ"), Prince of Kiev [one canon (to Vladimir)]

(ff.117-123v) 20th July, Prophet Elias [one canon; parœmiæ]

(ff.123v-130) 24th July, SS Boris and Gleb [one canon; parœmiæ]

51

(ff.130-131) **25th July, Dormition of St Anne** [defective (the beginning and end only); one canon]

(ff.131-136) **1st August, Procession of the Holy Cross; the Maccabees and their teacher Eleazar and their mother Solomonia** [two canons, one for each commemoration]

(ff.136-138v) **5th August, Forefeast of the Transfiguration** [one canon]

(ff.138v-145v) **6th August, Transfiguration** [lacking the end; two canons; parœmiæ]

(ff.146-148) **14th August, Forefeast of the Dormition**

Defective: begins with the words: нь написаѥмь. Трⷪце сⷮаа съроднаа.

[one canon]

(ff.148-151v) **15th August, Dormition** [two canons; lacking the end]

Language: Church Slavonic; most of the scribes follow Middle Bulgarian orthographic norms to a greater or lesser extent, except for the first and third, whose practice is much more consistently East Slavonic.

Provenance: written in the Ruthenian area. Purchased from Mariu Nicora of Cinkota together with Quart. Eccl. Slav. 7 and Fol. Valach. 6 (a Rumanian Gospel book) on 31st August 1925.

Plates 26, 27, 28

21. FOL. ECCL. SLAV. 10
Festal Menaion, 16th century (last quarter)

Paper. Watermark: coat of arms: Habdank (fig.74), similar to Laucevičius 1029 (1575-9), Budka 60 (1581), Lichačev 535 (1581); eagle (fig.75); coat of arms: Rogala (fig.76); coat of arms: Jelita; coat of arms: Lubicz. In the additional (first) gathering, two-headed eagle (fig.77), similar to Laucevičius 473 (1715). In the flyleaves, oak-twig (fig.34) also found in the endpapers of Fol. Eccl. Slav. 6 and 16.
ii+8+363+ii=ii+371+ii leaves; modern stamped foliation, [i-ii], 1-371, [327-373]. Size of leaves: 295×188 mm.

Collation: I-II⁸, III⁸(-2), IV-IX⁸, X¹⁰, XI⁸(-4?), XII-XXIII⁸, XXIV⁸(-8), XXV-XLV⁸, XLVI⁴. Gatherings signed in the lower margin on the first recto and the last verso of each gathering, а҃-м҃ѕ, level with the text's outer margin; XLVI signed on the recto only. A later unsigned gathering has been added before I.

Layout: 28 ruled ll./p., written area 231×135 mm.

Hand: semiuncial, x-height 3 mm, clear practised bookhand with a calligraphic effect given by the downward elongation of the stems of the letters on the bottom line and their transformation into foliar motifs. Majuscule titles. Ff.1-8 (the additional gathering) written in a degenerate late Ukrainian bookhand.

Ink: black; red for the titles and rubrics.

Binding: reddish-brown ornamented leather on bevelled boards, 315×195 mm, restored. Sewn on four cords with raised bands on spine, traces of two fastenings. Blind tooling. On the upper cover a border of eight-petal rosette (snowflake-like) stamps; at its inner side a linear cresting runs along the centre panel; the centre-piece is a lozenge of foliate ornament with a fleur-de-lys on top, enclosing a small oval medallion with the Crucifixion; around it are impressed stamps of the border rosette, smaller round rosettes and composite ornaments of the two. Tripartite flower motifs are stamped at the corners. The lower cover has the same border; the centre panel is divided by triple fillets into four vertical strips ending in two horizontal ones and filled in with the border stamps; in the middle of the horizontal strips are cross-like figures composed of the two small rosette stamps. The binding is probably contemporary with the added gathering, i.e. early eighteenth century. Two modern flyleaves at each end.

Condition: well preserved, restored at the time when the additional gathering was added to the manuscript: many leaves have been mended with the same paper. Both the leaves and binding have subsequently undergone modern restoration.

Decoration: one headpiece in the original part of the manuscript, and red initials.

f.9: a rectangular headpiece (65×135 mm) at the beginning of the Menaion, of the Balkan interlaced style; double, intertwined vegetal stems with stylised interlaced endings compose two circles and an ellipse; the outlines are red, while the interstices are coloured in ochre and blue, or left blank.

f.1: at the beginning of the added gathering, a ∏-shaped headpiece, filled with a lattice of vegetal stems with flower-like motifs at the intersecting points; a small primitive drawing of an angel's head at the centre of the upper frame; outlines in black ink, the interstices filled with red.

Numerous pen-flourished initials of the Neo-Byzantine type, four to ten lines, mainly at the Biblical readings in the original part, decorated with abundant ornament of small elegant branches with tendrils, wavy leaves, and small gemmæ on the stems of the letters. Smaller initials of the same kind at the liturgical entries.

Contents: Selective Festal Menaion for the whole year, following the Jerusalem Typicon. All services are provided with parœmiæ and unless otherwise stated two canons (in the case of a double commemoration, one for each), intercalated. Synaxarion readings are given for the Elevation of the Cross, Synaxis of the Bodiless Powers, St Nicholas, Nativity, Theophany, Annunciation, St George, SS Peter and Paul, Elias, Transfiguration, Dormition and the Beheading of John the Baptist. The Menaion begins on f.9; the first eight leaves are a later addition.

(ff.1-8) **Мⷭ҇ца ѡктоврїѧ въ ді҃ | Прпⷣбнїѧ мтⷬ҇е нⷲ҇еѧ Параскевїи. Нарїцаемїи | пѧтки Теⷬ҇новскїѧ**

Incipit: **Пощенїю пꙋть въсприеⷨши жїтейскиѧ любве избѣже параскевїѧ слав'наѧ.**

(ff.9-25v) **1st September, Beginning of the Indiction and Commemoration of St Symeon Stylites and the Forty Women** [three canons, one for each commemoration]
(ff.26-39v) **8th September, Nativity of the Mother of God**
(ff.40-52v) **14th September, Elevation of the Cross**
(ff.53-64v) **Dormition of St John the Theologian**
(ff.64v-81v) **26th October, St Demetrius the Martyr, and Memory of the Great Earthquake**
(ff.82-89v) **8th November, Synaxis of the Bodiless Powers**
(ff.90-105) **21st November, Presentation of the Virgin**
(ff.105v-121v) **мⷭ҇ца тогожде** [sic!] **6th December, St Nicholas**
(ff.121v-138) **25th December, Nativity**
(ff.138-150v) **1st January, Circumcision; St Basil the Great**
(ff.151-176v) **6th January, Theophany**
(ff.177-188) **2nd February, Presentation of Christ in the Temple**
(ff.188-200v) **мⷭ҇ца тогожде** [sic!] **25th March, Annunciation**
(ff.201-210v) **на малѣ̑ веⷱ҇рни въ сѫботѫ | веⷱ҇рь. Ст҃го праведнаго лаӡарѧ**
(ff.210v-222v) **Слꙋⷤ҇ба стыⷯ҇ стрⷭ҇тєи**
(ff.222v-239) **въ стⷹ҇ѫѧ великѫѧ сѫⷠ҇тѫ веⷱ҇р҇ | при чаⷭ҇їмь**
(ff.239v-253v) **23rd April, St George**
(ff.253v-266) **Ascension Day**
(ff.266v-277) **въ пѧⷦ҇ и́ веⷱ҇ памѧть | сътварѣемъ въсѣⷨ иже ѿ вѣка | оусъпшиⷯ ѡⷮцъ нашиⷯ и братїи | православныⷯ** [Only one canon, by Theodore Studite (including the second ode), but a rubric prescribes that the canon for the patron of the church in which the service is held should also be sung.]
(ff.277-297) **Sunday of Pentecost**
(ff.297-313v) **29th April, apostles Peter and Paul**
(ff.313v-322) **20th July, Prophet Elias** [one canon]
(ff.322-337v) **6th August, Transfiguration**

(ff.337v-353) 15th August, Dormition of the Virgin

(ff.353-371) 29th August, Beheading of St John the Baptist [three canons, one to the Mother of God and two to St John, the second of these by Andrew of Crete]

Language: Church Slavonic, closely following Middle Bulgarian Tărnovo norms. The additional gathering (ff.1-8) was evidently written by a Ukrainian in the eighteenth century.

Inscriptions:

inside front cover: Zékány Lajos | Zékány | Lajos

ff.13v-14: вѡ имѧ ѡца й сина и свѣтаго дѹ̂ха амнⁿ | [The second part of the inscription has been erased.]

A later hand has added running titles.

Provenance: of Moldavian or Transylvanian origin, with a later additional gathering written by a Ukrainian. One of 14 manuscripts donated by Antal Hodinka in 1904.

Plate 29

22. FOL. ECCL. SLAV. 15

Festal Menaion, 17th century

Paper. Watermark: stag with the letters ID (fig.78), cf. Piccard Hirsch 1299-1372 (1622-59);basilisk or griffin (figs.79, 80); eagle, small and rather faint; ?a coat of arms, toofragmentary to permit identification.

ii+305+ii leaves; modern stamped foliation [i-ii], 1-305, [306-307]. Size of leaves: 308×90mm.

Collation: I^8 (-1), II-III^8, IV-VI^4, VII^8, VIII-IX^{10}, X^8, XI^{10}, XII^8 (-1), XIII-XIV^8, XV^{10}, XVI-XIX^8, XX^{10}, XXI-XXII^8, XXIII^{10}, XXIV^8, XXV-XXVI^{10}, XXVII^2, XXVIII-XXIX^{10}, XXX^8, XXXI-XXXII^{10}, XXXIII^2, XXXIV^8, XXXV-XXXVI^{10}, XXXVII^8, XXXVIII^8 (-8). Unsigned.

Layout: 24-26 ll./p. for the first scribe; 26-29, 32 ll./p. for the second; 24-25 ll./p. for the third; 25-27 ll./p. for the fourth; varying for the fifth. Written area correspondingly: 264×60 mm; 260×55 mm; 250-255×55 mm; 265×55-60 mm; 90×60 mm. From f.165 to f.181v two scribes share the same page, dividing it in two horizontally, each writing a different text.

Hand: a variety of rather irregular hands. 1. (ff.1-53, 89-146v, 167.18-182v, 213-221v, 263-305): large semiuncial, x-height 5-6 mm, letters of elongated shape sloping to the right; 2. (ff.54-56v, 72-77v, 222-247): straight, very irregular script, x-height 3 mm; 3. (ff.57-71, 78-88, 147-149.14, 183-210v, 251-260v): a hand similar to the preceding one, also irregular, x-height 3-4 mm; 4. (ff.149.14-164v, 247v-250v) another large irregular semiuncial, x-height 4-5 mm; 5. (ff.165-167.17, 167v-181v) a small semiuncial, x-height 2 mm, sloping to the right, sharing leaves with the first scribe. On ff.211-212 a later hand had added a missing part of the text. All the scribes use majuscules for the titles, but only the first scribe puts elementary decoration to them.

Ink: brown-black, used by the majority of the scribes, with the exception of the second scribe, who writes with yellowish ink (the colour may be due to oxidation, however). Dark-red (tile-red) is used for the titles, initials and rubrics. Black ink is used for the later addition.

Binding: ornamented leather on bevelled boards, 315×94 mm, restored with another ornamented leather. Sewn on four cords with raised bands on the spine, two fastenings, now lost. Blind tooling. On the upper cover an incised border of triple fillets framing the central panel (270×40 mm), whose angles are connected to those of the border; on the lower cover the scheme is similar, but the centre panel is divided into three strips, terminated by two horizontal oblongs; the strips are roll-stamped with an interlaced cresting with foliate ends. The binding appears to be original. Two flyleaves at each end, one in each case of the same patterned paper as the pastedowns.

Condition: leaves missing at both front and back; much staining; old repairs to most of the leaves, some becoming detached.

Decoration: simple and rustic, consisting of headpieces (only one of which has survived), numerous initials, mainly in the parts written by the first and third scribes, and tailpieces.

56

f.178: reading for 23rd May: a framed headpiece, 28×58 mm, outlined in red and divided into three compartments, and the two flanking ones comprising medallions with interlaced frames; a short bar with simple floral endings decorates the upper edge; small foliate endings at the corners.

f.182: a simple bar between two texts.

f.213: reading for 29th June: a small fragment of headpiece, the rest is completely destroyed.

Red three- to ten-line initials, at the Old Testament readings, differing in their ornamentation and construction. One group consists of linear initials with elementary ornamentation of dots, small geometric elements and tendrils (more elaborate on ff.215, 215v, with foliate finials, dots, short lines, tendrils and "fringes"). A second group includes initials with painted or outlined composite stems and more complicated ornamentation of tendrils, foliate finials, small trefoils; the outlined initials are more particularly ornamented. In the parts of the manuscript written by the second scribe there are both linear and outlined initials, simply decorated.

f.35: ink drawing at the end of the entry, representing a human head with a cross atop, surrounded by the letters і͠с х͠с ни ка́, illustrating the priest carrying the cross on the feast of the Exaltation of the Cross.

f.53: a tailpiece consisting of a red-ink drawing of a small twig.

Contents: Selective Festal Menaion, also including material from the Lenten and Festal Triodia and part of the Acts of the Apostles. Parœmiæ are provided for all services except for that to the Prophet Elijah on ff.231–240; a reference is given for the parœmia for the first service, for the Nativity of the Mother of God, but the text is not written out. Unless otherwise stated, each service is provided with two canons (in the case of a double commemoration, one for each), intercalated.

(ff.1–18v) Services for the Nativity of the Mother of God [The beginning is missing.]

(ff.18v–35) На в̾ꙁдви́ние ує̄тъна́ и͂ ҂ꙵ͠ѡ въ|тво́рꙗщаꙷ крꙺта г͠нѣ [one canon, by Cosmas]

(f.35v) [blank]

(ff.36–53) мꙉа ѡктеврїа д͂і препо͂|бнъїа м͂тре ншеа пе꙼кьі [two canons, one to the Mother of God and one to St Petka]

(f.53v) [blank]

(ff.54–71v) съвѿ҆ архистратига | михаила́. и прочи͂х͏꙼ | беспльтнь͏ꙷ [one canon]

(ff.72–88v) прп҆бна͂ и в͂гносна͂ꙵ| ѡꙉа нше͂ архїера|ха и ую͂твоꙷца ни|кольі [one canon, byTheophanes]

(ff.89–118) еже по пльти рожꙵества́ | г͠а б͠а сп͠са нше͂ і͠с х͠а [F.97v is blank.]

(f.118v–136) мꙉа г͂еварїа а͂ е͏꙼ по͏꙼ | пльти ѡбрѣꙁание | г͠а б͠а сп͠са нше͂ і͠с х͠а | и па́ма꙼ иже въ с͠ть͏ꙵ | ѡꙉа нше͂ василїа ве|лика́ꙵ

(f.136v–164v) с͠тое в͂гоꙗвленїе г͠а б͠а и сп͠са́ | нше͂ і͠с х͠а

(ff.165–181v) Services for Palm Sunday

(ff.167–170) въ с͠тꙋ́ѫ велꙵкꙋѫ | сꙗвотꙋ [This text occupies the lower part of the pages, the upper part continuing to be occupied by the services for Palm Sunday; one canon.]

(ff.170–176) въ с͠тꙋ́ю велꙵ|кꙋꙍ не́ꙷ пасхьі [This text, like the previous one, occupies the lower part of the pages only. It is incomplete, breaking off in the middle of the Easter Homily of St John Chrysostom. One canon.]

(ff.178-182v) мца апри҃ к҃г ст҃го сла҃|на҃ велі́комѣ́ника х҃ва | геѡ҃ргі́ѧ [This text also occupies the lower part of the pages only, and is incomplete.]

(ff.183-197) въ че́ д҃ не҃ пра́не҃ в'|знесе́нїѧ г҃а нш҃е і҃с х҃а

(ff.197-212) въ не́ д҃ н҃ [i.e. Whitsun; the end is missing and has been supplied on two additional leaves. F.212v is blank.]

(ff.213-230v) мца і́юна к҃ѳ сты[х҃ъ] | великы́х҃ и в'ѣ҃хѡ҃ны́х҃ | й хвалны́х҃ а҃п҃ль пе҃|тра й павла҃

(ff.231-240) Ст҃ого прѡр҃ка҃ и҃лїи [one canon]

(ff.240-260v) Ст҃ое прѣ̑ѡвра҃д҃м҃ нїе г҃а нш҃е і҃с | х҃а [The end is missing.]

(ff.261-262v) [blank]

(ff.263-280) мца а҃вг҃у е҃і у҃спенїе пре҃|ст҃ыѧ в҃ца

(ff.281-305) Д҃ѣ[ѧннѧ] | а҃п҃ль съписа[на апо]|столѡ҃м҃ е҃гла́тѡ҃м҃ лу҃кож [incomplete: from the beginning to ch.7, v.58]

Language: Church Slavonic, broadly following Bulgarian orthographic norms but with marked East Slavonic and even local dialect features in both language and orthography, and somewhat carelessly written.

Inscriptions:

f.182v: Коре҃н҃ оу҃ченїѧ горокъ | есть плоды же | сладн суть

ff.287-291, 293-303, rectos: Сїю кнйгу реко́мую | минею превазова́д҃ | сц҃ины Іере̑ іѡ҃сиф҃' | градо̑вскїн на то̑ | зо҃таю҃уй на гѝжи [?] | за стара҃нїемь | его҃ мл҃ти микоу | йва́нъца нинового|го | и с'своею га҃зъ̑тафкею | оу҃уй҃ памать | своимь родичо̑м҃ | пре̑тавшійсѧ | а собѣ телеснаго | з'дравїа наипаче | дш҃внаго сп҃нїа | аминь

f.303v: ïoseph grado

f.304: вру҃чѣлѣта е зро́к хѕі | а҃ѱі҃еі [1715] мць ю҃н | дн҃ъ н҃і

f.305v: за дорошенка гекмана пу҃|ста украина [...] [a long inscription, largely illegible due to damage and staining of the paper]

Provenance: written in the Ruthenian area. The words на гѝжи on f.291 conceivably refer to the village of Chyža (Kistarna), Vynohradiv region, Transcarpathian oblast'. Given by Antal Hodinka on 11th June 1907.

Plates 30, 31, 32, 33

Festal Menaion for November, 1707

Paper. Watermark: coat of arms (fig.81), very similar to Laucevičius 1404 (1697); small horseman with a tree (fig.82), type Laucevičius 2779-80 (1681-5); à la mode (fig.83), very indistinct, type Laucevičius 31 (1704).

72 leaves; modern stamped foliation 1-72. Size of leaves: 310×190 mm.

Collation: (2 leaves), I-XI⁶, XII⁶ (-5-6). Unsigned.

Layout: 27 ll./p., written area 222×140 mm. Catchwords. Running titles.

Hand: a fine practised semiuncial, influenced by print.

Ink: black; red for titles, rubrics and initials.

Binding: disbound.

Condition: incomplete, but the surviving pages are in very good condition.

Decoration: majuscule titles, with some græcising letter-forms similar to those of Ukrainian printed books, ornamented with floral motifs; larger and smaller initials of the same kind at the subdivisions of the text with modest decoration of buds and tendrils.

Contents: Menaion for November, lacking the beginning and the end. Services according to the Jerusalem Typicon. No lessons of any kind, but where more than one saint is commemorated, canons to both are provided, intercalated. Includes services for Nov. 15th (f.1, Gourias, Samonas and Abibus), 17th (f.5v, Gregory of Neocæsarea), 18th (f.11, Plato and Romanus), 19th (f.18, Obadiah; Barlaam), 20th (f.23, forefeast of the Presentation of the BVM; Gregory of Decapolis; Proclus, Patriarch of Constantinople), 22nd (f.30v, Philemon and his companions), 23rd (f.35v, Amphilochius of Iconium; Gregory Agrigentinus), 24th (f.42v, Mercurius), 25th (f.46v, apodosis of the Presentation of the BVM; Clement; Peter of Alexandria), 26th (f.53, Alypius the Stylite), 27th (f.57, James the Persian; Palladius) and 28th (f.65, Stephen the New Confessor; Irenarchus).

Language: Synodal Church Slavonic.

Inscriptions:

f.5: Roku 1770. wszędzie po Wołyniu wszczęte | morowe powietrze poryletney, wiele ludzi | oboiey płci osmierć przyprawiło, nawety | w powiecie Włodzym-, w Ofsie dobrach JW | Wojewody Wołyń-: co dla pamięci tuzię za|pisało ręką własną dyta Bohusza Prbra WK | dz. 24. 9bris vs. Roku jako wyzey~

ff.57-60, rectos: Ста́ Мине́й Написа́хъ въ Ст҃о́й Оби҃|тели Мѣле́цкой. А҃зъ Ра́бъ Б҃жїй ‖ Сщ҃енноі҆нокъ Ѳеѡ҆кти́стъ . Кото́ры҆е Надалю̀ | За ѡ҆пꙋще́нїе грѣхо́въ . до Бг҃оспаса́емаго Гра́да ‖ Ковла̀ . до Ц҃ркви Ст҃о́й Собо́рной. Заложе́|нїѧ Воскресе́нїѧ Гд҃а нш҃его І҃с Х҃а. Абы̀ ‖ При то́й Ц҃ркви ст҃о́й. Вѣ́чными Ча́сы | Зоставаа́ли. Рокꙋ Бж҃ого ҂аѱ҃з. [1707] мц҃а сє̏: | дн҃ѧ г҃і.

Provenance: the inscription on ff.57-60 records that the MS was written in Mielec (near Sandomierz) in 1707. Bought from Miklós Pastinszky for 300 forints on 28th April 1960.

Plate 34

24. Fol. Eccl. Slav. 26

General and Festal Menaion, 18th century (second quarter: 1726?)

Paper. Watermark: à la mode (fig.84), type Laucevičius 30 (1740); coat of arms (fig.85), similar to Laucevičius 1759 (1724); cross (fig.86); coat of arms (fig.87). In the endpapers, coat of arms (fig.20).

i+446+ii leaves; modern stamped foliation [i], 1-447, [448]; original foliations а̄-ѵ҃д by the first scribe on ff.1-94 and а̄-ѕ̄, ѕ̄-ѷ҃д by the second scribe on ff.95-101, 102-149; ѷ҃д-сд҃ѻ, ѿ-т҃ѻѕ by the other scribes on ff.150-364, 365-441. Size of leaves: 286×175 mm.

Collation: indeterminable: the present gatherings are made-up ones, constructed at the time of the restoration, and do not necessarily reflect the original composition of the book.It seems quite probable that it was originally predominantly in twelves. Unsigned.

Layout: scribe 1: 30 ruled ll./p., written area 242×142 mm ; scribe 2: 27 ruled ll./p., written area 238×131 mm ; scribe 3: 27 ruled ll./p., written area 238×130 mm ; scribe 4:29 ruled ll./p., written area 239×140 mm. Calendar data are indicated in the upper margins; all the scribes except the third use a ruled outer margin in black ink.

Hand: a variety of late and slightly degenerate, though regular and consistent semiuncials. 1. (ff.1-94v, 413v.14-446) very small, regular semiuncial; 2. (ff.95-150.2) regular, slightly more conservative and larger (x-height=3mm) semiuncial; 3. (ff.150.3-153) upright semiuncial; 4. (ff.154-413v.13) small, slightly variable semiuncial. The first and fourth scribes use majuscule titles.

Ink: yellowish-brown for scribe 1 and black for the rest; orange colour (minium?) for titles, initials, and rubrics.

Binding: ornamented leather on thick bevelled boards, 310×185 mm, restored; five raised bands on the new flat spine, two new clasps. Blind tooling. On the upper cover a double-framed border with baroque ornament, now faint; big centre-piece of oval shape 108×88 mm, with the Resurrection within a garland. On the lower cover an incised and roll-stamped border of acanthus scroll; the centre panel is divided vertically by triple fillets into five strips, each stamped with the same scroll motif; the strips are terminated by two rectangles divided into triangles. The binding is from the eighteenth century, perhaps a little later than the manuscript, since the inscription on ff.95-111 has been cropped. One modern flyleaf at each end, and one old one at the end.

Condition: leaves missing at both front and back; ff.114-115 detached from the main body; the manuscript has been restored.

Decoration: very modest, on the model of contemporary printed books.

Three headbands outlined in black ink and filled in with red-orange linear floral motifs, two at the services for the Elevation of the Cross (f.112, with the Cross in the centre, and f.113, stopping at a framed representation of the Cross with the instruments of the Passion), and one on f.145 for 14th October, St Petka's Day, with the Cross in a round medallion in the middle. On f.125 the space provided has been left empty.

Numerous red or black penwork initials, many of them outlined and others double-outlined or framed, mainly at the Old Testament lessons. Shadowed and extremely large are those on ff.275v, 276v, 411v, 412, 412v at the Gospel lessons for the blessing of the waters, whereas the great majority of the initials are small and with no ornamentation.

Contents: General Menaion on ff.1-94v, followed by Festal Menaion on ff.95-446v. The services follow the Jerusalem Typicon. Parœmiæ are provided for only a minority of the services in the either part; in some of the other services references are given for parœmiæ which are not written out. All the services in the General Menaion and the majority of the services in the Festal Menaion have a single canon; exceptions are noted. Where more than one canon is given, they are intercalated. The services for the weeks preceding Christmas and Epiphany (December 20th-24th and January 2nd-5th) have two separate canons, one at Compline and one at Mattins; the former is normally called трипѣснєцъ, even though it may contain the full eight odes.

(ff.1-5) **Common Service for one prophet** [parœmiæ]
(ff.5v-9v) **Common Service for one apostle** [parœmiæ]
(ff.9v-14v) **Common Service for two apostles** [parœmiæ]
(ff.14v-20v) **Common Service for one saint** [parœmiæ]
(ff.20v-24v) **Common Service for two saints** [parœmiæ]
(ff.24v-28v) **Common Service for one saint who is a monk**
(ff.29-33) **Common Service for more than one monk-saint**
(ff.33-37) **Common Service for one martyr** [parœmiæ]
(ff.37-40v) **Common Service for two or more martyrs**
(ff.41-44v) **Common Service for one priest and martyr**
(ff.45-48v) **Common Service for more than one priest and martyr**
(ff.49-52v) **Common Service for a martyred monk**
(ff.53-55) **Common Service for martyred monks**
(ff.55v-58v) **Common Service for one female martyr**
(ff.59-61) **Common Service for female martyrs**
(ff.61-64v) **Common Service for a saint who was a nun**
(ff.64v-66v) **Common Service for more than one saint who was a nun**
(ff.66v-68v) **Common Service for martyred nuns**
(ff.69-71) **Common Service for a priest and confessor**
(ff.71-74) **Common Service for Anargyroi**
(ff.74-76v) **Common Service for Holy Fools**
(ff.76v-81) слꙋжба Ѻбща Іѡанꙋ прєⷣтєчи [parœmiæ]
(ff.81-85v) **Service for Angels and other Bodiless Powers**
(ff.85v-89v) слꙋжба Ѻбща свѧтимъ ѿцємъ [parœmiæ]
(ff.89v-91v) Канѡна два прⷮѣй бⷢци. пѣвдємⷮи в᾽праⷣ|ники нарочитиⷯ стыⷯ
(ff.92-94v) **Parœmiæ for the Prophet Elias**
(ff.95-102v) **1st September, the New Indiction, St Symeon Stylites and his mother Martha, Synaxis of the Virgin in the Monastery of Miasena, St Aeithalas, 40 Women martyrs and Ammon, their teacher, Martyrs Callistus, Evodius and Hermogenes, commemoration of Joshua, and commemoration of the Great Fire** [parœmiæ, canon for the New Year, by Joseph]
(ff.103-112) **8th September, Nativity of the Mother of God** [parœmiæ, two canons, the second by Andrew]
(ff.112-125) **14th September, Elevation of the Cross** [parœmiæ]
(ff.125-137v) **26th September, St John the Theologian** [parœmiæ, three canons, the second by Theophanes]

61

(ff.137v-145) 1st October, Protection of the Mother of God, apostle Ananias, Romanus the Melode

(ff.145-153) 14th October, St Parasceve, called Petka [parœmiæ, two canons]

(f.153v) [blank]

(ff.154-156v) 26th October, St Demetrius; Commemoration of the Earthquake [parœmia, canon for the earthquake]

(ff.157-160) 20th November, Forefeast of the Presentation of the Virgin, Gregory of Decapolis, Proclus, patriarch of Constantinople

(ff.160v-171) 21st November, Presentation of the Virgin [parœmiæ, two canons, the first by George]

(ff.171v-177v) 9th December, Conception of the Mother of God

(ff.178-181) 17th December, Prophet Daniel; Ananias, Azarias and Misael

(ff.181v-185v) Sunday of the Forefathers

(ff.186-196) Sunday Before Nativity, of the Fathers [parœmiæ, two canons]

(ff.196v-201) 20th December, Sunday Before Nativity, St Ignatius Theophorus

(ff.201v-205v) 21st December, Forefeast of the Nativity; St Juliana; St Peter, Metropolitan of Kiev

(ff.205v-211) 22nd December, St Anastasia

(ff.211-215) [23rd December], Forefeast of the Nativity; the Nine Martyrs of Crete

(ff.215v-226v) 24th December Forefeast of the Nativity; St Eugenia [parœmiæ]

(ff.227-236v) 25th December, Nativity of Our Lord [parœmiæ, two canons]

(ff.237-238) [26th December], Synaxis of the Mother of God; St Joseph; Euthymius of Sardis [no canon, but a reference to that of the previous day]

(ff.238v-242) Sunday after Christmas, St Joseph; King David; St James the brother of Our Lord

(ff.242-250v) 1st January, Circumcision; St Basil [parœmiæ, two canons (one for each commemoration)]

(ff.250v-256) [2nd January], Forefeast of the Epiphany; St Silvester

(ff.256v-261) 3rd January, Forefeast of the Epiphany; Prophet Malachi; St Gordius [two canons at Compline and one at Mattins]

(ff.261v-266) 4th January, Forefeast of the Epiphany; Synaxis of the 70 Apostles; St Theoctistus

(ff.266v-272) 5th January, Forefeast of the Epiphany; SS Theopemptus and Theonas; St Syncletica

(ff.272v-277v) Послѣдованїе часовомъ стыхъ | въꙗвленїи [parœmiæ]

(ff.277v-282) 6th January, Epiphany [parœmiæ, no canon]

(ff.282-295) Blessing of the waters [parœmiæ, two canons]

(ff.295-300) Synaxis of St John the Baptist

(ff.300v-303v) 1st February, Forefeast of the Presentation of Our Lord

(ff.303v-311v) 2nd February, Presentation of Our Lord in the Temple [parœmiæ]

(ff.312-315v) 3rd February, St Simeon

(ff.316-319v) 24th March, Forefeast of the Annunciation

(ff.319v-326v) 25th March, Annunciation

(ff.326v-327v) [26th March], Synaxis of the Archangel Gabriel [parœmiæ, no canon, but a reference]

(ff.328-337) 3rd May, St Theodosius of the Caves; SS Timothy and Maura [two canons, both for Theodosius]

(ff.337v-340) 6th May, Job; St Barbarus

(ff.340v-348) 21st May, SS Constantine and Helena [parœmiæ]

(ff.348-354v) 8th June, St Theodore Stratilates

(ff.355-362v) 2nd July, Deposition of the Robe of the Mother of God in Blachernæ [two canons]

(ff.362v-372v) 10th July, 45 Martyrs in Nicopolis; Dormition of St Antony of the Caves [two canons, both to Antony]

(ff.373-378) Положе́нїе ри́зи г҃дны

(ff.378-382) 13th July, Synaxis of the Archangel Gabriel; St Stephen Sabaites

(ff.382-389) 15th July, Martyrs Cyriacus and Julitta; St Vladimir, prince of Kiev [two canons, both to Vladimir]

(ff.389v-392v) 22th July, St Mary Magdalene; St Phocas

(ff.393-398v) 25th July, Dormition of St Anne; St Olympias; St Eupraxia

(ff.398v-403v) 31st July, Forefeast of the Procession of the Holy Cross; St Eudocimus [two canons, one for each commemoration]

(ff.404-409v) 1st August, Procession of the Cross, the Maccabees and their teacher Eleazar and their mother Solomonia [two canons, one for each commemoration]

(ff.410-414v) Blessing of the waters [Epistle and Gospel readings, no canon]

(ff.414v-416v) 4th August, The Seven Sleepers of Ephesus

(ff.417-420) 5th August, Forefeast of the Transfiguration; St Eusignius

(ff.420-427) 6th August, Transfiguration [parœmiæ, two canons]

(ff.427v-433) 14th August, Forefeast of the Dormition; Prophet Micah; Translation of the relics of St Theodosius of the Caves [two canons, for the forefeast and for St Theodosius]

(ff.433v-438v) 15th August, Dormition of the Virgin [two canons]

(ff.439-446v) 16th August, Translation of the Image not made by hands; St Diomedes [parœmiæ, two canons, both for the icon]

Language: Church Slavonic of the East Slavonic recension.

Inscriptions:

ff.95-111, rectos: а҂ѱкѕ [1726] Ро́кꙋ Ѻктѡврїа к҃. дна̀ | Ѡбновиⷭ҇сѧ дрє́внаго трꙋдолю́бца | писа́нїе, мнѡ́го недостѡ́йныⷨ рабѡ́ⷨ бж҃їиⷨ| па́влѡⷨ стєфа́новичємⷤ . сїа̀ кни́га | гл҃ємаѧ мѣнє́а вели́каѧ ѡ҆бщаѧ | сѡѡ҆рꙋзиⷭ҇сѧ за стара́наⷨ и ко́штомⷤ | всє́й спѡⷧ҇не бра́тїй [...] | [...] | [...] | ѝ всє́й [...] | [...] | Свѧщє́нникꙋ хра́ма рож҇єстⷡ҇ва прⷭ҇ Бц҃ы | до хра́мꙋ тогѡ́жⷣє рож҇єстⷡ҇ва прⷭ҇тїа Бц҃ы | а҆бы̀ ю҆ной ѿ вишємє́нного хра́ма | нєва́жилсѧ ѿдали́ти [...] | прокла́тїа ст҃и Ѻ҃ц҃ъ . т҃. и ѳ҃і ижє въ | никє́й Пє́рваго Совѡ́ра а҆ми́нь

f.447: Писатель книги сія достоинъ | похвалы и награды за трудъ.

f.447: Sacerdos Joannis Lubaczevski. [These two last inscriptions appear to have been written by the same person.]

Provenance: written in the Ruthenian area. It is very possible that the inscription on ff.95-111 relates to the creation of the manuscript, and although the location of the community for which it was written has been obliterated, the date of 1726 is plausible as that of writing. Bought on 12th May 1962 from Oprics Miklósné for 300 forints.

Preserved with the manuscript are two conjoint leaves, 210×170mm, bearing a text in Rumanian in a late 19th-century hand, which apparently relates to a completely different book.

Plates 35, 36

Lenten Triodion, 1678

Paper. Watermark: all rather indistinct: ff.1-48, horn within a circle with letter B above (fig.88), similar to Laucevičius 2987 (1686); ff.49-55, horn on a shield with letters M+K above, cross below, reversed B above the shield (fig.91), similar to Laucevičius 2985-6 (1672-8); ff.56-145, coat of arms (fig.90); ff.146-246, à la mode (fig.89), similar to Laucevičius 24 (1687) and Dianova–Kostjuchina 1267 (1689). In the endpapers, coat of arms (fig.20).246 leaves; modern stamped foliation 1-246; original foliation on ff.1-40, а̃-м̃. Size of leaves: 300×185 mm.

Collation: indeterminable: the binding is very stiff, and some of the gatherings at the beginning and end have apparently been reconstituted during restoration (the leaves having become detached).

Layout: 27-42 ll./p., written area 230-250×130-145 mm. Catchwords and running titles, apparently original.

Hand: a variety of very degenerate small semiuncials, some with cursive elements.

Ink: brown, with various degrees of fading; red for titles and initials.

Binding: ornamented leather on boards, 315×190 mm, restored. Sewn on five cords, with raised bands on the spine; two new clasps. Blind tooling. On both covers the same rich composition of an incised double border, roll-stamped with interlaced cresting of dotted stems terminating in rich foliage, similar to Laucevičius 1976: 54, №162 (1595), and faintly similar to Laucevičius 1976: 60-61, №224 (1667) and Janc 1974, plate 91, Nomocanon ÖNB Slav. 21 (1686); at the top and bottom of the square central panel there are three shorter borders, two stamped with the same cresting and one blank. The frame of the central panel is roll-stamped with a classical palmette motif within double fillets; the centre-piece is a complicated quatrefoil composed of volutes and linear floral motifs. The original binding was completely restored in the twentieth century, but preserves on the upper and lower covers leather contemporary with the manuscript.

Condition: dirty; damage to leaves, particularly at the front; restored.

Decoration: rich but very naïve and archaising decoration of headpieces, initials and tailpieces, with anthropomorphic and zoomorphic elements; drawn in ink and red-orange colour (minium?).

Seven headbands in the part of the first scribe, at the opening of the manuscript and the main liturgical subdivisions of the text.

f.1: a framed headpiece drawn in pen and ink, 42×150 mm, with a large flower motif in the middle; two snake (dragon?) heads flank the central motif with another two at the upper corners.

f.9: a band of crossing stems (lattice) on an ink-painted background, interrupted by a central arched panel with the figure of Christ as priest within.

f.12: a band, with the figure of Christ (or a priest?) blessing within a central arched panel, flanked by busts of angels and prophets; rude interlaces with dragon-head endings terminate the composition.

64

f.16v: framed step-like composition, filled in with knot-motifs (a common type of the early Balkan interlaced headpieces).

f.29: a narrow band, filled with foliage sprouting from a crown, with a cross on the top.

f.39: a panel consisting of small intersecting concentric circles, crossed by strips, with dragon heads as endings; the whole composition is a poor imitation of the Balkan interlaced ornament.

f.45v: an ornamented frame-band around the title; three crosses at the centre of the upper rim.

Numerous initials of different kinds, placed at the beginnings of the main and secondary liturgical subdivisions; in several of the initials painted by the two main scribes, an animal motif (a donkey?) or dragon head is incorporated into the letters.

ff.9, 16v, 24v, 28, 33v, 34, 51v: seven anthropomorphic initials of a composite character occupying between four and ten lines, with human busts, an individual figure (f.24v), two figures leaning on the stem (f.51v), a hand holding the stem of the letter. Floral initials of varying sizes and shapes, sometimes also including interlaced motifs. Numerous geometric initials, prevailingly three- to five-line, with outlined stems filled in by simple geometric motifs or with additional floral or other ornamentation; a particular variety are the two initials П, turned into a rectangular frame around a chalice. Eleven interlaced three- to five-line initials; that on f.48v is particularly big, with a complicated pattern resembling a portico with a cross hanging between the stems.

f.40: one three-line zoomorphic initial, representing a two-headed dragon.

Common red or black penwork initials with floral or anthropomorphic ornamentation.

Tailpieces of various kinds.

ff.8v, 11v, 16, 28v: interlaced tailpieces of different patterns.

f.38v: a tailpiece formed of a hand holding a big flower with two long, twisted stems growing from it, incorporating the inscription ка[..]тъ попо[.]ичь цици во.

f.236v: an ugly drawing flanking the end of the text, representing birds and a tree (?);

f.246v: an eight-rayed star accompanied by the inscription: а̃ . Х̃ . О̃ . Й̃ . | 1.6.7.8.

Contents: Lenten Triodion: type IX according to the classification given by Momina 1985.

(ff.1-8v) **Sunday of the Publican and Pharisee**

(ff.9-11v) Притча о влѫдномъ сн҃ѹ

(ff.12-16) Сѫвота мѧсопѹстъ

(ff.16v-38v) Не́лꙗ мѧсопѹстнаꙗ [Also services for the week following; a major sectional heading is provided for Thursday (f.29).]

(ff.39-45) Вн҃е́ Сыірнѹю

(ff.45v-236v) Начало великаго поста [Services from Monday of the first week of Lent to the end of the Sixth hour on Friday of the sixth week. The text may proceed from one day to the next, or one week to the next, without any indication other than a change in the running title. Major sectional headings are provided for Friday of the second week (f.103), the second Sunday (f.109), the third Sunday (f.136), the fourth Sunday (f.169) and the fifth Sunday (f.213v).]

(ff.237-246v) В Ꙋетке́ е́ н҃ли: ВЕЛИКАГО КАНОНА: ЖИТЇЕ Н ЖН҃НЬ: |

преподобныѧ мⷬтре нишеѧ мⷬти Єгипетскои, списаное сⷮъⷮишиⷨ | софронїемъ патрїархоⷨ. |
Іерⷧимскимъ

Incipit: Танию царскую добре ѿтаити, дѣла же гⷩѧ проповидати ѩсно

Language: Church Slavonic with distinct Ukrainian influence.

Inscriptions:

inside front cover: Ta xiązka [nie added in pencil!] nalezy do Cerkwi Rokitno

f.1: Jezus Marya Jozef Modlitwy [......] [and others illegible]

ff.1-7, rectos: [...] wiecznemy cz[...]stawąc ‖ przy cerkwi Hrudenskiey [...] ‖ Ta xięga dla Zostawac wieczne[...] czaly Prz[...] ‖ [...]liwi Hrudenskiey ktorą Pod czas ‖ wizity Gneralney Podpisnie ‖ dnia 23 Augusta Roku 1726 ‖ Stephan Litwinko [...] | y officia[...]

f.2v: [......] na ymia Feodora | [.]opatilia maiu iemu dati Suleman Czubut z myta złoty 47 sza[...|.......]

f.8v: Cerkiew w Hrudni ufundowana Roku 1666.

f.14v: Leon Slubicza Zalensky

f.22: Pomoc moia od Pana Boga [...|...]

f.22: Zymy niebyło w Roku 1724 Do wtorku drugi niedzeli postu | mięsopustu Było niedzel 8 potym stała niedzel dwie

f.22: Krol Polski Nap Pan Miłoserny

f.30: Pan Gardy chleb Twardy Piwnica Na[...]

f.42: z Hruda nazwana Jest Pra[...] Postna Albo Triod | Na co si potpisnie dat w Hrudzie Dna z [...]

f.73v: Xondz Teodor Kaminsky Zasło wielkie pustki wrokitni | Ante Cserka[?] Barzo zła Było Klucilo Prawem rozne | a nie sluszne

f.74v: Xondz Rokitensky na goli grunt nastał Xondz Teodor Kaminsky | Tilko Sacz[?] [...] Zyta gwatłem na na[...]

f.118v: Roku 1773 Brastwo Cerkwi Rokitni wydalo Pyniendzy Ze skarbuni Złłotych [sic] Pentset dyko 50 na dzwun naorat | nadach Cerkwi gontowi na triod Postnę dzwun Zlotych 30 dyko trista ornat 10 dyko sto | Triod Taleri 4 dyko Cztiri repera się [..] dzwonili resta

f.139v: Roku tisioc sedmsetnego fturego podczaz wiosny szwedzi yszli bez brzesc y bez bialo do polszczy | Roku tisioc sedmsetnego piątego sasi stali wwitulinie y szmygielsky / tegoż roku moskale zimowali w tykocinie | Roku 1708 Sender podstawscy witielinsky | byl w cerkwy witulinskiey

f.140: Roku siedmsetnego siedmego Moskwa zimowala w biały pulk Jensky | Nakoniec tegoż roku przed bożym narodzieniem pulk stal smolensky Ci wyiedli pszenice | y żyto | [...] pod grodnem pobiło

f.147v: Ru 1772 Xiądz Theodor Kaminsky miał Prymilye na Niebo wzęcie Swiętey Anny | Introdokował Brat Jego X Hrudzki z ręki X Mitropolity

f.148: Ru 1772 Xdz Teodor Kaminsky miał Prymilye na Niebo wzęcie Swiętey Anny Introdukował Brat [...] | z ręki Xdza Mitropolity

f.148v: Roku 1772 Xyondz Theodor Kaminsky mał Primilie na w Nebo wzentie S. Anny

66

| Intradukował Brat Jego X Hrudzanski z renki X Mitropolity | Tegosz roku moskali odebrały Złłti 20 X Teodora

f.149v: Roku 1773 Wasili Zahor Dzwun ze gdanska wyprowadził nowy salowni 30 Zlotych dyko | Tristo Złłoty Swim Kostem Za Xiędza Teodora Kaminskiego

f.161: Roku 1733 mię. februara [..] pomarł Krol August

f.161: Kiedy Bogaty umierz[.] to wszytki hausługi A kiedy ubogy to iedę Albo drugy

f.161v: Dai boze Doczekaty woskresenya Chrystowa w Dobrym zdorowiu nam wsi[...] | azeby doczekali iaicia czerwonoho

f.162v: Day Boze Dozdaty Woskresienia Christa W dobrym Zdorowiu

f.184v: W roku 1701 Było zatmienie słonca Miesiąca fbruary Dnia 17 / Pomoc moa od Boga | W roku 1701 Było zatmienie słonca Miesiąca fbruary Dnia 17 / Pomoc moa od

f.191: Roku 1734 Koronacia była Krola fryderyka | Tego roku Moskwa zimowała w Brzysciu [written twice]

f.208v: Сїа книга названа тришдь постнаа до церкви Hrudzkoy wicznimy czasy nadanaa do chramu Ofiarowa|nia P mary

f.212v: Roku 1773 X Teodor Kaminski sprawił Ornat Partirowi Salon | Około Złoty Zapinondzę Sprowijanta

f.219v: Roku 1773 Moskwa Prowiantamy ludzy zgubila Tegosz Roku Xiędzu Teodorowy Kaminskiemu | W Brziscu konie zabraly musia piechoto do domu iscz

f.233: Roku 1733 Stali kozacy przed Bozym narodzienie | w Ianowie niedziele pięc

f.242v: w R^u 1795 Antoniego Kamięskiego z Mulnika wypądzon | ze falszywu Trymałsprawe w Kamierze Pruskiey | w Białym Stoku KK

f.242v: [...] 1779 Dnia 9 miesiąca marca wsk' w tym Roku pryzybyły przy[...] Xiążęta Radziwiłłowie | do Biały

f.243: [...] marca dnia 9 wsk' w tym Roku pryzybył prziechał [...] Xiążę Radziw[...]

f.243v: [...] się missia odprawiła w Klonownicy [...] XX Bazylianie z Biały[...]

f.244: Ru 1778 dnia 14 8bra jaksię missia odprawiła w Klonownicy [...] XX Bazylianie Bialskiey

passim: [frequent trivial inscriptions of the type "Proba Ręki i Piora" or of a few words of the text written out, and some more which are no longer legible]

Provenance: Ruthenian, very likely written in the same region of present-day Poland as the later inscriptions. The date 1678 appears on ff.135v and 246v, apparently in the hand of the scribe who wrote those pages. The villages of Rokitno, Hrud, Klonownica Duża, Janów and Witulin, all mentioned in the inscriptions, are in the powiat of Biała Podlaska, Lublin Province. The parish church at Hrud was indeed founded in 1666, by Michał Kazimierz Radziwiłł. Purchased in 1918 from Gyula Halaváts (1853-1926), geologist and palæontologist. Eight fragments extracted from the binding at the time of its restoration are kept separately in the library.

Plates 37, 38

Octoechos, 16th century (first quarter)

Paper. Watermark: boar (fig.92), very similar to Piccard Vierfüßler v.3, 50 (1511); oxhead with serpent above (fig.93), very similar to Mareş 292, similar to Briquet 15376 (1498); oxhead (fig.94), similar to Budka 38 (1504); oxhead (fig.95), similar to Piccard Ochsenkopf 197 (1505-1509).

i+320+i leaves; modern stamped foliation in the centre of the upper margin, [i], 1-320,[321]; earlier, to a great extent deleted foliation at the upper right-hand corner of theleaves, indicating their disorder before the restoration. Size of leaves: 275×195 mm.

Collation: originally probably in twelves, as indicated by the surviving signatures А̄-А̄Ӏ on ff.154-284v, but the gatherings have been reconstituted during restoration and do not now necessarily reflect their original state.

Layout: first scribe 30 ll./p., written area 217×140 mm; second scribe 29 ll./p., written area 230×140 mm.

Hand: two hands, both medium-sized, informal but consistent bookhands; the first scribe wrote ff.1-120v and the second ff.121-320. A misplaced leaf of the first scribe's is now f.318.

Ink: brown for the first scribe and yellowish-brown for the second. Red used for the titles, initials, and rubrics.

Binding: modern, 288×201 mm, green and brownish-pink marbled paper on cardboard, half-bound; four raised bands on the spine. One modern flyleaf at each end.

Condition: lacking the beginning and the end, with sporadic losses within. The leaves towards the end were seriously damaged before the restoration; the leaves throughout, most of which had become detached, have been mended, not necessarily according to the original bifolia.

Decoration: two very simple interlaced headbands outlined with red, in the part of the second scribe on ff.121 and 122. Titles of small (8 mm) and bigger (15 mm) majuscules, with simple forms of vjaz'. Red, two-to four-line penwork initials at the liturgical subdivisions in both parts of the manuscript; mostly without ornamentation, except on ff.71, 99v and 121 (almost destroyed) where where the letters have foliate finials.

Contents: Octoechos, tones 1-8. There are sporadic lacunæ.

(ff.1-16) **Tone 2** [the end only: incomplete material for Friday]

(ff.16v-69v) **Tone 3**

     Incipit: ВСꙖ̈ ВЕ̂НА МАЛѣИ ВЕ̂РНІИ НА ГꙊ҇ | възва́ стр҇ы. въскрꙖснꙗ̀. гла҇ Г҇

[Sectional headings are provided at the beginning of the stichera на ГꙊ҇ възвахъ for each day of the week: Sunday ff.17 (Great Vespers) and 23v, Monday f.30, Tuesdayf.38, Wednesday f.45, Thursday f.51v, Friday f.59.]

(ff.70-120v) **Tone 4**

     Incipit: ВСꙊ̈ НА МАЛѣ" ВЕ̂РНИИ НА ГꙊ҇ ВЪЗВА́ ПО҇ | стн҇ Д҇ й пое҇ стр҇ы. въскр҇ны, гла҇ Д҇

[Sectional headings are provided at the beginning of the stichera на ГꙊ҇ възвахъ for each day of the week: Saturday (Great Vespers) f.71, Sunday f.75, Monday f.83, Tuesday f.91v, Wednesday f.99, Thursday f.106v, Friday f.114v.]

(ff.121-177) **Tone 5**

Incipit: ВСӜ҃Ӗ ВЕ҃РЬ НА МАЛѢИ́ ВЕ҃РНИ | на Г҃и въӡва҆х по҃с҃ д҆ и поѥмь стр҃ы꙼. въскр҃ны. гла҃ ѐ

[Sectional headings are provided at the beginning of the stichera на Г҃и възвахъ for each day of the week: Saturday (Great Vespers) f.122 (most of Saturday and the beginning of Sunday are missing), Monday f.137, Tuesday f.145, Wednesday f.152v, Thursday f.159, Friday f.166.]

(ff.177-231) **Tone 6**

Incipit: ВСӜ҃Ӗ ВЕ҃НА МАЛѢИ́ ВЕ҃РНИ НА Г҃И В҃Ъ|ӡва҆х поставлѧ꙼ѣ҆ х д҆. и поѣ҅н стр҃ы꙼ въскр҃ны гла҃ ӡ

[Sectional headings are provided at the beginning of the stichera на Г҃и възвахъ for Saturday (Great Vespers) f.178, Sunday f.188v, but subsequent sections are signalled only by the use of red ink.]

(ff.231-281v) **Tone 7**

Incipit: ВСӜ҃Ӗ ВЕ҃НА МАЛѢИ ВЕ҃РНИ ПО҃С҃ д҆И ПО|ѥмь стр҃ы꙼х въскр҃ны гла҃ ӡ

[A major sectional heading is indicated only for Great Vespers on Saturday (f.232).]

(ff.281v-320v) **Tone 8**

Incipit: ВСӜ҃Ӗ ВЕ҃НА МАЛѢИ ВЕ҃РНИ НА Г҃И ВЪӡВА҃х | стр҃ы꙼ въскр҃ны. постави꙼н с҃ д҆ гла҃ и

[A major sectional heading is indicated only for Great Vespers on Saturday (f.282v). The end is missing.]

Language: Church Slavonic; in the part written by the first scribe there are very few traces of Bulgarian orthographic practice; it is much more palpable in the second scribe's part. The first scribe is also very sparing in his use of diacritics.

Inscriptions:

f.26: кирнелѐсоньки꙼кирнелѐсоньки꙼кирнелѐсонь

f.42v: помощь иже перв꙼ѣ ѡбразꙋ злато꙼мꙋ | перскою ут꙼ю д꙼ѣ

passim: [running titles have been added by a later hand]

Provenance: written in the Ruthenian area. One of 14 manuscripts donated by Antal-Hodinka in 1904.

Plates 39, 40

Octoechos, tones 1-4, 16th century (middle)

Paper. Watermark: boar (fig.96), identical to Mareş 346 (1551). In the endpapers, coat of arms (fig.20).

i+209+i leaves; modern stamped foliation, [i], 1-43, 47-100, 102-213, [214]. Size of leaves: 315×200 mm.

Collation: I^8, II^8 (-1.8), III-IV^8, (2 leaves), V-VII^8, VIII^8 (-7), XI-XXVI^8, (2 leaves). Three gatherings are missing at the beginning; the two leaves inserted between IV and V are from the last of these and originally came immediately before the present f.1. Some material (probably one gathering) is missing between XXV and XXVI, and also some at the end. Gatherings signed in the bottom right-hand corner of the first recto, but the only signatures to survive are д (on the first extant gathering), є (not original!), ѕ, ді, ѕі, кв, кг and кѕ.

Layout: 30 ll./p., written area 240×135 mm; the conventional indications of theotokia, etc., in the margins.

Hand: a small (x-height 3mm) practised bookhand; majuscule titles.

Ink: black; red for titles and initials.

Binding: ornamented leather on boards, 322×209 mm, restored; even spine, two new clasps. Blind tooling. On the upper cover a large double frame incised with triple fillets; within the outer border a frieze of heart-framed palmette stamps, cf. Janc 1974: plate 38/38 (16th century), while in the inner one the stamp is an eight-leaved rosette with pointed leaves. The centre panel, outlined with the same fillets, is divided crosswise into four square compartments, each of them divided diagonally; small circles are stamped at every intersecting point and near the corners; the free space is occupied by rosette stamps. The panel ends in two short borders at the top and bottom, consisting of another variety of the heart-shaped palmette stamps and stamped S-like figures, cf. Janc 1974: plate 35/22 (15thcentury). On the lower cover the pattern is identical except that one of the shorter borders is stamped with the rosette motif, and within the central panel instead of the separate rosettes, separate palmette stamps are impressed. One modern flyleaf at each end.

Condition: apart from the missing leaves, generally good. Occasional spotting with wax; some damage to the edges of leaves (restored); some pink staining on ff.73-77; part of f.167 missing (probably a headpiece has been removed).

Decoration: modest, of interlaced headpieces at the tones, of which only the second and third survive (the beginning of the manuscript is lost and the fourth headpiece has apparently been torn out).

f.47: three intersecting, concentric circles, crossed diagonally by double stems with fine foliate endings, the whole area 75×117 mm, red outlines, yellow, light green and blue interstices.

f.109: intertwined broad strips ("lattice" or "basket" type), 55×125 mm, with small beads at the intersecting points; a small cross with the usual inscription at the middle on the upper rim; red outlines with colouring of the sectors in ochre, bluish green and bright blue; the "white" parts of the ribbons are speckled with the same colours.

Contents: Octoechos, tones 1-4. There is text missing at the beginning and end.

(ff.1-43) **Tone 1**
[The beginning is missing. Sectional headings are provided for each day at the beginning of the stichera на гй възвахъ for Tuesday (f.6), Thursday (f.20v), Friday (f.28v) and Saturday (f.42). That for Wednesday was evidently on the missing leaf after f.14.]
(f.43v) [blank]
(ff.47-108) **Tone 2**

Incipit: На велицѣй вернн на гй възва͠| стрьі͠. въскрⷩ҇ы
[Sectional headings are provided at the beginning of the stichera на гй възвахъ for each day of the week: Sunday f.58, Monday f.65v, Tuesday f.74, Wednesday f.82, Thursday f.90, Friday f.98v, Saturday f.107v.]
(f.108v) [blank]
(ff.109-166v) **Tone 3**

Incipit: На велицѣй вернй на гй възва͠| стрьі͠. въскрⷩ҇ы
[Sectional headings are provided at the beginning of the stichera на гй възвахъ for each day of the week: Sunday f.119v, Monday f.126, Tuesday f.134, Wednesday f.141v, Thursday f.149, Friday f.157, Saturday f.165v.]
(ff.167-213v) **Tone 4**

Incipit: На вéлицѣй вéрнн на гй | възваⷯ͠ стрьі͠. въскрⷮѣсны
[Sectional headings are provided at the beginning of the stichera на гй възвахъ for each day of the week: Sunday f.179, Monday f.187, Tuesday f.195v, Wednesday f.203v (the beginning only: there is a lacuna probably of eight leaves), Thursday f.204, Friday f.212v; the end is missing.]

Language: Church Slavonic, written according to Middle Bulgarian Tărnovo orthographic norms, but evidently in an East Slavonic milieu.

Inscriptions:

f.1: Agreşul de jos

ff.100v-108: аꙋастъ кар'те ‖ оⷲ҇мꞁ кꙋпⷤрⷶⷮ‖ ѐоꙋ попа оꙋрсꙋ ‖ дела ш'цⷼефⷶⷩ ‖ х̃ лꙋй ѐнакне ‖ дн брете ‖ амꞁ датꞁꙇ шꙋштауи ‖ ванн ‖ шн ꙁ мнрце де мъладю ‖ шн г҃ снле де плꙋгъ ‖‖ мъладю кте д҃ шꙋштауи ‖ шн ѿмꞁ кꙋмператъ

f.118v: [...] шн прекⷡⷠниⷮ͠ дꞁно фрⷶ поⷫ͠ глигорие съ ꙁⷩ сънътоⷢ͠ | амн꙼͠--

Provenance: probably of Ruthenian origin, but later used by Rumanian communities. The inscriptions on ff.1 and 103 connect the manuscript respectively with the villages of Agrişu de Jos (Alsó Egres) and Bretea (Magyarberéte), both in the Betlen district of Szolnok-Doboka megye (now Bistriţa-Năsăud region in Rumania). The first of these is also mentioned in an inscription in Fol. Eccl. Slav. 27. Bought on 18th January 1956 from the widow of Szilárd Sulica (1884-c.1950) at the same time as MSS Fol. Eccl. Slav. 22 and Fol. Valach 8; Fol. Eccl. Slav. 27 and 28 were also obtained from her.

Found in the manuscript, and now kept separately, are three short documents in German and Rumanian, two of them dated 1860 bearing the name of Eremias Papp of the village of Alsó Egres.

Plate 41

71

Octoechos, 16th century (3rd quarter)

Paper. Watermark: arms of Cluj, similar to Mareş 159 (1565); arms of Cluj, identical to Mareş 158 (1565-7); bear, similar to Mareş 490 (1555); bear, type Mareş 431-4 (1559-64); fox, similar to Mareş 3 (1546); two indecipherable letters, possibly a countermark to the preceding mark. In the last two leaves a lion (resembling Seven Provinces) and a coat of arms (??a castle), apparently much later marks.

34 leaves; unfoliated. There are a number of very fragmentary leaves also: some at the beginning, three after f.19, at least eight after f.20 and nine after f.29. Size of leaves: 307×195 mm.

Collation: the manuscript is too fragmentary for any collation to be established. However, ff.1-11 probably represent a gathering of twelve with the first leaf missing, and ff.12-20 probably a gathering of twelve lacking the ninth, tenth and eleventh leaves. Ff.11v and 20v are signed ι and αι respectively. The last three leaves are additional, evidently added to replace lost material.

Layout: 22 ll./p., written area 230×140 mm.

Hand: a practised Moldavian semiuncial, sloping to the right; majuscule titles. Towards the end (ff.30-31v and the fragments preceding them), though the hand is very similar, it may be that of a different scribe, using a characteristic tall ъ. The last three leaves are written in a later, squarer, less elegant hand.

Ink: brownish-black; red for titles, initials and rubrics.

Binding: brown leather on boards, 305×185 mm, with grooves running the whole length of the edges. The headbands are sewn with blue and rose threads; the book sewn on four cords. Flat spine with some restoration, traces of two fastenings. Blind tooling. The upper cover has a double border of two different patterns between triple fillets; the outer border consists of roll-stamped palmette motifs in juxtaposed heart-shaped frames and the inner one of of pointed eight-leaf rosette stamps. The central panel has a row of trefoils at the top and bottom, with the same trefoils in each corner and twice along each vertical edge. The centrepiece is a cross made up of small circular stamps. The lower cover has the same double border, the central panel being divided into lozenges by triple fillets running diagonally with the circular stamps at the intersections. The binding is contemporary with the manuscript. No endpapers.

Condition: poor: very many leaves are lost, and others fragmentary, and those that survive are dirty with extensive spotting and staining. Binding severely damaged.

Decoration: titles in simple vjaz', 25 mm in height; on f.30v a four-line initial Б with modest decoration.

Contents: Octoechos, very defective, containing only the end of the seventh tone (it begins in the middle of the third ode of the canon for Friday) and parts of the eighth. The latter begins on f.9. There are surviving sectional headings for Wednesday and Thursday (ff.21, 28). The manuscript ends with the eleventh Gospel of the Resurrection, with following exapostilarion and sticheron; it is probable that there is nothing missing after this.

Language: Middle Bulgarian, two jers, two juses.

Inscriptions:

f.1: Agrisul de jos

last leaf, verso: [salutation to the Mother of God in Rumanian]

Provenance: of Moldavian or Transylvanian origin. The inscription on f.1 connects the manuscript with the village of Agrişu de Jos (Alsó Egres) in the Betlen district of Szolnok-Doboka megye (now Bistriţa-Năsăud region in Rumania). A similar inscription is found in MS Fol. Eccl. Slav. 23. Given in the 1950s by the widow of Szilárd Sulica (1884-c.1950), from whom MSS Fol. Eccl. Slav. 22, Fol. Eccl. Slav. 23, Fol. Eccl. Slav. 28 and Fol. Valach 8 were also obtained.

Plate 42

29. Fol. Eccl. Slav. 16

Octoechos, 16th century (last quarter)

Paper. Watermark: faint boar (fig.97), very similar to Mareş 374 (1578). In the endpapers, oak-twig (fig.34), which is also found in the endpapers of Fol. Eccl. Slav. 6 and 10. i+136+i leaves; modern stamped foliation [i], 1-136, [137]. Size of leaves: 286×185 mm.

Collation: I^8 (-1), II^8, III^8 (8+2), IV^8, V^8 (±5), VI-XV^8, XVI^4, XVII^8 (-8), XVIII^4. This collation represents the present condition of the book, which is a result of a complete reconstruction at some time in its history: all the leaves have been repaired at the hinges. It does not, therefore, correspond to its original construction. There are no signatures. The last leaf (f.136) is extraneous. There are occasional leaves missing.

Layout: 28 ll./p., written area 230×140 mm.

Hand: a practised smallish semiuncial/bookhand (x-height=3mm). Majuscule titles. F.38, which replaces a lost leaf, is in a different hand. On the final extraneous leaf, a larger, more formal semiuncial.

Ink: black; red for titles, initials and rubrics.

Binding: ornamented brown leather on thick boards, 300×205 mm, restored; four raised bands on the new spine, traces of two fastenings. Blind tooling. On the upper cover a broad double frame with triple fillets; the vertical outer borders bear a roll-stamped double-stem rinceau, while the horizontal ones are divided into triangles; within the inner border a different roll-stamped rinceau in the vertical sides and oblong beads in the horizontal ones. The centre panel has an incised wavy line running along the frame of triple fillets; the same fillets connect the panel corners with those of the borders. The centre-piece is a small lozenge with the Crucifixion, around which small rosettes are stamped; flower motifs are impressed at the angles and at the corners of the lozenge; for the composition as a whole cf. Laucevičius 1976 №19 (18th century.) On the lower cover there is the same framing but the centre panel is divided into four vertical strips stamped with the wavy lines in two rows, the double-stem rinceaux and the beads. The upper border is overlapped by another lozenge stamp, very faint, with Christ in an oval medallion. The binding is probably from the time of the manuscript's reconstruction (18th century?). One modern flyleaf at each end.

Condition: good, except for a large number of wax stains and some missing leaves at both beginning and end. At some point the manuscript was reconstructed, at which time the hinges of the leaves were repaired with paper. There is hardly any other mending, although the manuscript has been restored in recent times.

Decoration: titles of majuscule letters, 15-18 mm, forming simple vjaz'. Twenty-three red pen-flourished initials of the Neo-Byzantine type, occupying three to five lines. Those on ff.124v-135v are at Gospel and Epistle readings. The ornamentation includes fine leaves, tendrils and small buds, centred on the stems of the letters, and black dots. Two-line red initials with buds and tendrils are put occasionally at the tones. A small tailpiece on f.85v consists of a calligraphic ᴀ and red outlined stylised vegetal stem composed of joints.

Contents:

(ff.1-85v) **Octoechos for Saturdays and Sundays** [Material for Great Vespers on Saturday and for Sunday morning, arranged according to the tones. A major sectional heading is provided for each of them: Tone 2 f.12v, Tone 3 f.23v, Tone 4 f.28v, Tone 5 f.40v, Tone 6 f.51v, Tone 7 f.53 and Tone 8 f.74. The beginning is missing.]

Defective: begins with the words: ꙗзьци съ веселїемь. х̂с в̂ъ б̂ъ нашь. на крът̑ѣ | приꙿгвозꙿди гр꙯ѣхы наша.

(ff.86-126) **Octoechos for weekdays** [A major sectional heading is provided for each of them, each commencing with Vespers on the previous day, thus for example the section for Monday (Tone 1) actually begins with Sunday Vespers (Tone 8): Monday f.86, Tuesday (Tone 2) f.93v, Wednesday (Tone 3) f.100, Thursday (Tone 4) f.106, Friday (Tone 5) f.112v and Saturday (Tone 6) f.118.]

Incipit: Въ нел̂ѣ ве҇ ст̑ры къ г̑ꙋ нашемꙋ іс̑ | х҇ꙋ. гла̂. й

(ff.126-130v) ел̂їа ꙋтр꙯нѣа въскр꙯наа [The end of the last Gospel reading is missing.]

(ff.132-135v) **Gospel readings for the Liturgy on Sundays** [Each is followed by exapostilarion, theotokion, sticheron, prokeimenon and Epistle. The beginning and end are missing, and only material for the second to seventh Sundays after Whitsun remains.]

(f.136) [The extraneous leaf. Possibly a fragment of another octoechos.]

Language: Church Slavonic, following Middle Bulgarian Tărnovo orthographical norms but with some East Slavonic elements.

Inscriptions:

f.1: ѿ с҇е в꙯жꙿг꙯жꙋ̂ вы҇ мц̂а а҇го҇ і дн̑ь ‚ач҇г

f.1v: 1912 Jacob Tanats

ff.17v, 18, 19, 20, 20v: ауа҇ст сф꙯ѣтъ ка҇те анꙋме | ѿтаю аꙋ плꙋти҇ пꙗ҇кꙋ съи фїе | де ле га҇адоаръ | поманъ пентрꙋ сꙋфлетꙋ̂ лꙋи | ши а пърицило̂ ши а мошило̂ ши а стрꙋмоши҇ лѣ̇ · а ·ѱ· л ·й· [1738]

f.27: г̑дь гръди҇ Противи҇те смире҇нꙗже да҇т бл꙯дь [The inscription is repeated in East Slavonic orthography in a later hand, which evidently wrote more, but this has been lost by trimming.]

f.27v: +ѣд евреи затворише въ гр꙯ѣвѣ животъ. разбоинни|къ же ѿрьꙁе аꙁыкомъ раи въпиа и гла. иже съ множ мене ради | распатса. съꙗвесимиса на др꙯евѣ. и ꙗвлѣеши ми са на пр꙯ѣстолѣ [...] [This sticheron is omitted from the text where it should appear on this page.]

f.28: де ꙋмигаю скривъ ши июнꙋшꙿко ла кꙋмꙗтꙋ мев ла кр꙯гꙋꙿ ш[...] | ена҇ къ съ вакъ вине ши ен три.мацꙿъ вани къ не стригъ де | ши васкъ в[...]

f.128v: [illegible]

f.133v: Burg Suseni in 20 April 1872 | Jacob Thanacs | cantor [...]

f.136: Писал июн꙯а҇ко ѿ вотꙋше҇ влѣ ‚зрн꙯г д҇ꙿ зиле лꙋ василие воевꙋ̂д влѣ ‚зрн꙯г [1645]

f.136: [..] д[..] ла симиꙋ ст꙯ъ҇нꙿ д҇ влꙿт‚зр꙯о҇г [1665]

f.136v: [a long but fragmentary and not easily readable text, apparently part of a service to St Petka]

passim: [occasional additions to the hymns]

Provenance: probably of Ruthenian origin, but later used by Rumanian communities. The inscriptions on ff.1 and 133v connect the manuscript with Susenii Bîrgăului (Felsőborgó) in Bistriţa-Năsăud region. Acquired in 1912 together with two Rumanian MSS.

Plate 43

Octoechos, 17th century (second quarter)

Paper. Watermark: arms, type Eineder 279-281 (1642-44); apostolic cross on three hills (in the first 19 leaves only); a very indistinct mark, possibly a sphere. 112 leaves; unfoliated. Size of leaves: 300×195 mm.

Collation: 19 leaves, I-II^{10}, III$^?$ (4 leaves), IV^{10}, V^8, VI^{12}, VII^{10}, VIII^8, IX^{10}, X^{10} (-10). The first 19 leaves certainly represent the remains of more than two gatherings. Ff.27, 40-41, 44-46, 58, 62 and 84 are fragmentary. Ff.20, 76, 86, 94, 104 signed centrally in the upper margin of the first recto, +.

Layout: ff.1-2v: 32 ll./p., written area 250×150 mm; ff.3-13v: 31 ll./p., written area 240×145 mm; ff.14-112v: 29 ll./p., written area 225×140 mm.

Hand: four distinct bookhands. 1. (ff.1-1v.24, 2v-13v) a medium semiuncial/bookhand; 2. (ff.1v.24-2) a fairly informal but professional bookhand; 3. (ff.14-75v) a semiuncial/ bookhand, similar to the first, but slightly thicker and more compact; 4. (ff.76-112v) an informal but clear and practised bookhand similar to the second (very likely the same scribe writing a somewhat larger hand).

Ink: black; red for titles, initials and rubrics.

Binding: brown ornamented leather on boards, 305×180 mm, with grooves running the whole length of the edges. Sewn on four cords; headbands sewn with reddish-purple threads. Flat spine. Blind tooling. Both covers have rather irregular borders. The central panels are rather crudely divided into lozenges with double fillets; foliar and cresting rosettes stamped in the spaces. No endpapers at the front; at the back, the pastedowns are leaves from an octavo psalter.

Condition: many leaves are lost, and others fragmentary; the remainder are dirty and stained. Some eighteenth-century repairs. Binding worn and damaged and almost detached.

Decoration: titles written within the text-block with only their initial letters bigger (by three times) than the text, so that they do not make clear divisions between the parts of the book. Simple red, three-to four-line initials, modestly decorated with tendrils, buds, and short lines crossing the stems, and sometimes with foliate finials of irregular shape; much more modest in the part written by the second main scribe.

Contents:

(ff.1-75v) **Octoechos for Saturdays and Sundays** [Material for Great Vespers on Saturday and for Sunday morning, arranged according to the tones. The beginning (including all of the first tone) is missing, and there are sporadic lacunæ throughout. Major sectional headings were provided for each tone; those that survive are: Tone 3 f.7, Tone 4 f.13v, Tone 5 f.22v, Tone 6 f.37v, Tone 7 f.47v and Tone 8 f.61v.]

(ff.76-112v) **Octoechos for weekdays** [A major sectional heading is provided for each of them, each commencing with Vespers on the previous day, thus for example the section for Monday (Tone 1) actually begins with Sunday Vespers (Tone 8): Monday f.76, Wednesday (Tone 3) f.91v, Thursday (Tone 4) f.99v, Friday (Tone 5) f.106v. Tuesday evidently began on the fragmentary f.84. The end is missing: the text breaks off near the end of the Friday canon.]

Incipit: **КЪ НЄ҇ЛѢ вѣрь стр̑ы покаа́ы | гла̑. н҃.**

Language: Middle Bulgarian, two jers, two juses.

Inscriptions:

inside front cover: [illegible]

inside front cover: + лѱц҆ ѱлг і҆в҃ ѡѱⲉвⲣв нⲉ кцѧ ѣ ввⲣв зцѱцⲩⲃ | з̑к фцѱⲣв ивⲙ[.] цⲉ҃ ⲣв
[This may perhaps be deciphered as: лтⲣꙋ тож уи[н]стици прѣювⲛⲅи дрⲁⲅⲓи ми фⲣⲁци вⲛⲅрⲉⲱⲅⲓ.]

inside front cover: Є҆рмона̑ а́тонїе є́рⲉⲙкоⲥ́кⲓ | ди҃ по҃трⷩ҇ ѿ вⲉⲥⲉⲣⲓка· влⲉ: ҂зскз [1718]| мⷰ҇: д̑ ꙃ̑?

ff.7-11, rectos: ※ Сїе книга рекѡмⷧ҇їе ѡхта[...]‖ ѿ сⲉⲗѡ Ꙗ́ка· и кⲩⲡⲓ́ сїе кнⲓ҇ ѡ́дⲁ̑ⷢ[...] ѿ [...]‖ сⲉⲗⲉⲃⲉ́трⲃ да си знаⲉ́ⷩ и́ дадⲉ [...] вⲃ мⲱⲛⲁ҃[...]‖ прѣⲥⲃⷬⲃⲧⷷ вⲅⷷ· аⲩⲉ ктⲱ възⲉⷩ сїⲉ ‖ ѿ свⷷта мⲱⲛⲁ҆ⷩ вⲉ влⲅⲱⲥⲗⲱⲃⲉⲛⲓ̑ⲉ

ff.48-56: + синⷩ҇тате дⲉ лꙋ хⷵ до́нⲗⲁ꙰ воаⲥⲧⲣⲉ | прⲉ҃ци ши дїако́нⲓ ши дїⲁ́уⲛ ши то҃ⷮ | клⲓⲣⲃ҃ свⲓ́тⲉⲛ мⲄⲛꙗстⲓⲣⲉ҆ ра́к꙰ꙋ | съ ⲩⲓⲅⲓ къ а́уⲁⲥⲧⲄ ка̑тⲉ а́нⲱⲙⲉ̀ а̑гⲓⲗⲉ̑· | фⲓⲛ҃дⲃ дⲉⲗⲉга́тⲄ ше нⲉгⲣⲓфⲓⲧⲄ· | ши датⷮ помⷨ҇ⲉ́нⲃ· а̑вⲉⲩⲓⲁ вⲉ́уⲓⲗⲟ꙰ | съ ⲩⲓⲅⲓ молⲓⲧⲃⲉⲗⲉ воⲁ́стⲣⲉ дⲉ́а̑уⲁⲥⲧⲁ. | ⲉ҃ⷮ попа тоⲁⲇⲉ҃ⷬ ди҃ ꙋ́шⲱⲁ̑ а́ нⲉⲃⲟⲛⷩ | ши а́ стⲣⲄжⲇⲟⲛⷮ к꙰ꙋ тоⲁⲧⲄ нⲉⲃⲟⲛⲅⲁ | дⲉⲱ́ⷣ лⲉга꙰ⷮ ди҃ вⲉⲕю а̑доа лⲉⲅⲄⷮꙋ́ⲣⲄ ‖ ши ⲉ́ⷬ лⲁ ⲥⲄⷮ фⲓ̑ⲉ ши мⲓ́ⲉ помⲉⷬнⲄ ши сⲟ́цꙋ̑ мⲉ́ | ши фⲓ̑ⲛⲗⲟ꙰ мⲓ̑ⲉⲛ дⲉ свⲓⲧ̑ⷮ р꙰ꙋгаⲩⲓ́ⲛⲓ | уⲉ съ во꙰ фа̑ⷣ дⲉ прⲉⲇⲓ́нⲥꙗ дⲉ молⲓ́тⲃⲉⲗⲉ воⲁ|стрⲉ съ а̑вⲉ́шⲓ нⲟⲛ помⲉⷬнⲄ ши ⲉ́тⲁⲣⲉ дⲉ пꙋ̑каⲧⲉ̀. лтⲣꙋ вⲓ̑ⲛⲅⲁ дⲉ вⲉ́уⲓ дⲉ лⲁ до́нⲟⲗ хⷵ ⲉ́тⲁⲣⲉ пꙋкатⲉⲗⲟ꙰ ⲉ҆рⲉ́ⲛ тоⲁⲇⲉ҃ⷬ и пⲁпⲁⲇⲓ́ⲉ ‖ ⲉго а̑нⲟ́ⲅⲉ и уⲉⷣди и҃. въ жизⲛⲃ вⲉ́уⲛⲓ̑ⲁ | ҂ⲁⲭⲩⲉ [1695] мⲅ̑ⲁ мⲁⲓ̑ к̑ⲉ дⲛ̑ⲃ амⲓ̑ⲛⷩ

ff.105v-106: [illegible]

Provenance: of Moldavian or Transylvanian origin. The town of Orşova is in Mehedinţi county near the Serbian border (formerly Orsova, Temes vármegye). The most probable location of the monastery mentioned in the inscription was at Râncu in the Prahova district, though there are many places in Rumania with similar names. Given in the 1950s by the widow of Szilárd Sulica (1884-c.1950), from whom MSS Fol. Eccl. Slav. 22, Fol. Eccl. Slav. 23, Fol. Valach 8 and Fol. Eccl. Slav. 27 were also obtained.

Found with the manuscript were some school essays on French literature, dated 1935 and 1936, on the back of which are written some notes about this manuscript, dealing particularly with the inscriptions, and also about another manuscript (a Rumanian octoechos). Also found were two Rumanian newspapers (Astra Reghin) dated 1937, one of them addressed to Dr Ioan Bozdag of Tîrgu Mureş.

Plate 44

Euchologion, 16th century (middle)

Paper. Watermark: boar (fig.98) very similar to Mareş 354 (1553); boar (fig.99) very similar to Mareş 355 (1553); boar (fig.100) similar to Mareş 356 (1557); boar (fig.101) similar to Mareş 359 (1557); coat of arms (fig.102).

i+181+i leaves; modern stamped foliation [i], 1-133, 1 unnumbered, 134-159, 1 unnumbered, 160-179, [180]. Size of leaves: 190×135 mm.

Collation: I² (13 leaves), II-VIII¹², IX² (11 leaves), X¹²? (-1-2), XI-XIV¹², XV² (7 leaves), XVI² (8 leaves). I-IV signed а̃-д̃, but the rest of the signatures are lost, except for a fragment on f.141v. Because of restoration, the composition of the outer gatherings and IX-X is uncertain.

Layout: variable: ff.1-34, 39v-45v, 172-179v, 21 ll./p., written area 155×100 mm; ff.34v-37v, 21 ll./p., written area 155×105 mm; ff.38-39, 46-85v, 17 ll./p., written area 160×100 mm; ff.86-96v, 131-131v, 19 ll./p., written area 150×110 mm; ff.97-108v, 19 ll./p., written area 150×105 mm; ff.109-119, 19 ll./p., written area 165×150 mm; ff.119v-130v, 22ll./p., written area 150×100 mm; ff.132-135v 19-20 ll./p., written area 155-170×110 mm; ff.136-171v, 20 ll./p., written area 170×110 mm.

Hand: a number of small to medium-sized informal bookhands, often tending to be rather coarse. The following scribes can be identified with reasonable probability: 1. ff.1-34, 39.9-45v; 2. ff.34v-37v; 3. ff.46-84v and probably 38-39.8; 4. ff.85-85v, 97-98v, 105-108v, very professional hand(s), contrasting sharply with the rest of the manuscript; 5. ff.86-96v and probably 99-101.5; 6. ff.109-119 semiuncial with extensive use of diacritics; 7. ff.119v-130v, small squarish semiuncial, slightly sloping to left; 8. ff. 131-131v, another more elegant hand, distinct from 4. but writing in a similar style; 9. ff.172-179v, a somewhat finer hand than most of the others. On ff.101.5-104v, 132-171v two or more scribes (one of whom is probably the same as 6.) alternate, frequently changing in the course of a page; the hand varies from a small square semiuncial to an informal bookhand. Sometimes there is a clear disjunction between hands, sometimes not. There are majuscule titles of varying degrees of skill at the beginnings of major sections.

Ink: varies from brown to black; red for titles, initials and rubrics.

Binding: modern (1953), tan leather on boards; some leather from an older binding on the back cover. One modern flyleaf at each end.

Condition: somewhat dirty and stained, with leaves missing at both front and back.

Decoration: simple, of numerous red or red-and-black pen-flourished initials some of which belong to the Neo-Byzantine type but the great majority of which cannot be ascribed to any particular type.

Particularly richly ornamented are the initials in the parts of the first and the third scribes, with irregularly shaped foliage with buds and tendrils, and also dots and short lines around the stems; their abundance often blurs the forms of the letters. Many of the initials are of a large size. On f.52 the letter is enclosed by a large irregular frame held by a human hand. Elegant Neo-Byzantine initials in the part written by the seventh identified scribe, some with large foliate finials. The rest of the initials are of a small size, with plain decoration.

Contents:

(ff.1-5v) **Proskomidia** [The beginning is missing.]

(ff.5v-33) вожⷭ҇твенаа слѹ҇вⷣа | иже въ сты҇ ѿ҇ца нашего Іѡ҇ⷩ злаⷮ҇у|стаго

(ff.33-65v) вожⷭ҇ств'наⷣа слѹ҇вⷣа иж҇е | въ сты҇ ѿ҇ца нашего василиа вели|каго

(ff.65v-88v) наѵало веⷱ҇ⷩⷯни [Proceeds without a break into morning prayer on f.81v.]

(ff.88v-91v) **Dismissals for weekdays, major festivals and other occasions**

(ff.91v-95) уиⷩ҇ врⷶⷶтотворенїⷶⷶ

(ff.95-95v) **Prayer for a midwife**

(ff.95v-97v) **Prayers for a woman after childbirth**

(ff.97v-112v) Послѣдовⷶнїⷷ ⷷже сътво|рити ѿроѵа Ѡглашенно . й крⷭ҇тити тⷪ҇

(ff.112v-115v) **Prayers for the fortieth day after the birth of a child** [F.114 is blank.]

(ff.116-125v) послⷷ҇ⷣⷪ҇ванїⷷ сты҇а паⷩ҇де|саⷩⷩница, въ неⷣлю стⷢ҇о дⷯⷶ

(ff.125v-132) послⷷ҇ⷣⷪ҇ванїⷷ ѿсцⷩ҇енїⷷ воⷣ҇ | въ ⷶ҇ авгⷭ҇ мца

(f.132-138) уиⷩ҇ лⷷтопровожⷩ҇енїⷶⷶ

(ff.138-146) послⷷ҇ⷣⷪ҇ванїⷷ просвⷷщенїⷶⷶ стⷩ҇[..] | вгоⷶ҇вленⷷⷩⷩⷩⷩⷩⷩⷩⷩⷩⷩⷩⷩⷩ

(ff.146-152) уиⷩ҇ ѿврѹѵенїⷶⷶ ѿтроковицⷩ҇и | къ мѹжѹ

(ff.152-161) **Prayers for sundry occasions**

(ff.161-171v) уиⷩ҇ како пⷱⷩ҇ⷷⷶⷷ творити паⷩ҇|маⷶⷶ҇ оⷷⷷⷷ҇ оⷷсⷷⷷ

(ff.172-179v) уиⷩ҇ покаⷶⷩнїⷶⷶ хотⷶⷷⷩⷷ | каⷶ҇ти [The end is missing.]

Language: Church Slavonic; orthography somewhat variable, but partly conforming to Tărnovo norms: ь is normal finally, ъ medially after liquids; ѫ is frequently confused with оу.

Inscriptions:

passim: [occasional liturgical notes in the margins; also occasional trivial inscriptions of the type "помощь моа ѿ господа"]

Provenance: written in the Ruthenian area. One of fourteen manuscripts donated in 1904 by Antal Hodinka. Restored in December 1953 by Magyari Lászlóné.

Plates 45, 46, 47

Euchologion, mid-16th and early 17th centuries

Paper. Watermark: in the first section, Lubicz (fig.105), identical to Dianova–Kostjuchina 1074 (1604); in the remaining sections, boars, all very hard to see, but two of which (figs.103, 104) can be identified as very similar to Mareş 342 (1531) and 351 (1557). In the pastedowns, three crescents (fig.106), similar to Velkov-Andreev 217 (1661).

245 leaves; modern stamped foliation, 1-245. Size of leaves: 195×130-140 mm.

Collation: I⁸, II¹², III¹⁰, IV-VI¹², VII¹⁰, VIII⁵ (5 leaves), IX-XII¹², XIII¹² (-1-8), XIV² (2 leaves), XV¹⁰, XVI¹⁰(-9-10), XVII¹⁰ (-1-2-3-10), XVIII¹², XIX⁵ (10 leaves), XX-XXII¹², XXIII⁵ (3 leaves), XXIV¹², XXV⁸ (-8). Later signatures in reverse order (!) on II-XXV, КД-а̄ (except for VIII, XIII, XIV and XVII, which lack their first leaves). III is also signed КД (!) in a different hand, and there are additional, fainter signatures on ЅI (X, f.82) and Ѕ (XX, f.188). There is an older (possibly original?) signature БI in the lower right-hand corner of f.106 (the first leaf of XI/БI). The manuscript is a composite, consisting of ff.1-30 (I-III), 31-76 (IV-VII), 77-139 (VIII-XIII) and 140-245 (XIV-XXV). The first section was certainly written to replace material missing at the beginning of the second, though it itself is now defective (there is a lacuna between ff.20 and 21), as the text follows on exactly from the end of f.30v to the beginning of f.31. The other sections do not match so exactly.

[FIRST PART, FF.1-30]

Layout: 19-20 ruled ll./p., written area 140/153×110 mm.

Hand: small bookhand strongly influenced by cursive, 3-4 mm. Majuscule titles.

Ink: black fading to brownish-black in places; red for titles, initials and rubrics.

[SECOND PART, FF.31-76]

Layout: 20 ruled ll./p., written area 142×90 mm.

Hand: small semiuncial, 2 mm, with long "tail" for the letter з. Majuscule titles.

Ink: brown; red for titles, initials and rubrics.

[THIRD PART, FF.77-139]

Layout: 21 ruled ll./p., written area 148/150×100 mm.

Hand: small semiuncial, x-height=2 mm, changing pen, sloping to the right. On ff.117v.3-118v.7 it is replaced by another hand of similar type. Majuscule titles.

Ink: black; red for titles, initials and rubrics.

[FOURTH PART, FF.140-245]

Layout: on ff.140-159, 21 ruled ll./p., written area 148/150×100 mm. On ff.160-182v, 185-226v, 19-22 ruled ll./p., written area 148/155×100/105 mm. On ff.183-184v, 20 ruled ll./p., written area 160×115/118 mm. On ff.227-245v, 20 ruled ll./p., written area 148×100 mm.

Hand: a variety of small semiuncials/bookhands, by four scribes. 1. (ff.140-159v.6) A hand very similar to that of the third part, but slightly thicker and less formal, x-height=3 mm. 2. (ff.159v.7-182; 185-226v) Small informal semiuncial, x-height=3 mm. 3. (ff.183-184v)

A smaller, compressed semiuncial, x-height=2 mm, sloping to the right. 4. (ff.227-245)
A somewhat irregular, informal, vigorous bookhand with thick strokes, x-height=3 mm.
The second and fourth scribes use majuscule titles.

Ink: brown for the first two scribes (the first one noticeably darker); black for the other
two. All the scribes use red for titles, initials and rubrics.

Binding: leather on boards, 195×135 mm, restored; three raised bands on the spine;
traces of two fastenings. The leather is very worn and with some deep cuts on the front.

Condition: extensive staining and grime, and some damage to the edges of the leaves,
partially restored at various periods. Only a fragment of f.1 remains. There is evidence
that the paper was mended at a time prior to the last restoration, possibly when the manuscript was rebound.

Decoration: simple, consisting of crude pen-flourishing red initials, varieties of the
Neo-Byzantine type corresponding to the different scribes. In the first part, two- to four-
line initials with buds and foliage, drawn by an unaccomplished hand; three- to four-line
initials in the second part, modest but elegant with fine arrow-like buds with tendrils
centred on the stems; three-line initials with plain ornament of single or double buds are
used in the third part, at the Biblical readings; in the fourth part (particularly the second
and fourth scribes) there are larger, six- to nine-line letters, with complex ornamentation
of heavy buds, tendrils, small linear branches and short lines; on f.236v a palmette is inscribed in the round part of the initial. The most conspicuous initial, on f.177v, precedes
the prayer for the blessing of wine.

Contents:

(ff.1-5v) ꙋ́стⷶ бж҃тⷱнꙇ[...] [Proskomidia: the first leaf is fragmentary.]

(ff.6-24) бож҃твенⷶаꙗ слꙋ́ба йже въ ст҃ꙑ | ѿ҇ца наше́ йѡа́на ѕла́ꙋстаго

(ff.25-43v) бож҃ⷮвнⷣаꙗ слꙋ́ба иⷯ в̾ ст҃ꙑ ѿ҇ца наⷲго васиⷧа велика́ [Although the second
physical part of the manuscript begins on f.31, the text continues without a break.]

(ff.44-55v) бж҃ⷮвнаꙗ слꙋ́ба преⷣдесⷡ҇цⷲе|нⷣ̾а

(ff.55v-59) наⷧо вѣⷬнꙇ прⷩ заходⷮѣ слъ҇|нечноⷨ

(ff.59-62v) и пѡ сиⷯ бⷤіваеⷮ литиꙗ

(ff.62v-67) млⷮтвꙑ вечернаꙗ

(ff.67-73) млⷮтвꙑ ꙋ́трнꙇй

(ff.73-76v) **Dismissals for weekdays and major feasts** [lacking the end]

(ff.77-87) **Service for Whitsun** [lacking the title and initial rubrics]

    Incipit: Пр҇ꙋте, несквернѣ. безначалне, невидиме.

(ff.87-95v) послѣдованꙇ̀ просвѣꙻщенꙇꙗⷯ ст҇ꙇ | бⷢгоꙗвленꙇи

(ff.95v-99) послѣдованꙇ̀ ѿ причꙗще|нꙇй ст҃ꙑа во́дꙑ̀

(ff.99-106v) послѣⷣⷣ҇ванꙇ̀ ѡсⷡ҇щенꙇ̀ водꙑ̀ | въ а҃ а҆вго́ӱ꙯та мⷰꙁа

(ff.106v-110) ун҇ⷩ братотворенꙇю̀

(ff.110-117v) ун҇ⷩ лѣтопроровꙋчⷯ ҇нꙇю̀

(ff.117v-127v) ꙋ́стⷶⷶ и ун҇ⷩ ѡ̈бр꙳ченꙇ꙳ | ꙗв̈ꙸнꙋа́нꙇю̀ цⷬⷩ и кнꙗꙁⷣ҇ и всѣⷧⷠ | хⷬ꙯ꙗноⷨ

(ff.127v-139v) Послѣдованꙇ̀ бꙑва|емо · и́꙯ творити ѿроуати ѡгла́шено . и крⷮꙇ то
[lacking the end]

(ff.140-145v) **Order for Confession** [lacking the beginning]

(ff.145v-152) ун҇нь поноⷡ҇ленꙇю̀ покаꙗнꙇю̀

(ff.152-159v) A penitential nomocanon

Incipit: аще который ино҃ распоⷣсоуѥ́тⲥⲙ и спи҃

(ff.159v-166) чи҃ како поⷣваѥ҃ пѣти по|нахидоу́ оусъпши҃

(ff.166-177) правило мⷪлебно къ пр꙯ⷭⲧⷯⲏ в҃ци

(ff.177v-179) Млⷮва на́ слⷤ҃ вны҃ вино҃. мⷪ҃ на пасхⷤ дѣтѐ҃ дх҃овны҃.

(ff.179-180v) Мⷪ҃ на ржⷭ҃тво христаво[!] дѣтѐ҃.

(ff.180v-181v) Млⷮва на оу́нищеніѐ црⷦви ѿсквернен꙯ѣ ѿ еретикь.

(ff.181v-182) В нѐлю верⷠ̈ноγю мⷪ҃ на цвѣⷮо҃.

(f.182) Млⷮва на петрⷪ҃ дн҃ь дѣтѐ҃ дх҃овнымь.

(f.182v) Млⷮва на бл҃венⷯ̈ѥ домⷹ҃ и храⷨ҃.

(ff.183) Мⷲ҃ на ѡснованⷯ̈ѥ црⷦви новой. мⷪ҃ в҃ а тамⷹ҃. мⷪ҃ наⷣ ѿтⷤ҃ѿ҃.

(f.183v) Мⷪ҃ на потревлеⷲ̈ арⷮжса разровити в сⷤ҃ ѳоминⷤ сⷤпⷪ҃.

(f.184) Мⷲ҃ егда́ чтⷪ въпадеⷮ неѹ́исто въ вино.

(f.184v) Мⷲ҃ аще кто̀ въпадеⷮ въ поганыꙗ. мⷪ҃ наⷣ иꙗⷣ'ши҃ скⲅ'рънаа маса.

(f.185) Мⷪ҃ наⷣ ѿскверⲅ'ньшиⷭⲙ съсⷤдⷪ҃.

(ff.185v-226v) чи҃ выважⷤ̈ти стⷮити мало

(ff.227-245v) чи҃ попⷤ егⷣⷶ престáвиⷮⲥⲙ

Language:
all parts are written in Church Slavonic of an East Slavonic redaction, with very few traces of Bulgarian orthography.

Inscriptions:

ff.19v-22: [in various hands] помани г҃и марка іл҃їю василїа прокопиꙗ помани г҃и ереа илїю, васⷤ | домитрїа григорїа помани г҃и еленоу ѿгафїю настасїю | помани г҃и дш҃оу рабы҆ своеⷤ евдокыѝ | раба петра помани г҃и полагⷹ помани г҃и григориа || поманⷮ г҃и иѡанна век'лю

ff.35v-36: ѿ вⷢолюбиваⷢѿ | Ѥпиⷩⲫа Андреꙗ̀ | Бауинскый оу́ оуⷩ|гварѣ градѣ̀. | Маꙁ҃им Поповинⷹ | Паро́ⷯ Новосⷯѥлⲥⲕⲓⲓ | Аⷣмⷤнⷯⲥⲧⲣⲁⲧⲟⲣⲟ Лꙗхⷯвⲥⲕⲓⲓ | Посвꙗⷮⷯⲓⲗⲥꙗ Наⷣ презвитерствⲱ | рокⷹ ҂аѱпе [1785] здѣ зостал | Рокⷹ ҂аѱпе Ст҃а҃ Книга пренесена е҃ⷮ | из веси рипиногⷳ до веси Старо-го|лꙗтина їереⷨ Паⷩ́телеимон Лꙗховиⷩ | Котораꙗ /: книга :/ Прислⷹшает до веси Лꙗхⷪ[...] | Panteleimon Lacychow[...] | Parok O. Holatinskiy

f.41: Корⷯ үченⷯїа горⷪⷡ плоды же его сдады | сⷹⷮ [There is a similar inscription scrawled on f.75v; a few other fragmentary inscriptions of a similar kind have not been recorded.]

f.42v: [illegible]

f.56v: [...] ѿц҃ь нашⷮ гдⷮ і҃с хⷮ꙯ | [...] помилуи на амⷮнь | рⷪⷡ в҃ ахла великⷮи мⷹ҃ наⷭ[...]

f.66: [...]те мⷯѣ грⷯѣшьнаго бл҃вите

ff.78v-81v: рокⷹ бж҃го ҂ахки [1628] || + попъ микⷤла повⷯѣдаѥ дⷯѣтелⷨ | своимъ же маютъ пювⷮ ланⷤ | волⷮного на горⷯвⷯ: изъ полꙗми | во то ꙗ оуⷢⷯⲥⲕ бывⷮ сⷯѣⲅ на тото | + ҂ахчⷣ [1694] | попⷮ перⷮ̈ро так'же повⷯѣдаѥ | дⷯѣтелⷨ' своиⷨ' же вол'но есть имь | тамⷮ сⷯⲅ'ти а корол' немаѥ таⷨ' дⷯѣла

f.100v: пакаштавати пера ци добра писати | ѿ горе валⷮ законици акова застеклоⷰь [?]

f.101v: пакоштова пера цѐ | черьнила каламара

f.104: оуⷢⲅⷯⲓⲛⲓ̈ андреⷩ хрыⷩ'тⷮи тⷪⷦ'

f.105v: А̀ ты ѿⷢⲥⲉ петре прошⷹ сего дⷯѣл | а ты ѿⲅⲉ лала спрошⷹ тⷤ сего дⷯѣла | пиши евсто [?] не лⷯѣниⲥⲙ варьꙁе ниска нехилиⲥⲙ дивиⲥⲙ

82

f.128: [an alphabet]

f.226v: [some crude drawings of churches, one labelled стӥ҃ бца | храмь]

ff.244v-245: [......] рокЪ божого ҂аѱкз [1727] ‖ щосъ дѣало попъ василии | оу новоселицю пришовъ

Provenance: all parts were written in the Ruthenian area. The villages mentioned in the inscriptions, Ó-Holyátin (Holjatin, Tarfalu), Ripinye (Repynne), Lyahovec (Liskovec', Lengyelszállás) and Novoselycja (Új-Holyátin, Tarújfalu), are in the Mižhirja region of the Transcarpathian oblast' of the Ukraine (formerly Ökörmezői district, Máramaros megye). One of fourteen manuscripts donated in 1904 by Antal Hodinka.

Plates 48, 49, 50

Liturgicon, 16th century (third quarter)

Paper. Watermark: anchor (fig.107) very similar to Mošin Anchor 922 (1565); scales (fig.108), similar to Briquet 2520 (1555); hat (fig.109), similar to Dečani 174 (1561); anchor (fig.110) similar to Mošin Anchor 1858 (1565-75); anchor (fig.111) similar to Mošin Anchor 1175 (1570-80). In the endpapers, coat of arms (fig.20).

i+215+i leaves; modern stamped foliation, [i] 1-11, [11a], 12-53, [53a], 54-202, [202a], 203-210, [210a], 211, [212], the omitted leaves (other than the flyleaves) having been numbered subsequently in pencil. Size of leaves: 205×150 mm.

Collation: I^8 (-1 ±2), II-III^8, IV^8 (4+1), V-XXVI^8, XXVII^8 (-8). The leaves of the last gathering are disrupted: the correct order should be ff.211, 206, 208, 207, 210, 209, 210a. F.27 is an extraneous piece of paper, 162×101mm, stuck onto f.28, and bears only inscriptions. Although the hand of f.1 is indistinguishable from that of the following three leaves, it seems that it was not originally part of this book, as the title Ѹставь вожⷭ҇твнїє сл[...] which has imprinted itself in mirror-image on the verso does not match that on f.2. Gatherings signed centrally in the lower margin of the first recto and last verso, а҃-к҃з.

Layout: ff.1-54v: 22 ll./p., written area 152×105 mm; ff.55-211v: 20 ll./p., written area 147×100 mm.

Hand: a variety of practised Serbian semiuncials. 1. (ff.1-4v) the most formal and restrained hand; 2. (ff.5-48) more vigorous but still elegant; 3. (ff.48v-50.8) similar, but sloping very slightly to the right; 4. (ff.50.9-62v) a little coarser and more upright; 5. (ff.63-211v) a hand of similar type, upright, vigorous and professional. The fifth scribe has a characteristic angular loop on ȣ and triangular о. Occasional majuscule titles.

Ink: black on ff.1-48, rather more faded on ff.5-48; brown on ff.48v-211v, sporadically darkening to black in the later parts of the book. All the scribes use red for titles, initials and rubrics, that of the first and second scribes being somewhat stronger in colour than that of the others. In places, particularly near the edges of the leaves, where it has been more exposed to the action of damp, the red ink used by the latter three scribes has faded to blackish. There is some green ink on f.155v.

Binding: brown leather on boards, 215×155 mm, restored: only parts of the original leather remain. Three raised bands on the spine, no fastenings preserved. Blind tooling. On the upper cover an incised border of quadruple fillets enclosing rectangular palmette stamps; the central panel is divided crosswise by triple fillets, the four resulting compartments in turn divided diagonally; at the intersecting points are impressed small concentric circles and trefoils resembling fleurs-de-lys around them. The lower cover probably had the same pattern, but the borders are now missing. The design is common in South Slavonic bindings of the sixteenth and seventeenth centuries. One modern flyleaf at each end.

Condition: the manuscript has undergone a thorough restoration; before this the paper was evidently in a poor condition.

Decoration: numerous pen-flourished, three-and four-line red initials, of Neo-Byzantine type, in the parts written by the second to fifth scribes, slightly varying in shape and quality; ornamented with buds and tendrils grouped on the stems of the letters and occasionally with foliate finials.

Contents:

(f.1) **Prefatory rubrics**

Defective: begins with the words: или инꙋ утꙋ прикоснет'се

[This is followed by заповѣдь стго василїа for the consecration of an extra prosphora on Maundy Thursday.]

(f.1v) [blank]

(ff.2-6v) Ꙋстдвь божтвеныꙗ слоужбы. | въ нюйже и дїаконьс'тва

(ff.7-36v) божтвнд слꙋж'бд иже въ | стыꙸ Ѡцд ншего їѡанна злаꙋ|стдго

(ff.37-53v) божетвнд слꙋж'ба й҃е | вь стыꙸ Ѡцд нашего въсилїа вели|кдго

(ff.53a-54) Слꙋжбд вечер'нюꙗ | въз'глашенїю

(ff.54-56) Слꙋжбд ꙋтрѣници

(ff.56-64) **Dismissals throughout the year** [with associated prayers]

(f.64-64v) м҃, глюмд, нд҅ коливо҃. Въ пдмети | стыꙸ. й нд҅ ново҃ꙸ врдшню҃ꙸ. й в'сдко|мꙋ принӡшенїю. й ѡвощїю

(ff.64v-67) дп҃лы, й ев҃лїа. оꙋскꙿпшꙿꙗмь, й вꙿи

(ff.67-70) **Prayers for sundry occasions** [beginning with the grape harvest]

(ff.70-91v) ев҃лїа, стыхь страстей | гд бд й спд наше їꙋ хд

(ff.92-101v) ев҃лїа, въскрнд, д҃ї

(ff.102-174v) апостолы і ев҃лїа, прдз|д'никомь, гӡпод'скымь. й нароуи|тꙗмь стымь

(ff.173-209, 211) **Epistle and Gospel readings for Lent, Holy Week, Easter, Whitsun and All Saints**

(ff.210-210av) мѣтва, юже глють дрхт|ерей. или дхӡв'никь прӡщен'ноу, | зд грѣхы в'сѣ

[The end is missing.]

Language: Serbian Church Slavonic.

Inscriptions:

f.1v: [illegible; apparently in German]

f.1v: + сїю ꙗгоу прилѡжи дрдгӡло | зд свою дшоꙋ ꙗꙶ дд прости

f.1v: [...] | ши д҃ꙿискълиꙿ | Про҃ꙿпопъ Данилъ | ѿ Илїа

f.1v: + протопопъ данилъ ѿ илиѣ къндꙋ | дꙋ фостꙋ ѡ ·д·х·м· [1640] дни мес д | придри. ·к·ѕ· д҃ъ цюрдръ върсъꙶѣннии | кꙋ сътꙋ лꙑсате кꙋ либꙋ | де морте лорꙋ дд попа ионꙋ | дуесте кърци

f.1v: [illegible]

f.2: попд данила

f.6v: нꙋмитꙋлъ | преѿ миꙷ | михдлъ | поповиу | 799

f.6v: милсти вꙶꙗ прѣѡсфещиндго | [...] поꙿ ѡпрд дид вдм потоꙿ

f.6v: + съ се цте къ дꙋ дату уатꙋ сфнтꙿ летꙋꙷгуе | попа їѡꙿ дид върмд ши мотъвниꙶ ши ꙋ уаслове꙰ꙿ дꙋи попа цꙋрцꙋ дм върсъꙶ. съи фте помднꙿ | съ дꙿ помен꙰ꙿскꙿ· ши уине ле вд дꙋа де лд врꙿ|съꙿ съ фте прокле꙰ꙿ де тꙶ ши нꙷ де ѡцꙷ. | уе д꙰въꙷнектею· помени гꙷ дши рдвд | вꙶте ереи їѡꙿ й родителе его сероцꙷники кд҅де поимени нꙷ въ цртво | невꙿное й въ жизини вꙶнꙷе въ | ставленїе | грѣхӡꙿꙸ где просвꙷꙗдеть све꙰ꙿ лица твоє[...]

ff.7-36 passim: [numerous marginal glosses in Rumanian]

f.17: съ цꙷе къ ꙗ зиꙷ де пдци | дмъ възꙋтъ 2 соре

85

f.27-27v: помєнⷮ гⷡ҃и бє мⷪ҇ | дш҃є раба своєго | дань · ака · жⷮїє | нага · коуꙁмь · мьⷬⷮїнь | · мьрⷮїє · или|на · ака · днь · крь|стє · мьрⷮїє · прⷢⷮꙁи|тєлоу ꙍ҃ь | моисєи ака вавоура днь | цєфань тотора|нь · моисє· гровє | прости ‖ дань · ака · жⷮїє · ил|ина [in another hand on the recto:] ганошоу ана [in a third hand on the verso:] пмⷩ҇ гдⷣи рова тⷢ҇о | иѥрⷮⷢ́и їоань кꙋ҃ тоⷮ нѣмꙋл҇ лор | дꙋмнєꙁєу съи помєнѣ|скъ амꙟ҃.

f.52v: пъри ѧтрꙋ ѧтрꙋ

f.53v: писа аⷧ҇ꙁ шаѣн | ·ⷮ· д[...]живх[...] прьтⷩ҇

f.54: дуаⷭⷮ картє | ѧпрєшнⷩ кꙋ лєтꙍ|ргиє ши кꙋ уаⷭ|ловъ

f.63: Димитрⷢїє [...] ии 7̅9̅4̅

f.64: Anno D. 798 Дєкѐⷡ҇ⷡри 1° ꙁи датꙋ҇ⷢ | Михаилъ Поповичъ Парох [...]

f.102v-103: Лꙋꙋ даⷮ ѧ в҇ѫрсъꙋ ‖ 19 Іꙋню 1803 ѧ ꙁилєлє

f.102v: съ тръници кꙋ | сънътак | скрисаⷧ

f.105: ѧнѫлцатꙋлꙋи ѧпъраⷮ франциꙘк [...] ши ал доилѣ

f.105v: An 1803

f.111v: сънътоⷱⷳи съ фиⷱⷳи

f.126v: саꙋ искълит прин Прєшꙋлъ Михаилъ Поповиⷱⷳ Парох [...]

f.127: вєꙁи фратє тає сакꙋ уꙋмꙋтатє

f.177: прѣуинституⷧꙋи ши дє в꙼ꙋ нѣм

f.182v: ꙍрминдѣнъ[?] дънилъ дин в҇ѫрсꙋ

f.189v: Єꙋ амъ скри|съ попа Іано|ши динъ си|мєрѣ лъкꙋи|тори ѧ в҇ѫрсъꙋ 1794

Provenance: of Serbian origin, and evidently subsequently brought to Transylvania. The places mentioned in the inscriptions, Bîrsău (Berekszó), Ilia (Marosillye) and Banpotoc (Bánpatak, Bonbach), are all in the Hunedoara region of present-day Rumania (formerly Hunyad megye). Given on 22nd August 1912, together with Quart. Eccl. Slav. 14, by László Réthy (1851-1914), chief curator of the numismatics department of the National Museum and writer of indecent verse.

Plate 51

Euchologion, 17th century (first quarter)

Paper. Watermark: coat of arms (fig.112), similar to Laucevičius 1809, 1810 (1596-1600); two-headed eagle (fig.113), similar to Laucevičius 488 (1618); arms (Jelita) (fig.114), type Siniarska-Czaplicka 391-395 (1584-1614); coat of arms (fig.115), type Siniarska-Czaplicka 1096 (1596); three more fragmentary and unidentifiable coats of arms (figs.116, 117, 118).

i+310+i leaves; modern stamped foliation, [i], 1-95, [95a], 96-121, [1 unnumbered], 122-308, [311]; older foliation on ff.1-146, а̄-р̄ѕ, ра̄ї-р̄м̄ѕ. Size of leaves: 195×155 mm.

Collation: I-II¹², III¹² (9+1), IV¹⁴, V-VIII¹², IX¹² (12+1), X¹² (2 misplaced after 11), XI-XV¹², XVI², XVII-XIX¹², XX⁸, XXI⁴, XXII¹², XXIII¹⁰, XXIV? (23 leaves), XXV¹², XXVI⁸, XXVII? (11 leaves). Gatherings signed, I-XII а̄-б̄ї and XIII-XXVI а̄ї-к̄ѕ. The signatures are not original, and the collation as given reflects the present, not the original state of the book: some gatherings have been reconstructed, and some leaves are missing. There appears to be one gathering missing between XII and XIII.

Layout: 18 ll./p., written area 145×105 mm; on ff.147-169, 233-253, 17 ll./p., written area 138×105 mm.

Hand: a variety of slightly informal semiuncial/bookhands, all of the same general type. 1. (ff.1-37, 171-184, 298-307v); 2. (ff.38-75v) slightly more condensed; 3. (ff.76-111v) a smaller hand; 4. (ff.112v-146v) similar but squarer; 5. (ff.147-169 and 233-253); 6. (ff.185-232) a similar hand; 7. (ff.255-273v) a still less formal hand; 8. (ff.274-277v.7, 296v.8-297v and possibly 308) a vigorous, informal bookhand; 9. (f.277v.7-19) a much more compressed hand, but conceivably the same scribe as the previous section struggling to fit his text onto the page; 10 (ff.278-296v.7) somewhat smaller and more formal. Majuscule titles and initials are used by all the scribes.

Ink: ff.1-37, 147-184, 233-254, 256v-273v, 278-307v, black; ff.38-146v, 185-232, 255-256, 274-277v, 308 brown; red for titles, initials and rubrics.

Binding: black leather on boards, 210×165 mm, restored. Three raised bands on the spine with triple fillets around them, two new clasps. Blind tooling. On the upper cover triple fillets frame the borders and the central panel; eight-leaved palmette stamps, are impressed between the panel and the border as well as inside the panel; for a slightly similar motif cf. Laucevičius 1976 №138 (16th century). The decoration on the lower cover is almost identical, but the central panel is left empty. The leather of the lower cover is made of two pieces sewn together. One modern flyleaf at each end.

Condition: restored. Some leaves missing, and rather dirty in parts. The binding is damaged, so the ornament is very faint.

Decoration: simple, of various initials, not clearly distinctive for the individual hands; one tailpiece.

ff.23v, 47v, 87v, 195v, 200, 200v, 294v, 295v, 298, 303: five- to nine-line red interlaced initials.

ff.54v-75v: outline initials of geometric character, in part of the section written by the second scribe.

Numerous pen-flourished red initials of varying size and quality, varieties of the Neo-Byzantine type, with ornamentation of buds, tendrils or simple geometric motifs.

f.158v: a tailpiece at the end of the order for the blessing of the waters, composed of a hand holding a "tablet" with the end of the text, flanked by two knot motifs.

Contents:

(ff.1-6v) ૪ставь бжⷷтвеныхⷯ слૂжⷢ|бы. вънеже дїаконьства

(ff.6v-37) бжⷷтвенаⷶ слૂжⷢба иⷤ въ | стыⷯ ѿ҃ца нашеⷢ їѡⷶ ҙлаૂуста|гò [F.37v was originally blank.]

(f.38-38v) чинⷪ̈ блⷭвити вино

(ff.38v-44v) послѣдованїе бываемо|ⷷ на велицѣй вечⷳни. и вде|нⷨⷯ

(ff.45-48) послѣⷣⷣванїⷷ бываⷷмоⷷ на | ૪трⷲни

(ff.48v-49v) **Liturgical instructions**

       Incipit: о повъседневной вⷷрни и ૪троⷲ|ни. подобаеⷮ вѣдати и се

(ff.49v-50v) ѿпૂстыⷠ повъседневный

(ff.50v-54v) ѿпૂⷭⷮ на праⷩни влૂчна и порⷮыⷯ | бца и въ памⷶⷮ стыⷯ великыⷯ мⷩни

(ff.54v-75v) бжⷷтвенаⷶ лૂⷮргïа ижⷤ въ | стыⷯ ѿ҃ца нашеⷢ василïа велика|гò

(ff.76-108) чиⷩ бываⷺюⷳщи стⷮити масло

(ff.108-110v) чиⷩ наⷣ ૪мрьшиⷨⷨ младеⷨцеⷯ

(110v-111v) ૪ставь аⷳще преставиⷮⷲса | наⷣ стоⷷ въскⷬⷩⷣïⷷ

(ff.112-116) чиⷩ на йсхоⷣ дши въсакомૂ | хрⷷⷮïанинૂ

(ff.116-141v) чиⷩ погрⷷбанïю мирскомૂ

(ff.141v-146v) како подобаⷷⷮ творити памⷶⷮ | оૂсъпⷳшиⷯ. йзображено нико|форⷲ зовемыⷯ к҃сан'фополⷲ [The end is missing.]

(ff.147-158v) **Order for blessing of the waters at Epiphany** [The beginning is missing. Ff.151v-152 and 153v-154 were originally blank.]

(ff.159-169) Мⷭца авгૂста въ а̃ днь стыⷯ | ҙ мако|вⷹïй. чиⷩ на ѡсⷳщенïⷷ водⷷ [Ff.169v-170v were originally blank.]

(ff.171-184) чиⷩ йспоⷡѣданïю велика|го василïа. йже нареⷩь быⷭⷮ. ૂаⷣⷪ|послૂшанïа [F.184v was originally blank.]

(ff.185-191v) чиⷩ наⷣ ѿглашеныⷨⷨ сирⷷⷠ| хотаⷳщиⷨ крⷷⷳститиса

(ff.191v-202) послѣдованïе стⷢого крⷷ|ⷳщенïа

(ff.202-205v) послѣдованïе въⷩаⷤ ѡмы|ти крⷳтившаⷭⷲ въ и̃ днь

(ff.205v-208v) послѣдованïе бываⷷмо|ⷷ ѡбрૂⷣченïю

(ff.209-219v) послѣдованïе вⷷⷯⷹанïю

(ff.219v-222v) послѣдованïе на двобраⷳныⷯ

(ff.222v-225) чиⷩ братотворⷷнïю

(ff.225-226v) чиⷩ на ѿбновленïⷷ ѿтроⷷте

(ff.226v-229) чиⷩ въ третïи днь женⷷ по роⷤженïй ѿроⷹте

(ff.229v-232) **Service for a woman on the fortieth day after giving birth** [F.232v was originally blank.]

(f.233-253) внⷣлю стого дⷯа по литоⷢⷮïн слⷩцૂ | ҙстૂпиⷳшૂ спⷪлૂⷣне клепаⷷⷨ веⷹⷹни поскⷪри слૂⷢ|бы раⷨ колⷷⷩ|наго приклоненïа [Ff.246v-247 and 248v-249 were originally blank, as were ff.253v-254v.]

(ff.255-268) чиⷩ попૂ ⷷгⷣа приставиⷮⷲса

(ff.268-273v) а̃ се лⷮ на роⷤ хⷡо сⷩоⷨи ⷳрⷷ [followed by prayers for other festivals]

88

(ff.274-277v) мл҃твы лит҃їйны веле|гла҃но

(ff.278-297v) послѣ́дованї҄е ст҃о҄ причаще|нї҄а

(ff.298-302v) мл҃твы веѵе҄рнї҄й

(ff.303-308) мл҃твы у҄трьнѣ҄й҄

Language: Church Slavonic of an East Slavonic recension, with fairly limited traces of Middle Bulgarian Tărnovo orthography.

Inscriptions:

f.1: Книга слу҄жевникъ | дѣдо баба ку҄пили[...]

f.5v-6: Год' лу҄ка данйло мйку҄ла | романъ иванъ иванъ | ан҄ъдѣ҄ пилйпъ мигал҄ъ | раковц҄ѣ ферец҄ъ ‖ тимофей

f.11: ѿ горе ї҄линпи

f.24-23v: во й҄мга ѿц҄а и сн҃а и сватого д҃у҄х҄а | ам҄ѣнь сиш книга теслевиуого поп ‖ [...]скевнуь федоръ по

f.37v: [Later hands have added the troparion (incipit "ѿ у҄сть твои҄ г҄а̄ злато") and kontakion (incipit "ѿ нб҃съ пре|емъ вж҄ею влг҄ть") for St John Chrysostom; the opening words of the former have been written in still later hands on this page and also on ff.37, 38.]

f.55: иску҄пил | ни еси ѿ кл[.]|тви зако|[.......]

f.75v: [...]ви степе недвижи҆

f.79v: сп҃си ѿ вѣ́д раба своего гако у҄срдньно ктевѣ | првѣга҆. гако̄ мл҃твомъ избавителю. и во вь|сехь влд҄цѣ гд҄у нг҃у [repeated on ff.80, 80v, 82v and 83]

f.81: възнесиса на кр҃ть волею тезюимени

f.103v: ѿу҄е сты нцѣлителю дш҃а҆ и тело҆ | наши҆ посла҆ единоро҄наго сина | своего г҃а нашего ї҃с х҃с ивъ

f.115: придите таине цу҄лование дади҆ братцу҄ | мешему҄ похвалающе вога свои зи|де ѿ рожества своего коровъ привл[?]

f.148v: І҄реи стефа҆ ву҄коски

f.150v: покоцовати перо ци пише добре добре | иже покоцоват

ff.151v-152: [An eighteenth-century hand has added on these orginally blank pages a text entitled Пѣснь стои тройцй катехймо в҃ї.]

f.153v-154: [Three late and unpractised hands have added on these orginally blank pages a list of names for commemoration, an incomplete alphabet and what appear to be some writing exercises; also a drawing of a hand holding a branch.]

f.158v: [an imitation of the tailpiece on this page]

ff.159v-160v: зо д҃у҄х҄а ам҄ѣ҆ сиш кни ‖ теслевиовгго попа стефана ‖ си тревнн҆ теслевинуового попа | стефана [incomplete: at least one leaf is missing between ff.159 and 160. It is possible that the next inscription follows on from this one.]

f.161v-162: ву҄коского и да z҄а ню ‖ ѕ селгаку҄ [??] [...]

f.167v: приклони гос҄по у҄хо твое оуслиши[...]

89

ff.169v-171: [Later hands have copied the text of some prayers onto these pages, the first-three of which were originally blank.]

f.184v: Сюго рокъ гръмѣло | четверътой недѣлѣ у вели|кий постъ у понедѣлокъ | тыжденъ передь .и҃. сватыхъ | подъписавъ тото | А҃дрѣи Копанъскы | Поповичъ

f.184v: Сого рокъ гръмѣло | четверътой недѣлѣ ꙋ | поста у понедѣлꙋкъ | пере сорокъ сватихъ | ро҃ бо҃ ҂афки [1728] | поповичъ | ванкла [?]

f.196: [imitation of the initial Д on the opposite page]

f.206: Тебе вели҃а҃емъ в҃це

f.232-232v: [an additional prayer, incipit Г҃и Б҃е нашъ едъ҃ѣ҃ блг҃ы ꙋꙗколоꙋвуе]

ff.248v-249: [A later hand has added the beginning of the life of St Alexis [?], incipit единъ вы҃ мазимиꙗ҃ ц҃ръ, on these orginally blank pages.]

ff.253v-254v: [An eighteenth-century hand has added on these orginally blank pages a text entitled начало исповѣданіа на вели҃ по́тъ concluding in the margin of f.255.]

ff.266v-267: а҃гг҃ле а҃рхг҃гле михаиле | оуриле рафаиле рꙋганле ‖ вварѳоноиле пѳаи

f.291: Зачало премꙋдрости страхъ господень | воитиса вг҃а сйнъ премꙋдри҃ веселитъ | ѿца сйнъ везꙋмний плачь матери свое

f.292: тали же писони҃ [?] стесовичь | васили҃ попа стефана вꙋко|скго

f.297v: чесни ѿуе стефане вꙋкос

f.297v: Миръ вамъ ѿцеве [...]

There are also a number of crude and not entirely legible scribbles on ff.55v, 64, 78v, 88, 104, 106v, 111v, 135v, 147, 149, 183, 233-234, 242, 246v-247, 251v-252, 253, and on f.308v primitive drawings of two birds.

Provenance: written in the Ruthenian area. One of fourteen manuscripts donated by Antal Hodinka in 1904.

Plates 52, 53, 54

Euchologion, 17th century

Paper. Watermark: fleur-de-lys (fig.119), type Laucevičius 2044 (1632); shield with a lion rampant, surmounted by a crown (fig.120), type Laucevičius 2259 (1664).

i+284+i leaves; modern stamped foliation [i], 1-284, [285]. Size of leaves: 182×150 mm.

Collation: I' (4 leaves), II-VI¹², VII' (4 leaves, the first three and the last), VIII-XXV¹². Original signatures on the first verso and last recto of II-XXV in the lower margin level with the outer edge of the text, ꙇ-ла̃.

Layout: 16 ll./p., written area 125×105 mm. Running titles.

Hand: a very regular semiuncial, x-height=3mm. Majuscule titles.

Ink: black; bright red for titles, rubrics, initials and running titles.

Binding: leather on thick bevelled boards, 195×162 mm, restored; two new clasps; three raised bands on the spine, which is almost entirely restored. On the upper cover there are faint traces of blind tooling. One modern flyleaf at each end.

Condition: there are leaves missing at both the beginning and the end, but the surviving leaves, apart from being rather dirty, are in generally good condition. The original binding has evidently suffered great damage and wear.

Decoration: one headpiece and red penwork initials, based on models from printed-books.

f.4: a framed headpiece of the Balkan interlaced type, 66×104 mm, composed of two intersecting circles and a quatrefoil medallion with a coat of arms in the middle, crossed by vegetal stems. The pattern is copied from the Liturgicon printed in Venice by Božidar Vuković in 1519. Ochre background, red outlines with silver-blue fillings.

Red, two-to four-line penwork initials, the greater part of which are decorated only with double buds on their stems or buds with tendrils.

Contents: Euchologion, lacking the liturgies and probably other material as a result of the loss of material (about fifty leaves) at the beginning.

(ff.1-3v, 4v) **Prayers for a woman after childbirth** [Fragments; f.4 is bound back to front.]

(ff.4, 5-27) Послѣдова́нїе ꙗже сътвори́|ти ѿроуа̀ Ѡглаше́но и кр҃ти́ти то̀ [A small amount of material is missing after the first page.]

(ff.27v-30) послѣдова́нїе быва́емое | ѡбрꙋче́нїю

(ff.30v-43v) Чи́нъ вѣнча́нїю

(ff.44-49) Чи́нъ Вѣнча́нїю Второ|бра́чнымъ

(ff.50-67) Чи́нъ и́сповѣда́нїю

(f.67v) Чи́нъ поновле́нїю покаꙗ́нїа [The beginning only: a probable eight leaves are missing.]

(f.68) Чи́нъ покаа́нїю попѡ́мъ [the end only]

(ff.68v-71v) Чи́нъ ѥгда̀ ключи́тъсѧ во|скорѣ вѣлмѝ бо́лномоу да́ти при|ча́стїе

(ff.72-127) Послѣдова́нїе ст҃го ма́сла

(ff.127v-184) Послѣдова́нїе погребе́нїю | скончавшоусѧ комоу̀ ѿ правосла́|вныхъ (ff.184v 187) Уйнъ провожденїю младе|н'уескомоу

(ff.187-196v) Ука́ како подобаетъ пѣти | на́ кютїею оусóп'шимь ѿце́" | й братїамъ нашимъ

(ff.197-215) Въслѣдованїе малаго ѡсщенїа | воды. Мца августа в а̃

(ff.215v-234) Въслѣдованїе великаго | Осщенїа стыхъ вгоавленїй

(ff.234v-260v) внлю й стго дха по литоургїи, | санцю з'стоупившоу сполудне | клепле" вечéрни пóскоро, слоу"|вы ради колѣн'наго преклонéнїа

(ff.261-284v) Млтвы на всакоу потребу

Language: Church Slavonic of an East Slavonic recension, with clear traces of Middle Bulgarian Tărnovo orthography.

Inscriptions:

f.67: помолитеса гдви и вздадите

f.68: покаганію попомъ и жена́| поповымъ

f.68: [illegible]

f.68: Сию книгу купи"рабь бжи" гаврило | саницькыи излазоро"наплу. за зло"й | и службами которы"на престолѣ [..] | вцрькве квıато"ской. А тои требникь | посполу службами не мае" быти ѿда|леныи ѿ цркве квıато"ской вѣуными уасы, | а кторыи сщени" буде" сни" ѿравовати. тог'а | дожень е̃ мıати Га Ба за раба бжıа гаври|лиıа. и лазорıа. и за подружие и" ганусю | и ганю. и за и" потос̃тва. за и"ѿпу|щение грѣхw" и ѡ наслѣдие цртва | нбнаго

f.128: [An inscription has been erased.]

f.216v: бжн ѿуе будь похвале" вѣуны же сме того | уасу беспеуны по

f.217v: помощь моıа ѿ гда сотворшаго | нбо и землю стихъ възведох

f.250: помощь моıа ѿ гда сотворшаго | нбо и зе́лю

Provenance: written in the Ruthenian area. The village of Kwiatoń mentioned in the inscription on f.68 is in the district of Gorlice in modern Poland. One of 14 manuscripts donated by Antal Hodinka in 1904. Some fragments removed from the binding during restoration are kept separately in the library.

Plate 55

36. Fol. Eccl. Slav. 21
Liturgicon, 1835-1848

Paper. Wove, no watermark.

iii+76+i leaves; original foliation а҃і-о҃з, н҃-н҃з, modern stamped foliation, [i-iii], 1-76, [77]. Size of leaves: 290×210 mm.

Collation: I-III⁴, IV⁶, V⁴ (+1 at beginning), VI-XVII⁴, XVIII⁴ (4+1). Unsigned.

Layout: 15 ll./p., within a ruled border 160×125 mm. Catchwords. Running titles. The manuscript imitates the layout of a printed book, and is very likely copied from one.

Hand: late semiuncial in imitation of print.

Ink: black; red for titles, initials and rubrics.

Binding: beige velvet over brown buckram on card, front and back decorated with a gilt foliar border and a Latin cross in the middle. Three modern flyleaves at front, one at back.

Condition: ten leaves missing at the beginning; some old repairs; otherwise good.

Decoration: pen and ink illustrations, imitating engravings or lithographs.

f.5: above the beginning of Mattins a miniature representing Christ and Bartimæus.

f.19v: full-page ink and wash drawing of St John Chrysostom in full length.

f.20: a miniature representing the Resurrection.

Two- to three-line red penwork initials with rich foliate ornament, following the model of printed books.

f.58: a diagram showing the disposition of the particles of consecrated bread on the diskos.

Contents:
>(ff.1-4) **Vespers** [The beginning is missing.]
>(f.4v) [blank]
>(ff.5-18) Послѣдованїе оу́трени
>(ff.18v-19) [blank]
>(f.19v) [illustration]
>(ff.20-69) Бж҃е́ственнаѧ слꙋ́жба, | во ст҃ы́хъ ѻ҃ца на́шегѡ і́ѡа́нна златоꙋ́стагѡ
>(ff.69v-70) У҆и́нъ в҃лг҃вѐнїѧ ко́лива
>(ff.70v-71) Моли́тва в҃лгосло́вѐнїѧ ва́їа
>(ff.71v-72) М҃лтва на в҃лгословѐнїѧ грозді́ѧ
>(ff.72v-73) Є҆ѵлїе ст҃о́е па́схи, ѿ і҆ѡа́нна, зача́ло а҃
>(ff.73v-74v) ΤΗ ΑΓΙΑ ΚΑΙ ΜΕΓΑΛΗ ΚΥΡΙΑΚΗ | ΤΟΥ ΠΑΣΧΑ | Ἐκ τȣ χ᾽ Ἰωάννου
>(f.75-75v) St John Chrysostom: Ὀπισθάμβωνος εὐχή
>>Incipit: Ὁ Εὐλογῶν τȣς εὐλογȣντάς σε Κύριε

Language: Synodal Church Slavonic; on ff.73v-75v Greek, evidently copied by someone not very used to it.

93

Inscriptions:

f.76: [The Great Prokeimenon for Easter, written in a cursive cyrillic hand]

Provenance: presumably written in the Ukrainian territories of the the Habsburg empire during the reign of the Emperor Ferdinand I (1835-1848), who is mentioned on f.5. The stamp on f.1, A ZIRCZI APÁTSÁG KÖNYVTÁRA 1875, indicates that it was formerly amongst the manuscripts of Zirc Abbey, acquired by the Library in 1954.

Plate 56

37. QUART. ECCL. SLAV. 17
Services to the All-Merciful Saviour and the Kazan' Icon of the Mother of God, 17th century (last quarter)

Paper. Watermark: in the first part foolscap (fig.121), similar to Laucevičius 2581 (1663-4), Dianova/Kostjuchina 485 (1685), Heawood 2020 (1688), Lichačev 476 (17th century); Arms of Amsterdam with letters IM (fig.122), similar to Dianova–Kostjuchina 129 (1678-80); in the second part, Arms of Amsterdam (fig.123), similar to Heawood 387 (1689). 20+16=36 leaves; modern stamped foliation, 1-35 + one blank leaf. Size of leaves: 190×155 mm.

Collation: I^8 (±1), II^8, III^4 (±2), I-II^8. Unsigned.

[FIRST PART, FF.1-20]

Layout: 16 ll./p., written area 145×110 mm.

Hand: a rather heavy, somewhat rough but nevertheless competent semiuncial.

Ink: black; red for titles, initials and rubrics.

[SECOND PART, FF.21-36]

Layout: 18-22 ll./p., written area 155-165×135 mm.

Hand: a late, degenerate semiuncial, becoming more hurried and careless on the later pages.

Ink: greyish-black.

Binding: modern, paper on card.

Condition: excellent.

Contents:

(First part, ff.1-20) М҃ЦА А҃VГꙊСТА ВЪ а҃ Д҃НЬ | Слꙋ́жба всемл҃тивагѡ сп҃са

(Second part, ff.21-36) Слꙋ́жба ꙗвле́нїю і҆ко́ны пр҃тыѧ вл҃чцы | н҃шеѧ б҃цы каза́нскиѧ

Language: Russian Church Slavonic.

Inscriptions:

on a small piece of paper tipped in before f.1: Sec. XVI. MSS Extranea. | Russica №5 | Adoratio Clementissimi Servatoris D.N.I. Christi | Lingva Vetere Slavo Ecclesiastico | et Characteribus Cyrilicis Rubeonigris in Charta | Gossipina exaratus. __Acc. | Sacræ Festivitatis Sanctissimæ Reginæ | Matris Dei in Kazan Celebratio. pag. 28. | Litteris perinde Cyrilicis, sed Seculi XVIII scri|ptus codex in quarto. [This text has been copied out in pencil inside the front cover.]

f.1: A Celleberrimo Viro Joh. Godofr. Eichhorn | LL.OO. in Academia Ienensi D.D. O. | dono accepit | Georg- Ribbay | Ienæ d. 7 Oct 1781

Provenance: of Russian (Muscovite) origin. From the collection of Juraj Ribay (1754-1812), writer and collector, who acquired it while studying in Jena in 1780-2 from Johann Gottfried Eichhorn (1752-1827), professor of theology and one of the founders of the Higher Criticism. Ribay's manuscripts were bought in 1804 by Miklós Jankovich (1772-1846), whose collection, including nine Slavonic cyrillic manuscripts, was acquired by the Library in 1836.

Plate 57

95

Molebny, 17th/18th century

Paper. No watermarks are now visible, as a result of the damage to the paper and subsequent restoration; in the endpapers, an unidentified mark (fig.124).

33 leaves; modern stamped foliation, 1-33. Size of leaves: 210×155 mm.

Collation: now bound as a series of bifolia, one gathering of four (ff.25-28), and a singleton (f.33), but this reflects the mounting of the leaves after restoration, and not the original composition of the book. There are no signatures.

Layout: 24-26 ll./p., within a ruled border 195-205×135-145 mm. The layout imitates that of a seventeenth- or eighteenth-century Ukrainian printed book.

Hand: a late, rather upright and condensed semiuncial.

Ink: brownish-black; red (seriously faded) for titles, initials and rubrics.

Binding: modern, marbled paper on card, 220×165mm, half-bound.

Condition: seriously stained and corroded, and in many places the text is almost totally illegible. Heavily restored throughout.

Decoration: one miniature and rather crude pen-and-ink headpieces, initials and tailpieces. The style of the decoration is derived from that of printed books.

f.8v: a full-page drawing of St Basil, within an ornamented frame.

ff.1, 9, 12v, 17, 23, 24, 29: headbands with foliage or figure representations.

Red and black six- or seven-line outline initials with floral ornamentation; on f.29 a big, eleven-line letter.

ff.8, 12, 16v: tailpieces representing floral motifs and vases, and a baroque motif.

Contents:

(ff.1-8) Service of prayer for the healing of a sick man
(ff.8v-12) Service of exorcism
(ff.12v-16v, 17-22v, 23-23v) [three illegible texts]
(ff.24-25v) Послѣдованїе молебное ко ѿгнанїю уародѣанїѧ
(ff.26-27) Ѵинъ ѡсѱѣнїѧ новыхъ сѱѣнничҁскихъ Ѻдѣждъ
(ff.27v-28v) [blank]
(ff.29-33v) [an illegible text]

Language: Synodal Church Slavonic.

Provenance: written in the Ruthenian area.

39. Quart. Eccl. Slav. 6

Nomocanon, 16th century (second quarter)

Paper. Watermark: boar (fig.125), very similar to Mareş 341 (1528); in the endpapers, a fragmentary coat of arms.
[ii]+137+[i] leaves; modern stamped foliation [i-ii], 1-134, pencil foliation 135-137 on the three last leaves, [138]. Size of leaves: 200×145 mm.

Collation: I^{6}, $II\text{-}XI^{12}$, XII^{12} (-12). Unsigned.

Layout: 20 ll./p., written area 150×105 mm, except in the 7th gathering (ff.67-78v), which has 23 ll./p., written area 148×110 mm.

Hand: a regular upright semiuncial/bookhand; titles in majuscules or simple vjaz'.

Ink: black; red for titles, initials and rubrics.

Binding: modern, marbled paper on cardboard; half bound. One modern flyleaf at each end, together with one older one at the front.

Condition: severe damage to the last three leaves, and evidently some material missing at the end; otherwise minor damage, generally restricted to the edges of the leaves. Restored.

Decoration: one headpiece of the Balkan interlaced type, numerous red or red-and-black pen-flourished initials, and a border.

f.1: a headpiece of four intersecting circles formed of thick, double vegetal stems, ending with large half-leaves at the upper part and flanking a small cross; a thick hatched stem at the left side; the whole area 60×115 mm. Red outlines, dark brown and red interstices, green leaves.

Two- to eight-line linear and outlined initials at the articles and their subdivisions; the largest and most lavishly ornamented ones precede prayers, Biblical readings, Psalms and other texts on ff.102v, 124, 125, 125v, 126v, 127, 128v, 130, 131, 131v, 132, 133, 134v, 135, 137. All are precisely drawn; the ornament includes dense groups of arrow-like buds on the stems, fine vegetal finials, dots and strokes, and hatched foliage around triangular floral motifs. An "eye" is sometimes inscribed in the round parts of the largest letters, whose stems are of composite character.

f.1: A red-and-black penwork border starting from the initial and running through the lower and outer margins; it consists of hatched elongated leaves and tendrils ending in small triangle leaves, and ends in a head with a triangular hat (or crown?).

In several places small hands "holding" an inserted word in the lower margins.

Contents:

(ff.1-53) правила ст҃ыⷯ ап҃лъ и стыⷯ седⷨи събоⷬ | прп҃дныⷯ и бг҃оносныⷯ ѿць нашиⷯ ѿ еп҃пⷭкⷯ | и ѿ м'ниⷯѡ, и ѿ ереѡⷯ и ѿ людеⷯ мирⷭкыⷯ | заповѣди въсѧкїа и поꙋченїа всѣⷨ хрⷭтїаноⷨ

(ff.53-74v) пакы сѐ заповѣⷣⷨ йныѐ ѿ законныⷯ | книгаⷯ. ѿ сърѡⷣствїи. и ѿ ꙁапрѣщен'ныⷯ бра|цѣⷯ. и ѿ раꙁличен'ныⷯ степенеⷯ. словѡ

(ff.74v-87v) А сѐ пакы ѿ йнокѡⷯ їереѡⷯ и про | чаа главы ѿ смѣрен'номꙋдрыⷯ въсѣхъ

(ff.87v-94) поꙋченїе ст҃го и великаго василїа къ и|нокѡⷨ. слово бж҃ие

(ff.94-94v) ѿ правиⷧ. ст҃ого събора иже въ аг'гирѣ съшеⷣшиⷯсѧ ст҃ыⷯ ѿц҃.

(ff.94v-97v) Степени сърѡⷣствоⷨ.

(ff.97v-102) Изложенїе ѿ прави́ въ православнѣй врѣ. [sic]

(ff.102-104) Изложенїе дроуго͡ѐ. ѿ оу́стинїана изложено са́модръжца.

(ff.104-105) ѿ заповѣдей сты́ а́по́стлъ.

(ff.105v-112v) **Miscellaneous canons** [from various sources]

(ff.113-134) чи́н попѹ ѐгда прѣста́ви͡лса

Language: Church Slavonic of an East Slavonic recension strongly influenced by Bulgarian orthography: while the distribution of ъ and ь largely follows the Tărnovo norms, ж is used as the equivalent of оу/ю and [ja] is represented by ѧ or а.

Inscriptions:

front flyleaf: [...]гочи коли в[...]ъ добро [...|...]стити замѣшати оудонское мо| [.....]

front flyleaf: лѣкарство на костѹ | ложкѹ андрѣшь соль полфо͡чт[..] | полфоть вабакѹнѹ долганъ масло | ходь такое старое или новое Сѣр|ка за два дѣткы, на еднѹ пе|рсонѹ должанъ на табакѹ, и | сѣркѹ тажо, и соль тото | намѣшати оу масло и гѹсто | ѡбы твердыбыло, и тимъ | маститиса, и твердо грѣ|тиса и печиса разъ тоть | оуучинти, лишить, а коль | не погыбать и еще болше ма|стити треба, и печиса

ff.1v-2: по͡до̇влет ‖ порты

f.7v: шырота зѐнага а высота нѣнга[...]

f.67v: [...] напацьканга О[...] ивань писавь | [...] равѹвь [...] ижимѹ вь

f.112v: ѿцѐве сты́, ци видитѐ вы, | ꙗки вамь красны̇ погрѣвь | справѹю͡т. алѐ во бы то́ сѧ не та͡ | и вамь справовати́ догань | нѐ кѹрити та́бакѹ не врати́ | [...]

f.112v: [...] | маткѹ его сты́ю, ѡпѣкѹкѹ нашѹ [...] которага [...] завшитокь народъ х҃стга́скїи, моли͡т сн҃ѹ своемѹ любомѹ и вогѹ нашемѹ, миломѹ | за на҆ грѣшны̇ [...]

f.125v: мигаль | ааввгдежзз

f.137: з сига гри [..|..] ченш[...]

Provenance: written in the Ruthenian area. Given by Antal Hodinka in 1909.

Plate 58

40. Quart. Eccl. Slav. 19
Panegyricon, 16th century (c.1580)

Paper. Watermark: anchor (fig.126) very similar to Mošin Anchor 2469 (1570-80); anchor (fig.127) very similar to Mošin Anchor 2530 (1582); anchor (fig.128) similar to Mošin Anchor 1888 (1581); in ff.183 and 184, hart (fig.129), type Piccard Hirsch 902-903 (1638); it could, however, be an 18th-century mark, cf. Siniarska-Czaplicka 1983: 1105-1111. i+182+ii+i leaves; modern pencil foliation [i], 1-184, [185]. Size of leaves: 205×135 mm.

Collation: I-XV^8, (14 leaves), XVIII-XIX^8, (32 leaves). The order of ff.121-134 and 151-182 is very seriously disrupted; they have been made up into gatherings during restoration, but bear no relation to their original sequence. The complete gatherings are signed in the lower margin of the first recto and last verso, а̃-ѕ҃ї, їі, ѕ҃ї; there are also signatures к҃а on ff.151, 158v, к҃в on f.159 and к҃ on f.178.

Layout: 22 ll./p., written area 155×95 mm.

Hand: a small (x-height=2mm) informal semiuncial. Simple majuscule title on f.1; occasional red initials with rudimentary decoration.

Ink: brownish-black; red for titles and initials.

Binding: dark-brown ornamented leather on bevelled boards, 220×145 mm, restored. Three raised bands on the spine, two new clasps. Gold and blind tooling. Triple fillets at the edges, a roll-stamped rinceau border. A roll-stamped bead motif frames the centre panel and joins its corners with those of the border; the centre-piece is a lozenge with the Crucifixion; the corners have the images of the Evangelists with captions. Around the centre-piece are impressed four groups of four small rosettes in circles and four five-petal rosettes between them. The vertical and horizontal strips between the border and the panel are stamped respectively with the five-petal rosettes and big eight-petal ones. On the lower cover the composition is identical, except that the centre-piece has a medallion within a floral frame, fairly similar to Laucevičius 1976: №134 (17th century) and the corner pieces are impressed with a wavy palmette-like motif on a hatched ground, very much like those on Kiril Gomirec's binding of 1715, cf. Janc 1974: plate 105 and similar to MSPC Grujić 20 (16th century), cf. Janc 1974: plate 88. A lily-cross motif surrounded by the smallest rosettes is repeatedly stamped on the spine. The whole design has affinities with manuscript SA 4 from the Library of Serbian Orthodox Eparchy of Buda (16th century), cf. Sindik, Grozdanović-Pajić, Mano-Zisi 1991: 246. One modern flyleaf at each end; at the back, two old flyleaves, and a fragment of a third (or of a pastedown) stuck to the modern flyleaf.

Condition: a certain amount of staining and some disruption of the leaves; otherwise good.

Decoration: very simple, of red initials with dots (or buds) on their stems.

Contents: НА҃ЛО̀ СЬ Б҃МЬ СЬ̃ ПАГЄРИ̃ | сьбранно на госпо̃скїе праз҃никь̃. ѿ м҃ца | сѐ. до м҃ца а̀вгоу̃та

(ff.1-3) иже вь ст҃ы̃ ѿ҃ца наше̃ | їѡ̀ан҃на а̀рхїеп҃кпа кон҃стантина града. | ѕла̃ꙋста̃ слово вь наче̃ лѣ̀ йлик҃тоу

Incipit: У҃ю̃на православны̃ трьжа̃тва̀а · свѣ̃тлы̃ | м̃ннꙋ̃кы̃нѐ паметѝ

99

Explicit: блгоѣтїю и | уⷧколюбїе́ⷨ · гаⷣ нашеⷢ їѡуⷯа . емоуⷤ слⷶ и дрьжава сь | въ|значелныⷨ ѡⷰемь й прⷵтыⷨ й животворѣщимь дхⷪⷨ | й ннⷉа й прⷩо й вь | вѣкы вѣкѡⷨ аминⷤ

(ff.3-6) мⷰа сеⷢ вⷤ. и. слово на рожⷣьство прѣⷮтїе | влⷣце наше бцⷣе и прⷩо дⷣвы марїе. | иже вь стыⷯ ѡⷰа нашеⷢ а́ндрⷣѣа критⷪкаго

Incipit: Вьсакь улⷦь хотⷣѣи похвалити уто любо хвалить | лить

Explicit: и ми те поеⷨ, ѡⷰа славеще й сⷩа й стго | дⷯа · вь вѣкⷤ аминь

(ff.6-7v) мⷰа сеⷢ дⷣ днⷤ слⷪ на въⷣвижент́е уⷤтнаго | и животворⷣѣщаⷢ крⷪта. иже вь стыⷯ ѡⷰа нашего | архⷣїепⷦпа коⷩстантина граⷣ їѡ злаⷮгустаго

Incipit: Вьса претрьпⷣѣ хⷵ бⷣ нашь наⷤ ради

Explicit: и радоⷮти и веселⷣꙗ | всаукаа испльнивша. ѡⷰоу слⷶ сⷣно̇ⷨ й стымь | дⷯомь . й ннⷉа и пⷩно й вⷤ векⷤ вⷤкⷤ аминь

(ff.7v-9) вⷤ тажⷣе днⷤ слⷪⷢ їѡ злаⷮго уⷤтомоу крⷪтоу

Incipit: Гдⷣѣ ти а́де побⷣѣда · гдⷣѣ ти сьмрⷣьти желѡ̇.

Explicit: ѡⷰи видⷣѣще и покланꙗюще́ · ѡⷰоу слава | и сⷩоу сь дⷯѡⷨ стымь · вь | вⷣѣкы векⷤ а́миⷩ

(ff.9-15) мⷰа сеⷢ вⷤ кⷤ. иже вь стⷨⷣ ѡⷰа нашего | їѡанⷩа архⷣїепⷦпа коⷩстантина граⷣ | злаⷮго. слово похвалⷩое їѡанⷩоу бⷤгословⷣ

Incipit: Їѡанⷩь вь ефесⷣѣ асистⷣѣмь їѡанⷩь а́сискаа | похвала

Explicit: единь дⷯ стⷤ. просⷣщꙗе всⷤ · едино бⷤⷤтво · томоу слⷶ вⷤ вⷣⷤ а́миⷩ

(ff.15-22v) мⷰа ѡ̇. иⷤ. оугⷣпⷩїе | стго апⷧⷶ еⷮⷢⷣꙗⷩлиста | лоукы

Incipit: Аще правⷣѣнаго паметⷤ | хⷤⷨⷶⷣꙗти сьврⷣьшати

Explicit: блгодⷣѣтїю | й улⷦолюбⷣꙗемⷤ гаⷣ нашего їоухⷶ · емоуⷤ слⷶва | сь бⷣⷣзначелныⷨ | ѡⷰемь · й стымь й животворⷣещимь дⷯомь. и ннⷉа и прⷩо и вь вⷤкы [...]

(ff.22v-27v) моуⷤⷤⷩїе стго й славнаго велⷪкомⷪⷩⷣⷣⷶника | хⷤⷶ димитрїа

Incipit: Маⷤꙗⷣꙗнь иже їⷤⷤⷩⷢⷤꙗ покоривь гоⷤⷤⷤⷤꙗти й сьвроматⷣꙗⷣꙗти

Explicit: мⷰа ѡ̇ · вⷤ · кⷤ · црⷤⷶⷤⷤꙗюⷤⷤꙗⷤⷤꙗ нами гⷤⷤ наⷤꙗⷤⷤꙗ̇моу їоухⷤⷤꙗ · емоуⷤꙗⷤ | поⷤꙗⷤⷤꙗютⷤⷤꙗ слⷶⷤⷤꙗ уⷤⷤꙗⷤ и поклⷶ|нꙗⷤⷤꙗте · сь ѡⷰемь й стⷣⷤ дⷯⷤ̇ · вⷤ вⷣⷤⷤꙗ а́миⷩ

(ff.27v-28v) похⷤⷤ̇ⷶ стⷪмⷤⷤ велиⷤⷩⷩⷪⷤ̇коу димитрⷤꙗⷣ̇ю

Incipit: Днⷤ единогⷤⷤꙗ̇нⷤⷤ̇о въⷣⷤꙗⷤ̇пⷤⷤⷨ̇ рекоуⷤⷣⷤꙗⷤ̇ще · раⷤⷤꙗⷤ̇исе

Explicit: тройⷤ̇це · ѡⷰа й сⷩа й стⷤⷤꙗⷤ̇го дⷯа живо|творⷤⷤꙗⷤ̇ещⷤⷤꙗⷤ̇аго · и ннⷉа и прⷩо и вⷤ вⷣⷤ̇ | вⷣⷤⷨⷤ̇ а́миⷩ

(ff.28v-34v) мⷰа ноⷤⷤꙗⷤ̇мрⷤⷣꙗⷤ̇ꙗ вⷤ .и̇. слово похвалⷩое | уⷩⷩⷤⷤⷨⷤ̇оⷩаⷤ̇челⷩⷤⷤꙗⷤⷤꙗⷤⷤꙗⷤⷤꙗⷤⷤꙗⷤ̇никоⷤⷤꙗⷤ̇ⷨ михаⷤⷤꙗⷤ̇илоу и гаⷤⷤꙗⷤⷣⷤ̇рⷤⷤꙗⷤⷩ̇илоу. творⷤⷩⷤꙗⷤ̇те климента епⷦпа

Incipit: Наста праⷤⷣⷤꙗⷤ̇нолюбⷤꙗⷤ̇чⷤꙗⷤ̇и, прⷣⷤⷤꙗⷤ̇свⷣⷤⷤꙗⷤ̇тⷤⷤꙗⷤ̇лое трⷤⷤꙗⷤ̇ьжⷤꙗⷤ̇|ство

Explicit: млⷣⷤⷤꙗⷤ̇тивⷤꙗⷤ̇и влⷪⷣⷤ̇ко · тебⷣⷤⷤꙗⷤ̇ѣ во поⷤⷤꙗⷤⷣⷤ̇ютⷤ̇ⷤ всака | слⷶва уⷤⷤꙗⷤ̇асть й покланⷤꙗⷤ̇ꙗⷩте · сь | ѡⷰемь й стⷤⷤꙗⷤⷨⷣⷤ̇ дⷯⷤ̇ⷪ · й ннⷉа и прⷩо й вь вⷣⷤⷤꙗⷤ̇кы вⷣⷤⷤꙗⷤ̇кⷤⷤꙗⷤⷨⷤ̇ а́миⷩ

(ff.35-38) мⷰа ноемрⷣⷤꙗⷤ̇ꙗ. вⷤ. аⷣ̇і. повⷣⷤⷤꙗⷤ̇сть уⷤⷤꙗⷤ̇ти | житⷤⷣꙗⷤ̇ꙗ стⷤⷤꙗⷤ̇го великомⷪⷩⷣⷤ̇ⷩника вⷤ црⷣⷤ̇ | стⷤⷤꙗⷤ̇ефана срⷤⷤꙗⷤ̇ьⷪⷤꙗⷤⷤ̇кⷪⷤⷤꙗⷤ̇аго иⷤⷤꙗⷤ̇же вⷤ дⷤⷣⷤꙗⷤ̇ѣаⷩⷤⷤꙗⷤ̇е. сьпⷤⷤꙗⷤ̇писа|ⷩⷤⷤꙗⷤ̇но григорⷤⷣⷤ̇ⷨⷤ минⷤⷤꙗⷤ̇хⷤⷨⷤ̇ иⷤⷤꙗⷤ̇гоуⷤⷤꙗⷤ̇меⷩⷤⷤꙗⷤ̇оуⷤ̇ тⷪⷤⷤꙗⷤⷢⷤ̇ ОБИТⷤⷤꙗⷤ̇Еⷤⷤꙗⷤⷧⷤ̇И

Incipit: Бⷣⷤⷤꙗⷤ̇ѣше й се велика й славⷩⷤⷤꙗⷤ̇а срⷤⷤꙗⷤ̇ьⷪⷤꙗⷤ̇вⷤⷤꙗⷤ̇ькⷣⷤⷤꙗⷤ̇аго еⷤⷤꙗⷤⷤⷣⷤ̇зⷤⷤꙗⷤⷤꙗⷤⷤꙗⷤ̇ыка

Explicit: ꙗⷤⷤꙗⷤ̇ко все плодⷤꙗⷤ̇ꙗ жрⷤⷤꙗⷤ̇ьтвоу приⷤⷤꙗⷤ̇е̇тⷤⷤꙗⷤⷯⷤ̇ и̇. боⷤꙗⷤ̇у нашемоу слⷶва вⷤ векⷤⷤꙗⷤⷧⷤ̇ амиⷩ

(ff.38v-40) юⷤⷤꙗⷤⷣⷤ̇ѡ пришⷤⷤꙗⷤ̇ьⷤⷤꙗⷤ̇твⷤꙗⷤ̇и стⷤⷤꙗⷤ̇го николи кь стаⷤⷤꙗⷤⷣⷤ̇оⷤⷤꙗⷤ̇у вⷤ коⷩⷤⷤꙗⷤ̇танⷤⷤꙗⷤ̇ти граⷤⷤꙗⷤⷣ̇ посⷤⷤꙗⷤ̇еⷤⷤꙗⷤ̇ци емⷤⷤꙗⷤⷤꙗⷤⷤꙗⷤⷤꙗⷤ̇ зⷤⷤꙗⷤ̇еници

Incipit: Уⷤⷤꙗⷤ̇то еⷤⷤꙗⷤ̇же ѡⷤⷤꙗⷤ̇соⷤꙗⷤⷤꙗⷤ̇у пⷣⷤⷤꙗⷤ̇ѣтⷤⷤꙗⷤ̇ое лⷤⷤꙗⷤ̇ѣто тоⷤⷤꙗⷤ̇гоⷤⷤꙗⷤ̇ва прⷣⷤⷤꙗⷤ̇ѣбⷤⷤꙗⷤ̇ыⷤⷤꙗⷤ̇ва|нⷤⷣⷤꙗⷤ̇їⷤⷤꙗⷤ̇а

Explicit: й мⷩⷤⷤꙗⷤⷪⷤ̇ⷢ мⷩⷤⷤꙗⷤ̇ожⷤⷤꙗⷤ̇ьⷤⷤꙗⷤ̇тво ѡⷤⷤꙗⷤ̇роⷤⷤꙗⷤ̇уⷤⷤꙗⷤ̇жⷤⷤꙗⷤ̇еⷩⷤⷤꙗⷤ̇оⷤⷤꙗⷤ̇сⷩⷤⷤꙗⷤⷣⷤ̇їⷤⷤꙗⷤ̇ⷩ того ѡⷤⷤꙗⷤ̇кⷤⷤꙗⷤ̇роⷤⷤꙗⷤ̇уⷤⷤꙗⷤ̇жⷤⷤꙗⷤ̇аше

(ff.40-50v) мⷰа ноⷤⷤꙗⷤ̇. вⷤ. гⷤꙗⷤⷤⷣⷤ̇і. слⷪово коⷤꙗⷤⷤꙗⷤⷣⷤ̇мⷤⷤꙗⷤⷤꙗⷤ̇ы вести|ⷤⷤꙗⷤ̇ктора. [sic] ѡ̇ прⷤⷤꙗⷤ̇ѣнесⷤⷤꙗⷤⷩⷤ̇їⷤⷤꙗⷤ̇и моⷤꙗⷤ̇щⷤⷤꙗⷤ̇и їⷤⷤꙗⷤ̇ѡанⷩⷤⷤꙗⷤ̇а | злаⷤⷤꙗⷤⷢⷤ̇таⷤⷤꙗⷤ̇го архⷤⷣⷤꙗⷤ̇їⷤⷤꙗⷤ̇епⷦⷤⷤꙗⷤ̇па конⷤⷤꙗⷤ̇ьⷤⷤꙗⷤ̇стантина града

100

Incipit: Слышасе въсако валиь ѿ х҃олюбьі҆вое сьбранї҆е

Explicit: и҆миже ѿ ζемлѧ҆ вьзвишьсе, сь б҃ль | жити спо҃бытсе· е҆моуже слава и
дрьжава | вь в҃екы а҆минь

(ff.50v-57v) м҃ца но̅. вь к҃а д҃нь. слово с҃того епифа|нї҆а а҆рхї҆епк҃па к҃уприскаго. ѿ жити |
пр҃ест꙯ые б҃ци ,

Incipit: Ѡ҆ и҆зв҃естн҃е истинн҃еи б҃ци й про҃ д҃вы | марї҆е

Explicit: и тев҃е ради сь намїй· | въспеваеми сь ѡ҃це. и д҃хо꙯ с҃тыꙁ· вь в҃екы҆а҆мин꙯

(ff.57v-59) м҃ца но̅. вь .л҃. прои҆авлю҆нї҆е кр҃щенї҆а роу|ска ѿ с҃того а҆п꙯ла а҆ндреа. како пришь |
вь роусї꙯ю и б҃лвти м҃есто и кр꙯ть постави | й҆деже есть градь к҃іевь ѿноу꙯д

Incipit: С҃томоу а҆п꙯лоу а҆н҆дрею живоущомоу вь сино|п҃е

Explicit: ѿ зслословеще с҃тою тройцоу. ѡ҃ца и с҃на | й с҃того д҃ха· емоу꙯ сла꙯ й
дрьжава· υасть й покла|нѧнї҆е вь в҃екы҆ а҆минь

(ff.59-61v) м҃ца де꙯ .д҃. мн҃ї҆е с҃ты велиꙗ҆мн꙯ц вар҆варї҆и

Incipit: При маꙁ꙯їмї҆ан҆е в꙯еконейшимь ц҃ри | в҃е некто д꙯їѡскорь

Explicit: й вь коупели с҃тые варварїи · силою | х҃а б҃а нашего · емоу꙯ сла꙯ вь в҃екы
в҃еко꙯ а҆минь

(ff.61v-65v) м҃ца де꙯ вь .е҃. д҃нь житї҆е с҃того ѡ҃ца на|шего савы ї҆ер҃л҆м꙯каго

Incipit: Б҃лвень б҃ь· й҆ ѡ҃ць г҃а нашего ї҆оух҃а

Explicit: иже сьвише ѿ б҃а дан҆ное | емоу ѿ х҃а б҃а наше꙯· емоу꙯ сла꙯ сь ѡ҃це꙯ и с҃ты꙯
д҃хо꙯ а҆ми꙯

(ff.65v-69) м҃ца де꙯ вь .ꙃ҃. слово | похвал҆но ѻ̑ рож҆дⷣ|нїю и ѿ жити иже вь с҃ты꙯ | ѡ҃ца
нашего а҆рх҆їереа и υю꙯|творца х҃ва николи мир꙯|ликук꙯аго

Incipit: С꙯е настои꙯ т браті҆е, светлою праꙁ꙯анⷣ҃тво

Explicit: единомоу б҃оу · сь в҃еꙁнаυелны сн҃омь его ї҆оух҃х꙯мь, и с҃ты꙯ д҃хо꙯| и н҃нѧ и
пр҃но и вь в҃екы в҃екомь а҆минь

(ff.69-73v) слово на рож҆ество х҃во иже вь с҃ты꙯ ѡ҃ца на|шего ї҆ѡан҆на а҆рхї҆еп꙯кпа коньстантина
гра꙯дⷣ

Incipit: Υто̑ с꙯е ꙁнаменї҆е и пр҃ереканї҆е вижⷣ҃оу

Explicit: вса υ҃лколюб꙯ствї҆е꙯ | сьтвориль е҆си· теб҃е повⷣает слава й дрь|жава й
н҃нѧ и пр҃но й вь в҃екы в҃екомь ами꙯

(ff.73v-74v) ї҆ѡан҆на а҆рхї҆еп꙯кпа коньстантина гра꙯дⷣ слово на рож҆ество х҃во ѿ пр҆роу꙯тва

Incipit: С꙯е во в҃еꙁвеснаа и таинаа, пр҃емоуг҆роти | твою

Explicit: и ѡ҆дрьжанї҆е его концїи | ꙁемлѧ· томоу слава вь в҃екы҆ а҆минь

(ff.74v-76) ї҆ѡан҆нⷣ҃а е҆кьсар҆х҆а вльгар҆скаго на рож꙯тво | х҃во слово

Incipit: Х҆оу прав҃едномоу сл҃нцоу ѿ д҃вы въставшꙋ

Explicit: праведное сл҃нце· емоуже слава сь ѡ҃цемь | й с҃тымь д҃хомь и н҃нѧ и пр҃но
й вь веки ами꙯

(ff.76-78) вь. к҃ꙃ. слово на сьборь пр҃ес꙯тї҆ю б҃це | ї҆ѿ . ꙁла꙯γуста. тлькованї҆е е҆ѵа҆лї҆кое

Incipit: Б҃ь оуво мо҃ус꙯е꙯ пороугасе фараѿ҆ноу

Explicit: и҆стинномоу б҃оу и сп҃оу наше|мꙋ· емоу꙯ повⷣает слава и υа꙯ть й дарь вь
в҃е|кы в҃екомь ами꙯

(ff.78-82) м҃ца ге̅. вь .а҃. слово похвалное с҃том꙯ꙋ | василю҆ . творенї҆е гр꙯їгорї҆а в҃госло|ва
а҆рх҆їеп꙯кпа коньстанти꙯ града

Incipit: Принесоу ѿ василї҆а оуво многы꙯ вь ветхы꙯

Explicit: словесей достоино. | ѿ х҃е ї҆с҃е г҃и нашемь· е҆моуже слава й дрьжава· | сь
ѡ҃це꙯· сь с҃ты꙯ д҃хо꙯· й н҃нѧ й пр҃но й вь веки в҃ек:

101

(ff.82-86) мца гнѣварта. въ .ѕ. слово на стое | бгоꙗвлѣнїе їѡа́н'на [sic] архїе|пка коньстантина гра́ | ѯлатꙋ́ста.

Incipit: Источни еѵа́гкы҆ оу́ченїи ѿврьсти има́т || потокъ

Explicit: Прослави́м оу́бо ꙗвльшагосе ха̀ ба̀ | нашего. ꙗко томоу по́бает' вьсака слава | й црьво. съ ѡ҃це́м й съ сты҆м дхѡ̀. й нн҃га й пр҃:

(ff.86-87) въ таже дн҃ь слово ѿ еже колико соу́т крꙉенїи

Incipit: Пречтⷮою к҃щенїе га̀ ба̀ и спа̀ нашего їоухⷶ̀

Explicit: двои еста́тавь · бжⷮтва й улⷸⷮтва: | боу наш:

(ff.87v-89v) мца гнⷷ. а҃і. повⷷ ѿ ѡ҃ци ѳеѡ́си

Incipit: Оц҃ь нашь ѳеѡ́сїе измлада начеть бо|ꙗтисе ба̀

Explicit: емоуже изⷣлада [sic] по|слѣдовавь · томоу слава въ векы҆ а́минь

(ff.89v-92) мца гнⷷварта. въ .д҃і. дн҃ь июⷣ стго саве | архїепкпа срьбска ѿ раслаблꙗⷩнⷶ̀

Incipit: Въ врѣме же некое пришⷣшоу стомоу саве | съ самодрьж'цемь стефанѡ́м

Explicit: на дрьжавоу е́го | противно смꙗгахоу начинати:- боу нашем:

(ff.92-96) июⷣ стго саве ѡ҆ оувѣрⷷнїи оу́гарьⷶкаго | кралꙗ̀. й прочии е҆реси латиⷩ

Incipit: Испрьва ненавидⷷй добра дїаволь

Explicit: въ гро|бе лежаща имамїи · славеще ѿца и сна и стⷢ дха:

(ff.96-98v) мца гнⷷ. въ .ѕ҃і. дн҃ь слово ѡ҆ житїю стго | а҆нтонїа великаго

Incipit: При велицемь цри коньстантине бы҆ вели|кы҆ а҆нтонїе

Explicit: ꙗко вити емоу живота · р҃ѐ лѣть · ѡ҆ хѣ̀ | гсⷵе ги҃ нашⷷ. емоуⷤ слава съ ѡце́м й сты҆м дхѡ́м й нн҃:

(ff.98v-101) мца гнⷷ. въ .к҃. повⷷ ѿ стⷷ҃й евѳѵми

Incipit: Слиши ѿ всѐ, ѿ блⷤⷷнне евⷷ҃ѳими

Explicit: патрїархоу въ їерⷧⷶме соущоу | а҆настасїю. боу нашемоу слава въ вⷷ а́минⷩ

(ff.101-104) мца. фе́. въ .в҃. дн҃ь слово на срⷮѣтенїе | га̀ ба̀ й спа̀ нашего їоухⷶ̀ · иже въ сты҆ⷯ | ѿца нашего архїепкпа коньстаньтина гра́|да їѡа́н'на ѯлатꙋ́стаго

Incipit: Сѐ пакы свⷷтлое празⷣньтво наста · праⷤникь праⷤника прѣспеваю

Explicit: причестникѡ́м | бы́ти всемь сты҆мⷧь · й съ ними хвалꙋ̀ въѯⷶ̀|ꙗти · въкоупⷷ съ ѿце́м й съ сты҆м дхⷪ̀. и нн҃га и пр҃:

(ff.104-108) кѵрⷮла а҆рхїепкпа їерⷧⷶмьⷶкаго слово. | на срⷷтенїе хⷡ҃о

Incipit: Раⷣу́се зелѡ̀ дьщи сїѡна

Explicit: съ единороⷣнимь сно́м · й прѣстымь блⷢⷮымь | й животворⷷщиⷨ дхⷪⷨь. и нн҃га й прⷩ҃о и в:

(ff.108-111) мца фер'варта. въ .г҃і. дн҃ь. похвалꙗ҆|нїе й ѿчести житїа. прѣпо́бⷣна сꙋ́мешна | срьбⷶкаго. мѵрѡ́точⷶца

Incipit: Тогⷣа влⷣⷮвоующоу срьбⷶкымїи землꙗ|мїи · блⷢⷵⷮоу́тивомоу самⷪрьжцоу стефа|ноу́

Explicit: въ монастири гл҃емⷪ | хылⷶⷩⷶдарⷶ. славеще ѿца й сна · й стго дха и нн҃:

(ff.111-114v) слово ѡ҆ мѵрⷪⷮ҆иⷥлитїю прѣпо́бⷣна сꙋ́мешⷶⷶ

Incipit: Вьса възможнаа тебⷷ ги҃ · вѣмь елика аще | вьсхощешїи

Explicit: тако въ своꙗ имⷷ ко|гожⷣо ѿпоущаеⷮ. славеще ѿца и сна и стⷪ дха

(ff.114v-120v) мца ферⷶвⷶ̀. к҃д. дн҃ь. слово на ѿврⷷте|нїе глави оу́тнⷶ пррⷪка прⷷтⷶⷶуе и крⷮⷮлꙗ | їѡⷶⷩ'на ѿ тлькованїа

Incipit: Правⷷни аще постигнеть скончатисе | въ покой боу́еть

Explicit: нап҇а́теи | избавлга́ѥ́тъ. ѿ х҃ѕ і́се г҃и нашемь· ѥмоуже слава въ векꙑ̀
вѣкѡ҃мь а́минь

(f.121-121v) [blank]

(ff.122, 127, 162-3, ?182) м҃ца мар҇·ѳа .к҃ѕ. слово на ст҃ое благове|щенїе: иже въ ст҃ꙑ҇х ѡц҃а
нашего і҃ѡ | а̑рхїепк҃па коньтантина града [incomplete and disrupted]

Incipit: Цр҃кꙑ҇ таинь праз҇а́ньтво праз҇оуимь дн҃ь [The end is missing.]

(ff.129-131v) Martyrdom of St George

Defective: begins with the words: .....кр҃тнаго провор҇ца. гіеѡ̑г҇їе воиномь |
ѿроужїе

Explicit: га́ко да ра́ю̑ще̑ | славіимь, ѡц҃а и сн҃а и ст҃го дх҃а· и н҃н҃га и пр҃н:

(ff.131v-134v) м҃ца ма́га. въ .ѕ҃. дн҃ь. слово ѿ прѣнесе́|нїи мощїи ст҃го ѡц҃а нашего
чю҃̑творца | а̑рхїепк҃па мирлїкꙑ́каго николи ѿ ми|рьскаго града въ барь градъ

Incipit: Пр҃но дльжнꙑ̀ ѥ̑смїи братїе· праз҇никꙑ̀ | бж҃їе творꙗ̑ще [lacking the end]

(f.135-135v) **May 25th: Third Invention of the Head of John the Baptist** [the end only]

Defective: begins with the words: ....паю глъбоко. ѡ̑бличив҇ше ѥго ересь

Explicit: исповедані́е ѥ̑го съхран҇ше· прослави҇ | ѡц҃а и сн҃а и ст҃го дх҃а и н҃н҃га и
пр҃но и въ век:

(ff.135v-137v) м҃ца ію҃нга. въ .г҃і. память пр҃но помина|ѥмаго и благоро̑наго и кроткаго
кн҃ѕга | лазара и сн҃ꙑ҇ множ҃тво благоро̑дꙑ̀

Incipit: Тогда сїре̑ въ сїе лѣто̑· бѣ некто цр҃ь на вас|тоцѣ имен҃ѣмь а̑моурать

Explicit: прѣдаше въ роуце г҃оу і҃оухх҃оу· ѥмоуже слава | и дрьжава съ ѡц҃емь и съ
ст҃ꙑ҇ дх҃омь. и н҃н҃га и пр҃но и въ векꙑ̀ вѣкомь а́минь

(ff.137v-143v) м҃ца ію҃. въ .к҃д. дн҃ь слово на рож҃ьство | ст҃го и славна̑ пр҃рка прт҇че
кр҃тлга і́ѡан҇а | тлькованїе еу҃лга

Incipit: Сл҃нцоу семоу хотѣщомоу видомоу изити | изъ прѣдѣла земльнаго

Explicit: ѿ добра | главо оу́тнаа роука иже достоина бꙑ҇· и по|врьсе преѥ̑ти г҃а
наше̑ і́оухх҃а [...|...] н҃н҃га и пр҃но и въ:

(ff.143v-148v) м҃ца ію҃лга. въ .к҃ѳ. дн҃ь иже въ ст҃ꙑ҇х ѡц҃а наше̑ | і́ѡан҇на а̑рхїепк҃па
коньтантина града зла́у|ста̑ похвала ст҃ꙑ҇ врьховни҇ а̑п҇лѡмь петроу | и павлоу

Incipit: Нб҃оу и земли редь вижоу настоѥщаго ради | праз҇ника

Explicit: имже | и съ нимже б҃оу нашемоу слава· съ прѣ|ст҃ꙑмь и благꙑмь и
животворещимь дх҃омь | и н҃н҃га и пр҃но и въ векꙑ̀ векѡ҃ а́ми҇

(ff.148v-150) м҃ца ію҃нга. въ .л҃. на сьборь в҃і а̑п҇лъ. | сказанїе і́ѡан҇на б҃гослова како при
чьте|нїи бꙑ̑ше г҃мь наши҇ і́оухх҃мь въ слоуженїе ѥго

Incipit: Въ оутрѣиже пакꙑ̀ видѣ і́ѡан҇нь і̑с҃а ходѣща

Explicit: съ нами все днꙑ̀ до скончанїа века. ѡц҃оу | слава съ сн҃омь и ст҃ꙑ҇ дх҃о҇
въ бѣсконеунїе вѣкꙑ̀

(ff.150-150v, 178-178v) м҃ца і́оу҇ въ .в҃. слово похвалное ѿ ст҃ꙑ҇ | бц҃и иже въ ст҃ꙑ҇х ѡц҃а
наше̑ кѵ̑рїла а̑рхїеп҇ па | а̑лезан҇рьска на положенїе рꙑзи [complete, though disrupted]

Incipit: Ра́уисе марїе пр҃но дв҃о прѣч҇таа

Explicit: и вьса тварь ѡ тѣ | ра́уѥтсе. и сн҃оу твоѥмоу покланга́ѥтсе. съ ѡц҃е̑ | и
ст҃ꙑ҇ дх҃о҇. и н҃н҃га и пр҃но и въ вѣкъ вѣкѡ҃ а́ми҇

(ff.153-155v, 171-171v) м҃ца ію҃лга .к҃. дн҃ь житїе ст҃го пр҃рка | илїе. ѡгнѥносного [incom-
plete and disrupted]

Incipit: Н҃н҃га ст҃озарноѥ сл҃нце нев҇наго кроуга
[The end is missing.]

(ff.170-170v, 156-156v) мц҃а а҆в'гоу́та. въ .а҃. слово ст҃ыⰿⰈ | мак'кавѣⱳ. иже въ ст҃ӹ ѿц҃а нашего | григорїа вⰓослова [the beginning and the end]

Incipit: Ст҃ыⰉ макавⰈ҆и настоѥ҆щеѥ҆ трьжⰈ҆тво

Explicit: і҃с х҃с и тога̅ | вⰆра и дн҃ь· томоу слава и҆ дрьжава и покла|нⰊанⰊⰔ. сь ѿц҃емь и҆ ст҃ыⰿ дх҃ⰿ въ вⰔкы вⰆк:

(ff.179-179v, 151-152v, 169-169v, 175)мц҃а а҆вгоу́та. въ .ѕ҃. слово на прⰆѿбра|женⰊⰔ г҃а б҃а и сп҃а нашеⰌ і҆оу́х҃а. иже въ ст҃ӹ | ѿц҃а нашеⰌ прокла патрїарха коⰐьстань|тина града [apparently complete, but disrupted]

Incipit: ПридⰈ́те дроуꙃⰀⰊ дн҃ь і҆е҆ѵⰉⰀⰊскыⰿ неⰈⰆноⷩ|сⰐⰆ прикоснⰈⰿсе

Explicit: и҆ нⰈⰉ|слⰔдованⰊⰉ поути е҆го· томоу слава и нⰐ҃га | и прⰐ҃о и҆ въ вⰆкⰊ вⰆкомь а҆минь

(ff.175v) а҆настасⰊа мниха слов на прⰆⱳⰉбраженⰊⰔ | ст҃оⰌ и свⰆтлое х҃во [the beginning only]

Incipit: Ѡ нⰊемже ре̅ лоука е҆ѵⰉⰍⰈⰍⰄⰈ. моⷱси и ⰊⰍⰊⰀ

(ff.172-172v, 157-158v) мц҃а а҆вгоу́та .е҃ⰊⰄ. дн҃ь. слово похва|л'ное на прⰆставлⰊⰔⰐⰊⰔ прⰆⱱ'тыⰔ бⰈⰍⰏⰊⰈ | наше бⱌⰈ и҆ прⰐ҃о дв҃ы марⰊⰔ сьтворено | климⰈⰐ'толь е҆пⰍⰍⰉⰍⰈ [disrupted]

Incipit: СⰈ нⰐ҃га свⰆтло праꙁⰀⰐⰈⰏⰍⰈ ликаствоⰔⰔ|щⰈ

Explicit: и҆ цр҃тво нⰈⰁⰐⰊⰔ и҆спросе|щⰊⰉ оў сн҃а своего. и г҃а нашего і҆оу́х҃а· е҆моⷤ | поⷣбаⰈⰔⰈ҆ть всака слава [...|...] й нⰐ҃га и҆ прⰐ҃о и҆ в:

(ff.158v-161v, 164-166, 168-168v, 173-173v) житⰊⰔ и҆ оусⰈⰍⰍⰐⰉⰕⰈⰐⰊⰔ уⰀⰏ̆ⰀⰄ҆наго прⰐ҃рⰍⰀ | и прⷣтуе и крⱄⰊⰈⰀⰉⰀ і҆ѡⰀⰐ'на. сьписан'но | ѿ оу҆ченика е҆го разоумна і҆ѡⰀⰐ'на сирⰆ | нарицаемаго мар'ка [disrupted]

Incipit: И҆спльнⰊⰐⰉⰍⰊⰍⰈ лⰈⰍⰕⰕⰈ пⰆть тⰊⰍⰍⰔⱅⰊ | и петⰊⰍⰈ столⰈ

(ff.167-167v, 174-174v, 176-177v, 180-180v, 123-124v, 126-126v, ?125-125v) въ соу́ⰍⰍⰍⰈⰎⰍⰍ а҆каⰍⰊⰎⰍⰍⱅⰈ поⰃⰆ польꙃⰐⰀⰀ | ѿ дрⰈⰌ'ныⱄ повⰈⰍⰍⰕⰈⰍ сьбраннⰀⰀ. й въспо|минанⰊⰔ ⱄⰀⰈⰊⰀⰔⱬⰊ иⰉⰈ прⰈⱄⰎⰀⰃⰐⰈ бⰊⰀ|вⱅⰀⰍⰎⱖ уⰔⰉⰈⰍⰊ. въⰐⰊⰈⰌⰀ перⱄⰉⰈ й варварⰊⰔ | цⰉⰊⰃⰉⰈⰀ бранⰊⰔⰂ̆ⰍⰉⰁⱖⰎⰊⱌⰈ. иⰉⰈ й погⰊⱖⰁⰉⰍⱄⰈ бⰈ̆Ⱅ̆ⰀⰂⰐⰉⰍ соуⰄⰉⱄ҆ и҆скоуⱄⰈⰐⱅⰊⰍ бⰊⰀⰂ̆ⰍⰈ. | град҃ь же нⰈⰂⰉⱖⰈⰍⰊ бⰊⰀ мⰊⰀⱅⰂⰀⰍⰊ бⱌⰈ. | й мⰊⰈⱖⰐⰉⰔ ⱳⱅⰉⰎⰈ поⰊⰈⱅⱄⰈ, блⰈⰃⰉⰀⰄⰈⰐⰊⰔ | несⰆⰄⰈⰎ'ное дн҃ь и҆меⰐⰉⰂⰉⰂ'ше [disrupted]

Incipit: Въ лⰈⱅ̆Ⰸⱖ и҆ⰉⰉⰀⰍ̆ⰎⰉⰀ цⰉⰀ грⰈⱖⰍⰉⰀⰃⰉ· хⰉⰉⱖⱄⰉⰉ | иⰉⰈ перⱄⰍⰉⰔ

Explicit: неизⰉⰈⱖ̆Ⱀ'ны̆ блⰈⰃⱄ полⰉⱖⱅⰊⰍⰊⰎⱖ· | блⰈⰃⰉⰈ̆ⱅⰊ̆ⰉⰔ и҆ уⰎ̆ⰍⰉⰎⰊⰉⰁ̆ⰊⰈⰍⰈ г҃а нашего і҆оу́х҃а | е҆моуже слава и҆ дрьжава въ вⰆкы вⰈⰍⰉ̆Ⰽ̆ ⰀⰌⰊⰐ̆

Language: Serbian Church Slavonic.

Inscriptions:

inside front cover: радꙋиса прⰈⱖⰍⰊⱄⱅⰀ дⰈⰂⰉ [repeated; also some other indecipherable scrawls]

inside front cover: ПачⰈⰎⱖ і҆ⰌⰀⰐⱖ

f.1: ⰔⰀⰍⰉ гⰈ і҃с х҃с | вⰀⰎⰀⰂⱖ ⱳⱌⱖ а҆минⱖ мⱖꙁⰀⰍⰉⰐ| г҃нⱖ ꙁп҃ⱁ [7089 = A.D.1581] лⰈⱅⰉ

f.121: СⰊⰀ книⰃⰀ глⰀⰃⰉⰎⰀⰀ поуⱖⰍⰈⰐⰊⰔ | ⱄⱅⰊⱅⰀⰎⱄⰍⰉⰈ при храⰍⰈ ст҃ыⱄⱖ | а҆плⰉⰂⱖ ПетⰉⰀ и҆ Па́вла, въ веⱄⰉ | титⰉⱅⱅ̆Ⰸ при ӗпⰍⰍⰈ а҆рсⰈ̆ⰐⰊⰉ Ра́дивⰉⰈⰂⰉⰍⱖ БудимскⰀⰃⰉ и҆ Сенⱅ|А҆ндрⰈⰉⱄⰍⰀⰃⰉ: СтолновⰈⰎⰈⱄ: СⰈⰃⰈⱅⱄ: | и҆ МⱖⰍⰀⱖⰍⰉⱄ: и҆ проⱖⰐⰉ̆

f.121v: СⰊⰀ Книга поⰂⱖⰍⰈ|нⰊⰔ храⰍⰀ | Ст҃ыⱄⱖ А҆пⰈⰎⱖ | петра и҆ павла в' СⰈⰎⰈ

f.183: поуⱖⰍⰈⰐⰊⰔ ⱄⱅⰊⱅⰈⰎⰈⰎⱄⰍⰉ

f.183: СⰊⰀ книга глⰀⰃⰉⰈⰍⰀⰀ поуⱖⰍⰈⰐⰊⰔ | стⰀ̆ⰍⰉⰈ при храⰍⰈ ⱄⱅⱖⱄⱖ перво|вⰈⰉⰍⰉⰂⰐⰊⱄⱖ а҆тⱁ́Ⰾⱖ пⰈ̆ⰉⰀ и҆ па́вла | и҆же есⱅⱖ в'селⰈ титⰉⱅⱅⰈ | лⰈⱅⰀ г҃дⰐⰀ 1784⁰ марта 207

104

f.183v: Благоро́днїи | Ста́ кни́га глаго́лемаа Поꙋче́нїе | ст҃ителское при хра́мѣ ст҃ыхъ | ап҃лъ петра й па́vла, 773°

f.184: Два́ днесь пресⷭ҇ще́ствена|гѡ ро́ждаетъ, й землѧ вертепь | непристꙋ́пномꙋ прино́ситъ, Аггли | сь паⷭ҇ⷮ҇рⷨми славословѧ́тъ, волсви | со ѕвѣ́здою пꙋтешествꙋютъ, на|съ во ра́ди роди́сѧ | отро́va младѡ превѣ́vныи в҃гь | амѝнь | 1774° | [..] Ное́мврa 19° | ꙗ̈ титошꙋ ве́си вⷢ҇оспасае́мїа

f.184v: marco[??] pawlowitz

f.184v: Ста́ кни́га имен꙰ема | поꙋче́нїе

f.184v: Ста́ кни́га йменvема́а Поꙋче́|нїе ӓще ю̈ кто́ ꙋ̈кра́детъ | Не бы́ло ѡ̈проще́нно Ни бла|гослове́но, в'селѣ титошѣ, | при хра́мѣ ст҃ыхъ ап҃лъ | петⷬ҇а й па́vла лѣ́та 1766° | ӓvгꙋ. 29°°

f.184v: Іере́й Пантелеи́монь

f.184v: монастирь ст҃ь вoꙗ́ни

last flyleaf: Да́димъ | Стефа́нъ же исполнь | вѣ́ри й сили творѧ́ше ꙁна|менна и ꙋ̈ꙋ́деса | в'лю́дехъ | в'лю́де́хъ ж живоτворѧ́щиⷯ

Provenance: of Serbian origin. The inscription on f.1 indicates that the manuscript was in existence by 1581; judging by the watermarks, it cannot have been written long before this date. The inscriptions indicate that in the eighteenth century the manuscript belonged to the Serbian community in the village of Titoš (Töttös, about 12 km south-west of Mohács); another inscription (on f.184v) mentions the monastery of Bodjani (Bogyán, in the former Bodrog megye, now in Serbia). Purchased on 29th August 1973 from János Krajcsovics.

A fragment of a Slavonic printed book, evidently one of those printed in Venice in the sixteenth century but bearing too little text to permit of a more precise identification, was extracted from the binding during restoration and is now kept separately, together with the old headbands.

Stefanović 2003.

Plates VII, 59

Miscellany, 17th century (1679?)

Paper. Watermark: three crescents (fig.130), similar to Nikolaev 249 (1673), Szentendre 104 (1665-75); crown surmounted by a star and crescent (fig.131), type Mošin-Grozdanović-Pajić VIIA, (1668-79).
93 leaves; modern stamped foliation, 1-87; the last six leaves are blank and unfoliated. Size of leaves: 197×142 mm.

Collation: I-X^8, XI^8 (-8), XII^8 (-7-8). Unsigned.

Layout: 25 ll./p., written area 150×95 mm; on ff.65v-74v, tables.

Hand: a small calligraphic Serbian bookhand. Elegant majuscule titles on ff.1 and 2. The scribe has been identified as Hristofor Račanin.

Ink: black; red for titles and initials. Red ink is also used extensively in the tables and occasionally for punctuation. Gold is used for the title on f.2. On ff.52-54 the scribe has used a different black ink, which has faded badly.

Binding: brown leather on card, 195×140 mm, Turkish in style except that there is no flap. Deeply impressed gilt tooling. On the upper and lower covers the pattern is identical: a thin triple border of "rope" kind framing the panel; a centre piece of an almond-shaped medallion with a smaller one inscribed in it, each bearing a different kind of rumi ornament. The corners are stamped with the same motif as the small medallion. The gold has been applied alternately on the ornament and on the backround. The inner sides of the covers are covered with bluish paper stamped with quadripartite floral motifs in black, consisting of tulip, carnation and another flower twice repeated. The binding could be contemporary with the book block; a possible place for its production is Sarajevo, but other arguments make both suggestions uncertain, cf. Kacziba 1999: 72-76.

Condition: very well preserved.

Decoration: refined, consisting of headpieces of the Balkan interlaced type, initials of two kinds, and illustrative tables; gold is extensively used. The decoration places the manuscript within a group of manuscripts written from the second quarter to the late 17th century in Serbia (Rača and Plevlja monasteries) and Bulgaria (Etropole and Sredna Gora region). The script and decoration the manuscript indicate that it is the work of Hristofor Račanin, cf. Kacziba 1999.

f.1: headpiece at the opening of the book consisting of a symmetrical floral motif of two composite leaves, whose intertwined stems are raised in between to form a cross-like figure; black, green, blue, red and carmine outlines, gold fillings.

f.2: a headband with a human mask in the centre, with vegetal stems growing from it; two of them form a pointed "hat" with a trefoil on top while another two coil in both directions into interlaces and circles with inscribed four-petalled flowers. The colouring is the same as above.

f.41v: a floral motif similar to that on f.1; red outlines, yellow and dark blue colouring.

Titles of red majuscules, with a limited number of ligatures and fine vegetal ornamentation.

f.2: a six-line interlaced initial of the Balkan type, with multi-coloured outlines and golden background.

Numerous two-to three-line red pen-flourished initials, a distinctive variety of the Neo-Byzantine type, known from Serbian and Bulgarian (Etropole School) manuscripts. The fine ornament consists of small buds, elegantly waving tendrils and leaves, and hatched lozenge-shaped buds, all set in intricate motifs at the bases of the letters.

f.65v: a table showing the phases of the moon; red-and-gold sun with a human face in the centre, surrounded by the phases of the moon, coloured in gold and blue.

ff.66-71v: twelve arch-framed calendar tables, each accompanied by a tinted drawing of the appropriate sign of the zodiac; the images are carefully depicted inside rectangular frames and are situated either on the step of the arch or outside it. Curious images are that of Virgo, on f.68v, represented as a girl seated on a massive chair, with the moon sign on her left, and Sagittarius on f.70, a moustached archer in contemporary armour with a plumed helmet.

f.72: a table for calculating times and seasons, surmounted by a big motif of combined interlaced and floral elements; green, blue, carmine and red outlines, gold and yellow fillings in between the ornaments.

f.72v: a table indicating the points of the compass and the winds, represented by eight solar images; red outlines, red, gold, carmine and blue colours.

ff.73, 73v, 74v: tables with simple golden frames.

f.74: an arch-framed table, outlined in gold; in the vault is inscribed an interlace motif with floral endings; red outlines, gold and blue background. Similar tables and ornamental devices are known from Hristofor's other manuscripts.

Contents: Miscellany. The first half of the manuscript contains a Slavonic translation of the *Fiore di virtù* attributed to Tommaso (Tomaseo) Gozzadini. After this come a number of items taken from or closely connected with the *Хронограф*, followed by a calendar with associated astronomical information, and miscellaneous religious texts including various brief commentaries and glosses. The prototype of the collection was evidently Russian, as all the texts are known to have been current in the East Slavonic area, and some have known Russian sources, for example the printed Кириллова книга (Moscow, 1644) for the anti-Armenian articles and the Книга о вѣрѣ (Moscow, 1648) for the titles of the Patriarchs and the Sermon against Drunkenness. The manuscript is very similar in its contents to another manuscript written by Hristofor, formerly belonging to P.J. Šafárik and now MS IX H 23 of the National Museum in Prague (Vašica/Vajs 1957: №156).

(f.1-1v) ѠГЛАВЛЮ́НІЄ | вещїй ѡбрѣтаємыхь въ кни́зѣ сѐй [contents to the *Kniga cvĕti* only]

(ff.2-41) КНИ́ГА ЦВѢ́Т Ы ДАРОВА́НІѠМЬ

Incipit: да́ръ любви, глава̀ ,а҃. | Любо̀ вѣ́рнаа съ ра́достїю й чисты́ сꙸр҃цємь ѥ де́лова́нїє

Explicit: въ се́мы дн҃ь почѝ бъ | ѡ въсѣ дѣ́лъ свои · ємꙋ сла́ва й дръжа́ва, съ | вѣначе́лнымь ѥго̀ ѻ҃цємь, й съ прѣсты́мꙿ й бл҃гымь й животворе́щимь дх҃омь, нн҃іа й прн҃ꙋ | й вѣко́нъчꙋныѥ вѣ́кы а́мінь:- Конꙿ се́мꙋ-

(f.41) григо́рїа мни́ха го́ры сінай́скїє | ѻ строе́нїи мнишъ́скꙷꙷ

Incipit: Постриже́нїє вла́сꙷꙷ оꙋ́бѡ гавла́єть въсѣ помы|шлю́нїи. й печа́ли житѣйски ѿе́тїє

107

Explicit: аналⷢⷵже ꙗго еуⷢⷧїа хⷭⷶ

(ff.41v-46v) Ꙩ родословїю ѿ лѣтописа꙳Сложено въкраⷮцѣ

Incipit: Адамъ прьвыⷨ уⷧⷦъ бывь лѣтомь, бⷧ. й роди сиѳа

Explicit: тѣмже й грамата прозвасе словен҆скⷶ

(ff.46v-47) Сказанїе Ꙩ четырⷷ великыⷯ морахъ въкраⷮцѣ

Incipit: Прьвое ꙋбо велико море начинаеть ѿ уⷧⷦъ йжⷷ имꙋще | пꙋⷭте главы

Explicit: й сⷮе дни нарицають алктⷧ|шнит҆скїе

(f.47) Ꙩ раю

Incipit: Райже ѥгѡ на въⷭтоцѣ насади | Бъ

Explicit: й смѣриши льва и тигра оукротиши, | Бꙋ нашемꙋ слава въ вѣкы аминь

(f.48-48v) родослѡвїе стⷶые вцⷩы

Incipit: Ѿ колѣна наѳанова, сⷩа двⷣва, мат҆ѳанⷾ їереи

Explicit: хрⷭ҇тосъ же, й їѡанⷿ прⷪⷮта, двоюрⷪⷣны се|стрⷶ дѣти

(ff.48v-50v) ѡ ѥллинскиⷯ мꙋдрьцⷷхъ йже ѿ утⷣⷹ | прⷪрⷭⷮствовахꙋ ѡ прѣвышнⷿемь бжⷮⷭвѣ, й ѡ рожⷣⷶ҇ⷭтвⷷ хрⷭ҇товѣ ѿ прⷮⷭыⷴе вцⷩы

Incipit: Повигшевосе улⷹⷶлⷦыⷴе [sic] вѣщи из҆Ꙩбрѣсти

Explicit: въ дⷩи же | константина й ирины ѡ слⷩце паки оузриши ме

(ff.50v-51) прⷪрⷭⷮтво Ꙩ хрⷭ҇тѣ, й ѡ прⷮⷭⷷй бцⷩи, въ кꙋми|рницⷷ ѥллин҆скагѡ кꙋмира аполⷧѡна

Incipit: Бывшꙋ гладꙋ въ ѥллинⷷⷯ великꙋ ѕѣлѡ

Explicit: пришьⷣⷺше влъⷭви глаголахꙋ | хрⷭ҇тꙋ, се ѥсть прⷮⷭⷭъ бжⷮⷭⷷи

(ff.51-52) Ꙩ арменской ѥреси

Incipit: Испрьва оубо армени бѣхꙋ съ нами въ съѥдинⷿнїи

Explicit: з҆весермѣны, бесермѣнⷷ. съ татары, татарⷷ. съ | хрⷭⷮїаны, хрⷭⷮїанⷷ

(f.52-52v) Ꙩ постѣ арменскомь, арцыбꙋровⷷ

Incipit: Въ нⷣлю въⷩнⷿже начинаетсе трїѡⷣⷪⷮ

Explicit: да | не съ ѥретикⷵ шⷠрⷵⷲемсе постⷷⷶщесе

(ff.52v-53v) Ꙩ лⷵⷵнⷷ оучители арменскомⷹ

Incipit: Повⷷда давыⷣь арменинⷿ, быⷭть реⷢⷱⷷ в арменⷷⷯ

Explicit: й послⷷⷣⷺ ѡ лⷹнⷷ, й ѡ скврⷵⷶⷵныⷴ дⷷлехⷿ ѥюⷴ

[a version of the Pope Joan legend]

(ff.53v-54) ѡ арменскомь дыбанⷿⷵ, сирⷷⷱь причⷷстⷵⷵ

Incipit: Шихъ йхꙋ оутаѥсе въⷭⷷ людеи въ полꙋнощи

Explicit: водꙋ прохоⷣ|дⷩⷺю пꙋщають на Ꙩвⷪⷱь, й дають хрⷭⷮїанⷵⷩⷺⷨⷵ

(f.54-54v) въ црⷭ҇тво авлиргїана цⷺра въ римⷷ

Incipit: При семь быⷧ манⷿ проклⷵⷷтый ѥретикⷵ

Explicit: противꙋ же на истинное ѥⷭтⷵⷭⷮвословⷵⷷ крамолꙋⷴ | ймоуⷮ

(ff.54v-57v) Ꙩ прⷷⷧⷭтницⷷ й прⷮⷭⷮꙋꙋⷵ антихⷭ҇товⷷ | махⷹⷲⷵⷷⷮⷵ. когⷣⷶ бⷷ й како. лютⷷⷵⷵⷵⷵⷵⷵⷵшїй ‖ прⷷⷧⷭⷭⷵⷵтникⷵ тоⷹрⷮⷮⷵковь ѥретикⷵ

Incipit: Бⷷ оубо межꙋ петыⷴ й шестыⷴ съборⷹⷵⷲ

Explicit: даⷶⷵще ктⷪ положить дⷩⷹⷺшꙋ свою za дрꙋⷹⷵга своⷷⷢ

(ff.58-63) [blank]

(ff.63v-65) тлъкⷪⷮванⷵⷵⷷ, бⷷⷮⷵⷵⷵⷵ зодїамⷵⷩⷺ

Incipit: Ꙩвⷵⷩⷺ, юнⷵⷩⷺцⷵь, близнⷵⷩⷺцⷵ, ракⷵⷩⷺ, львⷵⷩⷺ

Explicit: повелⷵⷵⷷ, | й създашесе · повелⷵⷵⷷнⷵⷵⷷ положи, и не мимоиⷵⷵⷵⷵⷵⷵⷵⷵⷵⷵⷮⷵⷵ

108

(f.65v) **A table showing the phases of the moon**

(ff.66-71v) **A calendar** [The calendar runs from March to February, with one page per month arranged in tabular form, and giving a variety of astronomical and other information.]

(f.72) мѹрда гра́ница се͠маго съво́ра [a table for calculating times and seasons]

(f.72v) **A table** [indicating the points of the compass and the winds]

(f.73-73v) **A table** [giving the indiction, solar cycle, annual letter ("сло́во ꙁнаме́но"), lunar cycle, epact ("ѳемелїѡ̈ "), celestial cycle, terrestrial cycle, siderial cycle, golden number and dominical letter ("епахтε лѣ́тѡ̈ ") for A.M.7187-7252/A.D.1679-1744]

(f.74) **СТЛ҆ПЬ СКА́РѢ** [A table plotting the lunar cycle (in the third row) against the solar cycle (in the first column), giving the annual letter. In the first row is the epact (themelion) and in the second row the date of Passover, in the last row is the golden number and in the last column, the dominical letter. Around the table are multiples of 532 from 1 to 15.]

(f.74v) **A table** [indicating, according to the annual letter, the day of the week of Christmas; the length of time, in weeks and days, from Christmas to Lent; the date on which the Triodion is begun; the date of Sexagesima ; the date of the Forty Martyrs (expressed as which day of which week in Lent); the date of the Annunciation (similarly); the date of Easter; the date of St George's day (relative to Easter); the date of Ascension Day; the date of Whitsun; the date of the beginning of St Peter's Fast; the length in weeks and days of St Peter's fast; the day of the week of St Peter's Day; the day of the week on which the Dormition Fast begins; the day of the week of the Dormition; the day of the week on which the Christmas Fast begins]

(ff.75-77) прεвла͠го͡ ѻ̈ц҃а наш͠е͡ го іѡа́нна дамаскѵ́на ѻ̈ бі́ти͡ ꙁодїа́

Incipit: Врѹ́хѹ се͠маго нб҃сε є́сть планї́тское ко́ло

Explicit: и́ нε и́маши слъга́нь вы́ти прїтꙋе́ю

(f.77-77v) оӱста́вь ѻ̈ съво́рнӧ съгла́сти ст҃ыми ап͠лы, ӥ вг҃о|но́снїими ѻ̈ц҃и оӱста́вл҃но

Incipit: Ӱтрънню пѣ́ти, ꙁанїε̈ ѿ оӱтра въскрсε х͠с в͠ъ ѿ мрꙋ̈|тивы́͡

Explicit: въ|са́кво пра́вѣй ст҃оε п͠ѣнїε. съ вл͠ь вѣседꙋ͡ёт ӥ съ ст҃ӹ͡

(ff.77v-78) **Sayings of the Fathers, on prayer** [Includes sayings of SS John Chrystostom, John Climacus, Macarius and Isidore.]

(ff.78-79) ст͠а́го іѡа́нна ꙁлатоꙋ̈стаго ѻ̈ мл͠твѣ

Incipit: Й͡коже вӧ тѣлꙋ св҆ѣ́ть сл҆́нцε, тако дꙋ́ши мл͠тва

Explicit: нεвнаго цр͠тва͡ нε | погрꙋ́шитε, мл͠тва͡ в͠а ӱ́колювї́ελ҆ · мл͠тва|ми прεꙋ́тыιε вцε · ӥ въсꙋ́хь ст͠ӹ͡, ӓми́нь

(f.79-79v) ст͠го іѡа́нна ꙁлаꙋ͡ста́͡ истлъкова́нна ѿ ап͠ла

Incipit: Хо́щꙋ пѣ́ть слове́сь гла́ти оӱмӧ своӥ͡

Explicit: въсꙋ͡ сꙋ̈́тεй вра́жїи͡ ѻ̈ х̈̈ ї͠с҆ъ г͠и наше́͡, ёмꙋ́жε сла͡͡ | въ вѣ́кы, ӓми́нь

(ff.79v-80) тлъкова́нїε, нεоӱ́довь поꙁнава́емӹ́. въ писа́ны͡ рέѵ̈͡

Incipit: Понιε̈͡ поло́жεни соу͡ рέѵи въ книга́, ѿ наѵа́лны͡ прεво́|дникь

Explicit: вла́ство праꙁ͡но|хожде́нїε

(f.80-80v) дрꙋ́гоε тлъкова́нїε ѻ̈ нεраꙁꙋ̈мεва́|ющи͡ слове́сꙋ̈͡

Incipit: ѱа́лтирь кра́снь | съ гꙋ́сльми, ѱа́лтирь ιε̈͡ оӱ́мь

Explicit: ӓпοста́ть ѿстꙋ́пни͡͡

(ff.80v-82) тлъкова́нїε вѣтхомꙋ ӥ но́вомꙋ ꙁа́вѣтꙋ

Incipit: У͠къ нѣ́кӹ͡ ӥсхо́жаше ѿ їερл͠їма въ їερихо́нь

Explicit: вѣ́ли ꙁꙋ́вы є̈го̀ па́ѵε | млѣ́ка. ꙁа́повѣдь ιε̈го̀ веспорόка ѵи́ста

109

(f.82-82v) Ст҃го є́фрє́ма ѿ цѣ́нѣ̀ хв҃ѣ, й срє́брьницѣ̀ˣ

    Incipit: Трѝ дє́сєти срє́врьникь й́же възє̈тꙑ̈ і́оу́да

    Explicit: й̀ нє скꙋ́пь на цѣ́нꙑ̀ ꙗ̈влꙗ́є̈ᵗсє

(f.82v) [A riddle]

    Incipit: въпро̂. что̀ є̈̂ улкь стⷶ́ростїю ѽдрꙋ̈жимь

    Explicit: оу́чєнїємь своймь въ̈ мі́рь просвѣ́тишє

(ff.82v-83v) ꙁⷶ́рⷶвицє, на трⷶ́пєꙁⷮѣ цр҃ꙋ московскомꙋ̈ [followed by others for the Voivodes of Moldavia and Wallachia and the titles of the Patriarchs of Constantinople, Alexandria, Antioch, Jerusalem and Moscow]

(ff.83v-87) ѽ ѽмрⷶ́чєнномь пїⷶ́нствѣ. глⷡⷶ́, є҃і

    Incipit: Хрⷭ̀тⷭ̀ь сⷭ̀псйтєль наⷲ̀шь ꙗ̈ко бъ̀ прⷺ́вѣдꙑ̈ въсⷶ̀

    Explicit: да въ | томь ꙋ̈годйвшє тєвѣ̀, сподо́вимсє чє́сти й̀ жⷬ̀ѣ́вїⷶ | йхь амйнь

(ff.87v-end) [blank]

Language: Church Slavonic, following predominantly Serbian (Resava) orthographic norms, but with a discernable Russian substrate. Both ъ and ь are used, the former predominantly medially and the latter predominantly finally. Both є and ю may be used in all positions, and both ꙗ and а after vowels. There are very occasional vernacular interpolations, and in the calendar occasional Turkish words.

Inscriptions:

ff.1-18: [Traces remain of an inscription, since erased.]

Provenance: written almost certainly in the monastery of Rača, probably in 1678 or 1679, the first year of the Paschalia. From the collection of Gyula Todoreszku and Aranka Horváth, given to the National Library in 1922. Transferred to the Manuscript Department in 1929.

Despite the shelfmark, the manuscript is in fact a quarto.

Kacziba 1999.

Plates VIII, IX, X, 60, 61

42. Duod. Eccl. Slav. 1
Dioptra, 1713

Paper. Watermark: horn (fig.132), but very fragmentary.

i+185+i leaves; modern stamped foliation [i], 1-57, 1 unnumbered, 58-185. Size of leaves: 145×98 mm.

Collation: I-V⁸, VI⁸ (±8), VII-XXIII⁸, (1 leaf). Gatherings signed with arabic numerals centrally in the lower margin, but only signatures 1-4 are legible; of the rest only occasional traces remain.

Layout: 14-18 ll./p., within a ruled pencil border 105-115×60-70 mm. Catchwords.

Hand: several hands, possibly as many as eight. They appear to succeed each other as follows, 1. ff.1-47v, 2. f.48-48v (the cancelled leaf), 3. ff.49-74, 4. ff.74v-88, 5. ff.88v-123, 6. ff.123v-128v, 7. ff.128v-151v, 8. 152-184v, though in some cases the discontinuity is much more apparent than others. The book is written throughout in a very informal late bookhand with many cursive elements.

Ink: brown.

Binding: plain brown leather on very thin boards, 152×100 mm. Triple incised lines around the edges of both upper and lower covers, and also on either side of the three raised bands on the spine. Traces of two fastenings. One old flyleaf at each end.

Condition: some leaves are missing at the end, otherwise reasonably good.

Contents: Philip Monotropus: *Dioptra*

The title page (f.1) reads: ДІОПТРА а́лбо | зе́рцало и҆ вирaжé|не живота людска́ | нà се́м свѣ́те. повтóре | съ и҆спрáвлѣ́нгe҆м видрꙋ́ско|ва́ное. | трꙋдолюбгe҆м инокꙋ. | ст҃ге ѡ҆бщежителнге | ѡ҆бители сьшаствге | прест҃го д҃ха животвó|рещаго. Apart from minor orthographical variants and the omission of the date and place of publication, this reproduces the title page of the edition of the Dioptra published in Vilna–Ev'e in 1642, from which one may infer that this book was copied. The end of the manuscript is missing: the text breaks off in the middle of chapter 40.

Language: Church Slavonic with strong Belarusian influence, and with further Serbian-influence on the orthography.

Inscriptions:

inside front cover: Dioptra | (speculum) operis | Virphinae Philotae

front flyleaf: Dioptra | (speculum) | operis | Virphinae Philotae | descriptio mundi humani. | Altera vice edita a Mo|nachis, coenobii ad S. | Spiritum 1713. Cod. | Sec. xviii, olim Protopre|sbiteri Budensis Nesto|ris Diaconi. | Adnotante Parocho | Nicolaio Milovanovich | Budae 23. Nov. 1735

f.185: Сгa книга Нестóра̀| дгaкa пгȼa ю | 1713 | лето | ꙋ табани | вꙋдимскои ва|роши

f.185v: Сгa книга ꙋ҆тнѣ́и|шаго гн҃a протопре́|витера воу́нимскге | ва́роши кꙋ́р нéстора | воу́м ймь многолѣ́т|ствге, по́писа̀ ю а́зъ | ма́нши въ сщéнницe | никóлае милова|нови́: 1735: но́e҆м 23 | въ вꙋдима̀:-

inside back cover: цр҃кою дгaдгмóю | престависe | ермóна̀х хр̃ | [...] | лето

111

Provenance: the inscription on f.185 implies that the manuscript was written in 1713 in Taban (Buda) by Nestor, clerk and subsequently archpriest of Buda, but this is somewhat at variance with the presence of several hands in the book, none of which seems to correspond to that of the inscription. The date 1713, however, is given both in the inscription on f.185 and on f.7v. One of nine Slavonic cyrillic manuscripts from the collection of Miklós Jankovich, acquired by the Library in 1836.

Plate 62

43. Quart. Eccl. Slav. 16
Passion Narrative, 18th century (last quarter)

Paper. Watermark: fleur-de-lys (fig.133), similar to Laucevičius 2090 (1736-7); letters WAP (fig.134); on ff.33-37, angel(?) (fig.135), similar to Szentendre 145 (1787), very similar to MSPC, Grujić 122 (1783) and MSPC, Grujić 3-I-17 (1784).
i+37+i leaves; modern stamped foliation [i], 1-37, [38]; apparently original foliation on ff.7-32, а҃і-л҃s and on ff.34-37, л҃д-л҃з. Size of leaves: 235×200 mm.

Collation: I³⁶ (-1-2-3-4), II⁶ (-6). Unsigned.

Layout: very variable, 16-24 ll./p., written area 190-210×170-185 mm. Ff.1-34 have ruled borders. Catchwords. Running titles.

Hand: six hands, all very irregular late degenerate semiuncials with some cursive elements. 1: f.1-2.9; 2: ff.2.9-5v.9; 3: ff.5v.10-22; 4: ff.22v-32v.10; 5: ff.32v.10-34; 6: ff.34v-37v.

Ink: greyish in the parts written by scribes 1, 2 and 5, dark brown for scribes 3 and 4, reddish-brown for scribe 6.

Binding: modern, 240×205 mm, green paper on card, red buckram spine. One modern flyleaf at each end.

Condition: dirty and faded, the first leaf almost illegible, probably four leaves missing at the front and an indeterminable number at the back.

Decoration: none except for a very crude ink-wash band on f.7 with simple flower motifs.

Contents: Страсти Христовы

The beginning and end are missing, and the extant text covers more or less the Gospel narrative. It is impossible to tell whether this manuscript originally contained the apocryphal elements frequently appended to this text.

Language: Ukrainian.

Provenance: written in the Ruthenian area. Bought on 23rd August 1891 from the antiquarian bookseller Dániel Kún, together with various other eighteenth- and nineteenth-century manuscripts. Quart. Eccl. Slav. 5 was also acquired from him in 1893.

Plate 63

Theological teachings, 18th century (first quarter)

Paper. Watermark: à la mode (fig.136), similar to Laucevičius 33 (1716).

174 leaves; original foliation on the third to 37th leaves, а҃-л҃е; modern stamped foliation on the third to 53rd, 1-51. Size of leaves: 200×160 mm.

Collation: I⁸ (1 and 2 are pastedowns, one on top of the other), II-VI⁸, VII⁸ (-6-7-8), VIII⁸ (-1-2-3), IX-XXII⁸, XXIII⁸ (7 and 8 are pastedowns). The stubs of the missing leaves from VII and VIII remain. Unsigned.

Layout: on ff.1-49, 2 cols./p., 25-30 ll./col., written area 170×140 mm. The text on f.50-51v is a later addition, written in a single column without ruling, and the rest of the book is blank.

Hand: two late cyrillic cursives: the first on ff.1-35, the second on ff.35v-49, both scribes providing titles in rather crude semiuncial.

Ink: black.

Binding: pink paper on card, half-bound, four raised bands on spine. Three incised parallel lines round the edges of the leather corner pieces and on either side of each raised band. The leather strip at the edges of the covers next to the spine is roll-stamped with an interlaced semi-circular cresting ending in a tuft of leaves, and alongside this another three parallel lines. The binding is very similar to those of MSS Quart. Eccl. Slav 2 and 4.

Contents: Lectiones | CLXXI [deleted, and **CXVII** written in] | **De Peccato Originali Adami, cum Insti|tutionibus Moralibus. Illyrice, et Valachi|ce**

This title is not original, and has been added, probably by Jankovich, on the first leaf. The work consists of parallel texts in Slavonic and Rumanian. The Slavonic begins: "ѡбꙋвѣнїе а҃ | Мно́зїи мно́гїта и разлиꙋнїта пре́|лагаютъ а҃даӎлю падѣнїю вини̇", and the Rumanian begins "Ꙗвъцъцъꙋтꙋръ а҃ | Мꙋлци мꙋлте ши демꙋлте | жѣлѡри де причини а҃да́ѡгꙋ къ|дѣрїн лꙋи а҃дамъ". The work appears to be unfinished: there is a title ѡбꙋвѣнїе рн҃і at the foot of f.49, but f.49v is blank; it is however possible that there was text on the six leaves immediately following that have been removed.

Language: Church Slavonic, strongly accommodated to Russian syntax, and Rumanian.

Inscriptions:

f.50-50v: [a text, largely illegible, but apparently in a mixture of Latin and German, written in brown ink in a Latin cursive hand, and beginning "1766 [..] 19 Maij"]

Provenance: evidently produced by the Serbian community in Hungary. One of nine Slavonic cyrillic manuscripts from the collection of Miklós Jankovich, acquired by the Library in 1836. It is likely that, like Quart. Eccl. Slav. 2 and 4 and Quart. Serb. 2, it had previously belonged to Arsenije Popović.

Plate 64

45. Quart. Eccl. Slav. 2

Liturgical treatise, orations and verses, 18th century (first quarter)

Paper. Watermark: à la mode (fig.137), type Laucevičius 39 (1711), 40 (1715). 88 leaves; modern stamped foliation, 1-88. Size of leaves: 200×165 mm.

Collation: I⁸ (-5-6; 1 and 2 are pastedowns), II-III⁸, IV⁸ (-4), V-VIII⁸, IX⁸ (3 and 4 are pasted together), X-XI⁸, XII⁸ (7 and 8 are pastedowns). Unsigned.

Layout: variable. On ff.3-36v, 2 cols./p., up to 33 ll./col., elsewhere 20-24 ll./p.; written area 170×140 mm.

Hand: a bewildering variety of late cursive hands, often more than one on the same page, alternating with great frequency.

Ink: black; brown on ff.85v-88v.

Binding: pink paper on card, half-bound, four raised bands on spine. Three incised parallel lines round the edges of the leather corner pieces and on either side of each raised band. The leather strip at the edges of the covers next to the spine is roll-stamped with rosettes, and alongside this another three parallel lines. The binding is very similar to those of MSS Quart. Eccl. Slav 1 and 4.

Contents:

(ff.3-36v) Сказаніе сщённаго храма

Incipit: Часть первая | ѿ храмѣ вжественномъ и сщен|ныхъ сосздѣхъ и ѿдеждахъ

[Parallel texts in Slavonic and Rumanian. The Slavonic text is also found in MS Quart. Eccl. Slav. 4.]

(ff.38-85v) привѣтсвїа различнаа [Formal orations for various occasions, and also some occasional verses. In Slavonic and Rumanian.]

(ff.1v-2, 37-37v, 85v-88v) [Various "орацїи" and "стихи"; apparently later additions.]

Language: Church Slavonic with some vernacular influence; Rumanian.

Inscriptions: the date 1762 appears inside the back cover.

Provenance: evidently produced by the Serbian community in Hungary. One of nine Slavonic cyrillic manuscripts from the collection of Miklós Jankovich, acquired by the Library in 1836. According to the title on f.1, apparently supplied by Jankovich, "Popovich Arsenii opera varia theologica". The name of Arsenius Popovich appears, among others, on f.4 of MS Quart. Eccl. Slav. 4, and is also found in Quart. Serb. 2. This, combined with the similarities in content and appearance between these manuscripts and MS Quart. Eccl.Slav. 1 (all from Jankovich's collection), suggests that he may at one time have been the owner of all four. However, the hand of the signature cannot be identified with certainty with any of the hands in which this manuscript is written; still less is there any internal evidence to identify Arsenius as the author of any part of it.

Plate 65

Miscellany, 1743?

Paper. Watermark: coat of arms with letters FPM (fig.138), very similar to SANU 136 (1740) or Szentendre 29 (1745), though the latter does not have the letters. 78 leaves; modern stamped foliation, 1-78. Size of leaves: 193×150 mm.

Collation: I^8 (1 is pastedown, -3+2-4-6-7-8), II^6 (completely removed, only the stubs of the pages remain), III^6 (-1-2), $IV-XI^8$, XII^8 (7 and 8 are pastedowns). The two additional leaves in I are a 19th-century bifolium. Unsigned.

Layout: very variable: 19-33 ll./p., written area up to 180×135 mm.

Hand: late cyrillic cursive on ff.5-39, 56-78v (at least four hands, alternating irregularly); latin cursive on ff.4v, 32v-52 (also more than one hand); both latin and cyrillic on ff.52v-55.

Ink: various shades of brown.

Binding: pink paper on card, half bound, 198×155 mm, three raised bands on spine. On the leather parts triple fillets round the edges and simple fillets on the spine. The binding is very similar to those of MSS Quart. Eccl. Slav 1 and 2.

Contents: miscellaneous religious and grammatical texts, reminiscent of a school notebook. According to the Latin title on f.3, "a Stephano Popowich 1743 exaratus", but this is not original (the very leaf is additional), and the hand of the signature "Stephanus Popovich" on f.4 can be identified only with the hand of ff.4v and 39v, which appear to be later additions, so the assertion is very much open to doubt.

(ff.5-39) Сказанїе сщенннагѡ храма, ризъ ѐгѡ, й внѐмъ со|вершаетса бжственнаа лїтꙋргїа, со ѻкрестностїю | ѐа, ꙋрѣзъ краткїа вопросы й ѿвѣты, | сочиненъ | во оꙋпотреблѐнїе сщеннослꙋжителен право|славнокаѳолическїа восточныа церкве [The same text is found in MS Quart. Eccl. Slav 2.]

(ff.40-52) **Notes on Latin grammar**

(ff.52v-64v) **A Rumanian-Latin-Slavonic-German vocabulary** [on ff.55v-64v, only Rumanian-Slavonic]

(ff.65-78v) **Miscellaneous sermons and other notes on religious topics** [in Slavonic]

Language: Rumanian, Latin, Slavonic and German.

Inscriptions: the inside of the front cover and f.1-1v are covered in short and largely meaningless inscriptions in various languages. An additional bifolium of different paper (ff.2-3) bears a Latin title for the volume. The same hand that signed "Stephanus Popovich" on f.4 has added some Latin and Hungarian sententiæ on f.4v and some additional grammatical notes on f.39v. On f.4 there appear the following inscriptions:

оꙋсапши. | Стоадн҃, ꙗнкѡ, неранжа, Іѡванъ. Милица. | живко радославъ. живи. ан҆ѳелїа. | оꙋсапши҃.

славнѡ ꙗ҃кѡ бг҃ъ

Stephanus Popovich

Arsenius Popovich

Stephan Petrov

Provenance: evidently produced by the Serbian community in Hungary. One of nine Slavonic cyrillic manuscripts from the collection of Miklós Jankovich, acquired by the Library in 1836. It is likely that, like Quart. Eccl. Slav. 1 and 2 and Quart. Serb. 2, it had previously belonged to Arsenije Popović, whose name appears on f.4.

Plate 66

Nastavlenie maloe, 1769

Paper. Watermark: coat of arms (fig.139), similar to Eineder 391 (1766). In the flyleaves, hart (fig.140).

i+38+i leaves; modern stamped foliation 1-39, [40]; original pagination 1-73 (the last three pages are blank and unnumbered, as were the flyleaves). Size of leaves: 192×155 mm.

Collation: I-XIX². Unsigned.

Layout: 20-23 ll./p., written area 155-160×135-145 mm.

Hand: small cursive.

Ink: brown.

Binding: paper with green and red pattern on card, leather spine, 200×160 mm. One flyleaf at each end.

Condition: good, apart from some worming in the spine, leading to the loss of a small part of the leather at the top.

Contents: Наставле́нїе малше | Христїянскимъ ѿтрокомъ то е́сть ка́ковымъ | ѡ́бразомъ надобно Хрⷭ҇тїански ѿтроковъ на|ста́вить ѿ хрⷭ҇тиянскимъ зако́нѣ

Language: Russian, with strong Church Slavonic and occasional minor Serbian influence.

Inscriptions:

f.1: Ла́зарꙋ Ко́ста

f.1: [first hand:] Brevis Instructio | qualiter | Proles Religione Christiana | imbuere oporteat | cxxvii Quæstionibus absoluta. | Lingva Vetero Slavica | vice Illyrica. | [second hand:] Descripta Strigonii A.1769 | per Gregorium Tiro | incolam civitatis L.R. Strigon. | [third hand:] Nastavlenia maloje | Christijanskim Otrokom, | to jest | Kanovim [sic] obrazom nadobno Christijanskich | otrokov nastavit o christijanskim Zakonye

Provenance: written in Esztergom in 1769 by Grigorije Tiro[vić]? (the end of his name is obscured by the alteration), as indicated by the final lines of f.38, which are written in the same hand as the rest of the book: 1769 Ма́рта 1го. во ѡ́строгонѣ | Преписа́ся сїя книжица [чрезъ мнѣ deleted, and the next three words altered from accusative to instrumental case] Григо́рїемъ | Тѵ́ро биватело́ⷨ Кралѣ́вскіа вароши | Ѡстрогонскагѡ. One of nine Slavonic cyrillic manuscripts from the collection of Miklós Jankovich, acquired by the Library in 1836.

Plate 67

48. Quart. Serb. 2
Miscellany, 18th century (after 1754)

Paper. Watermark: an extremely fragmentary imperial eagle.

123 leaves; modern pencil and stamped foliations, 1-123. Size of leaves: 204×162 mm.

Collation: I^8(-1-2; 3 is pastedown), II-V^8, VI^8(-5), VII-VIII^8, IX^8(-4-5-6-7-8), X^8(-1-2-3-4), XI^8(-3-4-5-6-7-8+1), XII-XVII^8, XVIII^8(6 is pastedown, -7-8). Unsigned.

Layout: variable: on ff.5-35, 19-22 (usually 21) ll./p. and ruled margins, written area up to 170×125 mm; elsewhere up to 32 ll./p., with or without margins, and a written area which can extend to cover the whole page.

Hand: a variety of cyrillic cursives: (1) ff.5-38, (2) ff.38v-40v, (3) ff.41-60, 71-78 (4) ff.61-63, (5) ff.64-69v, 79-93, (6) ff.96-back cover. Hands 3 and 6 are very similar, and may be the same. F.70 is written in a Latin cursive, very likely by the same scribe as wrote the third cyrillic hand.

Ink: varies from black to brown.

Binding: marbled paper on card, half-bound, traces of two fastenings, spine with three raised bands. The only decoration is a triple line incised rather roughly on the corner pieces, on the leather on the covers beside the spine and on either side of each of the raised bands.

Condition: good, apart from the binding which is much worn. The missing leaves have mostly been cut out quite neatly; the stubs remain.

Contents:

(ff.1-4v) [blank]

(ff.5-35v) Траéдѡкомéдïа | содержащия в'себѣ тринаде|сятъ дѣйствыи: [an allegory of Serbian history]

(ff.37-37) Стïхѝ разлѝчныя

(ff.37v-38v) Extracts from patristic writings

(ff.38v-40v) Стïхѝ воспоминáти смерть привѣтсвтомъ

(f.41-41v) Стïхи | ѡ сéдмъ тайнъ новáгѡ завѣта

(f.42) [blank]

(ff.42v-58) Разлѝчныя мнóю глаголáнныя ѝ писмéннѣя | посылáемыя привѣтствителныя ѡрáцïи | для лѵчшыя пáмяти здѣ порядѹ послѣ|дѵютъ ѝ вписаются. лѣта 1749го [Many of these are signed "Арсенïи Поповичь" and dated, the last being dated 1754.]

(f.58v) [blank]

(f.59) Мною сочинéнный Концéптъ писмà позивателнаго Монастѝрцевъ | фрѹшкогóрскихъ, к'прославлéнïю прáздника стáгѡ Архи-Стратѝга | Михаила

(ff.59v-60) Вторый, влѣтѣ 755ом мнóю сочиненый к'прослав|ленïю праздника стаго Архистратѝга, позивателный | Концéптъ

(f.60v) [blank]

(ff.61-63) ѡ Мѳери Бжïей

(f.63v) [blank]

(ff.64-69v) ὣ преизѧ́ществѣ и́ досто́инсіvѣ добрыхъ | Іереевъ, ѕѣлⱳ блгопрїѧтна бесѣда

(f.70-70v) **Epitaph on Franz, Freiherr von der Trenck** (1711-49) [in German and Latin]

(ff.71-95) **Miscellaneous sermons** [Ff.78v, 89v and 95v are blank.]

(ff.96-115v) Feofan Prokopovič: Панегирі́косъ | и́лѝ | Слѻ̀во похва́лное ὣ преславной над' | во́исками Свѣ́йскими | Побѣ́дѣ | пресвѣ́тлѣйшемv и́ великодержавнѣ́йшемv | госvда́рю цр̃ю и́ великомv кнѧ́зю | Петрv̀ Алеѯі́евичꙋ [This work was printed in Kiev in 1709 (Zapasko & Isajevyč, 853).]

(ff.116-123v) Feofan Prokopovič: ὣ сме́рти | Петра̀ вели́кагⱳ і́мпера́тора рⱳссі́искаго | Кра́ткая повѣ́сть [As noted inside the back cover, this work was printed in St Petersburg in 1726: see A.S.Zernova, T.N.Kameneva 1968: №1380.]

Language: mostly slavenosrpski, but a certain amount of Church Slavonic, and in the last items, Russian; on f.70, German and Latin.

Inscriptions: on f.1, in the hand of Miklós Jankovich, a summary of the contents in Latin. He adds: "MS hoc Autographum ab Actore Arsenii Popovics | ex Sclavonia, fors Carloviczio [...] exaratum est. | Fuerat is initio Miles Legionis Trenkianæ, dein | Castrensis Capellanus, post Eꝑꝑus Belgradensis ac Po|stremo Budensis Epp. Græci Ritus non uniti."

Provenance: it is possible that Arsenije Popović can be identified with the third scribe of the manuscript. One of nine Slavonic cyrillic manuscripts from the collection of Miklós Jankovich, acquired by the Library in 1836. Three others of his manuscripts (Quart. Eccl. Slav. 1, 2 and 4) appear also previously to have been the property of Arsenije Popović.

Plate 68

49. OCT. ECCL. SLAV. I
Sokraščenie istorii cerkovnija, late 18th/early 19th century

Paper. Watermark: coat of arms (fig.141), very similar to Laucevičius 3072 (1800). i+110+i leaves; modern stamped foliation [i], 1-110, [111]; original pagination 1-173, 247-314 on ff.3-75v, 77-110v. Size of leaves: 195×115 mm.

Collation: indeterminable (stabbed binding). No signatures. F.76 is extraneous, evidently a page from an account book accidentally bound into the present volume.

Layout: variable, but mostly 22-24 ll./p. within a ruled pencil border 155-175×85-95 mm.

Hand: small practised eighteenth/nineteenth-century cursive.

Ink: brown.

Binding: modern, blue cardboard, spine in maroon buckram; one modern flyleaf at each end.

Contents: Сокращéнïе Исто|рïи Церковнïа сила | либо крáткая разгла|голствïа На Исторïю | Церковнꙋю | къ тѣмъ | К⟨оторы⟩е желаютъ первен|ствꙋющïя Цéркве со|стоянïе навикнꙋти

Language: Russian, with strong Church Slavonic influence.

Inscriptions:

f.1: Едúна йзъ Кнúгъ [name deleted] | Каѳедрáлнагѡ Пароха | Новосáдскагѡ

f.1: Еѵлогïа Кꙋзмановичь | Iедïакона [sic] Крꙋшедол|скагѡ 1842

Provenance: first belonged to the Serbian clergy in the Vojvodina, amongst whom it was probably written, and subsequently to the Serbian Grammar School in Novi Sad, whose stamp is on f.1. In the library at least since 1948.

Plate 69

Songs, 1769

Paper. Watermark: postillion (fig.142); letters (fig.143).
21 leaves; modern stamped foliation, 1-14, followed by 7 unnumbered blank leaves. Size of leaves: 200×145 mm.

Collation: I^{22} (-22)

Layout: very variable, but on ff.2-13 consistently within a ruled frame 180×125 mm.

Hand: an eighteenth-century cursive; the additional song on ff.13v-14v added in a different hand, closer to semiuncial.

Ink: black.

Binding: fawn paper, enclosing an earlier cover of blue paper, enclosing a yet earlier cover of brown paper.

Condition: well preserved apart from a certain amount of staining.

Decoration: on ff.2, 3, 4, 5, 6, 6v and 7v, large titles and initials in pen and ink, with hatching and floral decorations in imitation of the large engraved capitals of printed books.

Contents: Пѣсми Разлиунта | Мнѣ діака ꙋ́ченика | Iлте Радишиуа | в'Будимѣ 769°. The songs are mostly on religious subjects. Another song has been added in a different hand on ff.13v-14v. The remaining pages are blank.

Language: Church Slavonic; slavenosrpski.

Inscriptions:

f.1: проба пери

f.1v: [a drawing of the head of a man, in cap and spectacles]

f.13: конецъ | такоже свѣтло солънце

f.[21v]: Domins [sic] qui expendit

Provenance: evidently written in 1769 in Buda by Ilija Radišić. Bought in 1893 from the antiquarian bookseller Dániel Kún, from whom Quart. Eccl. Slav. 16 had been purchased two years earlier.

Plate 70

51. Quart. Serb. 6
Miscellany, 1793-4

Paper. Watermark: horn on a shield, crown above, C&I HONIG below, countermark C&I HONIG.

i+48+i leaves; modern stamped foliation, [i], 1-49; earlier, possibly original foliation on ff.5-44: 6-44, 44. Between ff.48 and 49 are the stubs of about 110 leaves which have been torn out, and which evidently bore text. Size of leaves: 220×175 mm.

Collation: I⁷(5 leaves), II-VI⁸, VII⁸(-4-5-6-7-8). Unsigned.

Layout: a ruled border 165-170×130-135 mm; within this 13-15 lines of text.

Hand: varieties of late cyrillic. 1. (f.1) decorative capitals in imitation of printed books; 2. (ff.2-42v) cyrillic cursive; 3. (ff.42v-44) another, less elegant cyrillic cursive; 4. (ff.44v-48v) a rather more conservative cursive with elements of older bookhand.

Ink: on ff.1-42v brownish-black, slightly faded in the latter parts; on ff.42v-44, a stronger dark brown; on ff.44v-48v black faded to grey.

Binding: brown leather on very thin boards, 320×180 mm, five raised bands on spine, with a horizontal line on each side of each band, and between the bands a flower motif. Traces of two fastenings (now lost). Blind tooling: floriate patterns around the edges of both covers; on the front cover within a central medallion the name GEO[...] | ANTONI[.]S, and on the back 17|93. Flyleaves (one each at front and back) of coloured patterned paper.

Condition: poor; besides the fact that two thirds of the leaves are missing, those that remain are discoloured and brittle, and the binding is severely damaged.

Contents: Songbook, also including the Lives of St Sison and Prince Lazar.

(f.1) Пѣсни | различныя содержа|ются | Въ сей Книзѣ | Написата 1794 [F.1v was originally blank.]

(ff.2-9v) **Songs on religious subjects and occasions**

(ff.10-12v) Ірмоси на гⷣския и Бⷪгородичныя | Праздники

(f.13) Пѣснь Архїерею, ѡ Иншталаціи

(ff.13v-15) Житие Сⷮтагѡ Сисона; и страданіе | Сестре его Мелентіе

     Incipit: Бистъ воинъ сⷮти Сисонъ

     Explicit: Проће Страданіе Сестре | его Мелентіе

(ff.15v-27v) Житие | Святагѡ Князa Лазара, иже по|страда на полю Косовꙋ

     Incipit: Самодержецъ велики Князь Лазаръ бяше оте|чества рода племенита

[The end is illegible.]

(ff.28-42v) **A series of 25 songs on secular subjects** [mostly simply numbered, but the first entitled Пѣснь Беѡградская]

(ff.42v-44) **A song**

(ff.44v-48v) **Songs on religious occasions**

Language: mostly slavenosrpski, but with varying degrees of Church Slavonic influence, and probably some Russian influence too.

Inscriptions:

f.1: Αφτο το χαρτη ηνε δηκομ8 τ8 ττζηκα Χατζη, ιυ ἀγορασα | Απο γηοργη Αντοβιτζ ς8ς 1802: σεπτεβ: 12:

f.1v: Назначеніе 1865 Годинѣ | 1ᵍᵒ Октовера [sic] по Рімскомᵹ прстеновалисᵹсе | Младенці Гавріло съ Іюліаномъ у полъ 12. | Сати Вѣнчалисе 8ᵍᵒ Октобера по Рім: | у Недели преполдне у д. Сати лѣто 865

passim: [many scrawls and calculations at the beginning and end of the book, most hardly legible. The name Peter Poppovits can be discerned on f.49.]

Provenance: bought at auction, 30th June 1942.

Póth 1961. Prints the secular songs, on ff.28-44, and identifies the religious songs as being derived from the collection of songs (Pěsni različnyja) printed in Vienna in 1790 for Damjan Stefanović Kaulici (1760-1810), bookseller of Novi Sad.

Plate 71

52. Quart. Eccl. Slav. 18
Songs, 1835

Paper. Watermark: MITEL (fig.144), very similar to Decker 1190 (1822-39), Szentendre 126 (1830).

i+24+i leaves; modern stamped foliation [i], 1-24, [25]. Size of leaves: 200×165 mm.

Collation: Possibly three gatherings of eight. Unsigned.

Layout: 18-26 ll./p., within a ruled border 185-190×140 mm.

Hand: a very late and rough semiuncial.

Ink: dark brown.

Binding: new, yellowish paper on card, red buckram spine, one flyleaf at each end.

Condition: leaves worn and dirty, especially at the beginning and end.

Decoration: very poor, consisting of pen-and-ink dividing lines composed of scrolls or "meander" motifs, a very crude trapezoid tailpiece on f.24v, and occasional simply decorated outline initials.

Contents: songs, of a religious nature, for various occasions during the year or addressed to particular saints. The beginning is missing.

Language: a mixture of Church Slavonic, Ukrainian and Slovak in varying proportions.

Inscriptions:

f.8: Prta Selepetz | Bazily ı8нȣ | Vaszilykö

f.8v: Васйлкȣ сынȣ мȣн возмн ѿшель | Vazilkȣ Szыкȣ | 12345678910

f.8v: Polyanszky | istvan

ff.18v-19: писаль андрей шелепець | завалга ласпосъ [??] грабовскïн дакъ

passim: [traces of inscriptions along the foot of some of the earlier pages, mostly trimmed away so that nothing is now legible]

Provenance: written in the Ruthenian area. The date 1835 is incorporated into the tailpiece on f.24v. Given by Ernő Naményi on 29th September 1952.

Plate 72

Fragments of the Epistles, 13th century

Parchment. In I and II the recto is the hair side and the verso is the flesh side, in the others vice versa.

Seven fragments. I and II are complete (but slightly cropped) leaves, 152×95 mm, the remainder are much smaller. IV, V and VI were originally parts of the same leaf. IV and V are contiguous. The dimensions of the smaller fragments (which are all are slightly irregular) are, III: 99-96×117-119 mm; IV: 33×36 mm; V: 33×60 mm; VI: 37×55 mm; VII: 32×45 mm. The combined dimensions of IV and V are 33×91 mm. The smaller fragments clearly had the same layout at the whole leaves, and the fact that III has upper margins of 17 mm, outer margins of 30 mm, and inner margins of 12-15 mm while VI has a lower margin of 30 mm, suggests that the original dimensions of the leaves were not less than 167×123 mm.

Layout: 23 ll./p., written area 120×78 mm. Pericopes are indicated in the margins.

Hand: small semiuncial. ѵ asymmetrical, ѣ not far above the line (except when it is the last letter in the line), in some cases hardly at all; a single instance of т with a long stem, the penultimate character of IIv.14. Very high cross on ж, but not on и, ѣ, ю. Small serifs. "Initial" letters, i.e. slightly larger than the rest, may extend below the line but not above it, e.g. т IIIr.6, с IIIr.11, п IIv.8, Vr.1. Superscripts very few. Diacritics largely confined to the dot and the rough breathing (sometimes hard to tell apart), and two dots on ы. Four red marginal outline initials, 8 mm (=2 lines) high, О on Iv, П on IIr, л on IIv and л on IIIv.

Ink: black, red for the rubrics and the four marginal initials.

Condition: the fragments have suffered from their use as part of a binding, and are darkened and obscured in parts. The most legible parts are Iv, IIr, IIIv and IV/Vr.

Contents: fragments of a continuous text of the Epistles

    (1st fragment) **Romans i.8-21**
    (2nd fragment) **Hebrews vi.1-18**
    (3rd fragment, recto) **Hebrews vii.27-viii.3**
    (3rd fragment, verso) **Hebrews viii.6-10**
    (4th-5th fragments, recto) **Jude 4-5**
    (4th-5th fragments, verso) **Jude 9-10**
    (6th fragment, recto) **Jude 7** [fragment]
    (6th fragment, verso) **Jude 12** [fragment]
    [The original text of the seventh fragment is illegible, but it bears a mirror-image of the bottom four lines of IIIr, to which it was evidently once stuck.]

Language: Church Slavonic of the Serbian recension; early Raška orthography.

Provenance: of Serbian origin. The fragments were found in the binding of a manuscript collection of sermons by János Foktövi, written in Vác in 1614-15 (Oct. Hung. 380) and acquired by the library in 1886. They were removed when the manuscript was restored in the late 1950s or early 1960s. The two larger fragments (I and II) continued to be kept with the Hungarian manuscript, while the others were separated from it. These latter remained uncatalogued and unclassified. The two sets of fragments were reunited only during the preparation of the present catalogue. Together with fragments III-VII were kept two pieces of pasteboard, 158×100 mm, one of which (A) bears a mirror-image imprint of the text on Iv, and the other (B) a mirror-image imprint of the text on IIr. Slits for the thongs which attached the binding to the book are visible both in the parchment and in the pasteboard, and are also found in III, indicating that this was also stuck to board A, but on the opposite side to I and at right angles to it.

Also kept with the smaller fragments was another binding, of white ornamented leather with blind tooling. On the upper cover there is a large border of stamps with Renaissance images of Apostles and Evangelists supplied with Latin captions, identical with those on the cover of Quart. Eccl. Slav. 10; within the centre panel an oval medallion stamp with the Virgin with the Child standing within a frame of "flames", very similar to Laucevičius 1976:65, №248 (early 17th century); the lower cover is decorated with the impressions of the Renaissance stamps only, within strips separated by double fillets. This binding, however, cannot be connected with Oct. Hung. 380, being too large (185×115 mm); moreover, it has an accessions stamp, 1954, №138, which indicates a completely different provenance: it refers to a collection of 375 items, "Országos Könyvtári Központtól ajándék", none of which has anything to do with these fragments.

Király 1968 (the two larger fragments only).

Plates 73, 74

Fragment, 16th century

Paper; no visible watermark.

The lower part of a leaf of a quarto manuscript. Size of leaves: 117×175 mm.

Layout: 8 lines of text on each side, written area 80×115 mm. Margins: recto left 25 mm, right 37 mm, lower 38 mm; verso left 35 mm, right 25 mm, lower 40 mm. The book probably originally had 17 ll./p.

Hand: a professional semiuncial.

Ink: black; red initials.

Contents: the beginnings of the heirmoi of the seventh and eighth odes of the canon from the service на исходъ дѹши. Judging by the material missing and the size of the hand, there are about eleven lines missing between the bottom of the recto and the top of the verso.

Language: Church Slavonic, Middle Bulgarian orthography.

Provenance: from a Ruthenian manuscript.

The fragment is kept together with two other fragments, one apparently a fragment of a letter in a mixture of Latin and Hungarian, probably seventeenth-century, the other a bifolium from a fourteenth/fifteenth-century Czech MS. Kept in the same folder is a letter, dated 12th October 1955, to Péter Király from the Archbishop of Esztergom's secretary, evidently a covering letter when sending him the Czech fragment. This may possibly provide a clue to the fragments' provenance.

Plate 75

Fragment, ?17th century

Paper, no visible watermark.
1 leaf. Size of leaves: 282×194 mm.

Layout: two lines on the recto, eight on the verso, occupying an area 15×80 mm and 95×155 mm respectively, but both are later inscriptions and have no relation to the original layout of the book from which the leaf comes.

Hand: the hand on the recto is a late semiuncial, probably eighteenth-century Serbian; the hand on the verso is an informal Serbian semiuncial, probably of the sixteenth or seventeenth century.

Ink: black.

Contents: two inscriptions. The first, on the recto, reads: "Помѧни гди раба твоегw | петра Гєwргїєвича.".

The second, on the verso, reads: "дає има знатїи како ѡкупїи сїю | стѹ книгѹ глємїи єванћелїє првоє | драгићъ иѡсивь и марко и страйна | и метнѹшє ѹ црквѹ далѹжїй и кои вй | свєщєникъ проучатихо да има сваки | помєнѹти драгића иѡсива и марка | и страйнѹ и стоґака и аүйма и васъ | домъ бь да прости".

Language: Serbian, with Church Slavonic elements.

Provenance: evidently once part of a Gospel codex given to a church by the persons mentioned in the second inscription. A stamp on the recto records its acquisition by the library in 1936, №6; however, the five items recorded in the accessions register under this number bear no relation to it.

Kept with the leaf, and likewise stamped with the date 1936 and number 6, but equally unrecorded in the accessions register, are twelve leaves from a small Czech manuscript; there is also a single fragment with Hungarian text dated 29th June 1593.

Plate 76

Psalter, 16th century (first quarter)

The manuscript cannot be found at the time of writing; the present partial description is made from a microfilm, FM1/3150.

Paper.

152 leaves; modern stamped foliation, 1-2, 4-153. Size of leaves: 195×140 mm.

Collation: unknown. There are no signatures. Ff.1-2, 19-22 are later additions.

Layout: 20 ll./p., written area 145×115 mm. (On ff.1-2v, 13 lines/page, and on ff.11-13v, 19-22 lines/page.)

Hand: a fairly informal, rather square small semiuncial; there is certainly more than one scribe, but they all write similar hands and it is difficult to tell from the microfilm where one leaves off and the next begins. The additional leaves (ff.1-2, 19-22) have been written by later and much less professional hands.

Condition: the book is evidently dirty, with staining throughout, particularly at the upper corners; in places the ink has run or faded, especially the titles and initials.

Decoration: four-line initials at the beginning of each psalm, mostly plain or with simple nodes, but occasionally with a more luxuriant outgrowth of tendrils and dots.

Contents: Psalter and Canticles [There is evidently a leaf or two missing at the end: the text breaks off almost at the end of the Benedicite with the words "вѣвнте днднїѧ й дzарїа мнсаи".]

Language: Church Slavonic of an East Slavonic recension; ь is predominant finally, ъ medially, ѫ comparatively rare. Ff.1-3 were evidently written by a Rumanian.

Inscriptions:

inside front cover: A kisebbik könyv felső lapján: | Іереміа могнла воево|а а[...] | azt jelenti hogy: Jeremia Mogila Vojvoda Gos|podar. (M.Jeremiás moldvai vajda és uralk.) | ( ) ő ajándékoztatta a könyvet valamelyik | oláh egyháznak. A könyv tartalma: | Dávid zsaltára ó-szláv nyelven, a lapok alatt | és szélmi a szöveg forditása (töredekesen) késöbb|kori kezi által irva.

f.1: Іереміа могнла воево |алтннаръ

ff.5-9, rectos: [fragmentary inscription, comminatory in tone, beginning кенде о зйуе пöпа благовещенїй | дöмне атꙋнѣе весерка | де[с]кöперйта шй уерꙋлъ де [...]]

f.11: мцъ сѐ ймѧтъ дꙗн ѧ днъ | йматъ уасъ бі | а ноцъ бі | ѧ днъ сймеöнь [This is followed by the numbers ꙅ-ѕі on f.11v and ѕі-ѧ on f.12. There are similar inscriptions relating to the remaining eleven months on ff.12-32.]

f.21v: [.]v днеко ѧнушѵ дн добра скрнса молнтꙗн тале | [...] съ те цнне дꙋмнзеꙋ ѧ знле мꙋ|мꙋлате шн вꙋне дꙋпъ дꙋаста рогꙋ к[ꙋ?|...] паче мезнка

ff.32v, 33-39 rectos, 40-55, 56v-70: [the text of a Rumanian version of the so-called *Epistula e cœlo missa de servanda die dominica* (cf. BHG III, pp.120-121)]

f.38: Бѐ ꙋшнма нашеⷨ ꙋслншахоⷨ · ѡцн п[...]

f.55v: анча амȣ скрись єȣ поп[а] Ранаши [?] знѣ [...] ла анȣ ⌐1799¬ фебрȣарй к҃ȣ зиле єȣ амь скрйс чине щйє май бине | сль скрйє єȣ аша амь цйнȣть аша а скрис'

f.70: богъ да прӧстй

f.56: [illegible]

ff.70v-71, 72-75, 76, 77-85, 86, 87, 88: [the text of a Rumanian version of the *Dreams of King Şahaişa (Cele 12 vise ale lui Mamer)*]

f.94: л҃ зилеле ауеле Іȣ

f.96v: [numerals:] в г д̃ є ѕ̃ и ѕ̃ӏ а҃ӏ к л м н ч о̃ п ч̃ р̃ с̃ т̃ оу ф ѯ̃·ѱ [Exactly the same sequence is repeated on f.100v.]

ff.101v, 112v, 113v: [illegible]

f.123: [some more numerals, no longer clearly legible because of damage to the edge of the leaf]

f.129v: м҃лю б҃жѡ л҃ь

f.132v: ауаста карте че сь к̃ламъ ѱалтире сир[...]

f.133: є҇ днеко ѫнȣшȣ диѧ добра скриса моли. тале | пртопопъ даниль ѡ илие ·· рогȣмȣ съ мь лово | чи · съ ми словочи сь мь прёцескь · в[...] | наши г҃и помилон[.] г с҃ва [...]

f.144: [illegible]

f.152: ке ю̈шй̈а дй[.] гадȣлъ кӧпай̈еле мл҃^(шш) демеле | де пӧмȣн^(пь)а ши ва траѣе пькатӧшй | сȣп' сйне ѫ гадȣлъ ѡ вай̈рете. | де сȣхвлете пькатӧсе ши ѡс̈ндйте | че вӧръ фй ѫ мьткь хȣӧкȣлȣй | мȣй̈севӧръ вечй вькȣлȣй ѫмйнъ

Provenance: originally written in the Ruthenian area, but with three additional leaves and extensive inscriptions written in Rumanian, most probably in Bács megye. Given on 22nd August 1912, together with Quart. Eccl. Slav. 15, by László Réthy (1851-1914), chief curator of the numismatics department of the National Museum and writer of indecent verse.

Chivu 1978, 1997; Mareş 2003.

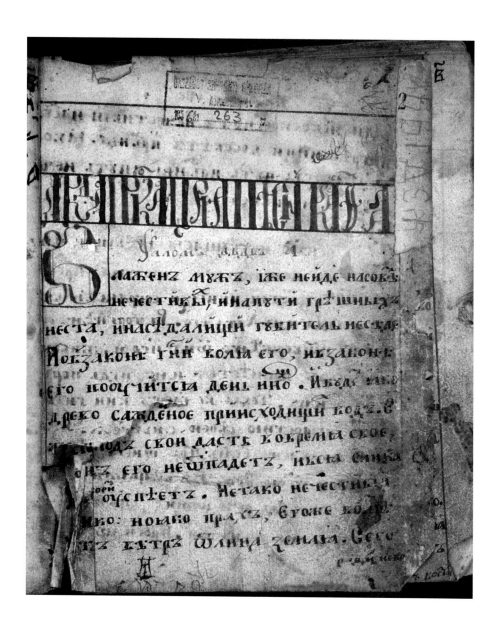

1. Oct. Eccl. Slav. 2, f.2 (cat. 1)

твоего · итогдапрозьриши изатиꙗсаꙗець
иже естьвъ ꙋ тесебрататвоего · нѣсо
древодобротворꙗи плодазла · ниⷣⱔ
возлотворꙗи плодадобрь · вьсѣⷦⷦоꙋбоⷣⱔⷡⷯ
воⷲплодасвоегопоꙁнаетьсѧ · неⷿтрьни
аботешꙋⷮьсловесь · ниꙋⷦалиⷩⷩⷩиⷡⷢⱃⷪ
здаⷲⷲьвьꙁемⷧⷮ · багьи тꙗвⱐⱕⷰ баⷢⱁ
скровищасрⷣцасвоего · иꙁноситьбагое
а ꙁльи тꙗвⱐⱕⷰ ꙁлагоскровищасрⷣцаско
его · иꙁноситьꙁлое · ѿиꙁбьит кавꙐⷣⷰⷣⷰ
гаⷮ рьꙋстаего · Ꙁⷪ · ꙁⷮ · втоⷬⷩⷬⷩⷦⷯ
Ꙋтожемꙗꙁоветеⷢⷥнⷢⷤ · аⷩⷬⷮⷡⷬⷱⷮⷡⷬⷱⷮⷮ
жеꙗꙁъгаⷧⷧ · вьсⷱⷭⷯꙐгрѧдⱐⷣⷯ кⷬⷨⱔ нⱔⷣⱔⷧⷱⱓ
шаⷩⷮ исловесамⷪ ꙋⷨⷩⱔ итворѧꙗ · скажⱙⷡⱔ
малⷪⷦⷪмоꙋ естьподобенⷭⷤ · подобенⱐⱕⷮⱐⷮ
ꙗⷡⷦⷪꙋ ꙁⷩⷣⷬⱔжⱔⷱⷪꙋ храмⷤⷤ нⱔⷣⱔ · иже искⷪⷪ
пⷪⷩⷦⷰⷣⱔⷧⷧⷩⷪⷮⷩⷯ иположⷩⷩⷦ ꙋⷤⷡⷱⷩⷪⷡ ⷩⷪⷡⷤ нⷩⷣⷪⷩⷩⷦⷮⱔⷣⷦⷯ на
каменⷭⱔ · наводⷩⱔꙋⷤⷡⷱⷩⷪ жеⷡⱔⷡⷯшⷪꙋ · приⷩⷣⷣⷣⷯⷯⷡⷯⷡⷤⱔ
каⷤⷡⷱⷩⷪ храмⱔⷩⱔⷣⷣⷩⷯⱐⱕ тⷪⷤ нⷩⷪⷩⷯⷡⷯⷡⷯⱐⷡⷯⷮ ⷤⷡⷱⷡⷯⷡⷯⷡⷯⷡⷯⷡⷯ
еⷤⷤ · ꙗⷡⷱⷡⷱⷡⷱ нⱔⷡⷱⷡⷱꙋ наⷡⷱⷡⷱⷡⷱ камⱔⷩⷣⷣ ⷡⷱⷡⷱⷡⷱ
ꙋꙗⷡⷱⷡⷱⷡ нⱔⷡⷱⷡⷱⷡⱐⷡⷯ · подобенⷭⱔꙗⷡⷱⷡⷱⷡⷡⷡⷡ
шⷤⷤ ꙋ храмⱔⷩⷣⷣⷩⷯ наꙁемⷧⷧⱔⷡⷱⷡꙁⷡⷤⷡⷡⷡⷡ
нⷩⷤⷡⷱⷡ · еⷤꙁⷡⷡꙗⷡⷱⷡⷱⷡⷡꙁⷡⷡ камⷤⷤꙗⷡⷤⷡꙗⷡꙁⷡⷡⷡⷡⷡⷡ
сⷤⷤ · с нⷤⷡ · ѿⷨⷨ · ҃ⷤⷡ стⷮⷪⷤⷤⷡⷡⷡⷱⷡⷱⷡ

2. Quart. Eccl. Slav. 7, f.87v (cat. 2)

Ѿ ѱⷤ ꙍ ⷩ истоеⷢ҃ѵⷢлⷣⷰє

Ꙁ наꙁаⷧ бѣ слово · и словобⷩ
кⸯбоⷮ, ибⸯ бⸯ слово · сѣⷤ н
сконⷰкⸯбоꙋ · вⸯсѣⷮ мⸯб⸉шⷴ.
ибеꙁнего, нитоⷤеб⸉, єⷤеб⸉
вⸯтомⷤⷤивотⷮⸯбⸯ, иⷤиⷩⷰ҃ⷩⷰ
бⸯсвѣⷮⷰлⷯⷦ. исвⸯбⸯтⷠⷩмⷮ
сⸯвⷮитⸯсѧ, итⸯмⷶꙗⷩ̀еⷩеобⷤⷶ꙽ ·

вⸯстⷮⷣлⷩ ⷩⷩвⷣ҃кⷣⷶ ⷩⷩⷩ пⷣ сⷯⷩ ⷣⷣ рⷢⷨⷩ ·

3. Fol. Eccl. Slav. 3, f.170 (cat. 4)

135

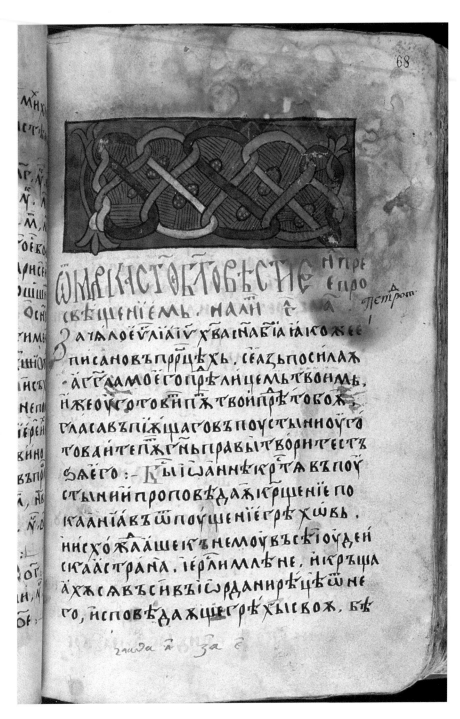

ѿ마르카ст облговесте и прє
єпро
сꙍвꙐщениемь. налй в̃ а̃   петрот

зачалоеѵліаітꙋ х꙰ва гнаблꙗ іако же є
писановъпр꙰ц꙰ѣхь. сеазъпосилаѫ
аг꙰г꙰ламоегопрѣлицемьтвоимь,
нже оуготовипѫтвоипрѣдꙇтобоѫ,
гласавъпіѫщагоѵъпоустинноуго
товаитепѫг꙰нꙗправытворитест꙰ъ
гꙗего ꙿ к꙰ꙑ і꙰ шаннькрꙿтꙗ въпоу
стꙑнии проповѣдаꙇкрꙋщеніе по
каанꙗвъ ѿпоущеніегрѣ хꙍвь.
иисхо жꙿдꙗашекꙿнемоувꙿсꙗꙇоудеи
скаастрана. іер꙰лимлꙗⷩне, икрꙋща
ахꙿжꙗсавъсивꙑꙇⷭꙿрданирѣцѣⷩѿне
го, исповѣдаꙇкꙿщегрѣхꙑсвоⷯ. бꙋ

гаꙿⷧда а̃ зꙗ є̃

4. Fol. Eccl. Slav. 20, f.68 (cat. 5)

136

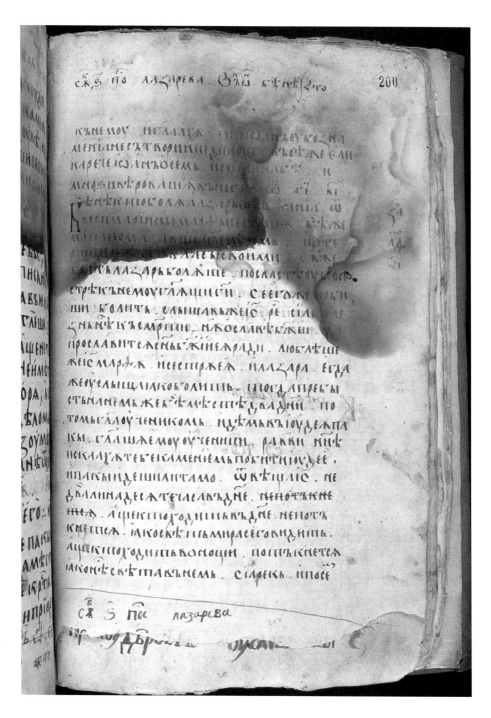

5. Fol. Eccl. Slav. 20, f.200 (cat. 5)

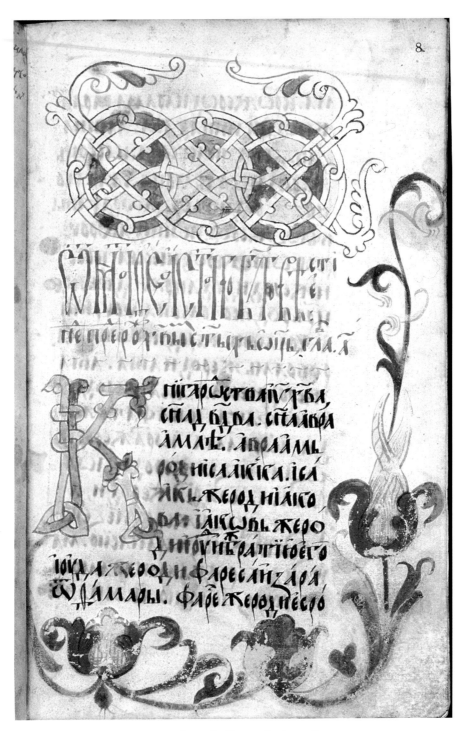

6. Fol. Eccl. Slav. 1, f.8 (cat. 6)

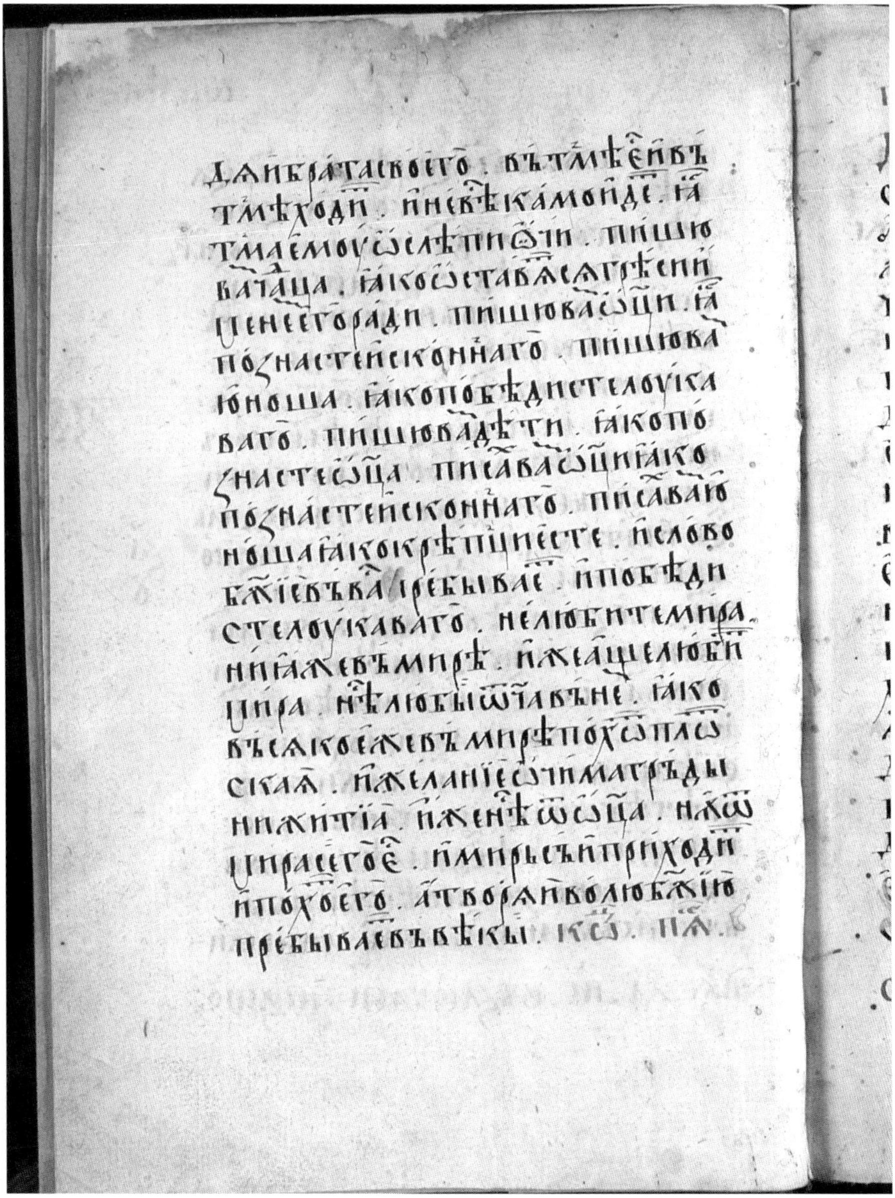

да иже расвоего въ тьмѣ еѱъ
тьмѣ ходи. и невѣкамонде. ꙗ
тьмаемоу иослѧпиоти. пишю
ватаца. ꙗкоиставлѧсаръени
ценесгоради. пишювасощи. ꙗ
познастеисконнаго. пишюва
юноша. ꙗкопобѣдистелоука
ваго. пишювадѣти. ꙗкопо
знастеоца. писавасощиꙗко
познастеисконнаго. писаваю
ношаꙗкокрѣпцинесте. ислово
бжиевъвасирѣбывале. ипобѣди
стелоукаваго. нелюбитемира
ниꙗжевъмирѣ. ꙗжеащелюби
ципра. нѣлюбыиотавьне. ꙗко
въсакоежевъмирѣпохотипло
скаꙗ. иꙗжеланиеотплаграды
нижитиꙗ. ꙗженѣоꙁоца. нашо
ципрасегое. имиресьипрѣходи
ипохоего. атворꙗиволюбжию
прѣбываесевъвѣкы. исо. пл.

7. Fol. Eccl. Slav. 11, f.3v (cat. 7)

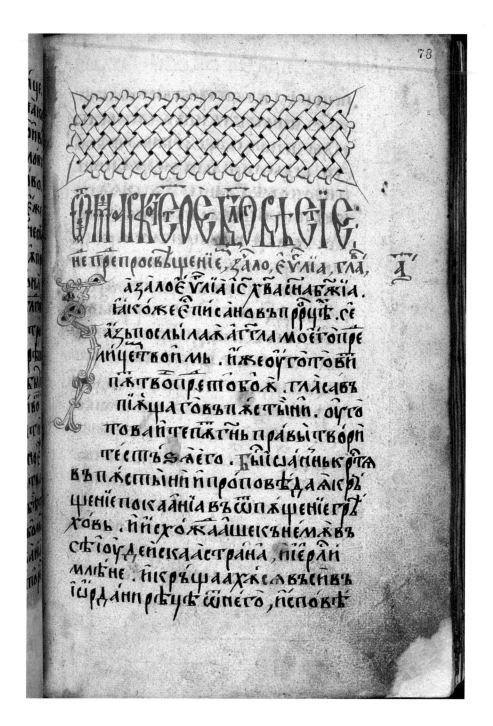

ѿ маⷬ҇ка єⷢ҇ꙋⷢ҇ сⷮое̏ е́

неⷣ пре́дъпросвⷮꙋщеніе, заⷬ҇о, еꙋⷢ҇лїа гла,
а҆ заⷬ҇лоє́ еꙋⷢ҇лїа і҆с х҃ва с҃на б҃жїа.
ꙗ҆ко́же є᷁ пис́ано въ пр́р́цѣⷯ .се́
а҆́зъ посылаⷣ а҆́г҃гла мо́его́ пре́
дъ ли́цеⷨ тво́и́мь . и҆́же оу҆́готови́
пꙋⷮ тво́и преⷣ тобо́ю . гла́съ въ
пѣⷣꙋща го́ въ пꙋⷤстыни . оу҆́го
то́ваи҆те пꙋⷮ г҃нь пра́вы твори́
те стⷮ҇зѧ е҆́го . бы́сⷮ и́а́ннъ крⷭ҇тѧ
въ пꙋⷤстыни и҆ проповѣⷣаꙗ к҃р᷁
щеніе пока́а́нїа въ ѿпꙋⷤщеніе грѣ
хоⷡ҇ . и҆́сходѧа́ше к нему̏ въ
сѧ́ і҆ꙋⷣе́иска́а стра́на . и҆̀ е҆рⷭ҇ли
мⷧ҇не . и҆ крⷭ҇щаа́хꙋ сѧ въ всиⷯ
і҆ꙋⷬⷣа́нⷯ рѣцѣⷤ ѿ него̏ , и҆́споⷡ҇

8. Fol. Eccl. Slav. 11, f.78 (cat. 7)

140

9. Fol. Eccl. Slav. 7, f.14 (cat. 8)

141

10. Fol. Eccl. Slav. 13, f.5 (cat. 9)

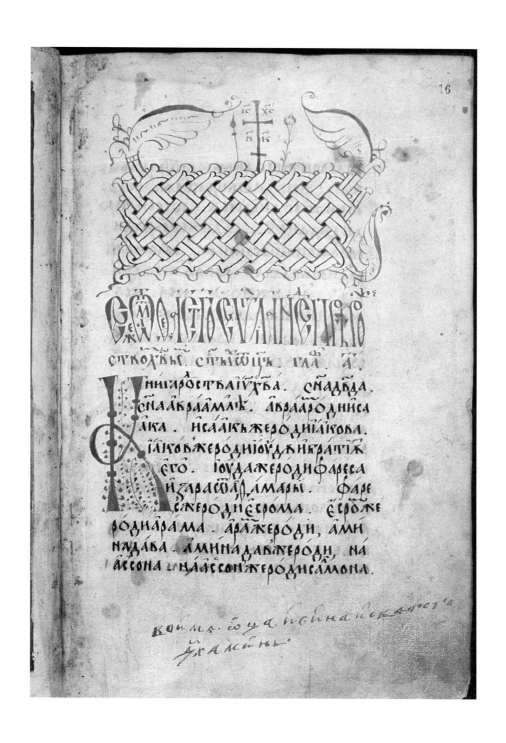

11. Fol. Eccl. Slav. 6, f.16 (cat. 10)

143

12. Fol. Eccl. Slav. 6, lower cover (cat. 10)

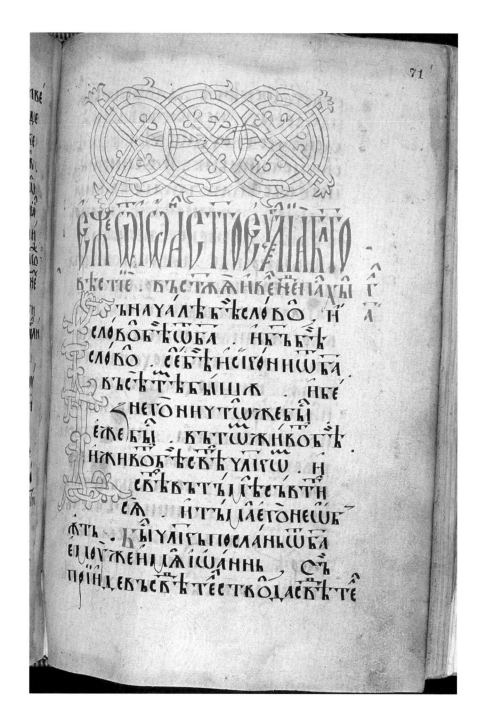

13. Fol. Eccl. Slav. 2, f.71 (cat. 11)

14. Quart. Eccl. Slav. 10, f.14 (cat. 12)

15. Quart. Eccl. Slav. 10, lower cover (cat. 12)

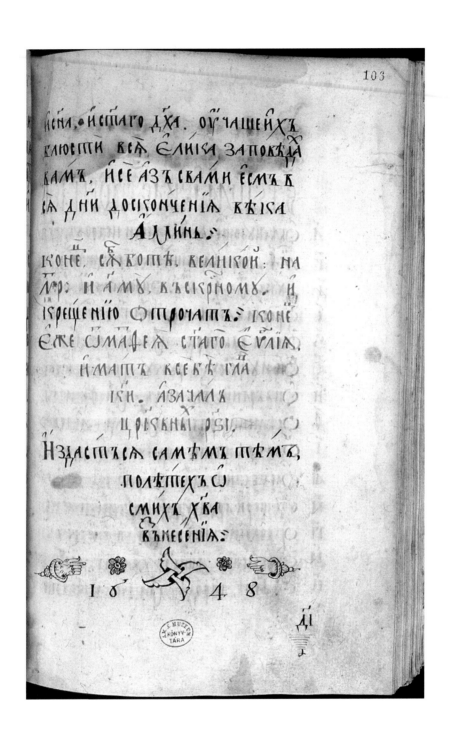

16. Fol. Eccl. Slav. 12, f.106 (cat. 14)

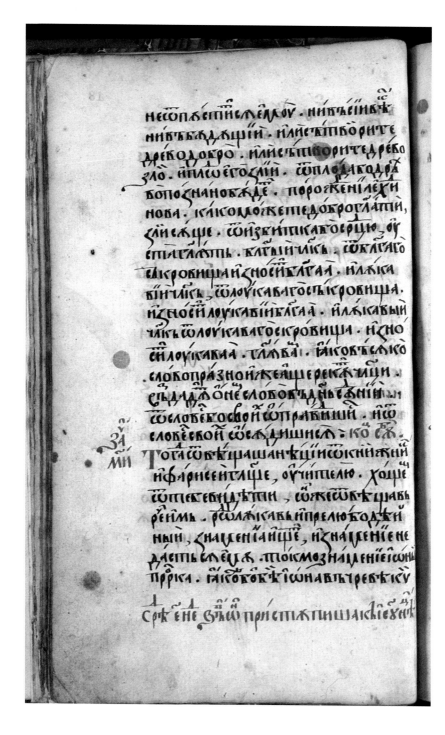

17. Fol. Eccl. Slav. 18, f.18v (cat. 15)

149

18. Fol. Eccl. Slav. 18, f.58 (cat. 15)

150

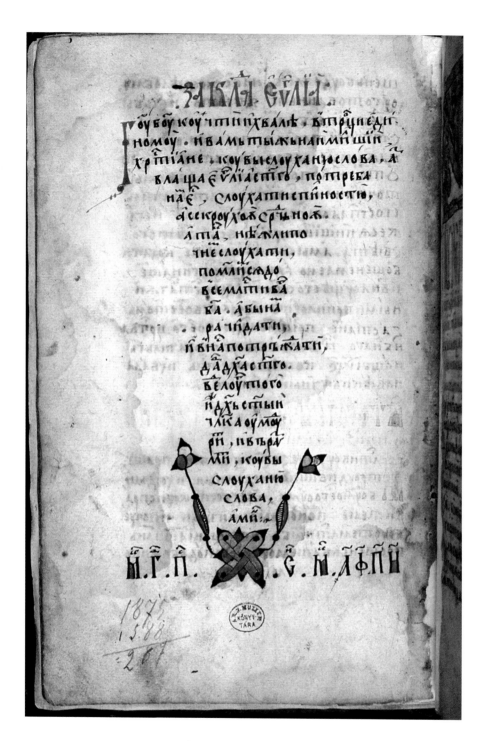

19. Fol. Eccl. Slav. 9, f.4v (cat. 16)

151

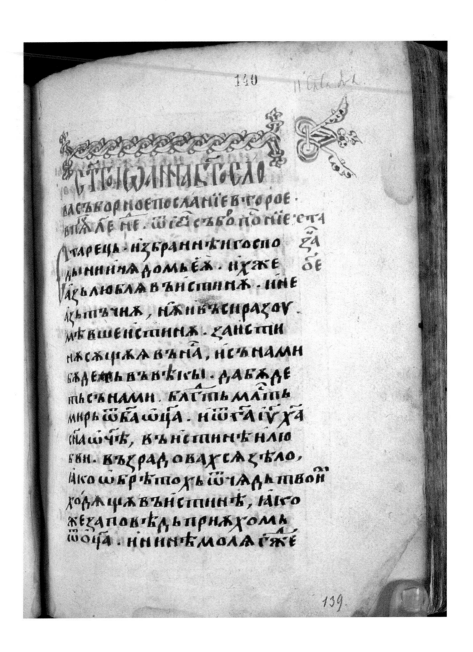

СТЫ ꙗⷩ҇ ГЛА Т СЛО

васъворноепосланїе второе ·

впⷤⷯлꙗе не · шⷯеⷭсъⷮбо поⷭгꙇе сⷮа
за
реⷰⷧ · изⷠⷠраннꙑⷯⷪ ꙇгоспо
ꙷⷣнининнадомьеⷯ · ꙇхже
б̾е
азⷤⷧлюблꙗвъꙇстинꙋ · ꙇне
азⷮⷰⷧꙇнꙗ, нꙗнвⷯаꙇнразоу
мⷡⷠвшенстинꙋ · занстин
нꙋⷤⷳꙇрꙗжавъⷩꙑⷩ, несⷮнамꙇ
бⷣꙺⷣемьвъвⷯкꙑ · дабꙋⷣе
тъснамꙇ · блⷢⷮⷮмлⷪⷮть
миръꙗⷳбⷢⷧⷶаⷪⷳца · нⷪⷮⷳгⷧⷶаꙇуⷧⷶхⷶⷮⷶ
наⷳчꙗⷮ, въꙗнⷮстⷮинꙋⷮꙇⷶⷧⷶлю
бⷡⷡи · възраⷣⷣовахⷶⷶⷶⷶⷶⷶⷶⷶ сꙗзⷢⷶⷶло,
ꙗкоꙗⷶбрⷯⷶⷶ

20. Fol. Eccl. Slav. 19, f.140 (cat. 17)

152

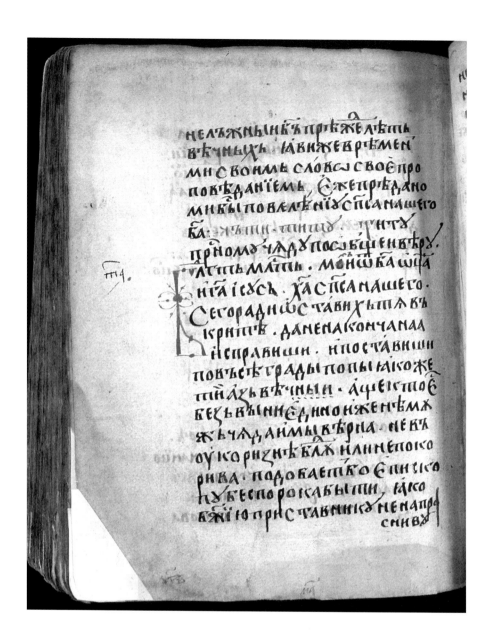

нелѣжны инѣ е прѣж е лѣти
вѣчныхь и авиж е врѣмен
ми своимь слово свое про
повѣ даниемь еже прѣдано
ми въ повелѣниꙗ спа нашего
ба · ꙗꙁѣти · типи · при ту
приному чаду посвѣщен вѣру
латть матть · мене ва Ѡца
ниꙗ исусь · ха спа нашего ·
сего ради Ѡставих та въ
критѣ · дамена кончанаа
исправиши · ипоставиши
повъсѣ грады попы накоже
ти азъ вѣчиныи · аще кто е
без выине диноиженѣ мж
же чада имы вѣрна · не въ
оукоризнѣ бл или непоко
рива · подобает ко е пи ско
пу бе спорока быти ꙗко
бжию пристaвнику не напра
снивꙋ

21. Fol. Eccl. Slav. 19, f.330v (cat. 17)

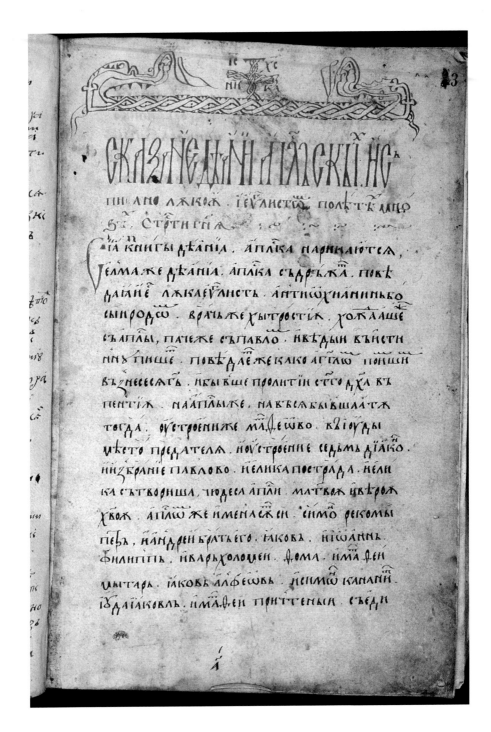

СКАЗ НЕⷣⷧИИ АПⷧСКЫⷯ НС

ПИСАНО ЛꙊКОⷤ . ІЕѵⷢАНСТОⷨ . ПОЛꙊⷮКА ЛѦⷤ
БꙀ̈ . СТꙋⷢ̈ТНГНА

СІА КНГЫ ДѢАНІА . АПⷧКА НАРНЦАЮⷮСѦ ,
ꙖЕⷧМАⷤЕ ДѢАНІА . АПⷧКА СЪДРЪⷤⷮА . ПОВⷢ̈
ДАꙖНⷮ ЛꙊКАЕѵⷢАНСТЬ . АНТНѶХНАНННЬКО
СЫНРОⷣⷭⷨ . ВРАѰⷤЕ ХЫТРОСТІꙖ . ПОХⷢАЛАШЕ
СЪАПⷧЫ , ПАѰЕⷤЕ СЪПАВЛО . НКꙖⷣЫН КЪНСТН
Иⷩⷤ ПНШЕ . ПОВⷢ̈ДАꙖ ЕⷤЕ КАКО АГⷧꙊ̈ ПОНШН
ВЪНЕСЕСѦⷮ . НБЫВШЕ ПРОЛНТІН ꙁⷭⷭⷭⷯ ДХА КЪ
ПЕНТГꙗ . НАⷦАПⷧЫꙖЕ . НАВСꙖⷣБЫВШАꙖТꙖⷯ
ТОГДА . ОУСТРОЕННⷤЕ МАⷱⷣЕШКО . Кꙁ̈ІОꙊⷣЫ
НⷨЕСТО ПРЕⷣАТЕЛꙖ . НОУСТРОЕННЕ СЕⷣⷨЪ ДІАⷦⷪ̈
ННꙁⷬⷬⷯРАНІЕ ПАВЛОВО . НЕЛНКА ПОСТРАⷣА . НЕЛН
КА СЪТВОРНША . ПꙊДЕСА АПⷩⷧ . МАⷮВБⷤ ЦⷡВⷮРОⷤ
ХВⷭⷬ̈Ꙗ . АПⷧꙊⷳ ЖЕ НМЕНАСꙖⷮ . СНⷨⷩ̈ⷪ РЕⷦⷪⷨЫ
ПЕⷮ̈Р , НАНⷣРЕН БРАТⷮ ЕГꙐ̈ . ІАКОВА . НІѠАННⷣ
ѲНЛНПⷪ̈ . НВАРⷯОЛОⷣⷨЕН . ѲОМА . НМАⷮⷫⷪ̈ЕН
ⷨⷩЫТАРꙖ . ІАКОВⷧ АЛѲЕОВЪ . НСНⷨⷩⷪ̈ КАНАⷩⷩ̈
ІꙊⷣАІАКОВⷧЬ . НМАⷮⷫⷪ̈ЕН ПРНⷰⷮⷮ̈ЕНЫН . СЪЕⷣН

А

22. Fol. Eccl. Slav. 22, f.3 (cat. 18)

154

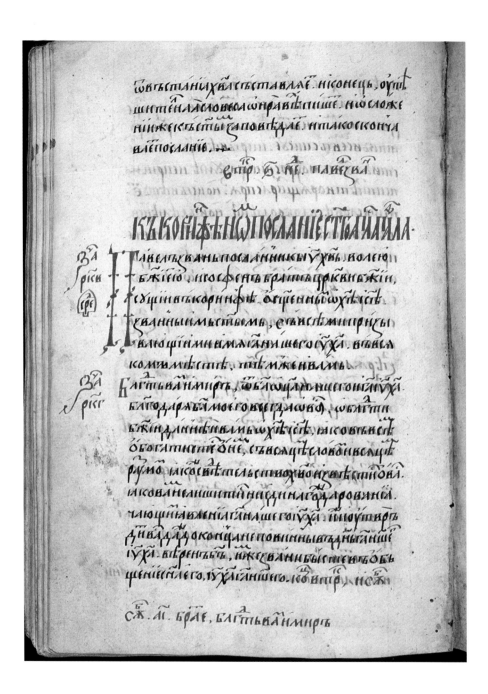

23. Fol. Eccl. Slav. 22, f.105v (cat. 18)

155

24. Fol. Eccl. Slav. 8, f.10v (cat. 19)

25. Fol. Eccl. Slav. 8, f.82v (cat. 19)

157

стꙑ сьздѣлѧ · т̾ съвьстѧ́нꙗ а́гг҃ловь прпⷣбне
сѵмеѡне · съ нимѝ ха҃ б҃а мⷧ҇и непрестанно
ѡбрѣтаꙗ ⁙ Ꙗ҇ко Сѵмеѡ́н оⷮ попоⷬ҇ ро́жⷣенїе
исꙑй ꙗ зꙑ̀чат̾ доболѣ е исⷢ҇да исꙿпоꙋвал̾
исꙿповѣдати · ѡбличе въсꙿпоꙗже і то мрⷪ҇
подобнаго страдⷣанїѧ · и подвигꙑ ніже на
земли ꙗ́ко свѣтилникь ꙗвлꙗшагосѧ
всеꙗко · мно́гꙑ трьпѣнїе бꙑнꙋꙿ а́гг҃ль
сть́й въ силꙿⷣаша · съ тѣмꙿ убо подⷣ непре
станно хⷵ· Аꙿое · Маꙗ непрестано обⷮⷭ҇ꙵ
наꙁⷨⷰ҇ септеврїꙗ а҃ · ПАМꙗ прпⷣбна
ѿц҃а нашего Сѵмеѡна ста҃пнⷫꙵ
лⷠ҇ꙗвнꙑй сѵмеѡⷩ҇сѣ · ѡ а́нⷮⷦ҇ оꙩꙵа сⷬ҇ъ
исⷪ҇а · на бꙑⷱⷮꙵ ѿ родⷣителю своего паⷭ҇н
ѡвцⷬ҇ · оꙋꙿпазнител̾ его ꙁимꙑ · въсеꙿхю
цⷬ҇ковьше · ег а тⷫ҇венаго еѵⷢ҇а слꙑш
бⷤꙵаще и хвалꙗ ше и ненавидꙗщꙵй мира,
и любꙗщꙵй · ѡставивⷣ родⷣителꙗ всⷩ҇
послѣдⷣова хс҃ⷱꙵ шⷤе блⷣгодꙋꙗ емх̾ ю ѡⷮра
ꙗⷡ҇мнꙵй · въ цⷭ҇рⷮⷠ҇во льва великаго · въ едⷣи
ного поꙗ лаврꙑ бⷤꙵаше прⷤⷮвѣ · и всѣ тⷭ҇
сꙋⷥꙵꙵ҇мнихо · добродⷣѣтелїю прес̾пⷠ҇ѣ ·
и тⷧ҇ло свое аꙵⷧꙵсанїе и жаждеⷮⷦ҇ оꙋдⷣрꙋчⷩꙵй
ѿꙁлобⷫꙵенⷣⷮꙵ · и постⷮнꙵсꙗ дⷩꙵй м҃ · ꙗже
иⷭ҇ стоꙗⷮꙵꙵ҇ше и іⷭ҇ сⷣꙗдⷣꙗше ѿⷮрⷮⷣа · послѣ
въꙁꙑⷫꙵде настꙗⷮꙵꙵ вꙑсоⷦꙵ · манеже мнⷢ҇ои
подⷣесⷨⷮꙵ твⷬ҇и, и белїй прⷣивѣбⷮⷰ҇ ꙗ́ко
и многꙑ ꙵⷮ погⷨꙵнꙑ и невⷮⷣрⷩꙵй собраⷮ҇и -
исⷠ҇ⷮⷰꙵ · и м лⷮ҇ работаⷮⷮꙵемх̾ · поꙋⷨⷮрⷮ, и
предⷣаⷧꙵб҃и своего дш҃ꙋ и погребенⷮ бꙑ того

26. Fol. Eccl. Slav. 5, f.4v (cat. 20)

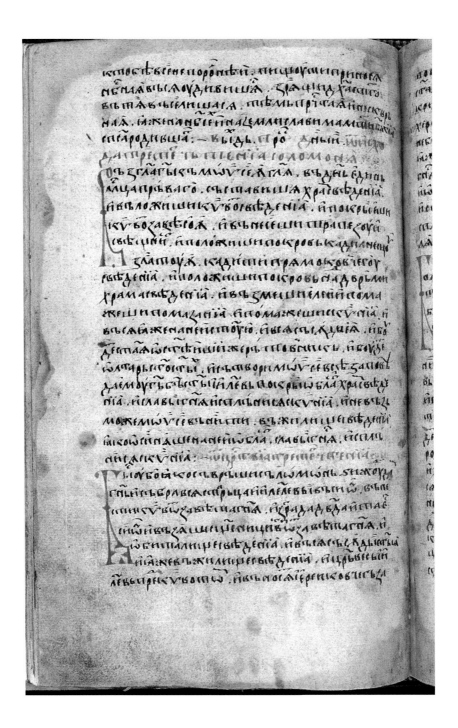

27. Fol. Eccl. Slav. 5, f.57v (cat. 20)

159

прьшⷣца . и прѣбывшиꙗженетлькема . порожⷣе
страⷣвоꙗ . тꙗжесⷧꙋⷦꙋнестиннопⸯсповѣⷣе .
прѣпⷦтаⷶ ⁖ пⷮк г ирмо Ⰰ оусилⸯныисⸯвкоⷬ
шисꙗ . дрьжавоꙗжⷮие . исилоꙗнемощии пⷬⸯпрⷬ
поꙗсаше ⁖ Ⰾⷮ тавеⷧꙗⷦотревⸯше . ꙗⷦоⷧкто
творець . истебедвоволеꙁⸯмладаꙁⸯнжетⸯсꙗ ⁖-
рⸯквошиⷬшиⷩⷩⷦⷡⸯпрославⸯи . имꙗжадавⸯне
бесⸯныираⷨ сꙗживе ⁖- Ⰸⷶꙁⷶлополⸯꙁⷮⷩⷩопрⷨꙗе и
рⷡⷦⷮѣⷩоⷩопⷮⸯꙗекевⸯкисⸯтⸯворе . мⸯтⸯнеꙗⷲии
прⷩоⷣвⷶꙗ ⁖- иⷩꙿ ирмо Ⱁ оутвр⸦꙽жаꙗⷮⷲⷬо ⁖-
ⷪ тⷧꙿⷦⷮⷩсⷨꙋⷨꙋпослⸯⷣовⷶⷨⷣⷡⷶⷬенїꙗ . паⷧⷭⷨⷤⷩⷶ
въ сⷮпрїⷩⷨⷡⸯⷡⷬⸯꙁⷨⷬꙙжⷨⷩⷦⷨⷫ . паⷮⷨⷲⸯсⷦⷫⷩⷶпⷮⷲⷨⷲⷩⷡⷪⷮ
мⷮ⸦ⷩⷡⷦⷬⷫ . ⷶⷮⷩⷧⷦ сⷦⷫⷩⷫⷦⷡⷦⷫⷫⷩⷦⷮ꙯ⷫⷩⷮⷨⷫⷶⷬⷨⷦⷮ ⁖-
Ⱀⷶсⷶⷤⷩⷦⷩⷪⷦⷣⷦⷡⷪ . прⷩⷦⷡ⸦ⷣⷩⷦⷣⷦⷶⷡⷦⷫⷨⷪⷮⷦⷦⷡⷪ
въⷡⷬⷦⷫⷨꙙⷡ꙯ⷩⷶⷨⷶⷮⷧⷶⷤⷩⷦⷦⷪⷫⷬⷪⷣⷶꙁⷦ . ⷫⷧⷪⷣ꙽ⷶⷪⷣⷪ
ⷬⷪⷣꙙⷮⷫⷧⷦⷮⷩⷦ . ꙗⷦⷪⷫⷮⷮⷫⷩⷪⷡⷦⷬⷶⷫⷦⷮⷫ꙯ⷮⷩⷦⷪⷫⷪ
ⷪⷨⷦⷦ ⁖- Ⰲ ⷮⷩⷫⷦⷮⷧⷧⷶⷣꙿⷡⷦⷬⷶ ⷡⷡⷧⷩⷦⷨ꙯ꙗⷫⷧⷦⷮⷦⷩⷦⷮⷩⷦⷬꙙⷨⷦ
Ⱀⷶⷡⷦⷧⷦⷶⷦⷩ . ипроⷡⷡⷦⷬ⸦ⷦⷩⷫⷫⷪⷩⷫⷪⷮⷦⷩⷪ . лоⷯⷶⷦⷦⷩⷫⷩⷶⷮⷫⷨⷩⷶⷮⷩⷮⷩⷶⷫ
ⷫⷨⷡⷩⷭⷮⷦⷮⷡⷦⷦⷮ . ꙗⷦⷦⷫⷦⷬⷩⷶⷫⷪⷮꙙⷫⷫⷦⷮⷡⷦⷮⷧⷪⷨ . ⷪⷮⷮ
ⷩⷶⷫꙿⷫⷦⷫⷪⷤⷩⷦⷮⷩⷶⷫⷫⷦⷫⷧⷡⷦⷮ ⁖-

28. Fol. Eccl. Slav. 5, f.109 (cat. 20)

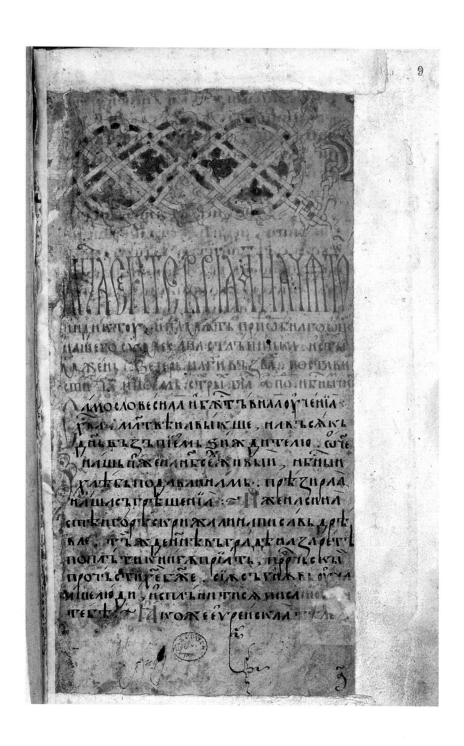

29. Fol. Eccl. Slav. 10, f.9 (cat. 21)

30. Fol. Eccl. Slav. 15, ff.65v-66 (cat. 22)

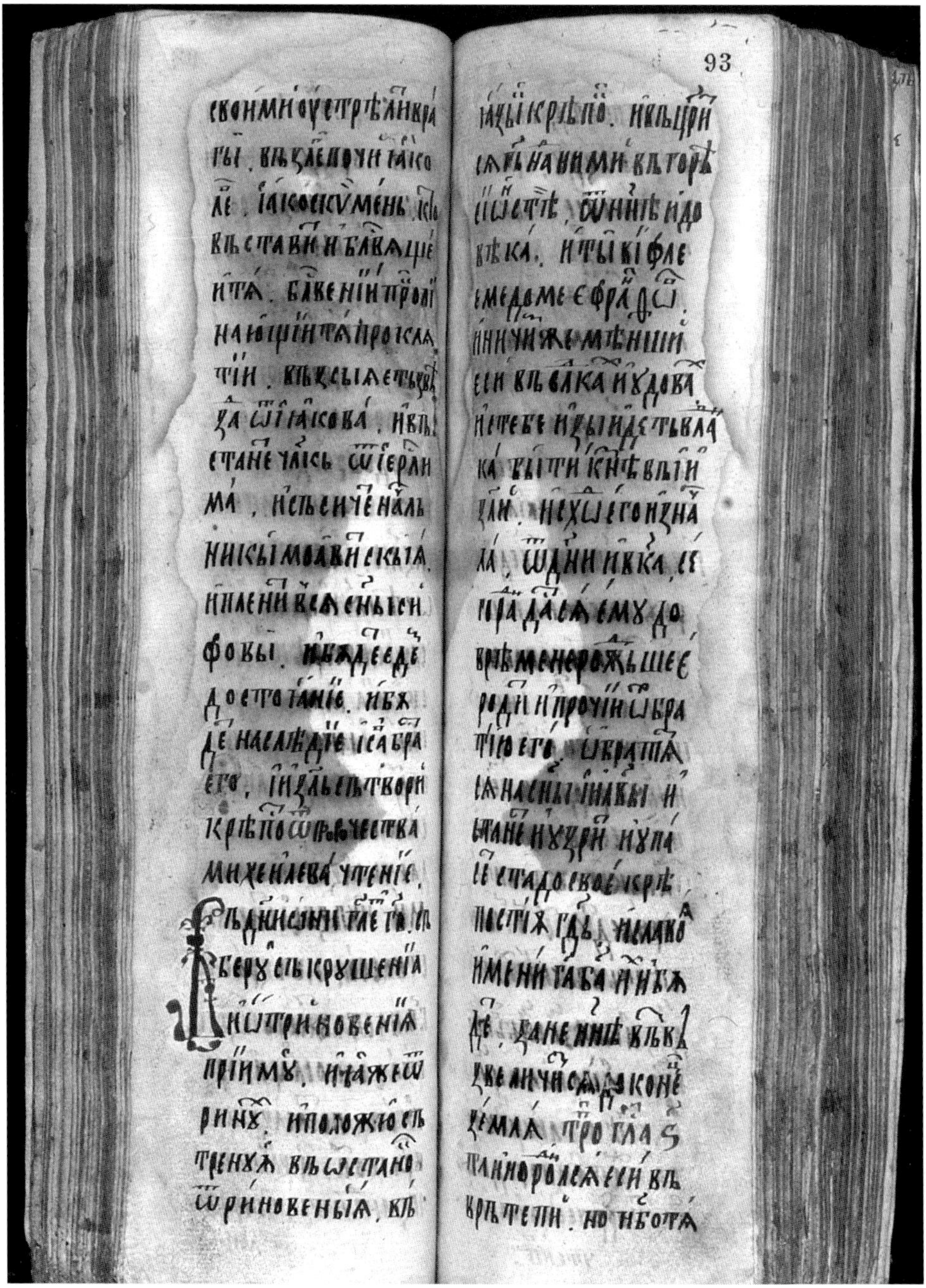

31. Fol. Eccl. Slav. 15, ff.92v-93 (cat. 22)

32. Fol. Eccl. Slav. 15, ff.167v-168 (cat. 22)

33. Fol. Eccl. Slav. 15, ff.216v-217 (cat. 22)

165

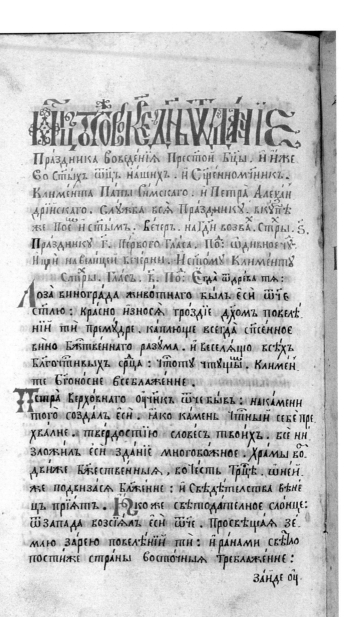

ПРⷣⷪⷮⷪОВКⷣⷬⷲⷰⷩⷥ

Праздника Бо̃ведⷷнїꙗ Престⷪ́й Бⷣⷰⷳ. и҆ и́же
Во Стⷯⷯ ѽⷳⷱ нашиⷯ. и҆ Сⷺⷩⷩомⷸⷮⷩⷩⷦⷯ.
Климеⷩта Па́пы Риⷨⷭⷦагѡ: и҆ Петра̀ Алеⷯⷩⷣ
дрї́нⷭкагѡ. Слⷹⷤⷠⷶ воⷳ Празⷣⷩⷩⷦⷯ. вкⷹⷣⷯ
же Поⷺ и стⷭⷪ́ⷨ. Вечеⷬ. на гⷭⷣⷩ возⷠⷶ. Стⷬⷣⷩ. ѕ҃.
Празⷣⷩⷩⷦⷹ г҃. Первого Гла́са. Поⷣ: ѽдивное чⷹ
И цⷬⷩ на велицеⷨ Вечеⷬⷩⷩ. И потомⷹ Климеⷩтⷹ
Стⷬⷩⷩ. Глаⷭ. в҃. Поⷣ: Ста̀ ѽдрⷷва та̀:

Лоза̀ винограда живоⷮнагѡ быⷧ ес҆и ѽⷡⷺ
стⷧⷶю: красно и́знⷪⷭꙗ гроздїе дⷯоⷨ повелⷷ
нїи ти҆ премⷹⷣре. капⷧⷶюще всегⷣа спⷭⷺнное
вино Бжⷭⷮвеннагѡ разⷹма. и҆ веселⷶⷳо всⷯⷯ
Блⷢⷪⷱⷮⷩⷡⷶⷯ срⷣⷰⷶ: чтⷪⷮⷹ чтⷱⷩⷶ. Климеⷩ
те Бⷢⷪносе всеблаже́нне.

Петра̀ верⷯоⷡнагѡ ѻ҆ⷱⷩⷦⷯ ѽⷡⷺбыⷡⷶ: на ка́менⷩ
тогѡ создаⷧ ес҆и. ꙗ҆ко ка́мень и́стⷩный себⷷ пре
хваⷧⷩⷺ. тверⷣостїю словеⷭ твоиⷯ. всⷺ ни
зⷧожиⷧ ес҆и зданїе многобѡжное. Храⷨы во
дⷡⷩⷤⷺ Бжⷭⷮвенныꙗ, воⷳ чеⷭть Трⷪ́ⷰⷷ. ѻ҆нⷩⷩ
же подⷡⷩⷨⷶⷱⷶ Блⷤⷩⷩⷩⷺ: и҆ Свⷷдⷷтеⷧⷭтва вⷷнⷺ
цⷺ прїаⷮ. Ꙗкоже свⷷтоⷣа́теⷧное слⷩ̈це:
ѽ запада возсїаⷧ ес҆и ѽⷡⷺ. Просвⷷщⷶꙗⷳ зе
мⷧю зарею повелⷷнїи ти҆: и҆ ранами свⷷтⷧо
постиⷤⷺ стра́ны восто́чныꙗ треблаже́нне:

ЗАиⷣе ѻ҆ⷱ

34. Fol. Eccl. Slav. 25, f.46v (cat. 23)

СЛУЖБА ОБЩАЯ СВ҃ЩЕННОИСПОВѢДНИКУ:

Вен на ли. ковач҃ в. Стри. Глас. д҃. По: Яко добла;

И стинъ ѡсновании. и вѣри оутвержение. и пощение приудачнаго ...

Я плом съ протолника. строгочирпаемъ равнообразнаго ...

Премрости тала ентъ оумножникъ всехвални. радости спо ...

Слава: Нинѣ: Бо: Скирвь ѡмий стрчнаго срⷣца моего ...

Православиа наставнни. и благочтиа оучатю и чотⷮ. всели ...

И лоучарни. Канонъ. Гла҃. ... по посⷧѣдⷣ̈...

Сеи ... свѣ воⷥгоⷬси сщⷣеннⷣии. Имⷦ: къ страданию
приложивⷮся крⷣпⷮко. скорⷣи ... и подвиги чрпⷮа ...
... съⷬрⷮи пищⷣ векоⷬнечнⷣⷢю. Кроⷬкими крⷮплении. Сла҃
... нⷣекⷣрⷣⷢтⷣа. скорⷣ оутолиⷧ еⷭи; рⷣка виⷧ еⷭи хⷭⷮа

надⷧⷣ

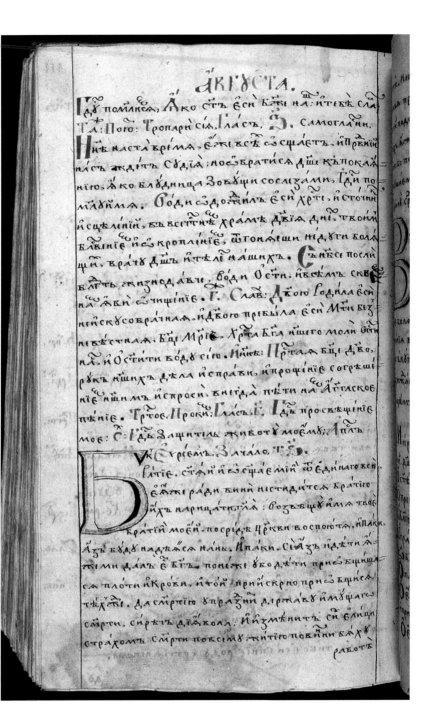

36. Fol. Eccl. Slav. 26, f.411v (cat. 24)

168

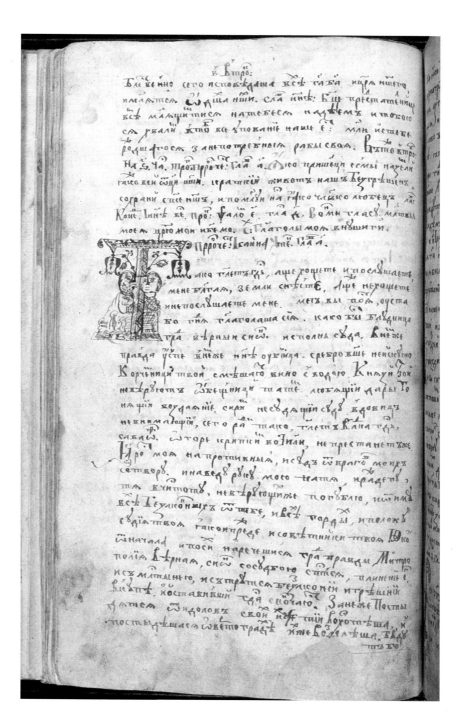

37. Fol. Eccl. Slav. 4, f.51v (cat. 25)

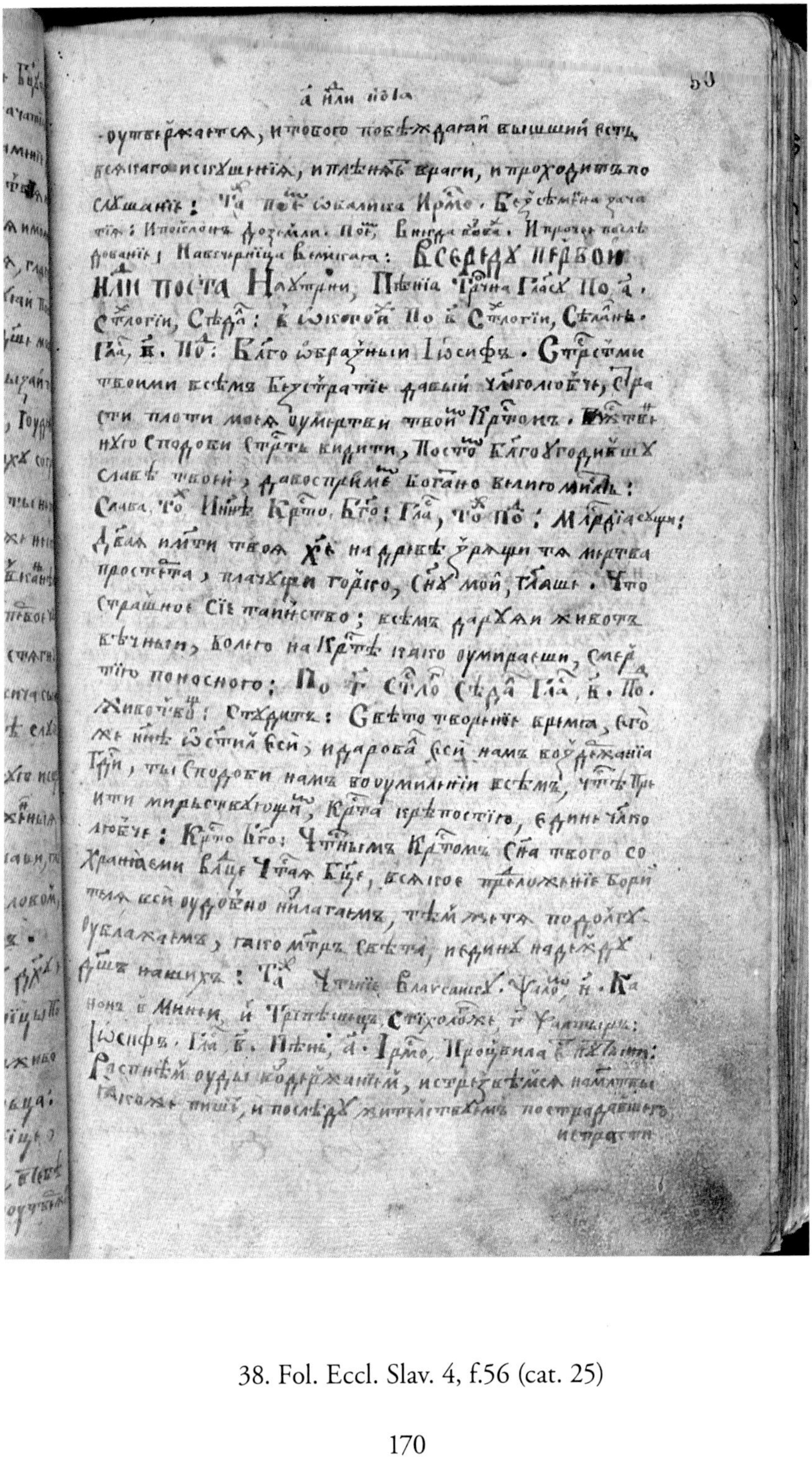

38. Fol. Eccl. Slav. 4, f.56 (cat. 25)

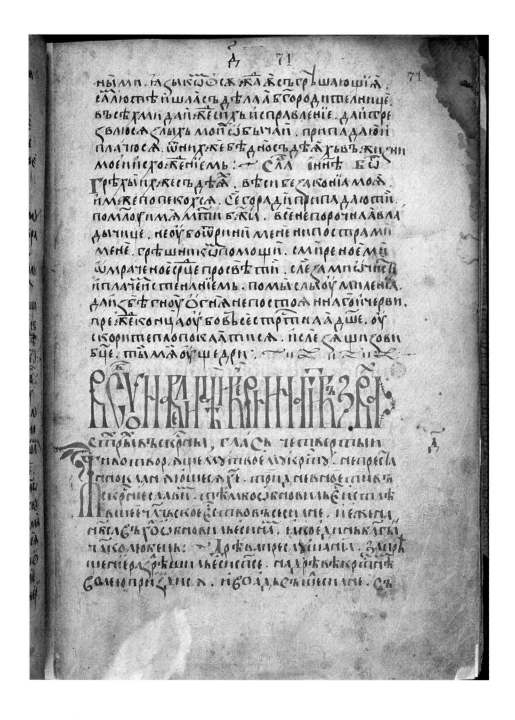

39. Fol. Eccl. Slav. 14, f.71 (cat. 26)

И҆ ке́пльны̏тьпрⷮѣмн҄ѡⷤка . о҆бнищⷶвъⷠгото́ты
меⷤ . е҆гⷪ҇рⷣⷪбн҄ищⷶвъⷩшⷶⷲѡⷠⷶти҆нⷭⷲⷶвⷩи҆ⷶпⷡⷩ
въⷯ . дⷶрова́ниⷨвъ҇҇ⷪвꙋⷯⷵⷩⷢⷨноⷠⷪⷢⷶщⷶⷲⷶⷲ
и҆ко́нⷰⷶ . бꙋⷣⷲⷡⷩⷶⷩⷢⷨⷩⷩⷢⷮⷩⷩⷢⷨⷡ҇ⷪⷩⷶⷥⷩⷶⷲⷩ
оу҆ра́ни҆съ . и҆а҆дⷪⷡⷩⷡⷮⷩⷵⷩⷩⷩⷡⷪⷭ҇ⷮⷩⷥⷩⷩ҇ⷢⷨ . и҆
оу҆ча́з҆ве́ноⷭⷣⷰ҇ⷯⷮⷶⷣⷶ . стъⷤⷤⷩⷩⷡⷡⷶⷠⷩⷶ҇ⷢ
и҆ⷤⷩⷩⷩⷶⷣⷩⷯ҇ⷯⷪⷢⷨⷵⷩⷶⷥⷩⷩ҇ⷢⷨⷢⷨ . а҆пⷭⷣⷮⷩⷡⷩⷩⷯ҇
лⷠⷶⷢⷨⷩ . и҆ⷭⷮⷢⷩⷡⷣⷩⷩⷩⷩⷩⷩⷩⷩⷶⷢⷨⷩⷡⷢⷶ . и҆ⷡⷡⷤⷩⷮ
мⷩⷮⷪⷠⷡⷶⷩⷯⷩⷡⷩⷭⷮⷩⷠⷵⷩⷩ҇ⷢⷩⷩ . и҆ⷮⷢⷨⷶⷡⷩⷩⷩⷩⷢⷪ
бⷩⷡⷡⷩⷡⷵⷶⷢⷩ . и҆ⷩⷮⷩⷮⷵⷩⷢⷡⷩⷩⷩⷩⷮⷯⷨⷩⷩⷩⷩⷡ . ⷭⷮⷩⷮⷩⷩ
ⷭⷨⷩⷮⷪⷢⷪⷩⷭⷩⷩⷠⷵⷡⷩⷩⷯⷩⷥⷢⷨⷶ . пⷩⷡⷵⷩⷣⷩⷮⷡⷩⷯⷩⷩⷩ
стⷡⷭⷩⷩⷶⷢⷨⷩ . ⷮⷩⷤⷡⷮⷩⷪⷢⷮⷩⷩⷩⷩⷯⷩⷶ . ⷵⷪ
а҆пⷭⷣⷩⷮⷪⷢⷨⷩⷩ . оу҆ⷭⷮⷶⷡⷩⷮⷩⷭⷮⷩⷮⷩⷩⷩⷮⷪⷩⷮⷩⷶ
чⷶ . и҆ⷶⷤⷩⷮⷩⷶⷣⷩⷩⷭⷪⷵⷩⷩⷮⷢⷩⷡⷯⷶⷪⷠⷪ҇ⷢⷨⷡ . и҆
сⷭⷮⷩⷩⷶⷩ҇ⷤⷩⷩⷮⷩⷭⷮⷩⷮⷶⷮⷩ҇ⷶⷭⷪⷶⷡⷶ ⷰⷶⷩⷶⷢⷩⷢⷪ : ⁓ і҆рⷨⷩⷩ
пⷩⷮⷩ҇ⷤⷩⷩ . Сⷮⷡⷩⷵⷩⷡⷩⷯⷩⷶⷶⷶⷣⷩⷢⷨⷩⷩⷮⷩⷡⷩⷩⷡⷡⷩⷢⷩ
пⷩⷮⷩⷠⷩⷩⷩⷩ . съⷡⷢⷩⷩⷮⷩⷡⷪⷪⷠⷩⷶⷥⷩⷮⷩⷡⷵⷶⷤⷩⷡⷩⷡⷩⷮⷯⷩⷶ
дⷶⷡⷡⷩⷮⷡⷪⷩ . и҆ⷯⷨⷶⷡⷶⷡⷩⷮⷩⷡⷮⷩ҇ⷢⷨⷡⷩⷪⷢⷨⷩⷩ . сⷩ
зⷩⷩⷣⷩⷡⷭⷮⷡⷡⷶⷡⷪⷩⷩⷩⷮⷩⷮⷩⷭⷩⷡⷩⷡⷩⷩⷶⷩⷡⷡⷪⷵⷩ҇ⷤⷩⷶ
нⷩⷩⷩ велⷩⷡⷩⷩⷩⷩⷩⷩⷩⷭⷩⷶⷡⷡⷪ : ⁓ И҆ⷤⷩⷤⷩⷩⷮⷩ҇ⷡⷩⷶⷢⷨⷶ
сⷩⷩⷪⷩⷶⷣⷩⷩⷮⷩⷡⷩⷡⷶⷥⷶⷡⷩ . и҆ⷩⷩⷡⷩⷮⷩⷡⷩ҇ⷡⷢⷩⷩⷡⷩⷯⷩⷢⷨⷡⷩⷪⷩ
пⷡⷩⷮⷩⷡⷮⷩⷩⷩⷵⷩⷩ . сⷮⷩⷡⷩⷮⷯⷤⷡⷩⷣⷵⷩⷩⷩⷪ . пⷩⷶⷵⷡⷩⷵⷮⷠⷡⷩ
шⷩⷩⷩ҇ⷩⷩⷯⷶⷡⷶⷭⷮⷩⷡⷩⷮⷩⷡⷡⷪⷭⷶⷪⷪⷮⷩⷵⷩⷶ҇ⷵⷩⷩⷩⷩ . о҆ⷰⷩⷪⷠⷡⷪⷡ
воⷭⷵⷩⷩⷵⷩⷩⷩⷩⷩⷩⷶⷡⷪ : ⁓ оу҆ⷩⷩⷶⷡⷪⷩ҇ⷪⷪⷠⷡⷩ҇ⷩⷩⷩⷩⷩ
въⷭⷩⷵⷨⷩⷩⷯⷩⷡⷩ . ⷮⷡⷩⷩⷩⷩⷡⷶⷡⷩⷠⷡⷩⷪⷭⷩⷡⷩⷩⷩⷮⷡⷩⷡⷩⷩⷩ
и҆ⷭⷪⷡⷡⷪ : ⁓ Оу҆ⷩⷩⷶⷡⷪⷩ҇ⷪⷪⷠⷡⷩⷶⷰⷩⷩⷶⷶⷡⷪⷵⷩ҇ⷶ҇ⷤⷩⷤⷩⷩ
нⷩⷩ . ⷮⷡⷩⷩⷩⷩⷡⷶⷡⷩⷭⷪⷮⷪⷪⷠⷡⷩⷯⷩⷩⷩⷯⷮⷩⷵⷩⷶⷡⷩⷩⷩⷩⷩ
и҆ⷭⷪⷡⷡⷪ . оу҆ⷮⷪⷡⷩⷡⷪⷩⷵⷮⷶⷡⷮⷩⷩⷯⷩⷩⷩ . о҆ⷩⷣⷪⷵⷩⷩⷩⷶⷡⷩⷶ
о҆ⷰⷩⷩⷶⷭⷮⷡⷩ҇ⷩⷩⷭⷮⷩⷶⷡⷪⷰⷩⷩⷭⷮⷡⷩⷭⷮⷡⷩⷵⷩⷶⷡⷩⷩⷣⷶⷵⷩⷶⷶ . ⷡⷶ

40. Fol. Eccl. Slav. 14, f.158v (cat. 26)

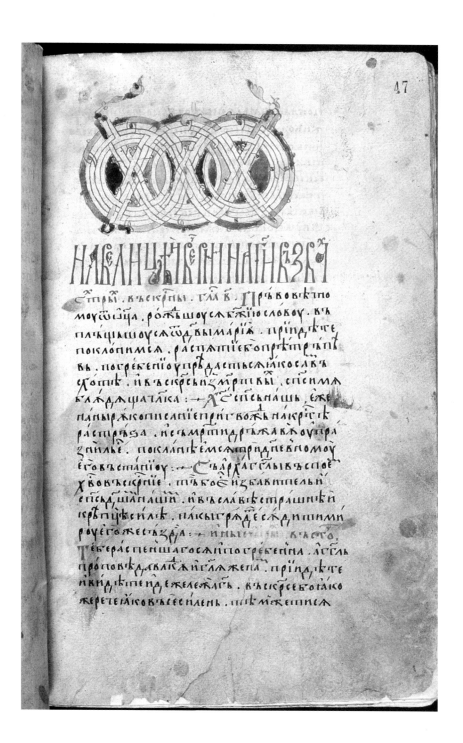

41. Fol. Eccl. Slav. 23, f.47 (cat. 27)

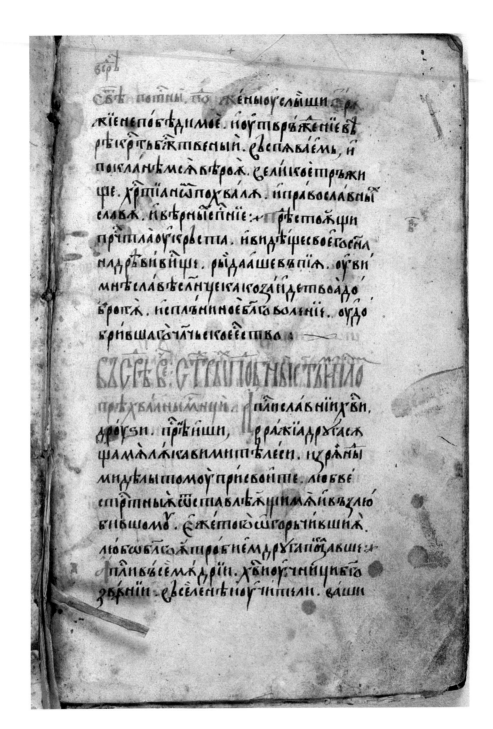

42. Fol. Eccl. Slav. 27, f.21 (cat. 28)

въ трїе ̈сщенїй славословима вѣрно : ҃ ꙗ
двери бжїꙗ . и҃ не же же проиде вѣтиꙗщен
дѣтелъ . запеатлѣннаа съхранивта · рꙑн
елеꙋкꙗчелестꙑꙗ · бжтвнаꙗнⷣⷣжⸯноⷭꙿсцꙑн .
рꙑнеꙗприктполе . ꙇꙗⷭⷭтвищеннаа · рꙑнеа
горо бжꙗнест꙼ꙗꙗсомаа . помꙗннꙗⷪ сⷪꙿпⷭ есе е ҃да при-

БⷭⷭⷶЛⷰⷢⷯⷱⷩꙖⷠⷷⷧⷩⷷⷱⷣⷩⷩⷩⷧⷢⷵⷩ

въ зⷡ҃ъ . стрⷣы ҃ . бⷭⷭꙿресрⷨⷬⷩⷩꙑ . глⷶ . аⷣ ҃ : +

Живⷪтворⷶщемоуꙋтвоемоусⷬⷬⷪⷧⷩⷩⷧⷦⷶⷣⷧⷩⷩⷩⷩⷧⷧꙋ . нестⷬⷳ꙼ⷭⷠⷶⷩⷩⷩⷩⷪ
слⷶⷩⷩ꙼ꙗⷳⷭⷩⷩ꙼ꙗꙿсахⷭ҃ . придневное тивⷭⷭꙿресрⷬⷣⷩⷩⷧⷩⷩⷪⷩⷩⷩⷧⷩⷦ꙼е
слⷶⷠⷩⷩⷧ꙼ⷧ꙼м . пⷩⷳⷷⷨⷠⷳⷷ꙼ⷩꙿновⷩⷩⷧⷠⷳ꙼ⷥ꙼꙼нⷧⷠⷳꙗ꙼сꙑ . ꙇⷭⷭꙿ꙼꙼꙼꙼꙼ⷧⷩꙗⷩ꙼꙼꙼꙼꙼꙼꙼кⷮ꙼꙼꙼꙼ⷱⷩⷦⷧ꙼꙼꙼꙼е
члⷮ꙼꙼꙼꙼꙼꙼꙼꙼꙼꙼꙼꙼꙼꙼꙼꙼꙼꙼꙼꙼꙼е

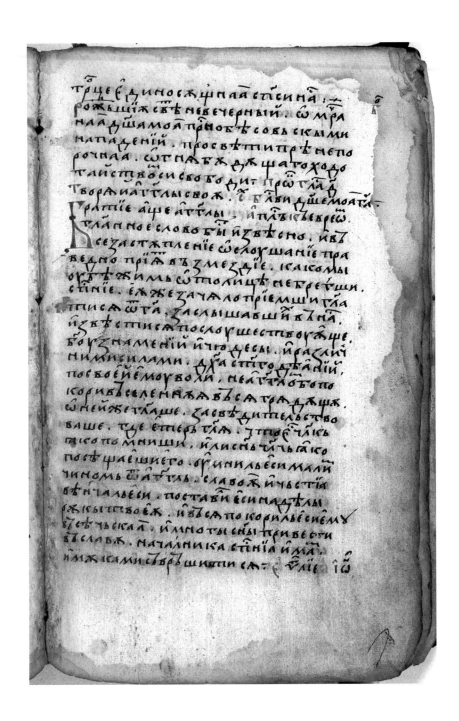

44. Fol. Eccl. Slav. 28, f.83 (cat. 30)

исходѧи дїаконъ. И таиноꙋ
ставленомъ есть. тайнъ єꙗсте
и иоꙋцевск совсѧ дшайсовъ
помышлѧнїа рꙋчьси. гнъсѣдъ
жипелю весоцьнашихъ поми
лоꙋнѧ беповелицем маттитво
ѣпрѣщевсь. ѣпгле маттвꙁпрѣпъ
ибенашь. прилѣꙗльноꙋюмо
боꙋснопеѝмисовоихъраба
помилоꙋнѝапоммоꙗ
ствоꙋмилотнитвоє
А. ипщеротытвоани
споснинаныипдвсалюди
твоꙗ. чающаꙗ ꙗꙗесотевч
богашоꙋюмлѧть. дїаконъ.
ѣщемолимъсѧаосоцинашемъ
ѝгоꙋменѣѝпсь. ѣщемонимъ

45. Quart. Eccl. Slav. 13, f.55v (cat. 31)

177

гпк свои . ипкавитипилашопастоа
идаіо прѣщеніа . люпгравсакоб*
ймитопситыи оу сльппип помлоуп
аюе рппомлоуп . ешемлисаве
сркилироса . ешемлисаавспокда
птх по окоусла ии комитивыипико
люкекеси . діакеи г оу помлиса оп
О лкотнеема , выскшпи славпыипико
люке . векдакемоуко проштивоу
прхдоштыисла . прпгастппкп
патворасвоетоцркитиа . пома
пивлкоклгынракксвоимлащп
са тт екпарипми , ткопмагев
члколюкев . ацедовккдкпепиа
мы . мпошаго рамаріатпвоетосиси
па . мыкоесмылюкетвопги . исыщ
паккитип гквоса . скспавпиалоки
паппипвса . испркгкыппашидоло
слоуженіа . паспгырюдокрыпи.по

46. Quart. Eccl. Slav. 13, f.134v (cat. 31)

178

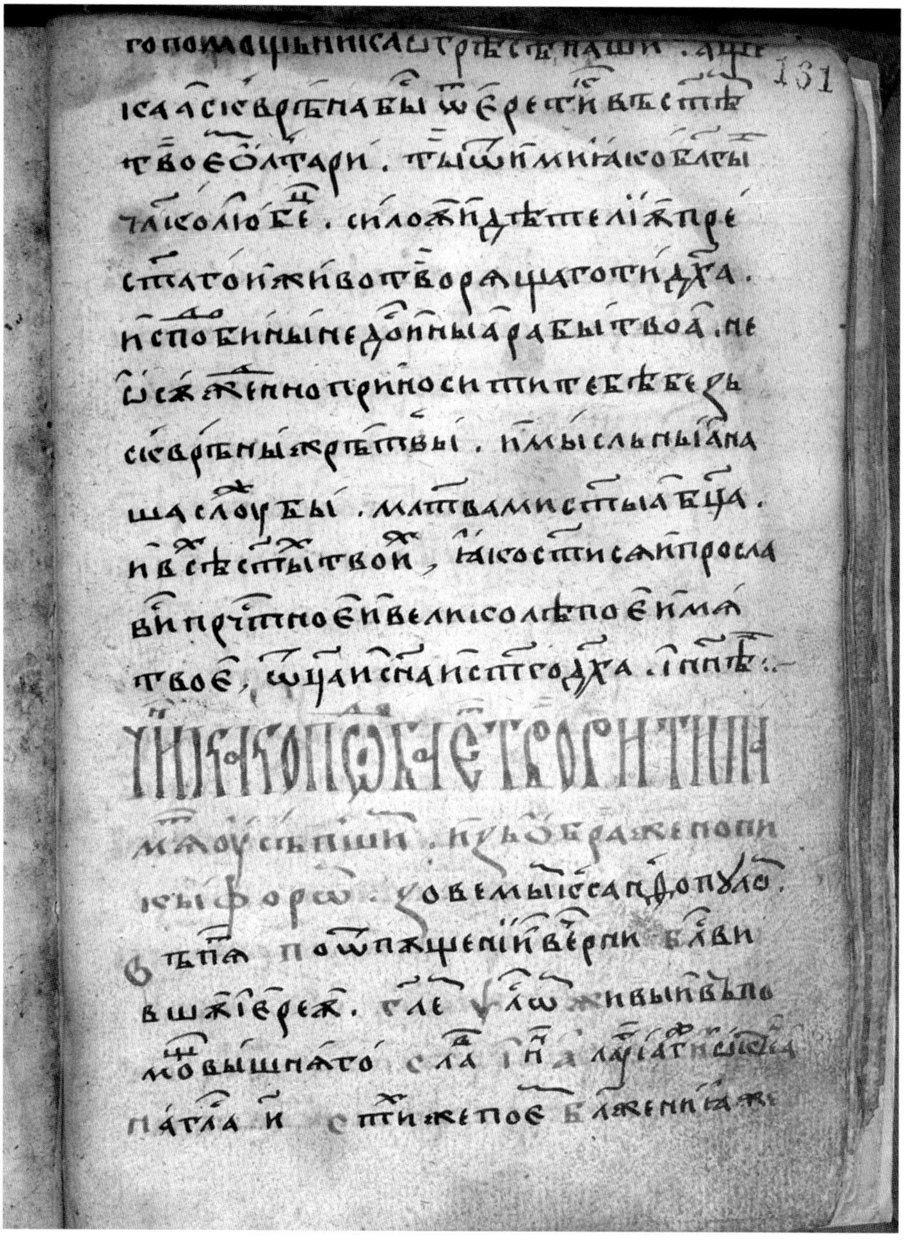

47. Quart. Eccl. Slav. 13, f.161 (cat. 31)

бжⷭ҇твнаѧ слꙋжба ст҃го іѡан҃а :

соⷡ васиⷧ҇їа велиⷦ҇а . ꙁа всеⷢ҇ пораⷣꙋ .
въ ꙁановⷧꙋ ꙋтосїи до мⷧ҇тⷡ҇ь
а атеѡслашⷩ҇ный ꙓставⷧⷩ҇й
тⸯвоӱ . сꙓ соуⷣꙋ поиⷭ҇тⷭ҇ов асилїа .
а рⷯнⷠ҇лⷧ҇аⷨ аⷧ҇тⷡ҇аⷦ҇ слашⷩ҇ный ⸱⸱⸱
и бенаⷠ҇ⸯⷲ҇ена нбⷭ҇е ⷤ҇ивы . прираⷣ
на вⸯсⷣⷨ влаⷭ҇воⷣ . априꙁⷣин арабы
тⸯвоⷣ еслашⷩ҇ныⷠ҇ꙗ . посⷧꙋшаⷣ
сⸯвоⷠ҇выⷣ . ӥданиⷱ҇ⷲ҇лесⷠ҇ысⷩ҇оⷣиⷭ҇о
тⸯвоⷱ҇ . сⸯтⸯворⷨ҇й оӱдӹ стⸯыⷣꙗ тⸯво
еⷯⷰ҇црⷣⷡ҇еви . иⷭ҇побиⷡ҇ⷡ҇анипаⷠ҇сⷨ҇выⷠ҇
тⸯыⷣ . сꙓставлеⷩ҇иⷰ҇срⷣⷯ҇хꙋ . иⷭ҇идеⷤ҇ⷱ҇ⷠⷲ҇
нетⸯлⷩ҇ныⷠ҇и въ раⷣⷨ҇мь тⸯвоиⷨ҇ истина
ба нашего . вⷭ҇сла ⷣ айтⷩ҇йⷡ҇ⷡ҇онами
славаⷩ҇ⷠⷱ҇честⷩ҇о . иⷡ҇елиⷦ҇оⷧ҇ⷦ҇ⷠ҇ⷲ҇оⷱ҇

48. Quart. Eccl. Slav. 12, f.25 (cat. 32)

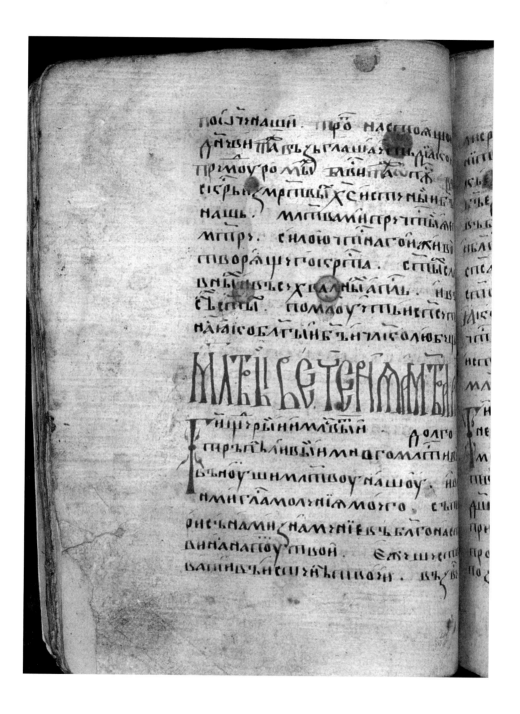

49. Quart. Eccl. Slav. 12, f.62v (cat. 32)

181

50. Quart. Eccl. Slav. 12, f.177v (cat. 32)

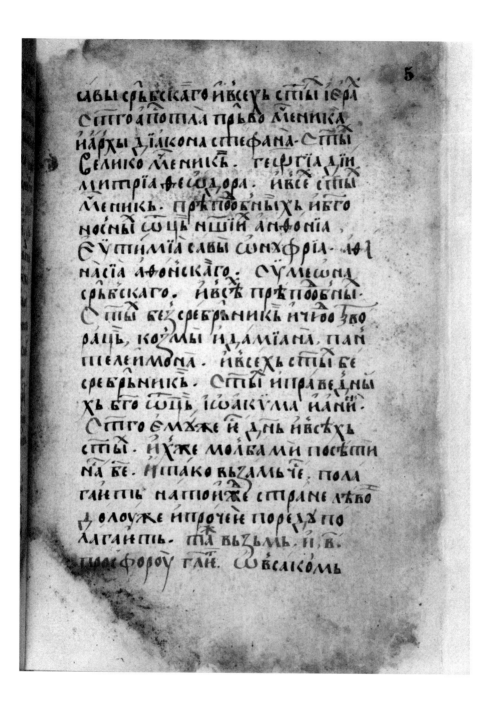

савы срьбскаго ивсеѧ стыѧ іера
стго апотла прьво леника
нархы діакона стефана · Стыѧ
Селико леникь · геѡргіа дїн
литрїа ѳеѡдора · ивсе стыѧ
леникь · прѣпоѡбныхь ивго
носныѧ соць нши́н анѳонїа
Ѧутимїа савы сонхфрїа · аѳ
насіа аѳонскаго · Сулешона
срьбскаго · ивсѣ прѣпоѡбны
стыѧ без сребрьникь ичюѡ бо
рань, козмы идамїана, пан
телеимона · ивсехь стыѧ бе
сребрьникь · Стыѧ иправедны
хь его соць ісоакула иани
Стго емхже и днь ивсѣхь
стыѧ · ихже молбами посѣти
на бе · Иппако вьзаль чте, пола
ганпь наппоиже стране лѣво
а олоуже ипрочен порѧдѹ по
лаганпь · Тꙑ вьзаль, и в
просфороу гли · Собсакомь

51. Quart. Eccl. Slav. 15, f.5 (cat. 33)

въ ҃г е поустой. и мае на стыс въса
и въвниманїе ... коневъстимъ
ха. и лично таковыхивымалы
а ... рипиды. бранисо кроце
... всими мыбжмвесцени. ...
ны спламивлкоулколюбечевъ
пїе нтле. стьесивъистинуи
ортьтыединороныитвосиь. и
дхтвоистыипртъ. ивеликоу
лепнаяславаткою. ижемизо
сицевъзлюбиеси. гакоснасвое
единороногодати. давъсавъру
живъннепогыбне. ноиматхиво
вны. ижеприше. ивъсееже со
насъмотренїесъврши. въно
вънюпредабываеши. паижесапре
даше. замискииживо. прїехл
бъвъстыской. ипрчтыйнепоро

52. Quart. Eccl. Slav. 11, f.24v (cat. 34)

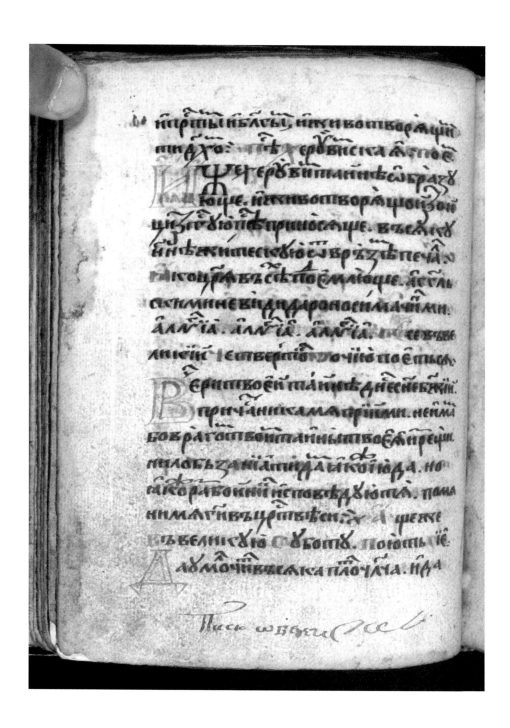

53. Quart. Eccl. Slav. 11, f.58v (cat. 34)

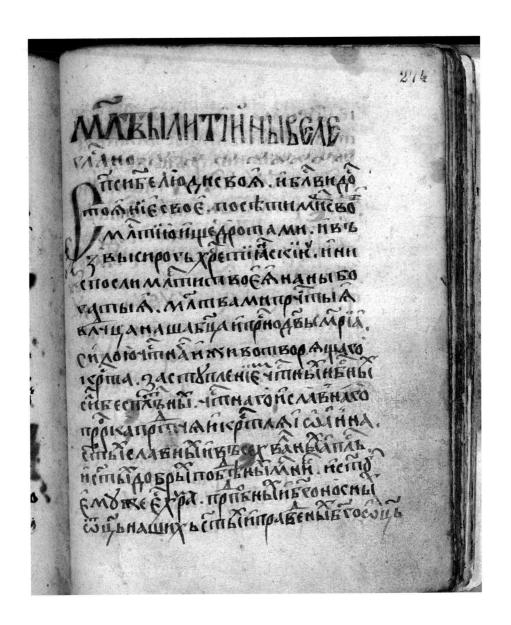

МлВЫЛИТІ́ННЫВЄ́ЛЕ
гла…

псивѣлюдиѥвоа̏ . иѣлѣидо
тоа̏нїѥ́своѐ . посѣти́ныи́своѐ
мл̏тїю̏и̏ще́дро́тами . пⷡ
выспроⷡхⷬестїаⷩскꙗ́и̏ . и̏ни
спослими́тисⷶвоѥ̏ндⷶныⷠⷠо
ѥⷣпиⷠꙗ̏ . мл̏тва́мипрⷶⷱ́тⷶⷠꙗⷶ
влⷱⷳⷶна́шаⷠⷣⷶи̏прⷪнⷪⷣвⷤⷤмⷬⷣꙗ̏ .
силою̏чⷭⷩꙗ̏и̏жⷤи̏вⷪтвⷪрꙗ̏щⷶⷢⷪ
креⷭⷶⷶ . застⷭⷪⷶⷶⷩⷶⷣⷱꙗ̏ⷩⷮⷩⷶⷩⷮⷩⷠⷩⷪⷠⷩⷩⷠⷩⷩ
…

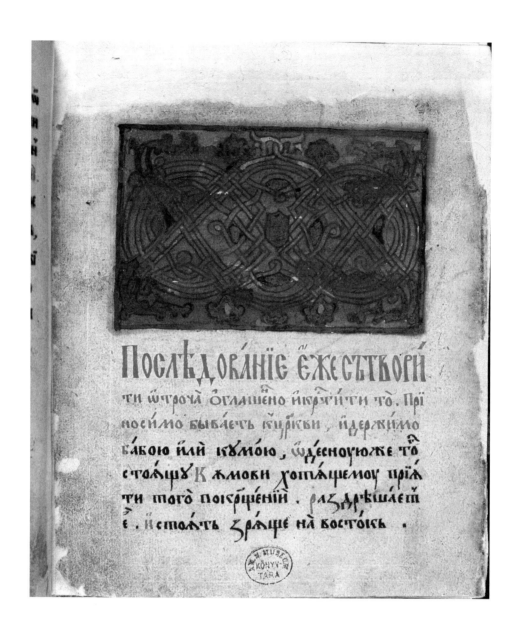

Послѣдованіе ѥже сътвори

ти ѿрочѧ ѡглашено йкрⷮи ти то. прі
носимо бываетъ кирⷦви, йдержимо
бабою йли кумою, ѡдеснꙋюже то
стоѧщꙋ к ꙁмокви хотѧщемоу пріѧ
ти того поⷦрщеній. раꙁдрѣшаетⷨ
 є. йстоѧⷮ ꙁрⷬще нⷶ востоⷦъ .

55. Quart. Eccl. Slav. 9, f.4 (cat. 35)

ПОСЛѢ́ДОВАНІЕ ОУ́ТРЕНИ.

По блгословéніи «Пріидѝте поклони́мсѧ, т̑ ѱал-
мы̀. Оу́слы́шитъ тѧ гдⷭ҇ъ, гдⷭ҇и си́лою: іерéй глаго́лет̑
Поми́лꙋй на́съ, бже по вели́цѣй ми́лости твоéй,
мóлимтисѧ, оу́слы́ши и̑ поми́лꙋй. Гдⷭ҇и поми́лꙋй, г҃:
Ещé мóлимсѧ ѡ Всепресвѣ́тлѣ́йшемъ и̑ держа́в-
номъ І̑мперáторѣ, и̑ Кралѣ̀ на́шемъ ФЕРДІНА́НДѢ І:
Ещé мóлимсѧ ѡ Преѡсвѧще́ннѣ Ар̑хіерéи на́ше
Ге̑ѡ́ргіи. Гдⷭ҇и поми́лꙋй. три́жды.

Ещé

56. Fol. Eccl. Slav. 21, f.5 (cat. 36)

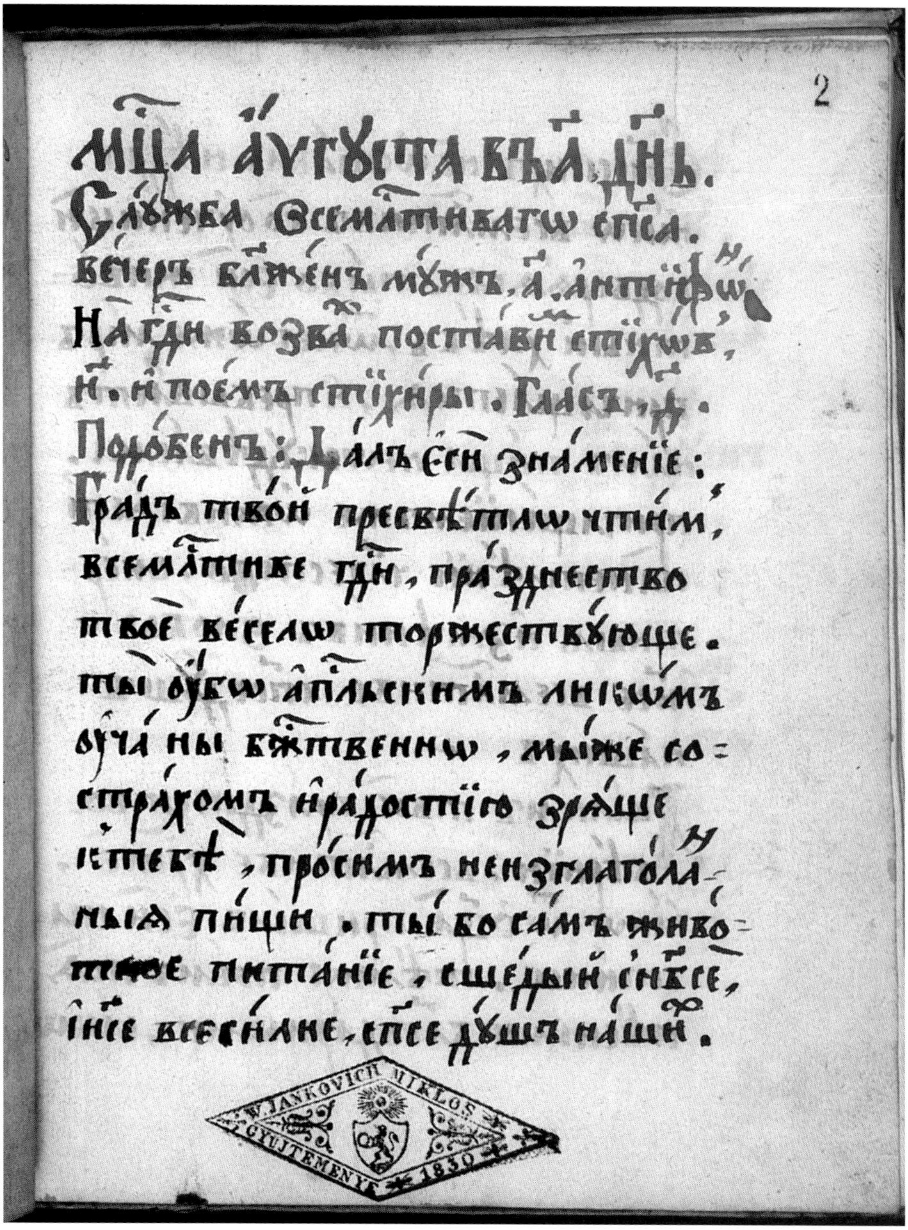

МЦА АѴГѸСТА ВЪ А ДНЬ.

Слꙋжба Всемлⷮтивагѡ спⷭа.

Вечерⸯ блаженⸯ мꙋжⸯ, а. антїфѡ

На гдⷭи возва постави стїхѡвⸯ,

і. и поемⸯ стїхиры. Глⷭасⸯ д.

Подобенⸯ: Далⸯ еси знаменїе :

Градⸯ твой пресвⷮтлѡ чтⷭнⷮм,

всемлⷮтиве гдⷭн, празднество

твое веселѡ торжествꙋюще.

ты ꙋбѡ апⷭльскимⸯ ликѡмⸯ

ꙋча ны бж҃твеннѡ, мыⷤже со=

страхомⸯ и радостїю зрⷶще

к тебⷮ, просимⸯ неизглаⷮгола=

ныѧ пищи. ты бо самⸯ живо=

тⷪое питанїе, еще́дый і нбⷭе,

і нбⷭе всесⷶлне, спⷭе дꙋшⷮ нашⷶ.

57. Quart. Eccl. Slav. 17, f.2 (cat. 37)

58. Quart. Eccl. Slav. 6, f.1 (cat. 39)

190

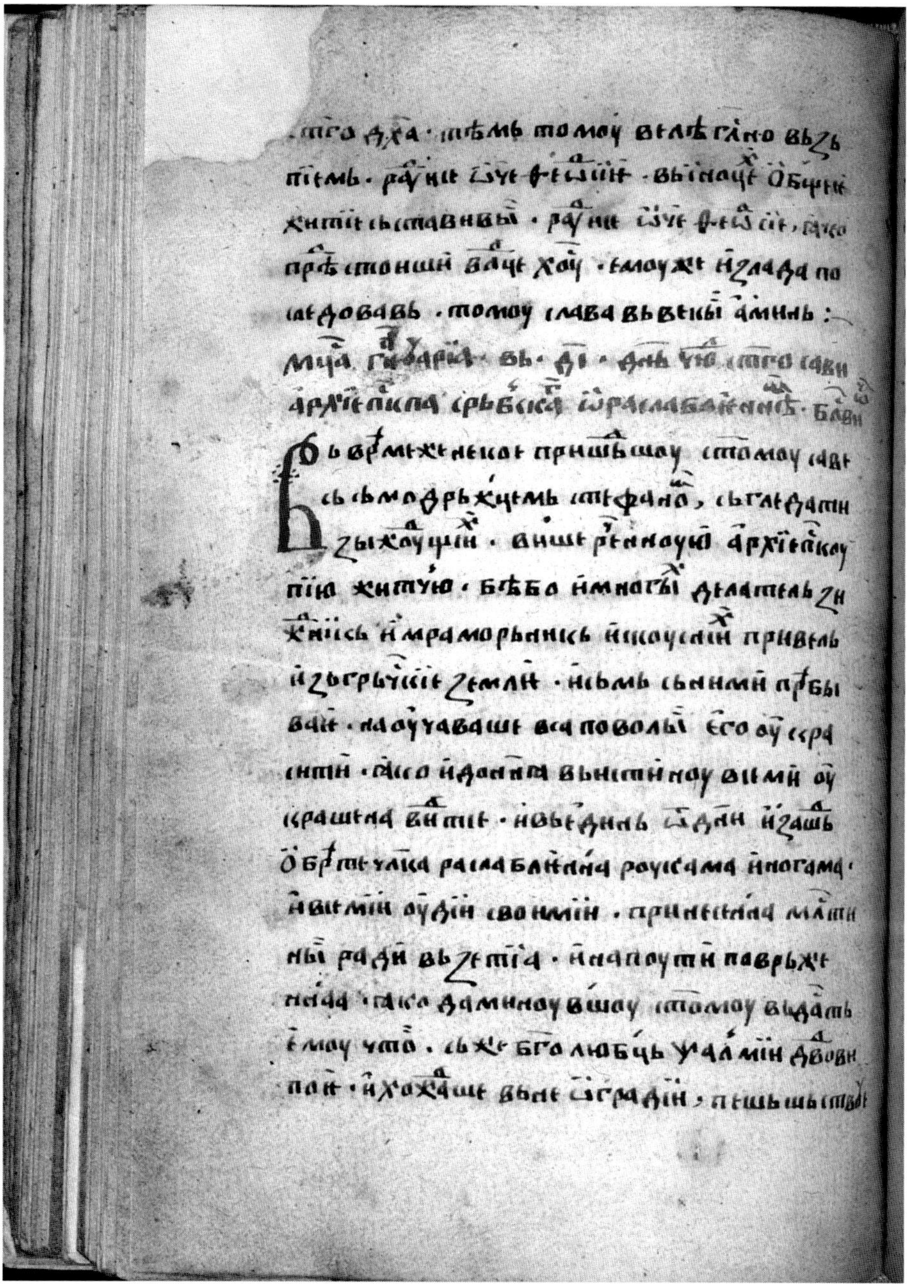

59. Quart. Eccl. Slav. 19, f.89v (cat. 40)

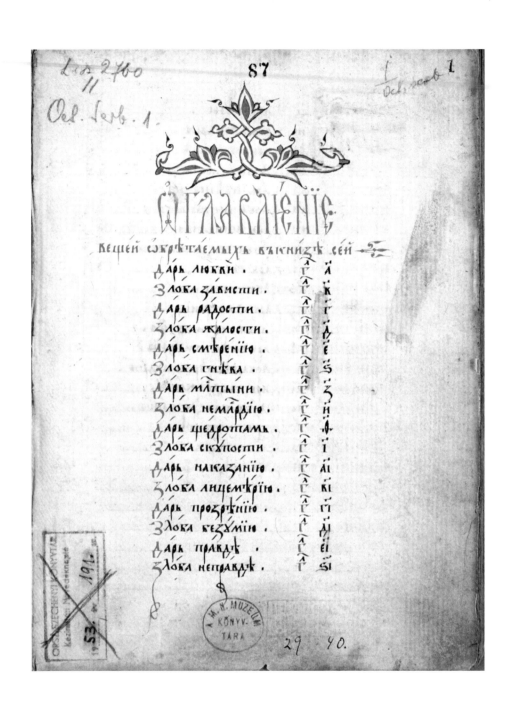

60. Oct. Serb. 1, f.1 (cat. 41)

61. Oct. Serb. 1, upper cover (cat. 41)

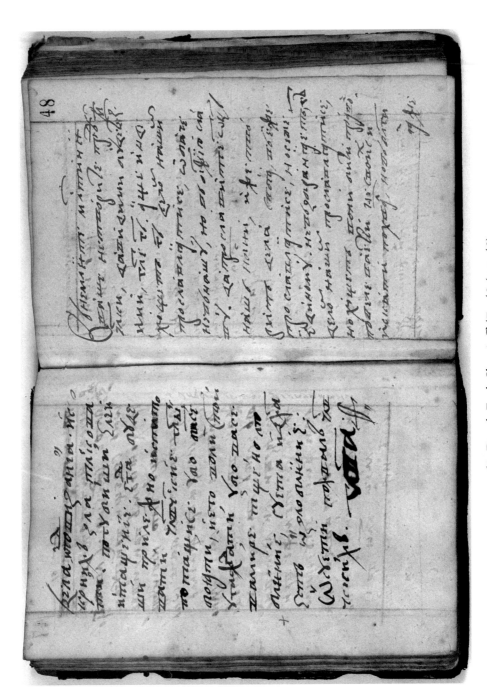

62. Duod. Eccl. Slav. 1, ff.47v-48 (cat. 42)

свою, то ёстъ ѡдѣ҆ѣнїе, и҆ взема лентїй
и҆ препоꙗсаса и҆влꙗ водꙋ во ꙋ҆мываи҆ницꙋ,
и҆почалъ и҆ми ногй ꙋ҆мыꙃатй, наи҆перш
и҆ноꙁѣ ꙋ҆мылъ, и҆ фартꙋхомъ ѡ҆теръ а҆
ѡ҆нъ даꙗ́сꙗ мꙋ҆ беꙁ жадного встидꙋ не
а
ба́ꙗчи ѡ҆томъ и҆ ѣ҆гꙋ ꙋ҆чи́тель ёстъ
потомъ і҃с прии҆де до стого петра, хотꙗ́чй
ногй ꙋ҆мытй а҆петръ реко́лъ гд҃й не ꙋ҆м
ꙋ҆меши нога мои зовѣ́кй, і҃с же реко́лъ петре

✿ ✿ ✿ ✿ ✿ ✿ ✿

ё҆сли не ꙋ҆мыю нога твои҆ха то неи҆маешъ
мѣтй частй со́мною во цр҃твїй не ё҆номъ
петръ реко́лъ гд҃й не ти́лко ногй, новсе
тѣ́ло мое ѡ҆мый, ти́лко а҆бымъ моголъ
бытй ꙋ҆частни́комъ цр҃твꙗ твего, и҆і҃съ
реко́лъ кнемꙋ҆, ѡ҆мытй нетребꙋꙗ́тъ ѡ҆мыта
нꙗ, ю же ви чи́стй ё҆сте а҆ле невсѣ, ти́лко
ё҆динъ

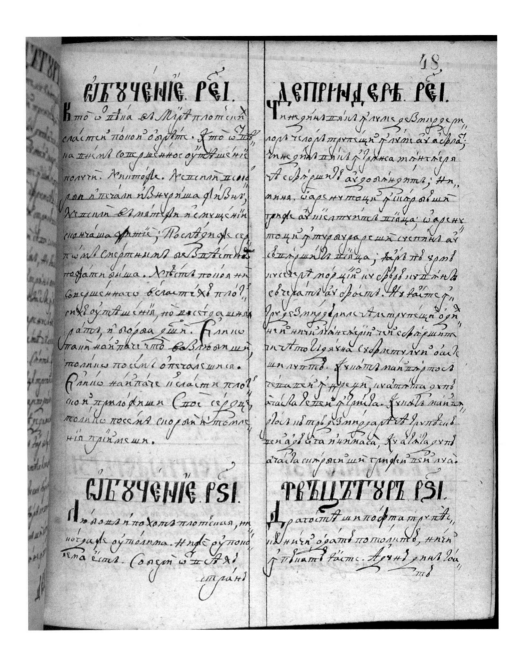

64. Quart. Eccl. Slav. 1, f.48 (cat. 44)

196

Въ толахъ, пⷬⷮри нашей по[...]
помнаніа ѡⷭⷮ. Сꙋⷬⷮгꙋпотⷬⷴа
прⷦⷴ рⷧⷹмірⷤ Сн҃ъ Бж҃ій Ба҃,
по распатꙗ съ[...] Аⷬⷴпоꙁоⷮⷭ
пⷬⷭⷤ нанⷪⷣрⷴ Хⷭ҃ стой сн҃аⷢⷴ
на Землю. Пⷬⷤре слыⷲⷪⷮще мⷮⷴ
всⷨ сіа прⷣⷴꙁⷮⷤннои лⷮⷹрⷢⷴ
тіи востоминаемаа, пⷬⷫⷮꙗꙁⷪⷮⷴ
разⷠⷦⷴⷠно о'ⷬⷤⷭⷴⷭⷪⷮ нашиⷬⷫⷮрⷮⷴ
ста[...]емаа. Нанонцⷮⷴ прⷬⷴⷦⷴ[...]
сⷬⷤхъ со[...]шаеⷣⷮⷭⷮⷦⷴⷯ, трⷫⷮ[...]
паⷲⷤ бл҃годарⷬⷬⷮⷸ дⷬⷮ, ꙗⷴ
[...] наⷬⷮ сіⷴ сⷧⷹⷲⷤ[...]
тⷨⷦ въ рⷮⷴ тⷪⷮ, ꙁ о'ꙋⷬⷪⷭⷴ
тⷮⷮⷲⷤⷨⷹ наⷬⷮ Ста҃то
Ха҃.

ВОПРОСЪ 69

Поⷮⷪ тⷤⷭⷮⷮⷴ дрⷤⷭⷮⷦⷸ наꙁⷬⷫ
въ неⷣⷹⷮⷦⷴⷡⷴ нⷮⷴⷦⷴ о'ⷬⷤ пⷬⷮⷪⷮ
сⷬⷤ Землⷮⷴ Сⷤⷦⷮⷮⷮ пⷮⷪⷬⷴ

ѾТВѢТЪ

Понⷤⷦⷴ поⷭⷮⷪⷡⷴⷡⷣⷬⷴⷡⷮⷴⷦⷮ Хⷬⷭ҃тоⷡⷤ трⷮ,
пⷮⷪⷬⷬⷤⷡⷴⷡⷤⷦⷴ воⷭⷮⷪⷮⷪⷫⷮⷬⷤⷦⷮⷤⷦⷮⷮ ⷭⷤⷦⷮⷪⷴ
[...] нⷮⷮⷦⷴⷦⷮⷴⷦⷮⷴⷦⷮⷦⷴ Ст҃о пⷮⷪⷮⷦⷴⷡⷮⷴⷦⷮⷴⷡⷮⷴ.

ВОПРОСЪ 70   Поⷮ

челоⷬⷴ дⷤⷮⷸⷮⷦⷴⷮⷤ дⷬⷤⷦⷸⷪⷴⷬⷬⷴ, шⷮⷴ прⷦⷴⷬⷴⷮ
нцⷮⷮ ноⷤⷮⷬⷮ адⷬⷹⷮⷬⷤⷦⷤ аⷮⷮⷬⷴⷦⷮⷤⷬⷤⷦⷴⷡⷤⷦⷴ.
Адⷦⷴⷤⷦⷪ, иⷤⷦⷮⷮⷹ авⷦⷴⷦⷮⷴⷦⷮⷤⷦⷴ дⷦⷴⷬⷤⷦⷮⷤ лⷤⷦⷮⷤ дⷬⷤⷦⷴ,
въ лⷬⷦⷴⷡⷮⷮⷦⷤ, пⷮⷦⷴⷦⷮⷦⷴ рⷬⷴⷡⷮⷦⷦⷮⷦⷴⷦⷮⷤ
аⷤⷦⷮⷴ. Кⷮⷦⷹ аⷹⷬⷤⷦⷠⷦⷦⷪ, ꙁaⷬⷬⷦⷴⷮⷤ
дⷬⷦⷹⷦ сⷬⷤⷦⷮⷮⷤ ꙁaⷹ погорⷬⷤⷦⷮⷦⷪ прⷤⷦⷮⷤⷦⷤ
мⷬⷦⷴⷦⷮⷦⷤ, дⷬⷬⷤⷦⷮⷦⷴ аꙁаⷮⷬⷤⷦⷮⷮⷹ аⷹⷬⷦⷤⷦⷤⷮⷦⷪ
шⷮⷴ аⷬⷴⷦⷮⷮ дⷤⷦⷮⷬⷦⷹ дⷬⷦⷮⷮⷦⷴⷦⷮⷤⷦⷤⷬⷤ лⷹⷮⷦⷹ.
рⷬⷦⷴⷡⷤ адⷹⷬⷦⷮⷮⷴⷦⷮⷮⷴⷬⷤ аⷮⷦⷮⷮⷦⷤ, шⷮⷴ ꙁaⷡⷬⷦⷹ
нⷬⷦⷹ пⷬⷴⷦⷦⷦⷮⷦⷮⷮ о'ⷦⷮⷦⷴⷦⷪⷡⷴⷦⷤ ноⷦⷮⷬⷬⷤⷦⷮ трⷬⷦⷴⷦⷬⷴⷦⷴ
нⷬⷦⷴⷮⷤ, лаⷦⷬⷦⷹⷬⷤⷦⷤⷦⷮⷹⷬⷤⷦⷮ тⷮⷦⷹⷮⷬⷬⷴⷦⷮⷬⷴ
аⷬⷤⷦⷮⷮⷪⷬⷤ ꙁⷦⷦⷦⷬⷴ сⷬⷴⷦⷦⷴⷬⷤⷦⷮⷤ иⷬⷤⷦⷴⷦⷬⷹⷦⷴ
мⷹⷬⷦⷬⷤⷦⷮⷮⷮ лⷹⷮⷦⷴ дⷮⷦⷮⷬⷦⷹⷦⷬⷮ ꙁ[...]ⷮⷦⷤⷦⷮⷦⷤ
аⷹⷦⷮⷦⷤⷦⷮⷤ ноⷬⷦⷹ аⷬⷤⷦⷮⷮⷤ аⷹⷬⷤⷦⷦⷹⷮⷬⷴⷤⷦⷴ аⷹⷦⷹ
шⷮⷴ ꙁⷦⷦⷮⷦⷮⷮ аⷹⷮⷦⷡⷬⷦⷮⷬⷦⷮⷮⷦⷮⷮ трⷹⷦⷮⷪⷦⷮ
сⷬⷦⷴⷦⷮⷦⷹⷦⷬⷴ Аⷬⷦ҃ⷦ.

ꙀТРЕВАРЕ: 69.

Пⷤⷦⷮⷦⷹⷬⷦⷹⷦ гⷬⷴⷡⷦⷮⷦⷴ трⷤⷦⷪⷮⷤⷦⷹⷦⷡ дⷬⷦⷮⷦⷦⷹⷦ
тⷤ дⷹⷬⷤⷦ дⷬⷤⷮⷦⷤⷦⷹⷦⷮⷤⷦⷴ, шⷮⷴ трⷤⷦⷮⷮ ⷭⷮⷤ
тⷮⷪⷮ нⷦⷦꙁⷮⷦⷹⷦⷦⷦⷦⷦⷴ тⷬⷤⷦⷬⷮⷦⷤⷦⷮⷮⷦⷤ.

РꙊⷭⷮПꙊⷦⷭⷤ:

Пⷤⷦⷮⷦⷹⷦⷦⷦⷹⷦ дⷹⷬⷦⷦꙁⷦⷦ сⷦⷦноⷮⷦⷹⷦⷤⷡ дⷬⷦⷦⷮⷦⷦꙁⷮⷴ
лⷹⷮⷦ Хⷦ҃ⷦтоⷤꙁⷦⷦ, адⷬⷤⷦⷦⷮⷦⷬⷴⷦⷤ аⷮⷦⷮⷮⷦⷦ дⷦⷦⷦⷦⷦⷬⷴⷦꙁⷦⷹⷦⷴⷦ.
рⷬⷦⷦꙁⷦⷦⷦⷮⷦⷦⷴⷬⷤⷦⷦⷮ лаⷦⷬⷦⷦⷦⷮⷦⷦⷦⷮⷴ.

ꙀТРЕВАРЕ 70:

Пⷬⷦ҃ⷦⷦ

---

65. Quart. Eccl. Slav. 2, f.35 (cat. 45)

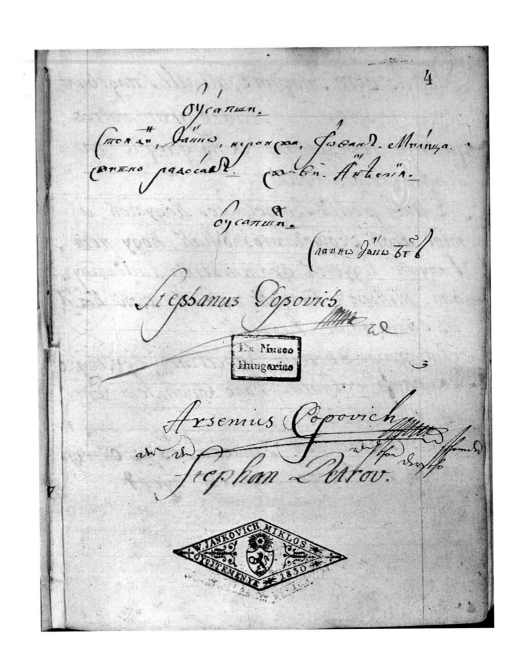

66. Quart. Eccl. Slav. 4, f.4 (cat. 46)

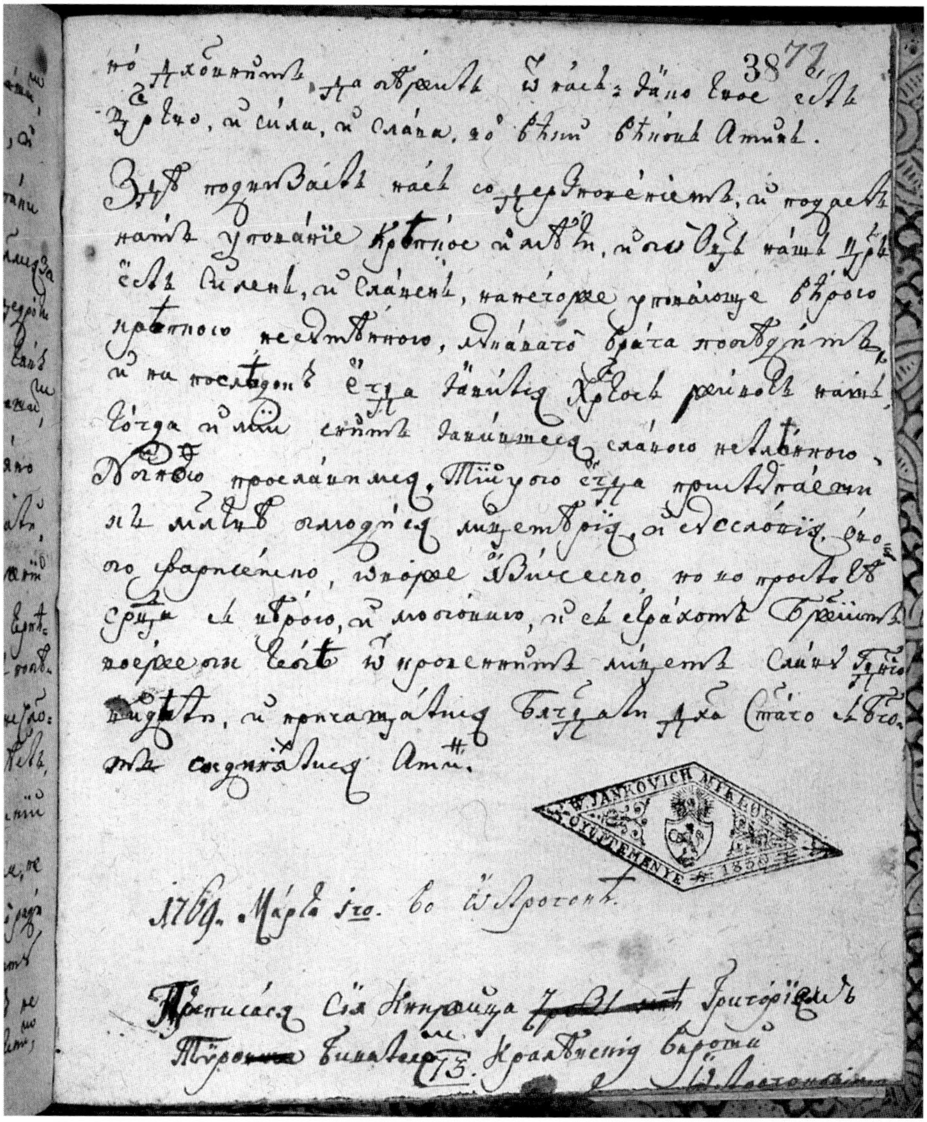

1769. Марта 1го. Во Апроет

[seal: S. JANKOVICH MIKLOS SZ. UDVARMENYE 1850]

[signatures, illegible]

Много сочиненныи концептъ ппста по дивательнаго Михаилу [...] Архангорскихъ, и прославлению праздника стаго Архи-Стратига Михаила и соборъ его, во остии дий под: лѣта 1744го.

Многажды о Возлюбленны сего свѣта соетныи чдый оубе исполнется радостии, п' та и огъ о стих: тах [...] оучеше, [...] оугробаю апо готовать и а при оугробляеотъ. Ко[...] горе сихъ поехать м Михаила Арх-Стратига па [...] а при [...] нашу соединающии надъ [...] а прославлению, сиграфже и пѣнию галовъ вса и при оуготовать пого [...] то же особ бать обще отщетъ и о бративи нашъ Враждами — Заблажшее [...] Возит [...] [...] Вратаса и потщетъ соорудии, о ради господии [...] иго то [...] Васкохъ Архисоигии соп[...]сов [...] и [...] о [...] ми Вкъ и прославли его патать пи [...] Праздникъ соси [...] лѣтии по Васка [...] Дию а апо прiатъ и наи о овкхъ Святиехии Вумии бать и о сохра [...] от Овкхи остихъ напа [...] сии по [...] [...] Воеи коп [...] а тенри наи при [...] и щедъ пикотти оупоование при [...] Ватъ [...] Архаггелом осѣниа Ваш и новѣсии под: бго, 744го лѣ.

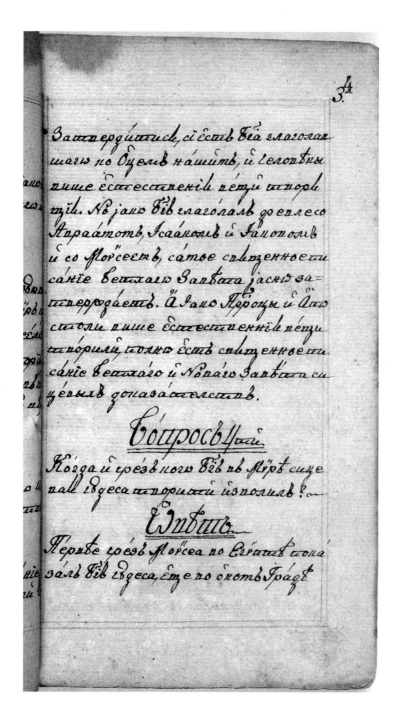

Заствердитися, сі єсть Бга глаголаа
шаго по Оцемъ нашимъ, и человѣчи
ниже єстественіи пети творе
тіи. Но їаю Бгъ глаголалъ древлесо
Авраамотъ, Ісааколъ и Іаковолъ
и со Мойсеєтъ, самое свщенностѝ
саніе ветхаго Завѣта ясно за=
ствердаетъ. А їаю Пророцы и Апо
столи ниже єстественіи пети
творили, полно єсть свщенности
саніе ветхаго и Новаго Завѣта си
цѣвылъ доказателствъ.

Вопросъ Цаїй

Когда и трезвного Бга въ Мѵрѣ сице
наи чудеса творилъ изполилъ? —

Отвѣтъ

Первѣ трезъ Мойсеа по Египетъ поа
залъ Бгъ чудеса, єже по окотъ Градъ.

69. Oct. Eccl. Slav. 1, f.4 (cat. 49)

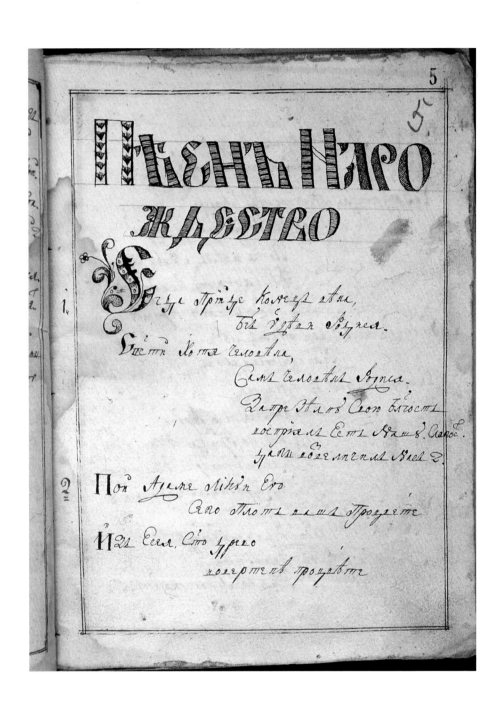

70. Quart. Eccl. Slav. 5, f.5 (cat. 50)

71. Quart. Serb. 6, f.15v (cat. 51)

203

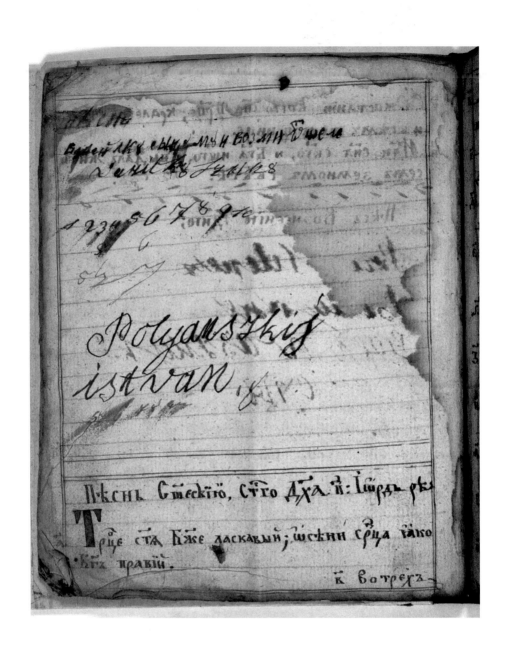

72. Quart. Eccl. Slav. 18, f.8v (cat. 52)

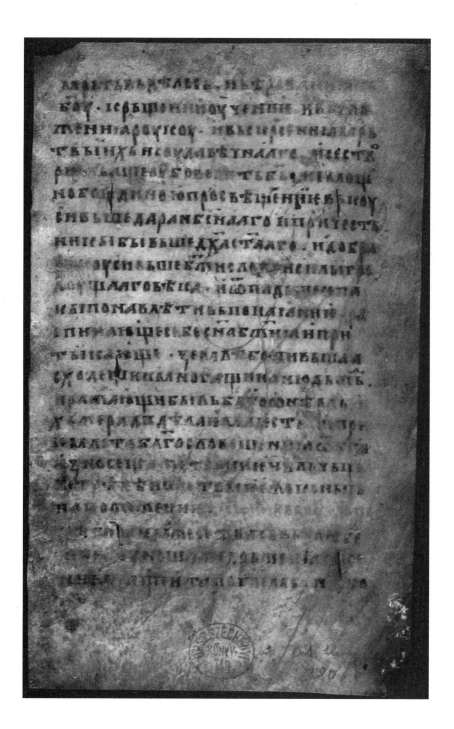

73. Frag. Eccl. Slav. 3, №II, recto (cat. 53)

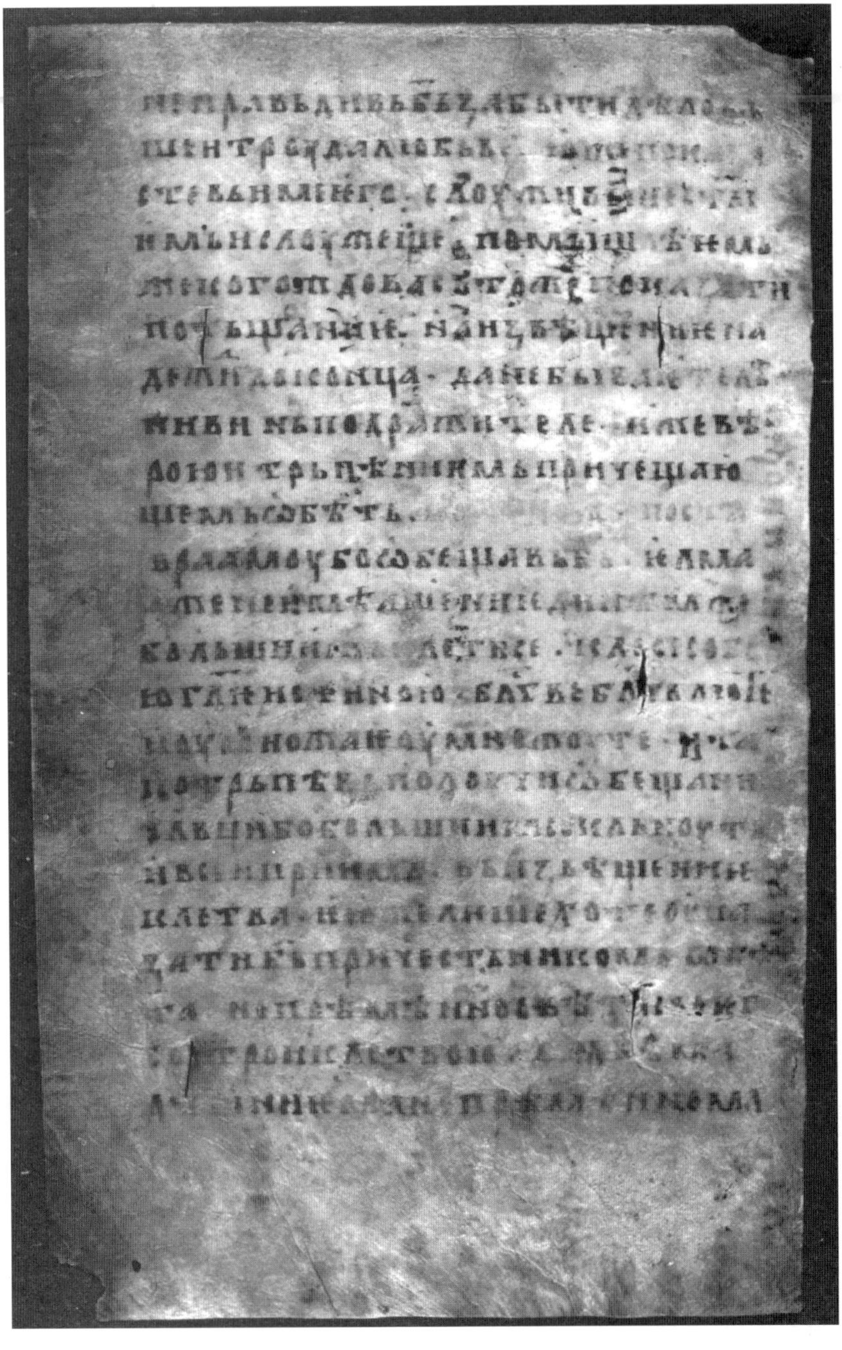

74. Frag. Eccl. Slav. 3, №II, verso (cat. 53)

75. Frag. Eccl. Slav. 1, verso (cat. 54)

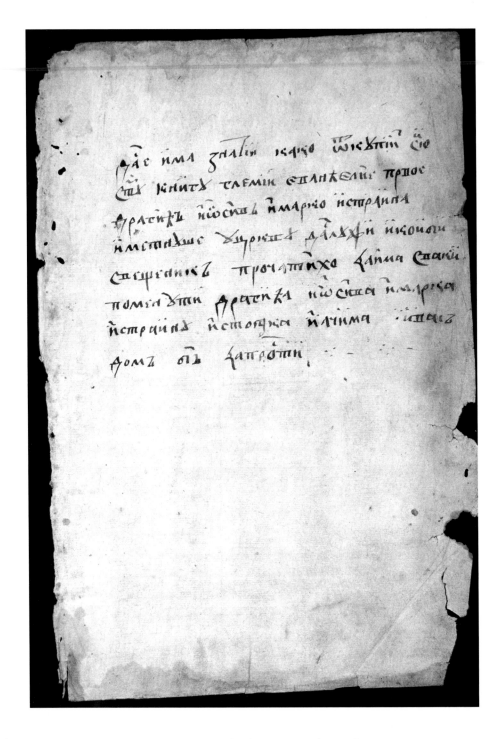

76. Frag. Eccl. Slav. 2, verso (cat. 55)

208

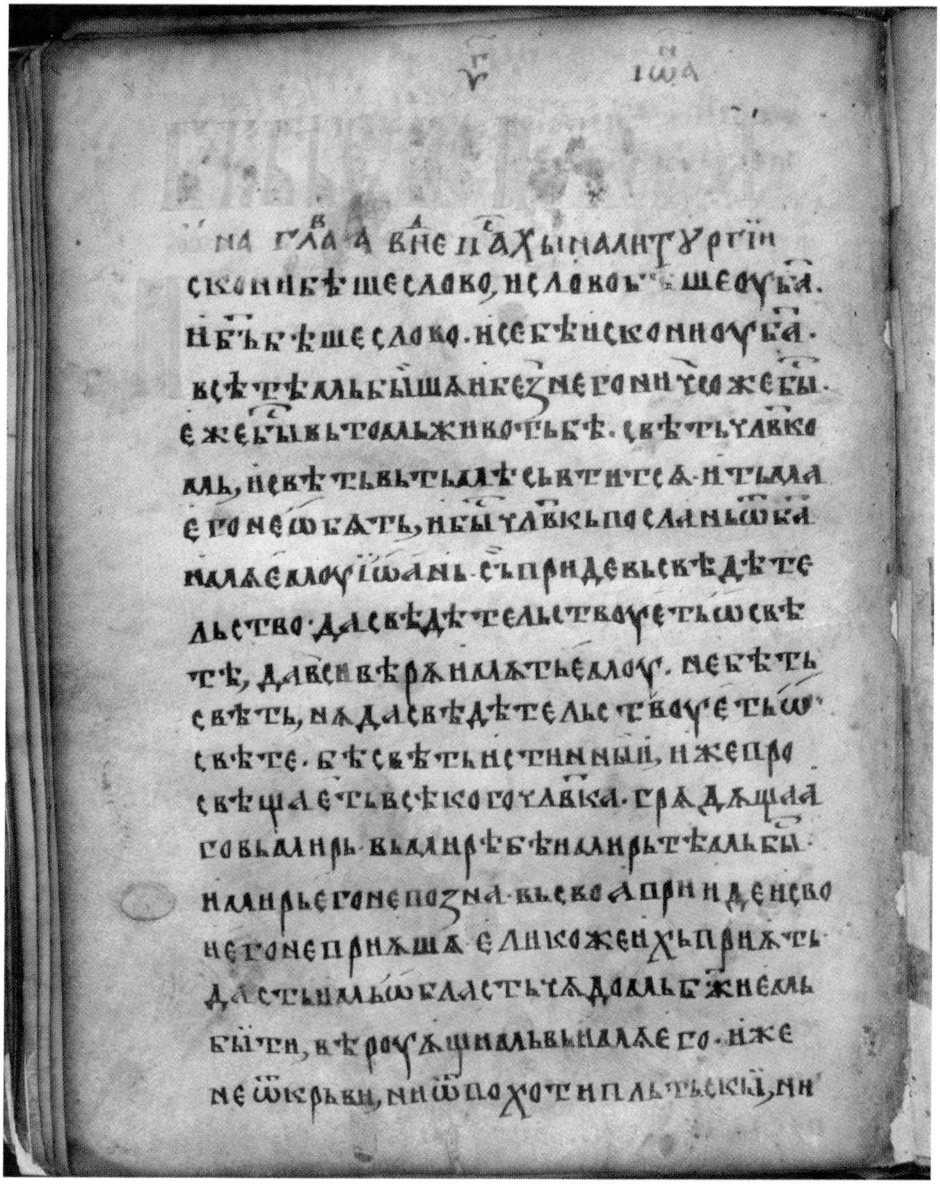

I. Quart. Eccl. Slav. 7, f.120v (cat. 2)

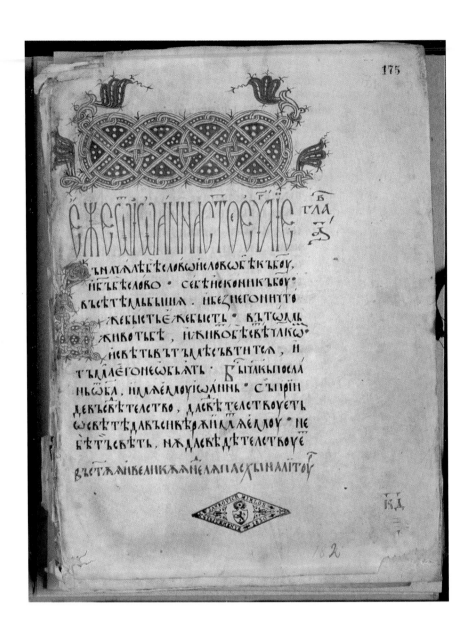

Е Ж Е Ѡ ІѠАННА СТОЕѴЛЇЕ ГЛА · В ·

ⱏ НАТⰀⰆⰝⰎ ВꙊ С ⰎОВѠ ИⰍⰎОВⰍⰎⰍ ⰆⰍ Ꙋ . ЇИⰍⰆⰍ СⰎОВО · СⰅ ⰆⰍ ИСКОⰐИⰍ Ꙋ Ꙋ · Вⱏ С ⰍⰎⰆⰑⰎⰍ ⰒⰍⰊⰡⰎⰉ · Ї ⰎⰅ ⰈⰐⰅⰃⰎ ⰐИⰍⰏⰎ ЖⰅ ⰍⰍⰑⰍⰎⰍ ЖⰅ ⰃⰍⰑⰍⰎⰍ · ⰆⰍ Ⱑ Ⱅ Ⱑ ⰐⰏⰍ ЖИⰍⰎⰑⰎ ⰀⰍ · ЇⰀ ⰐⰍⰉⰑⰍ ⰆⰍ ⰆⰍ Ⱅ ⰀⰍⰍⰑ ⰐⰍⰅⰍ ⰑⰍ ⰆⰍ Ⱅ ⰀⰍⰀⰍⰆⰍⰑⰐⰎⰅ Ⱑ · Ⰻ Ⱅ ⰍⰏ ⰀⰅⰃⰐⰅⰑ ⰡⰍⰆⰑ Ⱑ Ⱅ Ⱑ · ⰁⰍⰑⰍⰀⰍ ⰒⰑⰑⰎⰀⰍ ⰐⰍⰑ ⰍⰎⰎⰀ · ЇⰀ ⰎⰀⰅ Ⰰ ⰎⰑ Ꙋ ЇⰠⰀⰐⰐⰍ · СⰍ ⰠⰒⰍ Ⱀ ⰆⰅⰆⰍ С ⰆⰍ ⰑⰅ Ⰾ Ⱐ Ⱅ Ⰹ С Ⱅ ⰆⰑ · ⰆⰀ ⰍⰍ ⰆⰑ Ⱅ Ⰾ Ⱐ С Ⱅ ⰆⰑ Ꙋ ⰅⰑ Ⱐ ⰝⰍⰍ ⰆⰑ Ⱁ Ⱐ ⰎⰀⰍⰆⰑ ⰐⰅ Ⱐ ⰒⰍⰅⰎⰑ Ⱐ Ⱅ ⰑⰍⰍ Ⱐ ⰎⰑⰑ Ꙋ · ⰐⰅ ⰑⰍ Ⱅ Ⱐ С ⰑⰎⰑ Ⱐ · ⰐⰀ ⰆⰀ С ⰑⰍ ⰆⰡ Ⱅ Ⱁ Ⰾ Ⱐ С Ⱁ ⰑⰑ Ꙋ ⰍⰍ ⰆⰑ Ⱑ Ⱆ Ⱑ Ⱅ Ⰾ Ⱐ ⰆⰅ Ⱆ Ⰸ Ⰱ Ⰻ Ⱆ Ⱑ Ⱅ Ⱆ ⰐⰎⰑ Ⱑ ⰎⰑⰑⰎⰑⰎⰑⰎ ⰃⰍⰑⰍ ⰆⰑⰑ ⰐⰀ Ⰾ Ⱑ Ⱅ Ꙋ

II. Fol. Eccl. Slav. 17, f.175 (cat. 3)

III. Fol. Eccl. Slav. 3, upper cover (cat. 4)

IV. Fol. Eccl. Slav. 6, f.225v (cat. 10)

V. Fol. Eccl. Slav. 24, f.115 (cat. 13)

VI. Fol. Eccl. Slav. 9, f.5 (cat. 16)

214

VII. Quart. Eccl. Slav. 19, upper cover (cat. 40)

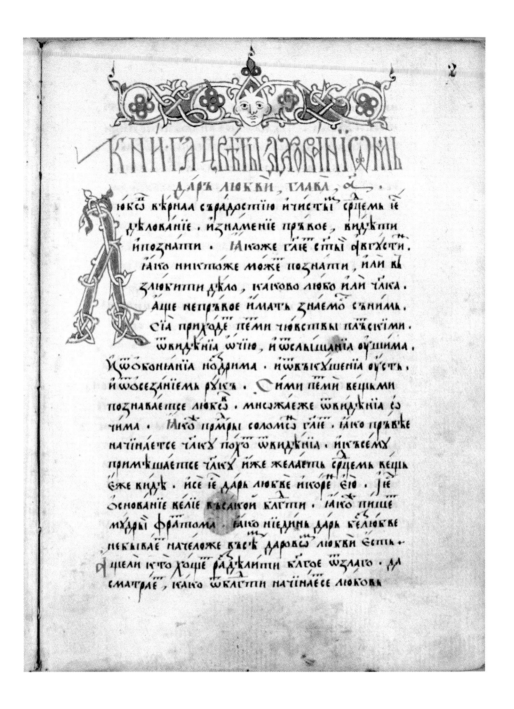

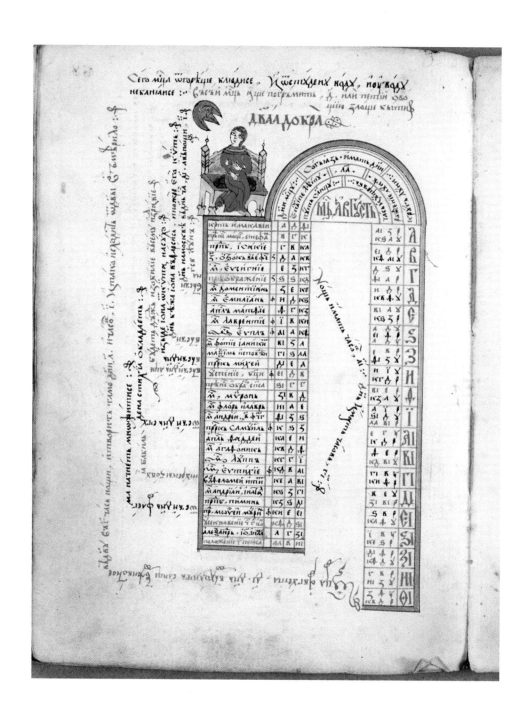

IX. Oct. Serb. 1, f.68v (cat. 41)

217

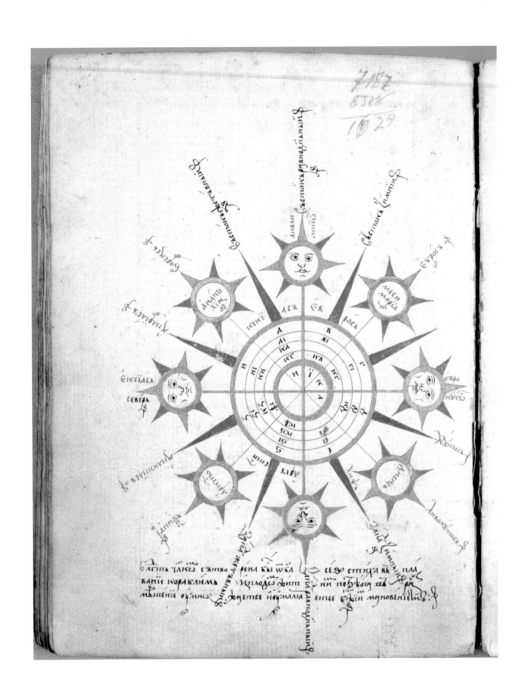

X. Oct. Serb. 1, f.72v (cat. 41)

5

8

6

7

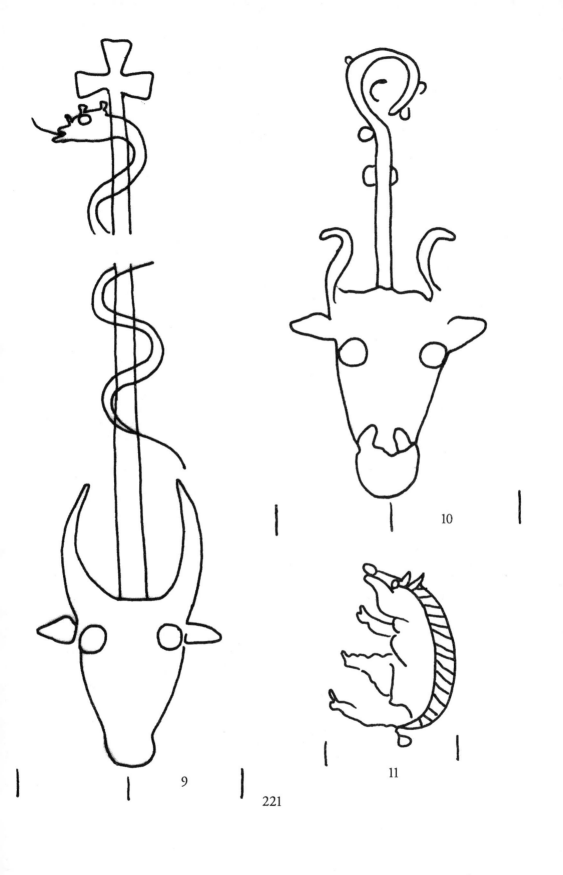

9

10

11

221

12

14

13

15

16

17

18

222

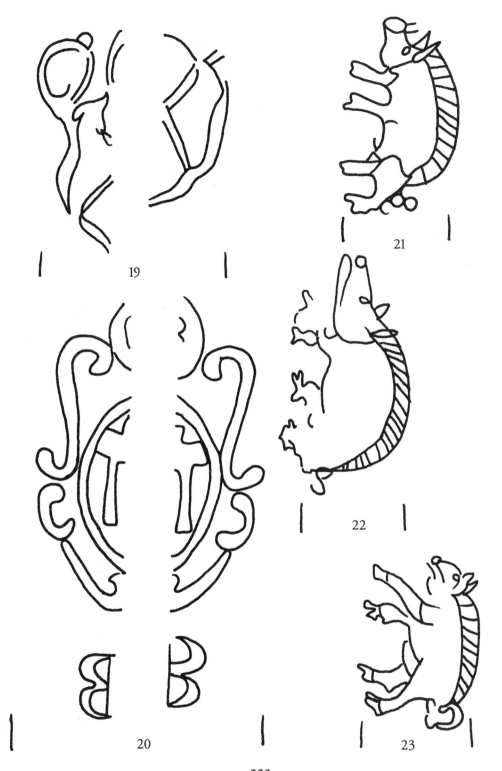

19

21

20

22

23

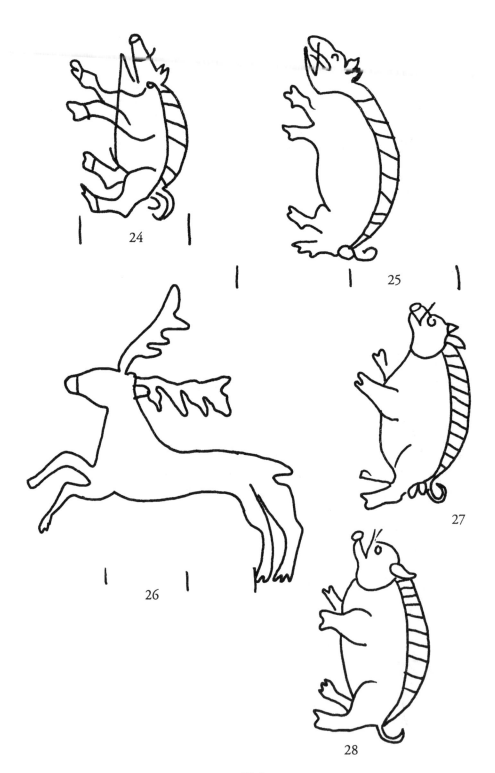

24

25

26

27

28

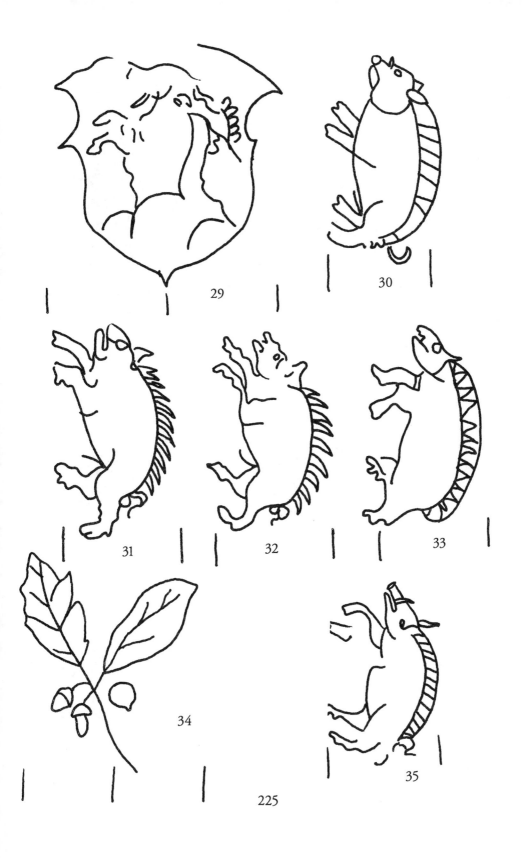

29

30

31

32

33

34

35

225

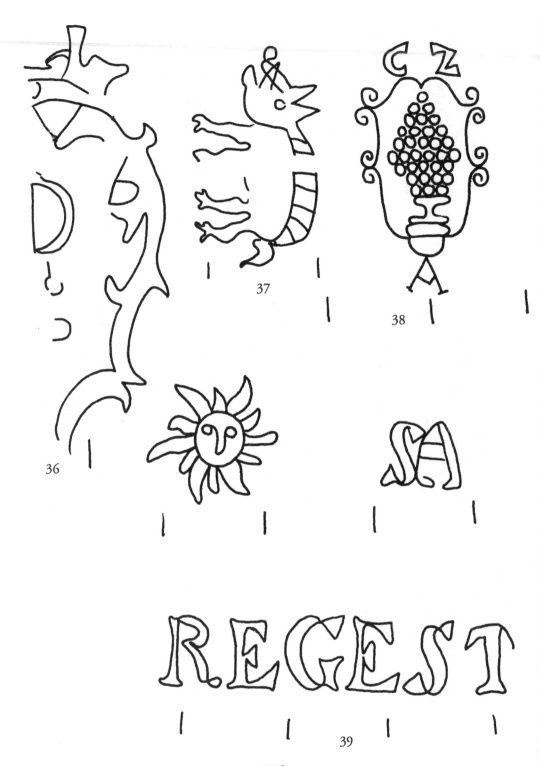

36

37

38

39

40

41

42

43

44

227

45   46

47

48

228

49

50

51

52

53

54

55

56

57

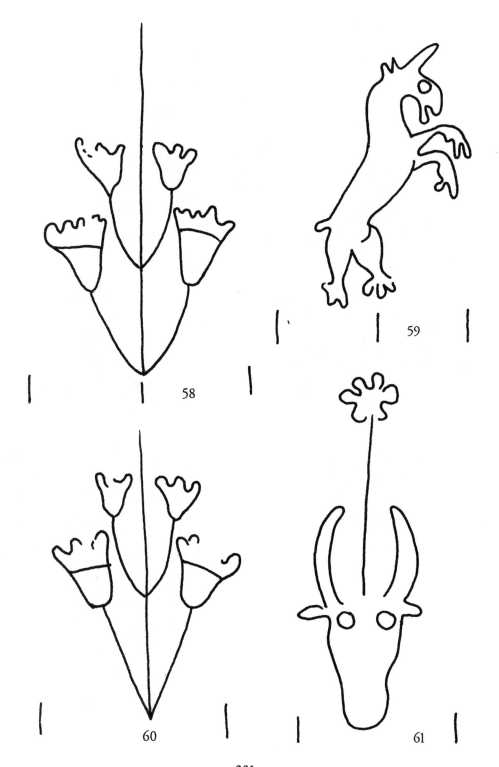

58

59

60

61

231

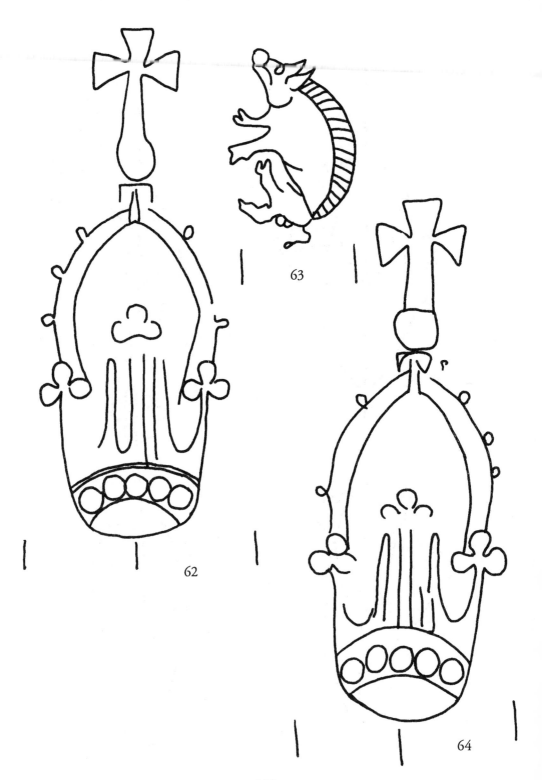

63

62

64

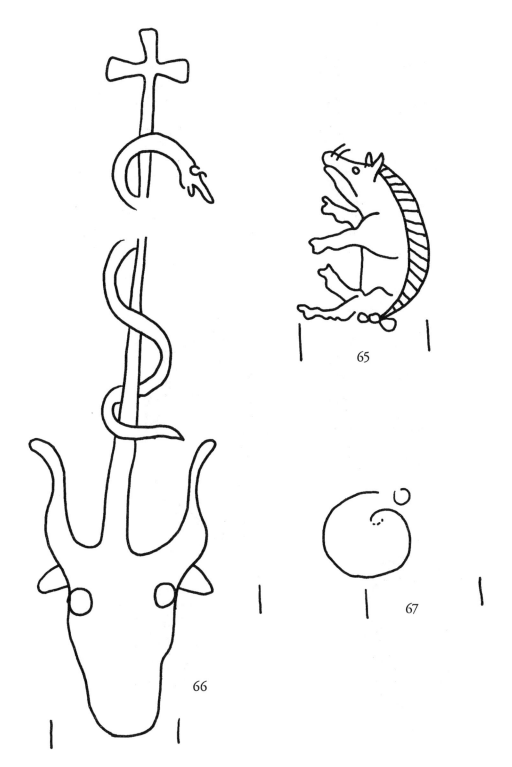

65

66

67

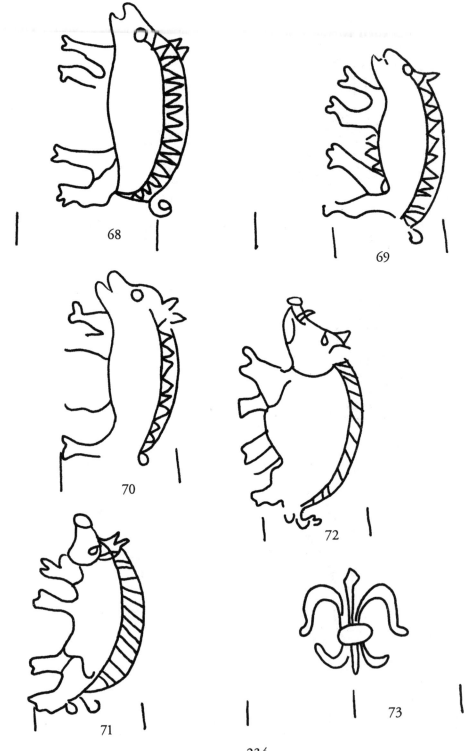

68

69

70

72

71

73

74

75

76

77

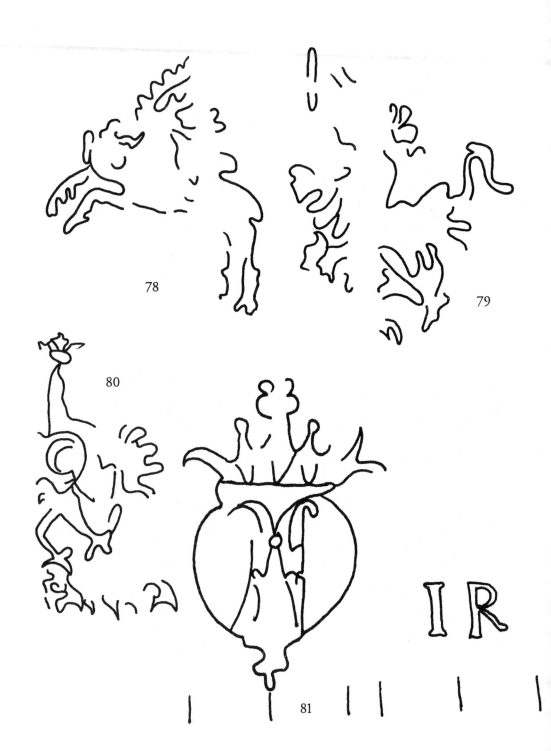

78

79

80

81

82

83

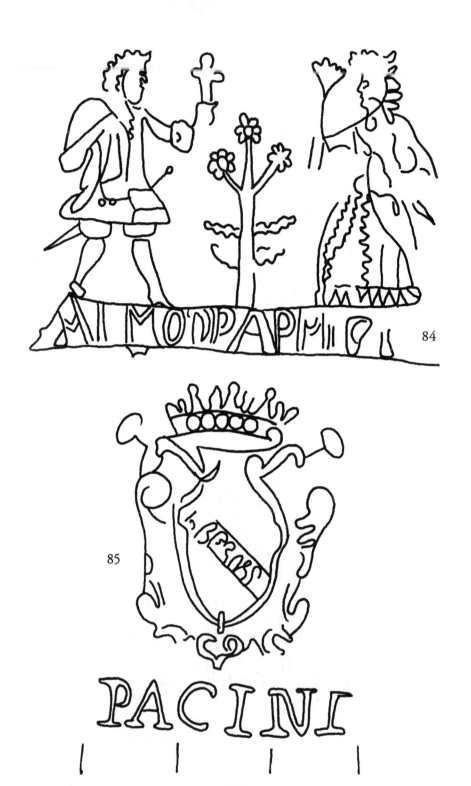

84

85

PACINI

238

86

87

88

89

239

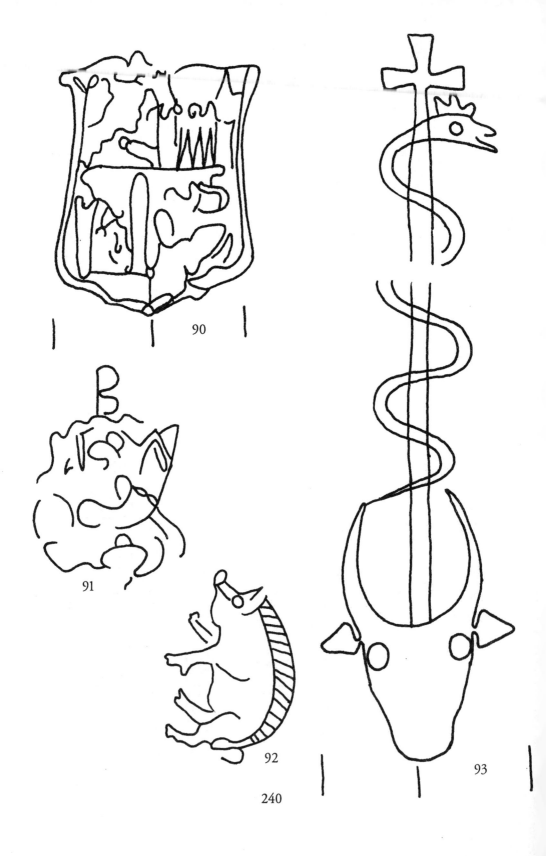

90

91

92

93

240

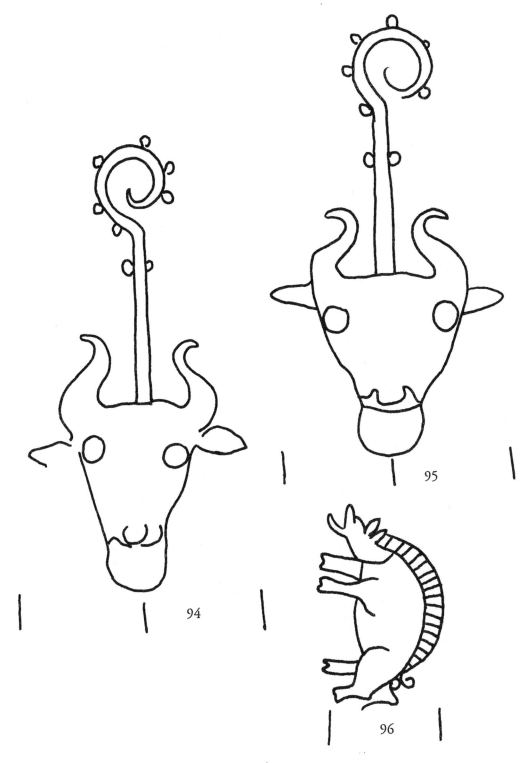

94

95

96

97

98

99

100

101

242

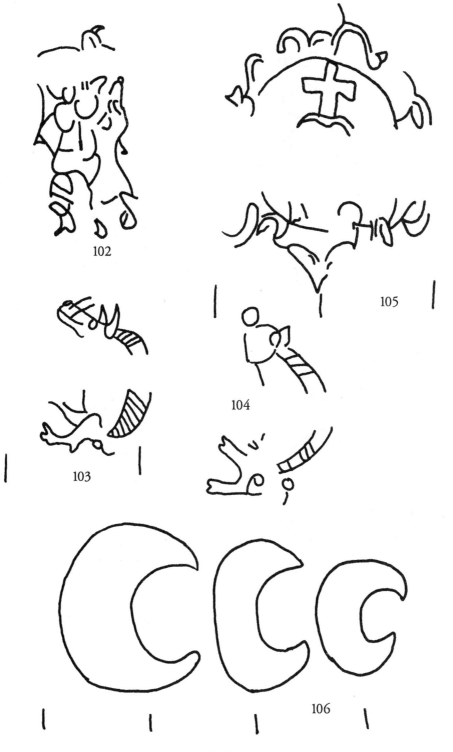

102

105

104

103

106

107

108

109

244

110

111

112

245

113

14

115

116

117

246

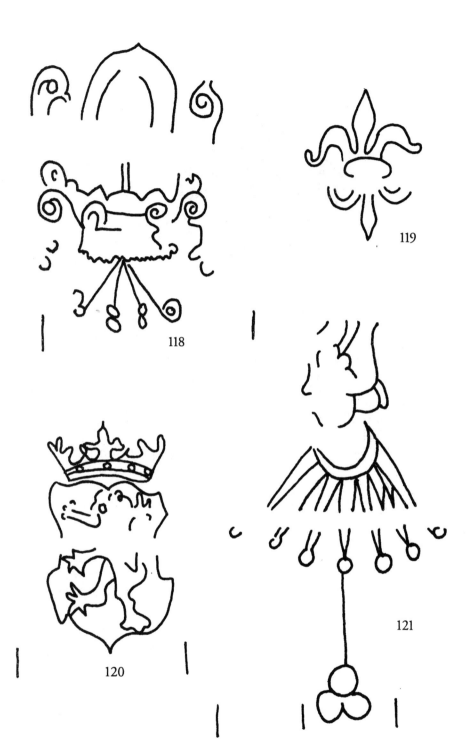

118

119

120

121

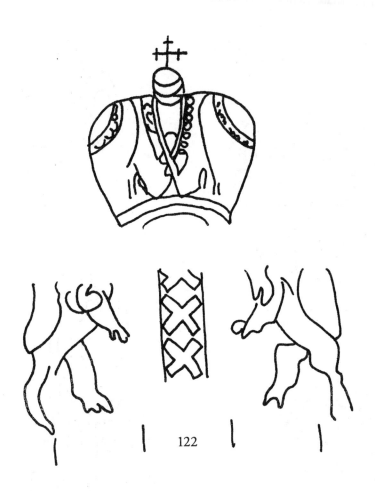

122

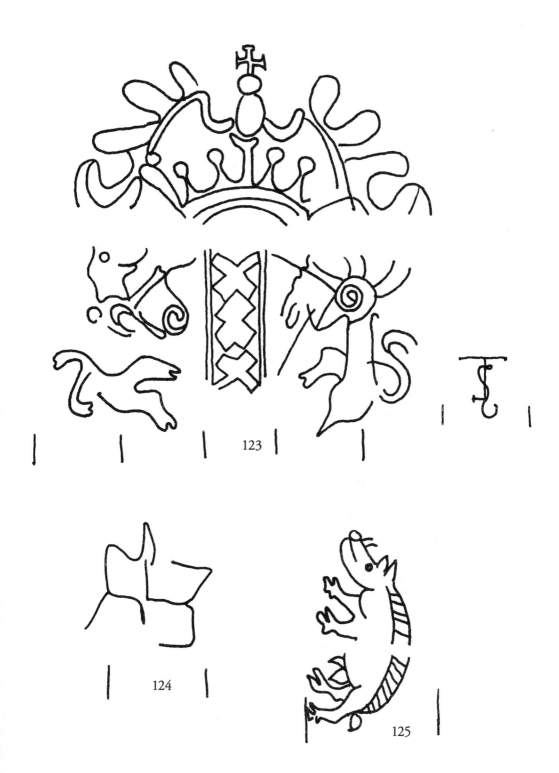

123

124

125

126

127

128

129

130

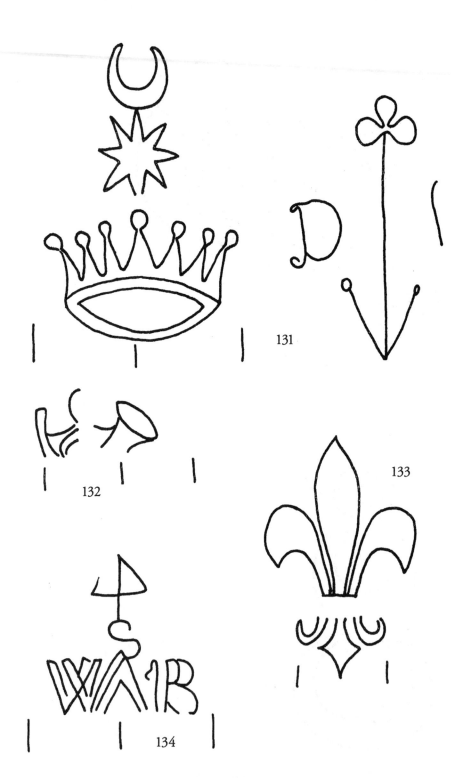

131

132

133

134

135

136

137

FPM

138

H

139

140

I RITSCHEL

SWI NITZ

141

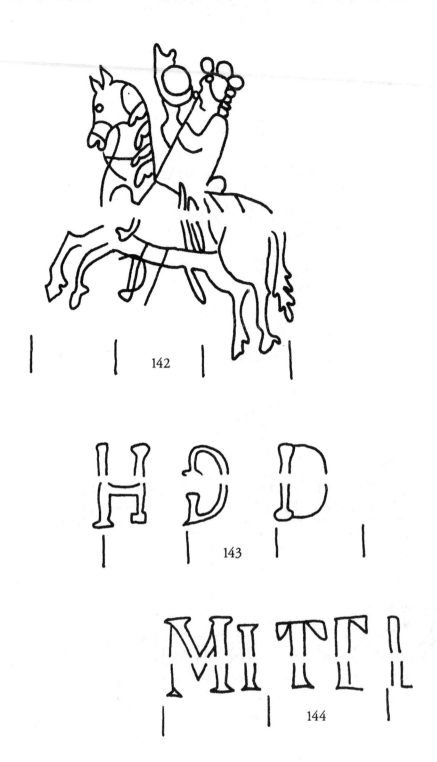

142

143

144

The numbers refer to figures in the Album; numbers in brackets refer to the catalogue descriptions in which the marks are found.

à la mode 83 [23], 84 [24], 89 [25], 136 [44], 137 [45]

anchor 107 [33], 110 [33], 111 [33], 126 [40], 127 [40], 128 [40]

angel 135 [43]

basilisk 79 [22], 80 [22]

boar 8 [5], 11 [5], 14 [6], 15 [6], 16 [6], 21 [7], 22 [7], 23 [8], 24 [8], 25 [8], 27 [9], 28 [9], 30 [10], 31 [10], 32 [10], 33 [10], 35 [11], 37 [12], 63 [18], 65 [18], 68 [19], 69 [19], 70 [19], 71 [20], 72 [20], 92 [26], 96 [27], 97 [29], 98 [31], 99 [31], 100 [31], 101 [31], 103 [32], 104 [32], 125 [39]

coat of arms 5 [4], 19 [6], 20 [6, 7, 9, 11, 12, 14, 16, 20, 24, 25, 27, 33], 29 [9], 36 [11], 42 [14], 49 [15], 52 [16], 53 [16], 81 [23], 85 [24], 87 [24], 90 [25], 102 [31], 112 [34], 115 [34], 116 [34], 117 [34], 118 [34], 138 [46], 139 [47], 141 [49]
    Amsterdam 122 [37], 123 [37], Habdank 74 [21], Hagel-Rune 43 [14], Jastrzębiec 7 [5], Jelita 114 [34], Lubicz 44 [14], 105 [32], Olkusz 6 [5], Rogala 76 [21], Ryba 40 [14], 41 [14]

cock 47 [15], 48 [15]

three crescents 106 [32], 130 [41]

cross 13 [6], 86 [24]

crown 62 [18], 64 [18], 131 [41]

eagle 50 [15], 51 [15], 77 [21], 113 [34]

fleur-de-lys 12 [6], 73 [20], 119 [35], 133 [43]

flower 58 [17], 60 [17]

foolscap 121 [37]

grapes 38 [13]

hart 26 [8], 78 [22], 129 [40], 140 [47]

hat 109 [33]

horn 18 [6], 88 [25], 91 [25], 132 [42]

Justice 45 [14], 46 [14]

ladder 4 [4]

letters
    FPM 138 [46]
    G 67 [18]
    HDD 143 [50]
    ID 78 [22]
    IM 122 [37]

    MITEL 144 [52]
    SA | REGEST 39 [13]
    SR 44 [14]
    SW 43 [14]
    W 17 [6]
    WAP 134 [43]

lion 120 [35]

mountains 54 [17], 57 [17]

oak-twig 34 [10, 21, 29]

oxhead 9 [5], 10 [5], 61 [17], 66 [18], 93 [26], 94 [26], 95 [26]

postillion 2 [1], 82 [23], 142 [5]

scales 3 [4], 108 [33]

star 56 [17]

sun 39 [13]

unicorn 55 [17], 59 [17]

Virgin and Child 1 [1]

LIST OF PUBLICATIONS AND OTHER SOURCES FOR WATERMARK IDENTIFICATION

Briquet – C. M. Briquet, *Les filigranes. Dictionnaire historique des marques du papier dès leur apparition vers 1282 jusqu'en 1600*, t. I-IV, Leipzig, 1923

Budka – W. Budka, *Papiernie w Polsce XVI wieku*. Prace Franciszka Piekosińskiego, Jana Ptaśnika, Kazimierza Piekarskiego, powtórne wydał i uzupełnił Włodzimierz Budka. Wrocław, &c., 1971

Decker – V. Decker, *Dejiny ručnej výroby papiera na Slovensku*, Martin, 1982

Dečani – М. Гроздановић-Пајић, Р. Станковић, *Рукописне књиге манастира Високи Дечани, књ.2: Водени знаци и датирање*, Београд, 1995

Dianova–Kostjuchina – Т. В. Дианова, Л. М. Костюхина, *Водяные знаки рукописей России XVII в.: по материалам Отдела рукописей ГИМ*, Москва, 1980

Eineder – G. Eineder, *The Ancient Paper-Mills of the Former Austro-Hungarian Empire and their Watermarks*, Hilversum, 1960 (*Monumenta chartae papyraceae historiam illustrantia*, Vol. VIII)

Harlfinger – D. & J. Harlfinger, *Wasserzeichen aus griechischen Handschriften*, Berlin, 1974

Heawood – E. Heawood, *Watermarks, mainly of the 17th and 18th centuries*, Hilversum, 1950 (Monumenta chartae papyraceae historiam illustrantia, Vol. I)

Laucevičius – E. Laucevičius, *Popierius Lietuvoje XV-XVIII a.*, Vilnius, 1967

Lichačev – Н. П. Лихачев, *Бумага и древнейшие бумажные мельницы в Московском государстве*, С-Петербург, 1891

Mareş – A. Mareş, *Filigranele hîrtiei întrebuinţate în ţările române în secolul al XVI-lea*, Bucureşti, 1987

Mošin, Anchor – V. Mošin, *Anchor Watermarks*, Amsterdam, 1973 (*Monumenta chartae papyraceae historiam illustrantia*, Vol. XIII)

Mošin–Grozdanović-Pajić – В. Мошин, М. Пајић-Гроздановић, "Водени знак 'Круна са звездом и полумесецом'", *Библиотекар* 15, 1 (1963), 11-20

Nikolaev – В. Николаев, *Водяные знаки Оттоманской империи. Водяные знаки на бумаге средневековых документов болгарских книгохранилищ*, т. 1, София, 1954

Piccard Frucht – *Wasserzeichen Frucht*, bearbeitet von G. Piccard, Stuttgart, 1983

Piccard Hirsch – *Wasserzeichen Hirsch*, bearbeitet von G. Piccard, Stuttgart, 1987

Piccard Ochsenkopf – *Ochsenkopf-Wasserzeichen*, bearbeitet von G. Piccard, Stuttgart, 1966

Piccard Vierfüßler – *Wasserzeichen Verschiedene Vierfüßler*, bearbeitet von G. Piccard, Stuttgart, 1987

Szentendre – Н. Синдик, М. Роздановић-Пајић, К. Мано-Зиси, *Опис рукописа и старих штампаних књига библиотеке Српске православне епархије будимске у Сентандреји*, Београд – Нови Сад, 1991

Siniarska-Czaplicka – J. Siniarska-Czaplicka, *Filigrany papierni położonych na obszarze Rzeczypospolitej Polskiej od początku XVI do połowy XVIII wieku*, Wrocław – Warszawa – Kraków, 1969

Siniarska-Czaplicka 1983 – J. Siniarska-Czaplicka, *Katalog filigranów czerpalni Rzeczypospolitej zebrany z papieru druków tłoczonych w latach 1500-1800*, Łódz, 1983

Velkov–Andreev – А. Велков, С. Андреев, *Водни знаци в османотурските документи, т.I: Три луни*, София, 1983

Voutova – Н. Вутова, *Филиграноложки проблеми на българските ръкописи от XIV и XV век (запазени в България)*, София, 1984

Zonghi – *Zonghi's Watermarks.* (Aurelio & Augusto Zonghi – A. F. Gasparinetti), Hilversum, 1953 (*Monumenta chartae papyraceae historiam illustrantia*, Vol. III)

MSPC - Muzej Srpske pravoslavne crkve, Beograd

NBCM – SS Cyril and Methodius National Library, Sofia (Slavonic Manuscript Collection)

SANU – Srpska Akademija nauka i umetnosti, Beograd

Zadar – Zadar, Državni arhiv

Anguševa, Dimitrova 1995 – A. Angusheva, M. Dimitrova, "Rare Bulgarian Manuscripts in Prague and Budapest", *Annual of Medieval Studies at the CEU 1993-1994*, Budapest, 1995, 250-254

Anguševa, Dimitrova 1997 – A. Angusheva, M. Dimitrova, "Рукопись Ms 10.403 Библиотеки Венгерской академии наук", *Studia Slavica*, 42 (1997), 37-44

Baleczki 1958 – Э. Балецки, "Эгерский рукописный ирмологий", *Studia Slavica*, 4 (1958), 293-324

Boynychich 1878 – I. Boynychich, "Két ó-szláv kézirat a Nemzeti Múzeum Könyvtárában", *Magyar Könyvszemle*, 3 (1878), 224-228

Chivu 1978 – Gh. Chivu, "Un manuscris cu o slovă neconoscută în scrierea chirilică românească: ⱔ", *Studii și cercetări linguistice*, 29 (1978), 399-409

Chivu 1997 – Gh. Chivu, "O versiune bănățeană a Visurilor lui Mamer", *Limba română*, 46, 1-3 (1997), 47-54

Cleminson 1995 – R. M. Cleminson, "The Cyrillic Manuscript Codices of Budapest University Library", *Полата къннигописьнаіа, кз-ки* (1995), 4-11

Cleminson, Moussakova, Voutova 2003 – R. Cleminson, E. Moussakova, N. Voutova, "Description of the Slavonic Cyrillic Codices of the National Széchényi Library", *Annual of Medieval Studies at CEU*, 9 (2003), 339-348

Conev 1927 – Б. Цонев, "Из една научна обиколка в чужбина", *Юбилеен годишник на Народната библиотека в Пловдив 1925*, София, 1927, 343-347

Čuba 2002 – Г. Чуба, "Текстологическая классификация украинских учительных Евангелий второй половины XVI века", *Славяноведение* 2002, № 2, 82-97

Dezső 1955 – L. Dezső, "Poznámky Dobrovského ke kodexu 'Acta Apostolorum'", *Studia Slavica*, 1 (1955), 415-418

Dobrovský 1790 – "Auszug aus einem Schreiben des Herrn Vicerektors Dobrowsky die Slavische Uebersetzung des N. T. betreffend", *Johann David Michaelis' Neue Orientalische und Exegetische Bibliothek*, 7. Theil, Göttingen, 1790, 155-167

Dogramadžieva 1993 – Е. Дограмаджиева, "Състав на славянските ръкописни четвероевангелия", *Palæobulgarica*, 17, 3 (1993), 3-21

Földvári 1995 – S. Földvári, "Egy a Székesfehérvári Püspöki Könyvtárban őrzött, szerb kéziratos Oktoich provenienciája", *Az ortodoxia története Magyarországon a XVIII századig*, Szeged, 1995, 71-75

Griesbach 1806 – *Novum Testamentum Graece*, Textum ad fidem codicum versionum et patrum recensivit et lectionis varietatem D. Io. Iac. Griesbach. Volumen II, Acta et Epistulas Apostolorum cum Apocalypsi complectens. Editio secunda, emendatior multoque locupletior, Halle–London, 1806

Hauptová 1961 – Z. Hauptová, "Debrecínský rukopís církevneslovanský liturgických mineji", *Slavica* (Debrecen), I (1961), 85-94

Janc 1974 – З. Јанц, *Кожни повези српске ћирилске књиге од XII до XIX века*, Београд, 1974

Jankovich catalogue – *Jankovich Miklós (1772-1846) gyűteményei: kiállítás a Magyar Nemzeti Galériában 2002. november 28 - 2003. február 16*, Budapest, 2002

Kacziba 1999 – Á. Kacziba, *Budimpeštanksi rukopis Hristofora Račanina: sadržaj, paleografski opis i pravopis*, Szeged, 1999

Király 1974 – П. Кирай, "Болгарское четвероевангелие в Будапеште", *В памет на професор Стойко Стойков (1912-1969). Езиковедски изследвания*, София, 1974, 527-536

Király 1968 – P. Király, "Budimpeštanski fragment apostola", *Зборник за филологију и лингвистику*, XI (1968), 109-117 + 4 plates

Kocsis 1994 – М. Кочиш, "Среднеболгарские черты в орфографии Сегедской минеи", *Szegedi bolgarisztika* (főszerk. H. Tóth Imre), Szeged, 1994 (*Hungaro-Bulgarica*, 5), 175-183

Kocsis 1997 – *Скотарське учительне євангеліє: український гоміліар 1588 року*. Текст рукопису підготував і видав Мігай Кочіш, Szombathely, 1997 (*Bibliotheca Slavica Savariensis*, IV)

Kocsis 1999 – M. Kocsis, *The Szeged minea: a Cyrillic manuscript from the late 16th century*, Szombathely, 1999

Kocsis 2004 – М. Кочиш, "К изучению наследия Константина Преславского (на украинском материале XVI века)", *Преславска книжовна школа*, 7 (2004), 114-121

Kočubinskij 1882 – А. Кочубинский, *Славянские рукописи Пештского музея*, Варшава, 1882

Kostjuchina 1974 – Л. М. Костюхина, *Книжное письмо в России XVII в.*, n.p., n.d. [Moscow, 1974]

Laucevičius 1976 – E. Laucevičius, *XV-XVIII a. knygu irišimai Lietuvos bibliotekose*, Vilnius, 1976

Mareş 2003 – A. Mareş, *Cărţi populare de prevestire: Cele douăsprezece vise în tâlcuirea lui Mamer; Învăţătură despre vremea de apoi a prorocului Isaia*, Bucureşti, 2003

Mathiesen 1972 – R. Mathiesen, *The Inflectional Morphology of the Church Slavonic Verb*, Ann Arbor–London, 1972

Momina 1985 – М. А. Момина, "Вопросы классификации славянской Триоди", *ТОДРЛ*, 37 (1985), 25-38

Nyomárkay 1990- – I. Nyomárkay (ed.), *Magyarországi szláv kéziratok*, I- , Budapest, 1990-

Ojtozi 1982 – E. Ojtozi, "Итоги и задачи исследования восточнославянских старопечатных книг и славянских рукописей в северовосточной части Венгрии", *Полата къннигописьнаіа*, 5 (1982), 30-39

Pandur 1990 – Ю. Пандур, "Кирилски ръкописни паметници в Библиотеката на Гръцко-католическата Духовна Академия в град Ниредьхаза", *Dissertationes slavicae: sectio linguistica*, XXI (1990), 347-352

Patera 1913 – A. Patera (ed.), *Josefa Dobrovského korespondence IV: vzájemné listy Josefa Dobrovského a J. Rybaye z let 1783-1810*, Praha, 1913

Pekar 1992 – A. B. Pekar, *The History of the Church in Carpathian Rus*, New York, 1992

Póth 1961 – I. Póth, "Eine serbische Liedersammlung", *Studia Slavica*, VII (1961), 347-361

Protas'eva 1980 – Т. Н. Протасьева, *Описание рукописей Чудовского собрания*, Новосибирск, 1980

Simoni 1903 – П. К. Симони, *Опыт сборника сведений по истории и технике книгопереплетного художества на Руси, преимущественно в допетровское время, с XI-го по XVIII-го столетия включительно*, С-Петербург, 1903

Sindik 2002 – Н. Р. Синдик, "Приновљене рукописне, старе и ретке штампане књиге у Библиотеци Српске православне епархије будимске у Сентандреји", *Археографски прилози*, 22-23 (2002), 401-443

Sindik, Grozdanović-Pajić, Mano-Zisi 1991 – Н. Р. Синдик, М. Грозданović-Пајић, К. Мано-Зиси, *Опис рукописа и старих штампаних књига Библиотеке Српске православне епархије будимске у Сентандреји*, Београд–Нови Сад, 1991

Somogy 1970 – Á. Somogy, "A piricsei óegyházi szláv kódex", *Művészettörténeti értesítő*, 19 (1970), 272-277

Stefanović 1998 – D. Stefanović, "Три ћирилска рукописа Универзитетске библиотеке у Будимпешти", *Studia Slavica*, 43 (1998), 203-250

Stefanović 2001 – Д. Stefanović, "Три ћирилска рукописа некадашње православне цркве у Адоњу", *Studia Slavica*, 46 (2001), 401-443

Stefanović 2003 – Д. Стефановић, "Вредан споменик словенске и српске духовности у Земаљској библиотеци Сечењи", *Српски календар за преступну 2004. годину*, Budapest, 2003, 214-216

Šul'gina 2000 – Э. В. Шульгина, *Русская книжная скоропись XV в.*, С-Петербург, 2000

Szarvas 1986 – М. Сарваш, "Среднеболгарский апостол конца XV - начала XVI вв. (о деятельности Иозефа Добровского и его связях с венгерскими личностями)", *Szlávok - Protobolgárok - Bizánc*, (H. Tóth Imre szerkesztő), Szeged, 1986 (*Hungaro-Bulgarica*, 2), 207-216

Tóth 1980 – И. Тот, "Задачи изучения и описания славянских кирилловских рукописей, находящихся в венгерских книгохранилищах", *Paléographie et diplomatique slaves*, [vol.1], София, 1980 (*Balcanica III: Études et documents, 1*), 56-59

Tóth 1983 – И. Тот, "Болгарское четвероевангелие в Будапеште", *Palæobulgarica*, 7, 2 (1983), 3-13

Vašica, Vajs 1957 – J. Vašica, J. Vajs, *Soupis staroslovanských rukopisů Národního musea v Praze*, Praha, 1957

Velčeva, Musakova 2003 – Б. Велчева, Е. Мусакова, "Един новооткрит ръкопис от Университетската Библиотека в Будапеща", *Пѣти достоитъ: Сборник в памет на Стефан Кожухаров*, София, 2003, 465-483

Zaimov, Tóth, Balázs 2003 – *Будапештское евангелие: среднеболгарский памятник XIII-XIV в.*, Szeged, 2003

Zapasko 1960 – Я. Запаско, *Орнаментальне оформлення української рукописної книги*, Київ, 1960

Zapasko, Isajevyč 1984 – Я. Запаско, Я. Исаєвич, *Пам'ятки книжкового мистецтва: каталог стародруків, виданих на Україні, книга друга, частина перша (1701-1764)*, Львів, 1984

Zernova, Kameneva 1968 – А. С. Зернова, Т. Н. Каменева, *Сводный каталог русской книги кирилловской печати XVIII века*, Москва, 1968

Zinčenko 2004 – С. В. Зинченко, "Методические рекомендации для описания, локализации и датировки средневековых кожаных переплетов с тиснением", *Рукописная книга Древней Руси и славянских стран: от кодикологии к текстологии* (отв. ред. А. А. Романова), С-Петербург, 2004, 5-18

INDEX OF PERSONS

Numbers refer to pages. Some inscriptions in the manuscripts consist of lists of names of persons to be commemorated; names from such lists have not been included in this index. These lists are found on pp.14, 21, 28, 38, 47, 49, 82, 86, 89, 116 and 129 of the catalogue.

Aeithalas, St, service to 61

Alexis, St, life of (?) 90

Alypius, St, service to 59

Amphilochius, St, service to 59

Ananias, St, the Apostle, service to 51, 61

Ananias, Azarias and Misael, service to 62

Anastasia, St, service to 62

Anastasius the Monk, *Sermon on the Transfiguration* 104

Andrew, St, journey to Kiev 101

Andrew of Crete, *Sermon for the Nativity of the Virgin* 100

Anna, *inscr.* 28

Anne, St, service to 52, 63

Anna, wife of János Simon, *inscr.* 37

Anoţe, wife of priest Toader, *inscr.* 77

Antonić *or* Antović, Georgije xiii, 124

Antony, St, of the Caves, service to 63

Antony, St, of Egypt, life of 102

Augustus II, king of Poland, *inscr.* 67

Augustus III, king of Poland, *inscr.* 67

Avram Ormenin, *inscr.* 8

Bačyns'kyj, Andrej, bishop of Mukačeve xxiv, 82

Balaž Ion, *inscr.* 21

Barbara, St , passion of 101

Barbarus, St, service to 62

Barlaam, St, service to 59

Baromić, Blaž xxix

Basil, St, service to 54, 57, 62

Basil, St, encomium to (Gregory Nazianzen) 101

Basil the Wolf, voivode of Moldavia 75

Boris and Gleb, saints, service to 51

Bozdag, Ioan 77

Bukoskij, Stefan, priest, *inscr.* 90

Burja, Hryhoryj, priest, *inscr.* 14

Callistus, Evodius and Hermogenes, saints, service to 61

Chryptin, Andrej, *inscr.* 82

Ćika Hadži (?), *inscr.* 124

Clement, St, of Ohrid
 encomium to SS Michael and Gabriel 100
 Sermon on the Dormition 104

Clement, St, of Rome, service to 59

Constantine and Helena, saints, service to 51, 62

Cornides, Dániel xxxi, 45

Cosmas Vestitor, *translation of the relics of St John Chrysostom* 100

Cyriacus and Julitta, saints, service to 51, 63

Cyril, St, of Alexandria, *Sermon on the Deposition of the Robe of the Mother of God* 103

Cyril, St, of Jerusalem, *Sermon on the Presentation of Our Lord* 102

Czubut, Suleman, *inscr.* 66

Damján, Vazul xxxvi, 8, 30

Daniel, prophet, service to 62

Danilă, archpriest of Ilia, *inscr.* 85, 131

David, king of Israel, service to 62

Demetrius, St, encomium to 100
 passion of 100
 service to 54, 62

Diomedes, St, service to 63

Dobrovský, Josef xi-xii, xxxi, 45

Dorošenko, hetman of the Ukraine, *inscr.* 58

Dragić, Iosif, *inscr.* 129

Dragojlo, *inscr.* 85

Egri, György xxxviii, 1

Eichhorn, Johann Gottfried xxx, xxxii, 95

Elijah, prophet, life of 103
 service to 51, 54, 58, 61

Ephesus, seven sleepers of 63

Ephraim, St, *Sermon on the 30 pieces of silver* 110

Epiphanius of Cyprus, *Sermon on the life of the Mother of God* 101

Eremkovski, Antonije, priest, *inscr.* 77

Eudocimus, St, service to 63

Eugenia, St, service to 51, 62

Eupraxia, St, service to 63

Eusignius, St, service to 63

Euthymius, St, the Great, life of 102

Euthymius, St, of Sardis, service to 62

Fedor, *inscr.* 33

Fena, wife of Petr Plešovskij, *inscr.* 24

Feoktist, hieromonk, scribe 59

Ferdinand I, emperor of Austria, 94

Fetion, Ioan, *inscr.* 44

Foktövi, János xl, 126

Francis I, emperor of Austria, *inscr.* 86

Gabriel, the Archangel, encomium to (Clement of Ohrid) 100
    service to 62

Gavrilo, *inscr.* 124

George, St, passion of 103
    service to 54, 58

Giurgiu, priest of Bărsău, *inscr.* 85

Gligorie, priest, *inscr.* 71

Gordius, St, service to 62

Gourias, Samonas and Abibus, saints, service to 59

Gozzadini, Tommaso, *Fiore di virtù* xvii, 107

Grabovskij (?), *inscr.* 125

Gradovskij, Iosif, priest, *inscr.* 58

Gregory, St, Agrigentinus, service to 59

Gregory of Dečani, *life of St Stephen of Dečani* 100

Gregory, St, of Decapolis, service to 59, 62

Gregory, St, Nazianzen
    encomium to St Basil 101
    Sermon on the Maccabees 104

Gregory, St, of Neocæsaria, service to 59

Gregory, St, of Sinai, *on monasticism* 107

Griesbach, Johann Jacob xii

Halaváts, Gyula xxxvii, 67

Hanja, wife of Lazor, *inscr.* 92

Hankuvskij, Petr, *inscr.* 24

Hanusja, wife of Havrylo Salnyc'kyj, *inscr.* 92

Hodinka, Antal xiii, xxxiv-xxxv, 14, 18, 22, 25, 28, 33, 38, 40, 42, 49, 55, 58, 69, 79, 83, 90, 92, 98

Horváth, Aranka xxxiii, 110

Hristofor Račanin, scribe xii, xiv, xvii, xxii, 106, 107

Humeni, János, *inscr.* 21

Ianăşi, priest of Simeria, *inscr.* 86

Ianuşu, clerk, *inscr.* 130

Iancu, *inscr.* 75

Ignatij, priest of Myrča, *inscr.* 21

Ignatius, St, Theophorus, service to 51, 62

Ion, priest of Vărmas, *inscr.* 85, 86

Ionaško, *inscr.* 75

Iosip, priest, *inscr.* 30

Irenarchus, St, service to 59

Isaiah, St, the Monk, service to 51

Isidore, St, apophthegmata 109

James, St, the brother of Our Lord, service to 62

James, St, the Persian, service to 59

Jankovich, Miklós xiii, xviii, xxiv, xxviii, xxix-xxxiii, 5, 45, 95, 112, 114, 115, 117, 118, 120

Jankovits, Ágoston, priest 33

Joachim and Anna, service to 51

Job, service to 62

John, St, the Almsgiver, service to   51

John the Baptist, life of 104

    sermons on 102, 103

    service to 61, 62

    Beheading of, service for 55

John, St, Climacus, apophthegmata 109

John, St, Chrysostom,

    apophthegmata 109

    encomium to St John the Divine 100

    encomium to SS Peter and Paul 103

    Sermon on the Annunciation 103

    Sermon for Christmas 101

    Sermon for Epiphany 102

    Sermon for the Exaltation of the Cross 100

    Sermon for the new Indiction 99

    Sermon on the Presentation of Our Lord 102

    Sermon for the Synaxis of the Mother of God 101

translation of his relics 100
troparion and kontakion to 89
John, St, Damascene, *on the Zodiac* 109
John, St, the Divine, encomium to (John Chrysostom) 100
service to 51, 54, 61
John the Exarch of Bulgaria, *Sermon for Christmas* 101
Jókai, Mór xxxii
Joseph, service to 62
Joseph, Palatine of Hungary xxx
Joshua, service to 61
Juliana, St, service to 62
Julijana, *inscr.* 124
Južikov, Oleksa, *inscr.* 33
Kamięski, Antoni, *inscr.* 67
Kamiński, Teodor, priest, *inscr.* 66-67
Kaulici, Damjan Stefanović 124
Király Péter xxxix, 128
Klenik, Matfej, *inscr.* 21
Kopanskij, Andrej, *inscr.* 90
Kopitar, Jernej 5
Krajcsovics, János xxxviii, 105
Krečun, Andrej, *inscr.* 24
Kún, Dániel xxxviii, 113, 122
Kuzmanović, Evlogije, *inscr.* 121
Lacychow *see* Ljachovič
Lazar, prince, life of 103, 123
Lazar, scribe xiii, 17
Lazor, *inscr.* 92
Lazarus, St, service to 54
Litwinko, Stephan, *inscr.* 66
Ljachovič, Panteleimon, priest of Holjatin, *inscr.*, 82
Lju(by)ckij, Feodor, priest of Karaszna, *inscr.* 37, 38
Lubaczevski, Joannes, priest, *inscr.* 63
Luka, priest of Myrča, *inscr.* 21
Macarius, St, apophthegmata 109
Maccabees, the, service to 52, 63, 88
Magyari Lászlóné 28, 79
Malachi, prophet, service to 62

Mamer, philosopher, 131

Mani 108

Mary, St, of Egypt, life of 65-66

Mary, St, Magdalene, service to 63

Mary, the Mother of God, services for her feasts 51, 52, 54, 55, 57, 58, 61, 62, 63, 95

Medvec'kyj, V., priest, *inscr.* 18

Mercurius, St, service to 59

Micah, prophet, service to 63

Michael, the Archangel, encomium to (Clement of Ohrid) 100
    miracle at Chonæ, service for 51

Mihály, priest, *inscr.* 11

Milovanović, Nikolaje, priest, *inscr.* xxxiii, 111

Mogila, Jeremias, voivode of Moldavia, 130

Mohammed 108

Molodec, Michail, archbishop of Máramaros xxiv, 35

Mykula, priest, *inscr.* 82

Naményi, Ernő xxxviii, 125

Nastasija, wife of Ioan Fetion, *inscr.* 44

Nestor, archpriest of Buda, *inscr.* xxxiii, 112, 113

Nicholas, St, encomium to 101
    service to 51, 54, 57

Nicora, Mariu xxxvii, 3, 52

Ninov, Mika Ivanec, *inscr.* 58

Obadiah, prophet, service to 59

Oleksej, *inscr.* 28

Olympias, St, service to 63

Onuphrius, St, service to 51

Oprics Miklósné xxxviii, 63

Ormindean, Dănilă, *inscr.* 86

Palladius, St, service to 59

Panteleimon, priest, *inscr.* 105

Papp, Eremias xxxvi, 71

Parasceve (Petka), St, service to 54, 57, 62, 75

Pastinszky, Miklós xxxvii, xxxix, 59

Pavlović, Marko, *inscr.* 105

Peter and Paul, saints, service to 54, 58

Peter, St, of Alexandria, service to 59

Peter, St, of Kiev, service to 62

Petr, cousin of János Simon, *inscr.* 37

Petro, priest, *inscr.* 82

Petrus, pastor Talaboriensis, *inscr.* 33

Philemon, St, service to 59

Philip, St, the Apostle, service to 51

Philip Monotropus, *Dioptra* xviii, xxxiii, 111

Phocas, St, service to 63

Plato and Romanus, saints, service to 59

Plešovskij, Petr, priest, *inscr.* 24

Polyanszky István, *inscr.* 125

Popović, Arsenije xviii, xxiv, xxxii 114, 115, 116, 117, 120

Popovič, Maksim, priest of Novoselycja, *inscr.* 82

Popovici, Mihail, priest, *inscr.* 85, 86

Popovits, Peter, *inscr.* 124

Popović, Stephanus 116

Premyko, Antonij, *inscr.* 14

Proclus, St, of Constantinople, *Sermon on the Transfiguration* 104
    service to 59, 62

Prokopovič, Feofan, *O smerti Petra Velikago* 120
    Panegirikos 120

Pudka, Ioan, *inscr.* 14

Radišić, Ilija, scribe xiii, 122

Radivojević, Arsenije, bishop of Buda, *inscr.* 104

Radziwiłł, princes, 67

Rákóczy, Ferenc, *inscr.* xxiv, 89

Réthy, László xxxiv, xxxv, 86, 131

Revnik, Ion, Paraska, Ivan and Marucja, *inscr.* 35

Ribay, Juraj xi-xii, xiv, xxx-xxxii, 45, 95

Romanus, St, the Melode, service to 51

Sabasko, *inscr.* 14

Sabbas, St, of Jerusalem, life of 101

Šafárik, Pavol Jozef 107

Salnyc'kyj, Havrylo, *inscr.* 92

Sava, St, of Serbia, miracles of 102

Seiden, Gusztáv xxxviii, 35

Šelepec, Andrej, *inscr.* 125

Šelepec, Vasilko, *inscr.* 125

Šelesnička, Anna, *inscr.* 24

Sigismund Augustus, king of Poland, *inscr.* 14

Silvester, St, service to 62

Simeon *see* Symeon

Simon János, *inscr.* 37

Sison, St, life of 123

Stanko Meškanin, *inscr.* 21

Stasov(?), Vasilij, *inscr.* 25

Stephen, St, of Dečani life of (Gregory of Dečani) 100

Stephen, St, the New Confessor, service to 59

Stephen, St, Sabaites, service to 63

Stefanovič, Pavel, *inscr.* 63

Stesovič, Vasilij, *inscr.* 90

Studenskyj, Vasilij, priest, *inscr.* 40

Sulica, Szilárd xxxiv, xxxvi, 47, 71, 73, 77

Symeon, St, service to 62

Symeon, St, of Serbia, life of 102

Symeon, St, Stylites, service to 51, 54, 61

Syncletica, St, service to 62

Széchényi, Ferenc xxviii-xxix, xxxii

Talamaskij, Vasilij, priest, *inscr.* 42

T(h)anacs, Jacob, *inscr.* 75

Teleki, József xxxi

Teslevič, Stefan, priest, *inscr.* 89

Thallóczy, Lajos xxxiv, xxxv

Theoctistus, St, service to 62

Theodore, St, Stratilates, service to 63

Theodore, St, Studite 54

Theodorovics, Marhea(?), priest, *inscr.* 18

Theodosius, St, of the Caves, service to 62, 63

Theodosius, St, the Cœnobiarch, 102

Theopemptus and Theonas, saints, service to 62

Theophylact, Archbishop of Ohrid, prefaces to the Gospels, 5-37 *passim*

Thuz, Osvát, bishop of Zagreb xxix

Timothy and Maura, saints, service to 62

Tirović, Grigorije, scribe xiii, xxxiii, 118

Toader, priest, *inscr.* 77

Todoreszku, Gyula xxxiii, 110

Tóth, Zsuzsanna 22

Trenck, Franz, Freiherr von der xviii, xxxii, 120
Trenck, Friedrich, Freiherr von der xxxii
Ursu, priest, *inscr.* 71
Vasilevjat', Demko Romančin, *inscr.* 21
Vasilij, priest of Karaszna, *inscr.* 38
Vasilij, priest of Novoselycja, *inscr.* 83
Vaynagi, Martinus, *inscr.* 33
Vladimir, St, service to 51, 63
Vuček, Oleksa, *inscr.* 32
Wolosiansky, Wasyl, priest, *inscr.* 38
Zahor, Wasili, *inscr.* 67
Zalensky, Leon Slubicza, *inscr.* 66
Zavadovskij, Ioan, priest, *inscr.* 38
Zékány, Lajos, *inscr.* 55

The numbers refer to pages.

Agrişu de Jos 71, 73
Alsó Egres *see* Agrişu de Jos
Bács megye 131
Baia de Criş 8, 30
Bánpatak *see* Banpotoc
Banpotoc 86
Berekszó *see* Bîrsău
Berezna *see* Velykyj Bereznyj
Beserica 77
Białystok 67
Bîrsău 85-86
Bodjani 105
Bogyán *see* Bodjani
Bonbach *see* Banpotoc
Botoşani? 75
Bretea 71
Brzyść 67
Buda 112, 122
Churches
    SS Cosmas & Damian, Myrča 21
    Dormition, Kronja 44
    Dormition, Putna 8
    St Michael, Černa 28
    St Michael, Iraşul de Sus 49
    St Michael, Karas 37
    Nativity of the BVM 63
    St Nicholas, Turka 33
    St Parasceve 11
    SS Peter and Paul, Töttös 104-105
    Presentation of the BVM, Hrud 67
    Presentation of Our Lord, Vičkovo 33
    Resurrection, Kowel 59
Chyža 58
Čorna 28
Drugetháza *see* Zaričeve
Esztergom 118

Felsőborgó *see* Susenii Bîrgăului
Fruška Gora 119
Gdańsk 67
Holjatyn 82-83
Hrud 66-67
Humenné 22
Ilia 85, 86, 131
Iraşul de Sus 49
Janów 67
Jena 95
Kapušianske Kľačany 38
Karas *see* Krásnovce
Karaszna *see* Krásnovce
Kis Rákóc *see* Malyj Rakovec
Kistarna *see* Chyža
Klonownica Duża 67
Kőrösbánya *see* Baia de Criş
Kowel 59
Krásnovce 37, 38
Kronja? 44
Kwiatoń 92
Lengyelszállás *see* Liskovec'
Liskovec' 82-83
Lyahovec *see* Liskovec'
Magyarberéte *see* Bretea
Magyarkelecsény *see* Kapušianske Kľačany
Malmos *see* Strojne
Malyj Rakovec 49
Máramaros megye 14
Marosillye *see* Ilia
Matejovce *see* Maťovské Vojkovce
Maťovské Vojkovce 21, 22
Mátyócz *see* Maťovské Vojkovce
Mércse *see* Myrča
Mere(si)cke 21, 22

Michalovce 22
Mielec 59
Mircse *see* Myrča
Močarany 21
Mocsár *see* Močarany
Monasteries
    Bodjani 105
    Fruška Gora 119
    Mielec 59
    Râncu 77
Mulnik 67
Myrča 17-18, 21, 22
Novoselycja 82-83
Ó-Holyátin *see* Holjatyn
Orşova 77
Pochov? 11
Putna 8
Rača 110
Râncu 77
Repynne 82-83
Ripinye *see* Repynne
Rokitno 66, 67
Rozália *see* Rozavlea
Rozavlea 49
Strojne 24-25
Susenii Bîrgăului 75
Taban 112
Talabor *see* Terebja
Tarfalu *see* Holjatyn
Tarújfalu *see* Novoselycja
Terebja 33
Titoš *see* Töttös
Töttös 104, 105
Turka 33
Tykocin 66
Új-Holyátin *see* Novoselycja
Ungvár *see* Užhorod
Užhorod 82

Vác 126
Velykyj Bereznyj 17
Vičkovo 33
Witulin 66, 67
Zaričeve 17, 18
Zaricsó *see* Zaričeve
Zirc 94

Numbers refer to pages.

Acts & Epistles 16, 43-49, 58, 85, 126
Bible *see* Acts & Epistles, Gospels, Psalter
Calendar 109
Cele 12 vise ale liu Mamer 131
Chronograph (excerpts from) 108
Dioptra 111
Encomium to St Basil (Gregory Nazianzen) 101
 to St Demetrius 100
 to St John the Divine (John Chrysostom) 100
 to SS Michael and Gabriel (Clement of Ohrid) 100
 to St Nicholas 101
 to SS Peter and Paul (John Chrysostom) 103
Epistula e cœlo missa 130
Epitaph on Franz von der Trenck 120
Euchologion 78-92
Festal Menaion 50-63
Fiore di virtù 107
General Menaion 60
Gospel Homiliary 41
Gospels 2-40, 85
Hieraticon *see* Euchologion
Kirillova kniga (excerpts from) 108
Kniga o věřě (excerpts from) 110
Lectiones de peccato 114
Legends
 St Andrew's journey to Kiev 101
 siege of Constantinople by the Persians 104
Lenten Triodion 64
Life (including miracles, passion)
 of St Antony of Egypt 102
 of St Barbara 101
 of St Demetrius 100
 of the Prophet Elijah 103
 of St Euthymius the Great 102
 of St George 103

of John the Baptist (John Mark) 104
of Prince Lazar 103, 123
of St Mary of Egypt 65-66
of St Sabbas of Jerusalem 101
of St Sava of Serbia 102
of St Sison 123
of St Stephen of Dečani (Gregory of Dečani) 100
of St Symeon of Serbia 102
of St Theodosius the Cœnobiarch 102
Liturgicon 84, 93, *see also* Euchologion
Menaion *see* Festal Menaion, General Menaion
Miracles *see* Life
Miscellany 106, 114-117, 119, 123
Molebny 96
Nastavlenie maloe 118
Nomocanon 82, 97
O smerti Petra velikago (F. Prokopovič) 120
Octoechos 68-77
Orations 115
Panegirikos (F. Prokopovič) 120
Panegyricon 99
Paschalia 109
Passion Narrative 113
Psalter 1, 130
Sermons
    miscellaneous 116, 120
    on particular subjects or occasions:
    Annunciation (John Chrysostom) 103
    Baptism 102
    Christmas (John Chrysostom) 101
    Christmas (John the Exarch of Bulgaria) 101
    Deposition of Robe of the Mother of God (Cyril of Alexandria) 103
    Dormition (Clement of Ohrid) 104
    drunkenness 110
    Epiphany (John Chrysostom) 102
    Exaltation of Cross (John Chrysostom) 100
    Invention of the Head of John the Baptist 103
    St Luke's Day 100

life of the Mother of God (Epiphanius of Cyprus) 101

the Maccabees (Gregory Nazianzen) 104

Nativity of the Mother of God (Andrew of Crete) 100

Nativity of John the Baptist 103

new Indiction (John Chrysostom) 99

Presentation of Our Lord (Cyril of Jerusalem) 102

Presentation of Our Lord (John Chrysostom) 102

Synaxis of Mother of God (John Chrysostom) 101

Synaxis of the Twelve Apostles 103

the 30 pieces of silver (St Ephraim) 110

Transfiguration (Proclus of Constantinople) 104

Transfiguration (Anastasius the Monk) 104

translation of the relics of St John Chrysostom (Cosmas Vestitor) 100

see also Encomium

Services

  for various persons and occasions:

    St Aeithalas 61

    to the All-Merciful Saviour 95

    St Alypius 59

    St Amphilochius 59

    St Ananias the Apostle 51, 61

    Ananias, Azarias and Misael 62

    St Anastasia 62

    St Anne 52, 63

    the Annunciation 54, 62

    St Antony of the Caves 63

    the Ascension 54, 58

    St Barbarus 62

    St Barlaam 59

    St Basil 54, 57, 62

    the Beheading of St John the Baptist 55

    blessing of the waters (Aug. 1) 81

    SS Boris and Gleb 51

    SS Callistus, Evodius and Hermogenes 61

    Christmas 51, 54, 57, 62

    the Circumcision 54, 57, 62

    St Clement 59

    the Conception of the Virgin 51, 62

SS Constantine and Helena 51, 62
Crete, nine martyrs of, 62
SS Cyriacus and Julitta 51, 63
the Prophet Daniel 62
King David 62
the dead 54
St Demetrius 54, 62
the Deposition of the Robe 51, 63
St Diomedes 63
the Dormition 52, 55, 58, 63
the great Earthquake 54, 62
Easter 54, 57
the Elevation of the Cross 51, 54, 56, 61
the Prophet Elijah 51, 54, 58, 61
Ephesus, seven sleepers of 63
St Eudocimus 63
St Eugenia 51, 62
St Eupraxia 63
St Eusignius 63
St Euthymius of Sardis 62
the great fire 61
the Forty Women 51, 54, 61
the Archangel Gabriel 62
St George 54, 58
St Gordius 62
SS Gourias, Samonas and Abibus 59
St Gregory Agrigentinus 59
St Gregory of Decapolis 59, 62
St Gregory of Neocæsaria 59
St Ignatius Theophorus 51, 62
image not made with hands 63
St Irenarchus 59
St Isaiah the Monk 51
St James the brother of Our Lord 62
St James the Persian 59
Joachim and Anna 51
Job 62
St John the Almsgiver 51

St John the Baptist 61, 62
St John the Divine 51, 54, 61
Joseph 62
Joshua 61
St Juliana 62
Kazan' Icon of the Virgin 95
St Lazarus 54
the Maccabees 52, 63, 88
the Prophet Malachi 62
St Mary Magdalene 63
St Mercurius 59
the Prophet Micah 63
the miracle at Chonæ 51
the Nativity of the Virgin 51, 54, 57, 61
St Nicholas 51, 54, 57
Nicopolis, 45 martyrs of 63
the Prophet Obadiah 59
St Olympias 63
St Onuphrius 51
St Palladius 59
Palm Sunday 57
St Parasceve (Petka) 54, 57, 62, 75
the Passion 54
SS Peter and Paul 54, 58
St Peter of Alexandria 59
St Peter of Kiev 62
St Philemon 59
St Philip the Apostle 51
St Phocas 63
SS Plato and Romanus 59
the Presentation of Christ in the Temple 54, 62
the Presentation of the Mother of God 51, 54, 59, 62
the Procession of the Cross 52, 63
St Proclus 59, 62
St Romanus the Melode 51
St Silvester 62
St Stephen the New Confessor 59
St Stephen Sabaites 63

Sunday of the Forefathers 51, 62

St Symeon 62

St Symeon Stylites 51, 54, 61

the Synaxis of the Bodiless Powers 51, 54, 57

the Synaxis of the 70 Apostles 62

the Synaxis of the Virgin at Miasena 61

the Synaxis of the Virgin (26 Dec.) 62

St Syncletica 62

St Theoctistus 62

St Theodore Stratilates 63

St Theodosius of the Caves 62, 63

SS Theopemptus and Theonas 62

the Theophany 54, 57, 62, 81

SS Timothy and Maura 62

the Transfiguration 52, 54, 58, 63

the Veil of the Virgin 51, 61

St Vladimir 51, 63

Whitsun 54, 58, 81

Skazanie sveščennago chrama 115, 116

Sokraščenie istorii cerkovnija 121

Songs, 121-125

Tlŭkovanie neudobǐ poznavemymŭ… rěchemŭ 109

Tlŭkovanie Větchomu i Novomu Zavětu 109

Tragicomedy 119

Verses 119

Vocabulary 116

Ада́мъ пръ҆вы҄ ч҃лкь бы́вь лѣ́томь, ѕ҃і. й роди́ си́ѳа 108

а́ще который ино҆к распоа́соу́ѥ́тсѧ й спи҆т 82

Аще правѣ҃наго паметь хвала́ми́й сьвр҆ьша́ти 100

Бл҃вень Б҃ъ· і҆ ѡ҃ц҃ь Г҃а нашего і҆ѵ̈у́х҃а 101

Б҃ъ оу́бо мѡ̈сѣ̈о́м поро́угасе фараѡ́ноу 101

Бы́вш҆у гла́д҆у въ ѥ́ллин҆х велик҆у ѕѣ́лѡ 108

Бистъ во́инъ ст҃и Сисо́нъ 123

Бѣ оу́бо мѣжд҆у пѣ́ты̆м й ше́сты̆м сьбо́рѡ́м 108

Бѣ́ше й се вели́ка҆р й сла́вна҆р срьбь҆скаго ѥ́зы́ка 100

Връх҆у се́магѡ н҃бсе ѥ́сть плани́тское ко́ло 109

Въ врѣме же некоѥ пришь҆шоу ст҃омоу са́вѣ сь сьмодрьж҆цемь стефа́нѡ́м 102

Въ лѣтѣ҆х и́ракліа цр҃а гр҆ьч҆скаго· хор҆со́й иже пер҆скою 104

Въ н҃лю вьн҆же наƔина́ѥтсе трі́ѡ́дъ 108

Вь оу́трѣиже па́кы̆ видѣ і҆ѡан҆нь і҆с҃а ходѣ́ща 103

въпро҆с Ɣто́ ю҆с ƔЃлкь ста́ростію О́дрьжи́мь 110

Вьса вьзмож҆наа тебѣ Г҃и· вѣ́мь ѥ́лика аще вьсхо́щеши́й 102

Вьса прѣтрьпѣ х҃с Б҃ъ на́шь на҆с ради 100

Вьса́кь ƔЃлкь хотѣ́й похвали́ти Ɣто любо хвалить 100

Гдѣ́ ти а́де побѣ́да· гдѣ́ ти сьмрь́ти жела҆ѡ. 100

да́рь люб҆ви, глава҆ ,а҃. Любо҆в вѣр҆наа съ ра́достїю й Ɣисты́м срдцемь ю҆с дѣлова́нїе 107

Дн҃ь единогл҃но вьзьпи́м рекоуще· ра́Ɣисе 100

Іѡ̈ан҆нь вь ефе́сѣ а́систѣ́мь і҆ѡан҆нь а́сис҆каа похвала 100

Испльньши́мсе лѣ́тѡ́м петь тисоу́щь и пѣ́тиль сто́ль 104

Исто́Ɣни҆к ѥв҆л҆ск̆ы̆х оу́Ɣе́нїи ѿврь́сти има́м пото́кь 102

Испрьва ненавидѣ́й добра́ дї́аволь 102

Испръва оу́бо а́рме́ни бѣ́х҆у съ на́ми въ сьѥ́динѥ́нїи 108

кто́ хоƔѥ҆т Ɣита́ти и́ли перѣпи́совати 42

Маѯі́мїань иже і҆ер҆коуга́ѥ поко́р-ивь гоѳ҆тї й сьвроматї́и 100

Наста праз҆д҆нолюб҆ци́й, прѣсвѣтлое трь́жьство 100

Нн҃а сто҆зарное сл҃нце нб҃наго кроуга 103

Нб҃оу и земли редь виж҆доу настоѥщаго ради праз҆ника 103

Ѿ извѣ́стнѣ истин҆нѣй б҃ци й пр҃но дв҃ы марі́е 101

Ѿ нюмьже ре҆Ɣ лоука ѥв҆л҆ст̆ь . мѡ̈сꙇ и і҆лꙇ҆а 105

о повъседневной ве҆Ɣꙿни и у҆тр҆ьни. подоба́ѥ҆т вѣдати й се 88

Овѣнь, юнѣць, близнѣць, ракь, лѣвь 108

Ѿ колѣна нафанова, сна двдва, матѳань іереи 108

Ѻць нашь ѳеѡсте измлада наћеть боатисе Ба 102

Повѣда давыдь армениньъ, бысть речѐ в арменѣхъ 108

Поⷣвигшебосе улуⷱлкыѥ [sic] вѣщи изⷢѻбрѣсти 108

Понѥⷤ положени суⷮ рѣчи въ книгаⷯ, ѿ начелныⷯ прѣводникь 109

Пострижѐнїе власоⷨ убѡ ꙗвлꙗеть въсѣхъ помышлѥнїи. й печалїи житейскиⷯ ѡюѐтїе 107

Пощенїю пѫть въсприеⷨши житейскиа любве избѣже параскевїа слав'наꙗ. 54

Праведⷩни аще постигнеть скончатисе въ покой боуⷣеть 102

При велицемь цри коньстантине быⷭ великыⷯ антонїе 102

При маⷯіⷦмїанѣ бѣⷥконейшимь цри бѣ некто дїѡскорь 101

При семь быⷭ мⷩань проклетый еретикь 108

Придѣте друзыⷨ днⷭ тевⷢлⷮскыⷨ нелѣносⷩѣ прикоснѣмсе 104

Принесоу ѿ василїи убо многыⷯ въ ветхыⷯ 101

Прⷭно длъжныⷩ есмїи братїе· празⷣникыⷩ бжїе творꙗще 103

Прⷭвое ꙋбо велико море начинаеть ѿ улⷦк иж' имꙋще пѣсте главы 108

Прѣсвѣтлое крⷭщенїе Га Ба и спа нашего іоуⷯха 102

Прꙋⷭте, несквернⷩѣ. безначалне, невидиме. 81

Радуисе зелѡ дьщи сїѡна 102

Радуисе марїе прⷭно дѣво прѣчⷭтаа 103

Райже его на въстоцѣ насади Бъ 108

Самодержецъ велики Кнꙗзь Лазарь бꙗше отечества рода племенита 123

Стⷪмоу аплⷪу анⷣдрею живоущомоу въ синопѣ 101

Стыⷯ макавѣи настоꙗщеѥ трьжⷭтво 104

Се бо бѣзвеснаа и таинаа, прѣмоуⷣрⷭти твоѥ 101

Се настоиⷮ братїе, свѣтлоѥ празⷣаньⷭтво 101

Се нꙑнꙗ свѣтло празⷣаньⷭтво ликаствоующе 104

Се пакы свѣтлое празⷣаньⷭтво наста· прⷣаникь празⷣника прѣспеваю 102

Слишасе въсако вамь ѿ хⷭолюбивыⷩое сьбранїе 101

Слишⷩи ѿ всеⷯ, ѿ влⷤженнеⷨ евⷭѳїмїи 102

Слⷩцоу семоу хотѣщомоу виⷣномоу изити изъ прѣдѣла земльнаго 103

Таниѕ царскꙑю добре еⷭ таити, дѣла же гⷩна проповидати гасно 66

Тогⷣа влⷣтвоующоу срьбⷭкыꙗⷨи земⷧꙗⷨїи· блⷢоуⷱтивомоу сьморⷣьжцоу стефаноу 102

Тогⷣа сⷩреⷱ въ сте лѣто· бѣ некто црь на вастоцѣ именѣмь амоурать 103

Три десети сребръникь иже възеⷮ іоуда 110

Утрьнию пѣти, занѥⷤ ѿ оутра въскрⷭе хⷭ Бъ ѿ мрътвыⷯ 109

285

Хо́щȢ пе́ть слове́сь гла́ти Ȣмо҃мъ сво́мъ 109

Хр҃то́сь сп҃си́тель на́шь ꙗ́ко б҃ъ пр⸱ѣ⸱вⷣѣⷣы̀ въса̀ 110

Х҃Ȣ праве́дномоу сл҃нцоу ѿ дв҃ы въста́вшȢ 101

Цр҃кы тайнь праⷥань́тво праⷥȢимь дн҃ѣ 103

Уа́сть пе́рваа ѿ хра́мѣ бж҃ественномъ й сщ҃енныхъ сосȢдѣхъ й ѡ́деждахъ 115

Ул҃къ ка́ждый хр҃тꙗ́н҆скꙑ̀. жа́ной р⸱ѣ҃чи 42

Ул҃къ н⸱ѣ́кꙑ̀ йсхо́жⷣаше ѿ ꙇ́ерл҃ꙇ́ма въ ꙇ́ери́хонь 109

Уто еже ѿсоуⷣ пѣ́тое л⸱ѣ́то тогова пр⸱ѣ⸱бꙑва́нꙇа 100

Утⷪ́ с⸱ѣ̀ ꙁнаме́нꙇе и пр⸱ѣ⸱река́нꙇе вижⷣȢ 101

Ую́на правосла́внꙑⷯ тръжа́тваа св⸱ѣ́тлꙑ̀ мⷩ҆ниꙋ́кꙑꙇ́е па́мети 99

Ши́хъ йхⷬ Ȣ́та́ꙇесе въс⸱ѣⷯ люде́и въ полȢноции 108

Ꙇ́коже бо̀ т⸱ѣ́лȢ св⸱ѣ́ть сл҃нце, тако дш҃ѝ мл҃тва 109

Ѱа́лтирь кра́снь съ гȢ́сльми, ѱа́лтирь ꙇ́еⷭ Ȣ́мь 109

Ὁ Εὐλογῶν τȣ̀ς εὐλογȣ̂ντάς σε Κύριε 93

Numbers refer to catalogue entries.

dated and datable MSS

1553 7
1588 16
1648-9 14
1678 25
1679? 41
1707 23
1713 42
1726? 24
1743? 46
1769 47
1769 50
1793-4 51
1835 52
1835-1848 36

undated MSS

13th century 53
14th century 2
15th century 3
15th century (middle) 17
16th century 54
16th century (first half) 18
16th century (first quarter) 4, 5, 26, 56
16th century (second quarter) 6, 39
16th century (middle) 8, 9, 27, 31, 32
16th century (third quarter) 10, 20, 28, 33
16th century (middle of second half) 12, 40
16th century (last quarter) 11, 19, 21, 29
17th century 22, 35, 55
17th century (first half) 15
17th century (first quarter) 13
17th century (second quarter) 30, 34

17th century (third quarter) 37
17th/18th century 38
18th century (first quarter) 44, 45
18th century (second quarter) 1
18th century (after 1754) 48
18th century (last quarter) 43
18th/19th century 49

INDEX OF MANUSCRIPTS BY ORIGIN

The numbers refer to descriptions.

Bulgarian MSS   2, 17
Hungaro-Serbian MSS   42, 44, 45, 46, 47, 48, 49, 50, 51
Moldavian MSS   3, 4, (11), 21, 28, 30
Russian MS   37
Ruthenian MSS   1, 5, 6, 7, 8, 9, 10, 11, 12, 13, 14, 15, 16, 18, 19, 20, (21), 22, 23, 24, 25, 26, 27, 29, 31, 32, 34, 35, 36, 38, 39, 43, 52, 54, 56
Serbian MSS   33, 40, 41, 53, 55